Subversive Meals

Subversive Meals

An Analysis of the Lord's Supper under Roman
Domination during the First Century

R. Alan Streett

PICKWICK *Publications* · Eugene, Oregon

SUBVERSIVE MEALS
An Analysis of the Lord's Supper under Roman Domination during the First
Century

Pickwick Publications
An Imprint of Wipf and Stock Publishers
199 W. 8th Ave., Suite 3
Eugene, OR 97401

www.wipfandstock.com

ISBN 13: 978-1-62032-018-1

Cataloguing-in-Publication Data

Streett, R. Alan

    Subversive meals : an analysis of the Lord's Supper under Roman domination dur-
ing the first century / R. Alan Streett.

    xii + 328 p. ; 23 cm. — Includes bibliographical references and index(es).

    ISBN 13: 978-1-62032-018-1

    1. Lord's Supper—History—Early church, ca. 30–600. 2. Sacred meals—Rome—
Comparative studies. 3. Emperor worship—Rome. 4. Religion and politics—Rome—
History. I. Title.

BV6 S75 2013

Manufactured in the U.S.A.

To my loving wife and best friend

Lynn Fenby Streett

Contents

Acknowledgments

SUBVERSIVE MEALS, ALTHOUGH RESEARCHED and written entirely by the author, was nonetheless a collective effort on the part of many individuals. It is my sincere joy to acknowledge these dear saints of God who offered support along the way.

To President Jerry A. Johnson and the Board of Trustees of Criswell College (Dallas, Texas) who approved a year-long sabbatical that enabled me to begin this work: Thank you for your confidence and generosity.

To Drs. William S. Campbell and Kathy Ehrensperger, my thesis supervisors at the University of Wales, Trinity Saint David, who provided expert academic advice and personal encouragement from day one: Thank you, Bill and Kathy. I could not have had better supervisors.

To Warren Carter, Carolyn Osiek, David Balch, Art Dewey, Reta Finger, and Andrew McGowan who in the earliest stages of my research directed me to resources: Thank you for taking the time to answer my emails.

To all the members of the Presidents' Class Bible Study, who prayed for me throughout this lengthy project and wondered if I would ever get finished: Thank you. I did!

To my wife Lynn: Thank you for loving and believing in me.

1

Introduction

THE THESIS OF THIS book is that the Lord's Supper of the first-century CE was an anti-imperial praxis. Whenever early Christians met for a communal meal they saw themselves as participating in subversive non-violent acts against the Roman Empire.

1.1 Statement of the Problem

What actually took place when a first-century church gathered to eat the Lord's Supper? Did its members, like their twenty-first century counterparts, take a bite of bread and a sip of wine in memory of their Lord? In recent times scholars have taken a fresh look at how and why the early church met around the Lord's Table. Thus far they have been successful at reconstructing the outward form of the Lord's Supper, but have not ventured into the political nature of the meal. Since all meals in the Roman Empire were political as well as social functions, what political function did the Lord's Supper serve? This book seeks to offer an answer.

1.2 Need for the Study

While most research on the Lord's Supper prior to the twentieth century had focused on the meal as a sacrament, with particular attention given to the nature and meaning of the elements, a shift in scholarship began to take place near the quarter-century mark when Hans Lietzmann advanced the theory that the nascent church met for a combined non-sacramental *agapé* feast and a symbolic sacramental Eucharist.[1] His position was embraced widely by scholars including D. Dix,[2] J. Jeremias,[3] P. Bradshaw,[4] and I. H. Marshall,[5] among others.

Nearly a half-century later V. Eller[6] proposed that the Lord's Supper or Eucharist was in its entirety a full evening meal without any distinction between sacramental and non-sacramental as Lietzmann suggested. R. Banks[7] and E. LaVerdiere[8] were two scholars who embraced this new understanding and continued to write about it.

Only within the past two decades, M. Klinghardt,[9] D. Smith,[10] and H. Taussig[11] have built a convincing case that the Lord's Supper was not only a full meal, but followed the structure of a two-course Roman banquet with a *deipnon* and *symposium.* They argued that from all outward appearance, there was little, if any, difference between a banquet eaten by Christians and their non-Christian counterparts.

During this same time frame, R. Horsley,[12] W. Carter,[13] and others began examining Jesus and his movement in the context of the Roman Empire. They showed the difficulty with which the early *ekklesiai* functioned within a domination system that claimed it had been chosen by the gods to rule the world, and used its power to guarantee its success. Proclaiming an alternative vision for the world, the churches stood opposed to Roman ideology and imperial rule. Building upon the work of these researchers and their predecessors, the author shows that when examined in the context of Roman imperialism an even sharper picture

1. Lietzmann, *Mass and the Lord's Supper.* Lietzmann's view was widely accepted among scholars until Smith's and Klinghardt's groundbreaking research. Since then only a small minority hold to separation of *agapé* and Eucharist, the most notable being German NT scholar Bernd Kollmann, *Ursprung und Gestalten der frühchristlichen Mahlfeier.*

2. Dix, *Shape of the Liturgy.*

3. Jeremias, *Eucharistic Words of Jesus.*

4. Bradshaw, *Eucharistic Origins.*

5. Marshall, *Last Supper and Lord's Supper.*

6. Eller, *In Place of Sacraments.*

7. Banks, *Paul's Idea of Community.*

8. LaVerdiere, *Dining in the Kingdom of God.*

9. Klinghardt, *Gemeinschaftsmahl und Mahlgemeinschaft.*

10. Smith, *From Symposium to Eucharist.*

11. Smith and Taussig, *Many Tables.*

12. Horsley, *Jesus and Empire* and Horsley, *Jesus in Context.*

13. Carter, *Roman Empire and the New Testament* and Carter, *Matthew and Empire.*

of the Christian meal emerges. While it followed the outward form of a Roman banquet, it functioned as an anti-imperial activity.

In light of James Scott's landmark research on how people living under oppressive regimes use hidden transcripts—behind-the-scenes actions to express their opposition and voice their hope for change[14]—this monograph postulates that the Lord's Supper might rightly be classified as a hidden transcript. This means that when first-century believers, especially the marginalized and disenfranchised, gathered together to eat a communal meal, they sought ways to express their resistance toward Rome, particularly during the symposium portion of the meal.

After searching databases, combing through the critical commentaries, querying leading academics in the field of Greco-Roman meals, and finding no scholarly work published on the subject, the author saw a need for such a project that would fill the existing void.[15]

1.3 The Importance of the Study

In conducting his research, the writer corresponded with many leading experts on Greco-Roman meals, including Andrew McGowan, Reta Finger, Art Dewey, Dennis Smith, Carolyn Osiek, and David Balch to name a few. Many offered sound advice and encouragement. A few were willing to brainstorm through email, but none was aware of any scholarly work dealing with the Lord's Supper as an anti-imperial activity; hence, the importance of this study.

This is also the first examination of the Lord's Supper through Scott's lens of "hidden transcripts," which adds credence to the thesis that the Lord's Supper is an anti-imperial practice.

When the Lord's Supper is placed within the historical context of a Jesus movement that nonviolently opposed the tyrannical practices of the empire, it becomes clear that it was an act of resistance and took on political significance. Believers not only gathered to eat and satisfy their appetites, they engaged in various kinds of anti-imperial symposium activities that included prophetic utterances, singing protest songs, and lifting a toast to a man whom Rome deemed worthy of a criminal's death.

14. Scott, *Domination and the Arts of Resistance*.

15. Three years after this research was underway, Taussig included a twenty-eight-page chapter on the Christian meal as an act of resistance to Roman imperial power (*In the Beginning*, 115–43). He devotes five of those pages to an argument that Christian meals were anti-imperial because believers made "libations" to Christ instead of to Caesar. This writer will challenge that assertion in chapter 2.

By failing to recognize the anti-imperial nature of first-century Christian meals, the modern church has eviscerated the Lord's Supper of its political significance. As a result, the Lord's Supper rarely serves the same function as it did at the time of Peter and Paul but has devolved into a symbolic act that offers spiritual solace to the partakers but does little to contest the policies of modern-day tyrants who rule their empires for the benefit of the few and to the detriment of the oppressed masses.

1.4 Objectives of the Study

The first objective of this study is to advance the scholarly understanding of Christian meals. Just as this writer's research was built on the work of Banks, Smith, Taussig and others, so he hopes his research will serve the same purpose for the next generation of scholars.

The second objective is to recreate in the historical imagination of the readers a more accurate and clearer picture of the political nature of the Lord's Supper than previously existed.

The third objective is to help exegetes, be they scholars or studious pastors, to look afresh at key passages which deal with Christian meals in order to help them more precisely interpret these texts.

1.5 Limitations of the Study

The writer limits his study of Christian meals mainly to the writings of Luke and Paul but occasionally refers to other gospels and letters for support and/or clarification.[16]

This study does not seek to reconcile or harmonize contradictory accounts that appear in the Synoptics, believing that each author tells his own version of the Jesus story, choosing to include and exclude specific events and details. Even when different gospel writers tell the same story, they often nuance it for their own purposes, remember it differently, and make it applicable to their particular audiences. Therefore, this is not an attempt to reconstruct the life of the historical Jesus.

This research is limited to the first-century CE. It examines documents and events from other periods only when they illuminate our understanding of the Lord's Supper as it was practiced in the first century.

16. An explanation as to why the researcher limited his discussion of meals in the Gospels primarily to the Gospel of Luke is found in chapter 5.

This research additionally limits its treatment of the Roman domination system to that information which is pertinent to the topic. It is not a full-fledged history of the Roman Empire, the Caesars, Roman military, etc.

This research is also limited to comprehending the anti-imperial nature of Christian meals and does not deal with the nature and substance of the elements, the order of the institutional words, or other sundry controversies surrounding the Lord's Supper.

1.6 Outline of the Study

Chapter 2 shows that Christian communal meals followed the same format as the Greco-Roman banquet, which was an important social institution in the first-century CE and used by Rome to enforce patronage and stratification. Christians, however, used their meals to promote the kingdom of God and resist the empire.

Chapter 3 identifies the Passover as a subversive, anti-imperial meal that the Jews ate as they anticipated divine liberation from Pharaoh's tyrannical rule. The author will trace the Passover—as far as can be discerned from biblical and other texts—from its inception to the first-century CE when Jews once more found themselves under foreign rule and sought encouragement in the meal, looking again for God's deliverance.

Chapter 4 critically examines the Roman domination system, which sought to control the lives of the masses through political, social, and military means, and provided the context for the anti-imperial nature of the Lord's Supper. Special attention will be given to the political and economic conditions of the time.

Chapter 5 analyzes the meal practices of Jesus according to the Gospel of Luke, showing how the Lukan Jesus used the symposium to speak against Roman and Jewish practices of stratification and to promote a kingdom ethic that included egalitarian table fellowship—a reflection of the eschatological banquet when people from all walks of life will sit at the table with Abraham in the kingdom. Jesus' table talks and examples served to inform the church how it was to eat its communal meals.

Chapter 6 examines the Lukan version of the Last Supper where Jesus infuses the Passover feast with eschatological meaning. It further explores the relationship between the Last Supper and the Lord's Supper.

Chapter 7 shows how the early church—living in the midst of Roman domination and drawing upon lessons gleaned from Passover, Jesus' mealtime teachings, and the Last Supper—practiced a pro-kingdom of God, anti-imperial meal ethic. It will focus on 1 Cor 11:23–26, women and slaves reclining at the table, the place of prayer and letter reading at the meal, and how the believers sang subversive songs and hymns to promote their beliefs and oppose the empire.

Chapter 8 takes an in-depth look at the gift of prophecy as an example of a symposium mealtime activity. Particular attention is given to the anti-imperial content of Christian prophecy, which exalted Jesus as Lord, offered hope to the oppressed, and spoke of judgment upon all powers that opposed God's kingdom.

Chapter 9 summarizes the study, drawing conclusions and making suggestions for further scholarly research on the Lord's Supper as an anti-imperial praxis.

2

The Roman Banquet as a Model for the Lord's Supper

—*Part 1*—

The Structures and Kinds of Roman Banquets

2.1 Introduction

A MODERN-DAY COMMUNION SERVICE in which a symbolic piece of cracker and a thimble-sized portion of wine are distributed to the faithful had no counterpart in the first-century church.[1] When early believers gathered in a home, courtyard, or hall to partake of the Lord's Supper they reclined at a table in Greco-Roman fashion and ate a full course meal. It was a joyous time for sharing food, honoring Christ, remembering the martyrs, and using their gifts, talents, and resources to minister to one another. A scholarly consensus exists among members of the SBL "Meals in the Greco-Roman World" Study Group that these Christian meals were similar, if not identical, in format to traditional Roman banquets held throughout the empire.[2] The communal meals eaten "in Jesus' name" differed mainly from other

---

1. As Jewett, "Tenement Churches and Pauline Love Feasts," 44, sardonically observes, "The purely symbolic meal of modern Christianity, restricted to a bite of bread and a sip of wine or juice, is tacitly presupposed for the early church, an assumption so preposterous that it is never articulated or acknowledged."

2. In typical first-century CE pagan banquets, participation at the table was limited to free males. Christian banquets, while following the outward form of the Roman meal, opened the table to all persons regardless of gender, economic, and social status. This will be discussed in more detail in chapter 7.

formal meals of the era in that they focused on Christian theology rather than Roman ideology. Otherwise, it would be hard to tell them apart.

The thesis of this chapter is that the Christian communal meal, popularly called the "Lord's Supper," followed the same structural format as the Greco-Roman banquet, which was an important social institution in the first-century CE.

2.2 The Roman Banquet: An Overview

The reclining banquet was arguably the most important social institution of the Roman Empire.[3] The term "social institution" refers to a system or entity that transcends the individual, in which all people of a given culture participate.[4] Family, government, public education, and religion are examples of contemporary institutions. By their nature social institutions preserve societal values, influence and regulate human behavior, define kinship, and transmit knowledge and beliefs from one generation to the next. The Greco-Roman banquet served in this capacity throughout the Mediterranean region during the first-century CE. It supported the core values of the Roman Empire, particularly the tradition known as patronage or benefaction, upon which the social structure of the empire was built. Patronage was the practice in which those of higher social status offered favor and provided economic assistance to those below them in exchange for honor, loyalty, and service. Caesar was considered the ultimate patron or benefactor, since he provided for the needs of all his citizenry. Therefore, everyone throughout the empire owed him homage and allegiance.

Banquets by nature were also sociopolitical enterprises that supported Roman ideology—the belief that Rome was chosen by the gods and given a manifest destiny to bring peace to the world. David Balch has done extensive research showing that frescoes depicting scenes of Roman imperial power graced the walls of many Roman dining rooms. As people reclined to eat they did so before grand visual displays that portrayed Rome's ideology, its mythical origins, gods, and bigger-than-life war heroes, all designed to ensure that diners honored Caesar and supported the state's imperial agenda.[5] Roman ideology was embraced by all from the highest in society to the lowest peasants in a similar fashion as most Americans, regardless of their station in life, believe the founding fathers

3. Smith, "The Greco-Roman Banquet as a Social Institution," 1–11.
4. Ibid., 1.
5. Balch, *Roman Domestic Art*, 202–9.

Strange comment / I wouldn't say most.

were called by God to cast off British ties and create a new republic. All diners throughout the empire were required to salute the gods and heroes of Rome. Any meal that did not devote a specific time to paying tribute to the empire was looked upon with suspicion.

As an important social institution the banquet encapsulated the Greco-Roman culture, its values, morés, and ideology. In a sense, each banquet was a miniature reproduction of Roman society and served as a venue where one's social status was recognized and formally solidified.[6] Hence, the banquet was a primary means for social formation throughout the empire. It served to identify and set boundary markers for those living within a stratified society. People with common interests or part of a certain social or ethnic network regularly dined together. Casual acquaintances became friends. Everyone had his place in the pecking order.[7] One's standing within the Roman hierarchy was determined by one's eating partners. Where one reclined at the table defined his ranking among his associates. Interpersonal relations at mealtime mirrored daily life within the empire. Rome used the banquet as a vehicle to promote imperial ideology, define community boundaries, and reinforce allegiance to the empire.

In essence, the banquet was one of Rome's important instruments of domination, guaranteeing that the aristocracy maintained its "social control of the *polis*."[8]

2.3 The Structure of Roman Banquets

In the first-century CE those living in the Roman Empire, elites and peasants alike, ate their main meal of the day sometime between midafternoon and dusk, a practice they inherited from the Greeks and adapted to their culture.[9] They called this meal the "*deipnon*" (δεῖπνον) i.e., supper. At

---

6. Plutarch, *Quaest. conv.* 615D. Taussig, *In the Beginning*, 26, 30, discusses the nature of the Roman banquet as a social institution.

7. The pronouns "him" and "his" will be used throughout this chapter to describe those who attended Greco-Roman banquets in the first-century CE, since guests were normally limited to adult males. The author is aware of the importance of contemporary gender issues and the proper use of inclusive language. In this rare instance, however, it seems more prudent to be exact by using precise gender pronouns, even at the expense of political correctness.

8. Burkert, "Oriental Symposia," 7.

9. Smith, *From Symposium*, 20. While the writer of this book will limit his description and analysis of the banquet rituals mainly to those of the first-century CE as practiced in the Roman Empire, he recognizes that Roman meals evolved out of Greek meal tradition. The key document from the classical Greek period, which deals

frequent intervals, people throughout the empire attended an expanded form of the meal, which included an after-dinner discussion and entertainment. A host summoned guests to an evening-long social event by way of formal written or oral invitations.[10] Smith calls this much more elaborate affair a "banquet" to distinguish it from the normal and less formal evening meal.[11] We, too, will adopt this usage.

Unlike the regular meals that people ate on a daily basis, which were concerned mainly with consumption of food, a typical Roman banquet was a much more elaborate affair. It followed specific protocols that encompassed the way one dressed, how the table was set, the order in which the meal was served, the types of food chosen, and the standards of acceptable behavior.[12] All banquets were similar in structure except for minor variations, which were dictated by the setting and particular purpose of the occasion. They usually lasted three to four hours and were divided into two major components: 1) a full course evening meal (*deipnon*) and 2) the symposium (*symposion*), a prolonged period of leisurely drinking that included entertainment in one form or another. The two segments were joined by the lifting and pouring out of a cup of mixed wine known as a libation in honor of the emperor, household, guild, national deities, or a benefactor.[13] Unlike Westerners of the twenty-first century who attend banquets infrequently, and then only on special occasions, those dwelling in the empire during the first century attended them on a monthly or even weekly basis, if not more often.

Dennis Smith and Matthias Klinghardt, independent of one another and an ocean apart, each concluded that the banquet was a well-established and respected "social institution" in the Mediterranean region of the Roman Empire during the first century in which people of all classes

with banquets and symposia, in particular, is Plato's *Symposium*, written in the late fifth-century BCE. Xenophon also penned a work entitled *Symposium* in the early fourth-century BCE, which sought to balance Plato's more idealized view of meals. Smith provides a comprehensive treatment of meals from 300 BCE to 300 CE. Also see Blomberg, *Contagious Holiness*, 87–90.

10. Xenophon, *Symp.* 1.27.

11. Smith, *From Symposium*, 20–21. The Romans also used the Latin *cena* interchangeably with the Greek *deipnon*. To maintain clarity and continuity, this paper will use only the term *deipnon* to describe the meal.

12. Ibid., 13. Roman elites, who did not labor for a living, spent their early afternoons in exercise, bathing, and dressing up for the evening banquet (21–22).

13. These aspects of the banquet will be examined in more detail later in the chapter.

participated as a normal state of affairs.[14] To dine with friends, associates, and peers was an expected part of life within the empire. Everyone attended banquets, whether of the elite or peasant class. Christians were no exception.[15] Scriptures seem to indicate that their weekly worship services revolved around the Lord's Supper, which took the form of a Greco-Roman banquet (Acts 20:7–11; 1 Cor 10:33).

Banquets operated according to recognized sets of rules and codes of ethics. Communal eating experiences were times of joy, friendship, and pleasure as the senses were stimulated and the camaraderie was strengthened.

The formal meal was considered an occasion for collective "good cheer" or "pleasure,"[16] which was also referred to as "festive joy" (*euphrosyne*) and looked upon as a gift from the gods. Festive joy was an essential and valued component of any proper meal, without which the meal was deemed less than successful.[17] One might liken festive joy to the exhilaration one experiences when invited to a victory party of a newly elected political candidate. The entire banqueting experience was designed to produce a pleasurable experience for everyone.[18] To ensure mutual pleasure, the evening's affairs were to be conducted "decently and in order."[19] To this end, invited guests had ethical obligations to one another, and agreed to

14. Smith, *From Symposium*, 2, 13, recounts how his and Klinghardt's findings paralleled each other (Klinghardt, *Gemeinschaftsmahl und Mahlgemeinschaft*). Smith's and Klinghardt's published findings gave impetus to the forming of the SBL study group: "Meals in the Greco-Roman World." Taussig, *In the Beginning*, 21, also tells how both researchers independently concluded that the Roman banquet was considered a major social institution in the Roman Empire.

15. Smith, "Greco-Roman Banquet," 11 states, "The banquet as social institution provided a social form, an ideology, and a literary model for a rich and ubiquitous banquet tradition. If we apply this model to the issue of Christian origins and ask the question, 'Why did early Christians gather at table,' the answer is simple. Early Christians gathered at table because that is what groups in the ancient world did. Christians were simply following a pattern found throughout their world. And in following that pattern, early Christian communities were being formed sociologically and theologically by table ritual and banquet ideology."

16. Blomberg, *Contagious Holiness*, 86. Also see Smith, *From Symposium*, 55.

17. Smith, *From Symposium*, 12.

18. Epicureans placed a high premium on pleasure. Their motto "eat, drink and be merry" can only be understood in light of banquet practices. Many Epicureans believed pleasure could be attained only when everyone was free to choose their own seating arrangements, regardless of status. They believed that status should cease to exist when one crossed the threshold of the dining room. The Epicurean push for "anti-status" banquets did not gain wide acceptance (Smith, *From Symposium*, 57–58).

19. Plutarch, *Quaest. conv.* 615–616B.

conduct themselves according to the principles of social etiquette, which were universally understood but also enumerated in the by-laws of the sponsoring society or guild. The goal of the banquet was for the group as a whole, and not just for the individual, to enjoy the banqueting experience.[20] Therefore, drunkenness, quarreling, and abusive behavior were discouraged.[21]

Although what is known about Roman banquets comes mainly from historical descriptions of elite banquets, all banquets, whether attended by elites or peasants, contained common features and served to bind people together.

2.3.1 The Deipnon (The First Tables)

Although the *deipnon* mainly involved eating supper, it was as ritually significant as the symposium portion of the banquet. Just about everything connected to the *deipnon* was meaningful: who was invited, where they sat, and what they ate. These arrangements were important because they reflected the order of Roman society and gave people a sense of where they fit into it.

Formal meals were sponsored often by a host, usually a patron, who often selected a *symposiarch* or president of the feast to choreograph all aspects of the evening's affairs.[22] Usually a different *symposiarch* was chosen for each meal. The position, therefore, was functional and not official or permanent. Because of this arrangement, no *symposiarch* ever gained more status than the host, who always remained the most powerful person

---

20. Smith and Taussig, *Many Tables*, 31–32.

21. Similar decorum is practiced in the modern Western world. At formal banquets, the host or sponsoring committee determines seating arrangements, name tags are often issued, alcoholic beverages are limited, and respect and courteousness are the expected table manners.

22. As the name implies, a symposiarch was one who ruled the feast. Plutarch, *Symposiacs*, 1.5, deals with the question, "What manner of man should a director of a feast be?" In Plato, *Symp.* 213E, Alcibiades assumes the position of symposiarch when the host does not appoint one. Xenophon, *Symp.* 2.27, describes an occasion when the host does not choose a symposiarch, and the guests mix the wine as they please. Davis, *A Day in Old Athens*, 186, describes a typical Greek banquet scene where Prodicus, the host, selects Eunipias to serve as the president or master of the feast. The latter's duties include, among other things, the mixture of the wine and the pouring out of libations to the gods and national heroes. Smith, *From Symposium*, 33–34, offers an excellent description of the role of the *symposiarch*, as does Taussig, *In the Beginning*, 79–82.

in the room apart from an occasional guest of honor.[23] When meals were held in homes it was not uncommon for the host himself to serve as *symposiarch*.

The Custom of Reclining

When free men gathered to eat a banquet they did not sit in chairs like modern diners. Rather they reclined on a couch around banquet tables. This was a universal Greco-Roman practice.[24] It "signified leisure, and therefore reclining together expressed a community of leisure."[25] Couches were constructed of masonry and covered with pillows to provide comfort for a full evening of eating and entertainment.[26] The dining couch was called a κλίνη, the same term used to describe a bed or funeral couch where a body lay in repose.[27] From this cognate the English word "recline" is derived.

Dining rooms, whether located in homes, temples, or association buildings, were "designed so that couches could be arranged around a central axis and diners could share tables and communicate easily with each other."[28] A typical dining room had enough room for three couches

---

23. Taussig, *In the Beginning*, 81.

24. By the time of Xenophon (ca. 430 BCE) and Plato (ca. 385 BCE) diners customarily reclined at banquets. See Xenophon, *Symp.* 1.20; Xenophon, *Anab.* 263; Plato, *Symp.* 174E. Neither Greeks nor the Romans, however, were the first to recline when eating. The origins of the practice can be traced back to the Assyrians in the eighth-century BCE (*ANEP*, 637). A relief found in the palace at Nineveh depicts King Ashurbanipal of Assyria, reclining at a banquet, while his queenly wife feasts with him while sitting in a chair. A photograph of the relief, which now hangs in the British Museum, can be found in King and Stager, *Life in Biblical Israel*, 63. The Greeks adopted the practice in the sixth-century BCE and institutionalized it. Reclining was also being practiced in Israel during the same century (Amos 6:4–7). It was not until a millennium later (fourth-century CE) that sitting in seats became the preferred method of dining. See Smith, *From Symposium*, 14–18.

25. Taussig, *In the Beginning*, 69, makes an insightful observation that reclining was contrary to one's ordinary experiences in life that were anything but comfortable.

26. Smith, *From Symposium*, 26–27. Couches were made of wool or horsehair.

27. Ibid., 26.

28. Ibid., 25. The Greeks referred to the dining room as an "*andron*" or "men's room" because here the *symposiarch* or *paterfamilias* wined, dined and entertained his invited male guests. Since the Roman Empire was Hellenized and most within the empire spoke Greek, these terms from the Hellenic period were still being used. White, "Taste and Space," 2, mentions that the *tablinum*, a room located off the atrium in the homes of wealthy Romans, also served a similar purpose.

configured in a horseshoe design, known as a *triclinium*, with each couch able to accommodate three persons.[29] Because the dining room was where one entertained friends and guests, it was the most lavishly decorated room of the house.

Guests would take their positions on couches and recline on the left elbow in a prone position, enabling them to eat with the right hand.[30] Low level tables were placed along side of the couches so guests could reach comfortably to retrieve food and drink.[31] All diners ate with their hands without the aid of utensils. Bread was used as a napkin to wipe one's face and hands, and was discarded by being tossed onto the floor.[32] Dogs were often on hand to devour the discarded crumbs, sinew, and bones.[33]

The Banquet Guests

To attend a banquet one must first be invited by the host of the dinner party, who usually sponsored and paid for the meal and entertainment and, when necessary, the facilities. He might be the head of a family, a benefactor, or even the president of a club or association.[34] The host or his courier, usually a slave, personally delivered initial invitations to desired guests in either written or verbal form just a few days prior to a banquet.[35] This allowed enough time for invitees to *RSVP* and for the host to send out additional invitations if someone declined.

Whom one invited to the banquet depended on the circumstances and purpose for the banquet. Certain rules applied to all banquets. First,

---

29. Jeffers, *Greco-Roman World*, 39–40. Larger banquets required that the couches be arranged end-to-end along a wall or in rows. Some facilities such as temples often had several banqueting halls of various sizes to accommodate the needs of their members.

30. Ibid., 40.

31. Jonge, "Early History," 210.

32. Taussig, *In the Beginning*, 82.

33. Smith, *From Symposium*, 28; Taussig, *In the Beginning*, 82.

34. Lucian, *A Feast of Lapithae* in *Works of Lucian of Samosata*, 5. In a sacrificial banquet, a god or goddess might be listed on the invitation as the host, although the cultic priest would be required to serve in that capacity on the god's behalf. See Smith, *From Symposium*, 81–84.

35. Jesus often drew his illustrations from the meal customs of his day. In the parable of the wedding banquet he tells how slaves are sent to invite guests to the feast (Matt 22:1–14).

reclining was extended only to free men, particularly citizens.[36] That means slaves were *persona non grata* at the banquet table, although they were on hand to serve the tables. When slaves got to eat, they normally sat on benches. Similar seating arrangements were made for women and children. Prior to the era of Augustus Caesar, if a woman attended a banquet, she sat beside her husband's couch, but did not recline herself.[37] However, by the mid-first century trends were changing—especially among the aristocracy in the western Mediterranean—and some women were beginning to recline with their husbands at banquets.[38] Smith concurs but claims they usually reclined at a special women's table.[39] Rarely did women attend the symposium portion of the meal.[40] Plutarch mentions one occasion when two women remained for a part of the symposium, but did not speak.[41]

Second, since banquets served to identify one's status in society and determined the boundary lines within which one might traverse, there was rarely a mixing of classes at the banquet table.[42] This means that elites ate with elites and peasants with peasants. Within the elite and non-elite categories there were additional gradations that further narrowed the range of one's associates. In this way, the banquet as a social institution reflected the culture. As part of the social fabric of the empire, Rome used meals as a tool to dominate people and keep them in their place.

Where and with whom one ate conveyed the sense that certain people were more important and powerful than others within a society. Even in contemporary culture meals may be viewed as a means to isolate and dominate people. This researcher is aware of private dinner clubs where participants attend functions by membership or invitation alone. Only those of a certain socioeconomic category are prospects. Exclusive country clubs in America serve a similar function. They identify and define a person according to status. Likewise, on the other end of the spectrum,

36. Smith, *From Symposium*, 10; Taussig, *In the Beginning*, 30.

37. Corley, *Private Women*, 28.

38. Ibid., 53–59, 147.

39. Smith, *From Symposium*, 43.

40. Plutarch, *Quaest. conv.* 612F–613A.

41. Plutarch, *Sept. sap. conv.* 150–55.

42. The exception to this rule occurred at banquets sponsored by guilds (similar to modern labor unions) and associations (similar to modern civic clubs or ethnic societies). Members of guilds or associations, regardless of rank were able to recline at the banquet table. In many cases, the banquet was the venue where individuals could rise to a higher status based on their achievements and contributions to the organization. See Taussig, *In the Beginning*, 30–31. This matter will be discussed later in this chapter.

meals served daily at the local rescue mission speak to the lesser status of its diners.

At Roman banquets the arrival of an unexpected guest often proved to be a problem. There were three main kinds.[43] The first was an invited guest who did not show up until the symposium course had begun. By the time of his entry his seat had been given to someone else. The next was the *epikletos*, an individual who had not been invited by the host but brought to the banquet by another guest. This too made for an awkward state of affairs especially since there was no space on the couch for a surprise visitor to recline. The third was *akletos* or party crasher who upon hearing of a banquet tried to gain entrance. The "uninvited guest" was a well-known literary device used in popular Roman writing,[44] but was likely based on real life situations.

The Role of Slaves at a Banquet

Slaves living in the Roman Empire were often well educated and ran the affairs of the elites, who did little or no work. Like others in Roman society, not all slaves were of equal status. Therefore, in the context of a banquet, slaves served in many capacities depending on their position, trustworthiness, and expertise. They wrote and delivered invitations, greeted the diners, controlled unruly guests who might drink too much, prepared and served food and wine, washed guests' feet and hands, cleaned up after the meal, and so forth.[45] They were subservient to guests, while at the same time directing and ordering guests around. This caused friction at times.

While slaves did not recline at banquets, on occasion they were called upon to entertain, even to recline next to a guest and provide sexual favors.[46] Such arrangements especially took place at banquets for the elites.

Peasant banquets, which were mainly sponsored by associations,[47] likely used fewer servants and looked to the association members themselves to serve in this capacity on a rotation basis.[48]

---

43. Taussig, *In the Beginning*, 83.

44. Smith, *From Symposium*, 22–23.

45. Plato, *Symp.* 175A; D'Arms, "Slaves," 170–74.

46. Roller, *Dining Posture*, 19–22.

47. A brief section is included later in this chapter on the nature of associations and the meals which they sponsored.

48. Taussig, *In the Beginning*, 82.

Seating Arrangements

While all diners reclined, and in this way they were equal, one's status was recognized and confirmed by where he was seated around the table. Each table had an "imputed ranking attached to it."[49] Guests were arranged according to social rank, which fluctuated by the ranking of the other guests present at a particular meal.[50] The host/*symposiarch* was in charge of formulating a guest list, providing a place to meet, choosing a menu, providing the food and drink, and determining who sat where. When a guest of honor was in attendance—often a political or community leader—he was given the highest ranking seat.[51] Otherwise, the host or *symposiarch* took the best seat with all others arranged to his right according to rank until the person of lowest rank found his spot at the other end of the horseshoe configuration facing the *symposiarch's* back.[52] In larger rooms containing differing elevations, the most important guests were situated on the highest level. "To honor a person's social rank was considered appropriate" and "was a sign of the 'good order' that should characterize a banquet."[53] This seating arrangement replicated the patron-client system that existed throughout the empire. In this way, the banquet preserved and reinforced the Roman social structure.[54]

A person could elevate his status if the host chose to place him at a more prominent seat than he had at a previous banquet. The raising of a client's status came as a result of honoring the patron in some way that endeared him to the client.

49. In Plato, *Symp.* 175C, when Socrates, the most important of the dinner guests, arrives at the banquet he is given a position next to Agathon, the host. Also see Xenophon, *Symp.* 1.8 as an example of seating arrangements. Smith, *From Symposium*, 32–34, 42–46 discusses the importance of status and seating.

50. 1QSa 2.11–22, the Qumran community followed a similar procedure and seated members according to rank.

51. The Gospel accounts give examples of where Jesus was invited to a meal as the guest of honor, most likely because he was considered a teacher or prophet.

52. Taussig, *In the Beginning*, 69.

53. Smith and Taussig, *Many Tables*, 33. While such an arrangement may initially seem strange today, in reality, there is little difference between this practice and the faculty ranking system used by most universities. Those professors with the highest rank and seniority are shown the most respect and afforded the most privileges.

54. In those situations where every banqueter was of equal societal status, there was still stratification due to age differences, with elders receiving more honor. Taussig, *In the Beginning*, 70, remarks, "Holding up the values of equality and stratification at the same time ritually reproduces the tension of these two values in the society at large."

The Menu

Roman banquet menus varied depending on the social status of the host and guests. At an elite meal, the host might serve a meat dish such as fish, game, or lamb, plus vegetables, bread, and mixed wine.[55] Guests of higher rank might be given larger portions or better fare than those of lesser status attending the same banquet.[56] One might liken the practice to the difference between first class and coach in the airline industry. First class customers are pampered with wider seats that fold back into sleepers, hot napkins, complimentary glasses of wine, a full course meal, dessert, slippers, and other comforts, while coach customers sit in narrower seats with little leg room and are served peanuts and a soft drink.

Banquets hosted and attended by peasants, while offering much simpler fare, nevertheless represented the best one had to offer. Even the poor made certain they brought out their best food for the guests.[57] What and how much one ate at a meal spoke more about the Roman social order than one's preferences regarding taste and diet.[58]

The Venue

Because most homes and other structures used for banquets had open windows, the activities going on inside were minimally visible to outsiders, depending on the location of the meal within the house. Hellenistic temples had many dining rooms, which usually surrounded the altar where sacrifices were made. People were coming and going at all hours of the day, so that even a private banquet was open to a quick glance. Occasionally strangers wandered into the banquet for a full view. Banqueters were always aware that as they celebrated an event they could be seen by

55. Romans diluted their wine according to traditional standards: five parts water to two parts wine or three parts water to one part wine. This enabled guests to consume several cups of wine without getting drunk. See Smith, *From Symposium*, 32.

56. Smith, *From Symposium*, 45. Pliny the Elder describes how the banquet host determined the quality and quantity of the food guests would receive based on their status. Banquets that were sponsored by associations or guilds usually served larger portions and better quality food to officeholders while the remaining guests received a lesser meal (See Taussig, *In the Beginning*, 72).

57. Since the host of a meal was usually the patron to the invited guests he was redistributing his wealth to those under him. In this way, the meal served an economic function. It also served as a means of domination, since those receiving the largesse became obligated to the host who provided it.

58. Taussig, *In the Beginning*, 72.

outsiders. One might liken the venue to a birthday party being held at a public park or a picnic in one's backyard, or a banquet in a hotel ballroom. While the affair may be private, it is not exempt from outside scrutiny.

Standardized Procedures

Proscribed rituals accompanied the meals. When a guest arrived at an elite banquet he was met at the door by a servant and escorted to the dining room. Another servant might remove his footwear, while yet another washed his feet. The guest was then conducted to the assigned couch, where he would be met by another servant holding a basin of water in which he would wash his hands. The host might greet him with a kiss. When time came for the banquet to begin, the host closed the door to deny others entrance and to provide an uninterrupted evening of feasting and festivities.[59] Slaves brought in trays of food, which were placed on the tables and shared among the guests. After the meal was over and the dogs devoured the bread crumbs, discarded bones, and inedible scraps, the banquet progressed to the next phase.

2.3.2 The Libation (The Transition from Meal to Symposium)

The offering of a "ceremonial libation" or drink offering marked "the transition from *deipnon* to *symposium*.[60] According to Smith it was the pivotal point in the banquet and involved a formal ritual abounding with meaning.[61] After the slaves cleared the tables, swept the floor, and passed around a basin of water for guests to rinse their soiled hands, the host or the designated *symposiarch* prepared a libation cup of unmixed wine to be offered to a Roman deity, usually addressed as the "good deity" (*agathou daimonos*) and often identified as Dionysus, the god of wine.[62] According to various local customs and depending on who sponsored the banquet and its purpose for being held, additional libations might be poured out in honor of numerous other deities, heroes, or events. Sponsoring associations and guilds customarily did likewise to the guild's patron god. "After

59. Jeffers, *Greco-Roman World*, 40. The practice of closing a door is the basis of Jesus' teaching of the five virgins who are excluded from entering a wedding feast (Matt 25:10).

60. Xenophon, *Symp.* 2.1; Plato, *Symp.* 176A; Plutarch, *Quaest. conv.* 712F–713A.

61. Smith, *From Symposium*, 28.

62. Ibid.

Caesar Augustus's military victory in Egypt, all meals were also to have included a libation in honor of the genius of the emperor."[63] It was a way of "dedicating the whole evening" to the gods, but rarely to one god alone.[64] There was no such thing as a nonreligious or secular banquet.

The Common Denominator

Regardless of the various customs, all libations included one constant feature. When the host first ladled the wine out of the central bowl, pouring it into a single cup, he pronounced the name of a deity over it. After spilling a portion onto the floor, he then took a sip of the remaining wine and passed the cup to his right until each guest from the highest to lowest took a sip and uttered a similar refrain.

This rite was followed by all in attendance singing a hymn to the deity in the form of a solemn chant or a victory song depending on the context and reason for the banquet,[65] but always the paean was addressed to a god.[66] The practice of a toast accompanied by singing has loosely been carried over into modern times.[67]

The Importance of the Libation

The libation was ritually significant for two reasons: first, as Taussig points out, it was located at the center of the banquet, and served as a hinge for the entire meal.[68] Without it, the banquet could not proceed to the next stage. In this way, the libation was essential to banquet ritual.

Second, the libation and the singing were entirely focused on and directed toward a patron or deity who was being honored. Joint participation in the libation produced a sense of identity among the diners and bound them to the patron/god honored and to each other. The libation

63. Taussig, *In the Beginning*, 75.

64. Ibid., 32.

65. Xenophon, *Symp.* 2.1, writes that after the tables had been removed, "the guests had poured a libation and sung a hymn." Also see Smith, *From Symposium*, 30; Klinghardt, *Gemeinschaftsmahl und Mahlgemeinschaft*, 11–129.

66. Plato, *Symp.* 176A.

67. While not libations, modern toasts often include a raised glass in recognition of a hero and the singing of "For He's a Jolly Good Fellow" or "Happy Birthday." So many contemporary customs can be traced back to the Greco-Roman culture.

68. Taussig, *In the Beginning*, 74 79.

was a ritualistic means used by the empire to induce the subjected masses to be loyal to their respective patrons and the gods of Rome. Whether such allegiance was ever achieved is doubtful.[69]

2.3.3 The Symposium (The Second Tables)

The second course of the banquet was known as the symposium or drinking party.[70] The Romans also referred to it as the *convivium* or "second tables."[71] It was the dessert and entertainment portion of the banquet that lasted about two hours, featuring nuts, fruits, sweet cakes and a never ending abundance of mixed wine.[72]

Additional Libation(s)

The symposium commenced with slaves placing a large mixing bowl (*krater*) in the center of the *triclinum* into which they poured wine and

---

69. Ibid., 109. While all libations to the honorees were understood to include a tribute to the emperor and empire (although not necessarily expressed verbally with each lifting of the cup), the question remained whether the conquered or oppressed people were really honoring the emperor or merely going through the motions. After all, if they honored tribal gods or national deities that were peculiar to their own ethnic roots and not directly associated with the empire, how could Rome know where their loyalties lay? This was a cause of some concern for Rome. Still, that the emperor required that a libation be made to him showed the pressure placed on the meal participants to be loyal to the empire.

70. Xenophon, *Symp.* 1.8, 9.2; Plutarch, *Quaest. conv.* 612E, 612F. In Plato, *Symp.* 223B–223D, all participants drink through the night until the sun rises the next morning. In some situations, a person might be invited only to the symposium portion of the banquet. Smith, *From Symposium*, 31, notes even in such cases the symposium never stood alone. It was always preceded by a *deipnon*.

71. Taussig, *In the Beginning*, 27. For purposes of clarity and continuity the word symposium will be used exclusively throughout this book.

72. Ibid., 32. In the Roman period, wine was also drunk at the *deipnon* as well as the symposium in contrast to the Greek tradition. It was common for Roman men to leave a banquet hall inebriated, a practice frowned upon by the Greeks. Most Romans were able to maintain a cultured façade and conduct themselves in a civil manner, despite overindulgence. When drunkenness and gluttony became widespread among banqueters, Pliny the Elder condemned the intemperance (*Nat.* 14.28). In the Julian era, Cicero preferred the use of *convivium* to symposium because the former emphasized the "communion of life" so important to Roman society rather than drinking. Despite his preference, drinking played a significant role in every Roman banquet. See Blomberg, *Contagious Holiness*, 91.

added water to dilute its potency.[73] The host/*symposiarch* determined how much water should be used to cut the wine, usually never less than three parts water to one part wine, bringing the alcohol content to less than 3 percent.[74] When it was thoroughly mixed, a single cup of wine was removed and brought to the *symposiarch*, who raised it in the name of Zeus Savior (*Zeus Dios Soteros*) and poured a portion onto the floor or into the fire. He then took a sip and passed it around to the guests.[75] At larger banquets where multiple mixing bowls were used, the host often gave additional toasts to deities and Roman heroes based on the number of mixing bowls in the room.

Other Symposium Activities

The additional libation(s) gave way to the symposium proper, which focused on eating desserts, drinking an abundance of mixed wine, and enjoying the entertainment or topic of discussion for the evening. Slaves brought wine and sweets to the tables. Drinking continued at a leisurely pace until sunset at which time the banquet ended. It was not uncommon for some guests to depart the banquet either high or inebriated, and in a joyous spirit.[76] However, many banquets had rules that discouraged or even forbade drunkenness, and some hosts employed enforcers to maintain civility, the equivalent of a modern-day sergeant of arms. The Lion's Club, to which this writer belonged many years ago, assigned the humorous title of "Tail Wagger" to a member whose sole responsibilities were to keep order at the dinner meeting and to make sure speakers did not use the venue to promote their business enterprises.

Every banquet included post-meal entertainment of some sort, which might include music, lectures, debates, philosophical discussions, lively discourse extolling emperor and empire, recitations, drama, the unraveling of riddles, dancing, party games, and the like.[77] The exact nature

73. Athenaeus, *Deipn.* 10.426.

74. Taussig, *In the Beginning*, 79. Some banquets may have allowed guests to determine the strength of the wine.

75. Smith, *From Symposium*, 29; Taussig, *In the Beginning*, 47.

76. The picture of banquets ending in drunkenness may be a caricature based on literary tradition rather than on reality. Plato's *Symp.* 223 B–D, for example, ends with the dinner guests in a drunken stupor. Many associations, however, had rules which limited the consumption of alcohol at banquets.

77. Xenophon, *Symp.* 2.1; 9.2–7. Smith, *From Symposium*, 12. One of the popular banquet party games was *kattabos*, which tested a contestant's prowess at slinging

of amusement depended on the setting and the occasion.[78] Usually the symposium included a large amount of group singing like one might experience in an Irish pub. Music and drinking naturally went hand-in-hand.

At banquets attended by elites, professional entertainers were usually hired. The three most popular were musicians (usually female flute players), singers, and orators/teachers.[79] The *symposiarch* supervised the activities, and if the symposium was the kind where dialogue or debate was appropriate, the *symposiarch* often chose the topic of discussion for the evening. All reclining guests were free to speak. Those making wise contributions might be elevated to a new status at the next banquet. At philosophical or purely religious banquets a teacher might be invited to lead the discussion.[80]

Topics of conversation ranged from lighthearted fare, dealing with arts and entertainment to more weighty issues, relating to current events, the world of politics, history, or philosophy. Ideally, all discussions were to be conducted in an orderly fashion, and designed to be profitable, instructive, and pleasant for all participants, leading to good deeds and charity.[81] While the ideal was not always achieved, it was the goal.

2.4 The Ethical Foundation of the Banquet

Since the banquet was not merely a meal but a social institution that defined and shaped the Greco-Roman culture, it expressed what it meant to be civilized. Three prominent attributes of Roman society were part of every well-planned banquet.

---

drops of wine at a target in the middle of the banquet hall (ibid., 34). Another common feature of symposia entertainment was a female flute player who provided a soothing musical atmosphere for the occasion, especially the sacrificial ceremonies (ibid., 35).

78. Some literary accounts and vase paintings of the period portray symposia as venues for sexual proclivity with female slaves and young boys providing erotic stimulation as part of the entertainment. More likely than not, these depictions were idealizations or aspirations of what one wished for a drinking party, rather than what really happened. Nevertheless, the ideal version of a banquet can be used to reconstruct an actual one. See Smith, *From Symposium*, 48. Thus the characterizations were likely based in part on the excesses that occurred within certain elite banqueting circles. For example, Smith cites that some sort of sexual prize might be given to the winner of a *kattabos* contest (ibid., 34, 36–37). On the whole, however, a typical symposium consisted of moderate drinking and sane discussion and entertainment.

79. Xenophon, *Symp.* 2.1, 21; Taussig, *In the Beginning*, 82.

80. Taussig, *In the Beginning*, 79.

81. Smith, *From Symposium*, 52–53.

2.4.1 Fellowship (Koinonia) or a Sense of Community[82]

Plutarch (ca. 46–120 CE) identified "fellowship" as the basic ingredient of the symposium.[83] He also charged that when guests served their own interests and did not share in the communal aspects of the meal, Dionysus was angered.[84] At banquets guests shared in the communal experience, eating from common food platters, drinking wine from a common bowl, and speaking on a common topic.[85] Individualism was discouraged.[86] The meal was the setting where people experienced community.

2.4.2 Friendship (Philia) or Bonding[87]

Plutarch also spoke of the "friend-making character of the table."[88] Sharing of food, drink, and conversation naturally created bonds between diners that did not previously exist. This social intercourse led to the strengthening of patron-client bonds and thus the social fabric of the empire.

2.4.3 Equality (Isonomia)

To a modern reader this concept might imply that every person had equal status, when in fact the opposite was the case. As already discussed, social stratification was essential to the smooth operation of the empire. It was no different at the banquet table. The principle that seating and eating arrangements were determined by social rank was accepted by all. In what sense then was each diner treated equally?

According to Roman values, equality did not mean impartiality or pure egalitarianism as conceived by those living in a modern-day democracy, but that one could expect to be a full participant in a banquet and be treated fairly according to one's specific social status and the rules

82. Taussig, *In the Beginning*, 26–27.

83. Plutarch, *Quaest. conv.* 615A.

84. Ibid.

85. Smith, *From Symposium*, 54.

86. The modern-day church potluck dinner where all guests eat from the same fare is closer to the Greco-Roman idea of *koinonia* than eating at a restaurant where each diner selects the fare of their own choosing off a menu and is then served their individual meals.

87. Smith and Taussig, *Many Tables*, 31. Also Taussig, *In the Beginning*, 27.

88. Plutarch, *Quaest. conv.* 612D; 614 A–B.

associated with banquets. Each could equally recline and speak freely, regardless of status.[89] Thus, two people who were not equal outside the banquet hall reclined as equals within it.[90]

Whenever these three features predominated, banquet harmony existed throughout the evening; thus, the banquet became a picture of the ideal society, a utopia in miniature. As each person comfortably reclined, consumed food and wine until satisfied, enjoyed the companionship of those around him, and the entertainment of the evening, he was able to get his mind off the dangers and banalities of life. At the conclusion of the meal, guests felt a sense of peace and wholeness. Even the OT prophets described the perfect kingdom in terms of a sumptuous feast (Isa 25:6–12).

2.5 Various Types of Banquets

Today, if individuals want to get together socially, they might grab a cup of coffee or tea, go out for a bite of lunch, or even have friends over for dinner and dessert. Unless they are independently wealthy, rarely do they host a party each week with a full course meal, open bar, and entertainment. In the Greco-Roman world, however, banquets were part of the fabric of society. They were held for many reasons and at various venues, and "marked virtually every special occasion."[91] Guests might include neighbors and family, fellow workers, patrons and clients, club members. Banquets were convened regularly on a weekly or monthly basis, but special banquets associated with birthdays, anniversaries or funerals were held when the occasion arose. The venue might be a home, temple, park, or associational clubhouse.

Personal banquets refer to those festive meals when family and friends gathered to celebrate a special occasion. Among peasants who lived in tenement apartments or one-room housing, such affairs involved great sacrifice since most earned only a subsistence wage.[92] Often one's patron would cover the expenses incurred for food and rental cost of a temple dining room in exchange for honor and loyalty. Elites, of course, held elaborate dinner parties without regard to expense. Regardless of

---

89. Plutarch made the case that everyone should feel comfortable in table talk. See Plutarch, *Quaest. conv.* 614E.

90. Taussig, *In the Beginning*, 69.

91. Jeffers, *Greco-Roman World*, 40.

92. Jewett, "Tenement Churches and Communal Meals," 23–43.

their purpose, every banquet had standardized features.[93] As mentioned previously, these included couches for reclining, tables, food, wine, entertainment, servants, and a *symposiarch* to give direction. All banquets paid tribute both to Jupiter and the emperor as patrons of the empire. The main differences between banquets were the kinds of foods served, the topics discussed, and the form of entertainment, all of which depended on the peculiar tastes of the host and the purpose of the banquet being held.[94] Banquets offered the guests few surprises.

While banquets were held to commemorate any number of occasions, here are a few of the more frequent reasons people came together for a formal meal.

2.5.1 Rites of Passage

Meals were regularly held on special occasions to recognize important moments in one's life. For example, friends and family assembled when a Roman boy gained the status of an adult and received a *toga virilis*. Such an event might be likened to a modern-day *bar mitzvah* celebration when a Jewish boy at age thirteen is declared to be a son of the law. On such an occasion, decorum is the rule and an established order or ritual is followed. The affair is lavish and includes rich food, music, toasts, recitations, and ceremonial pomp and pageantry.

2.5.2 Birthdays

Individuals of all social strata used the venue of the banquet to celebrate birthdays with relatives and their closest friends.[95] While peasant banquets were more austere than their elite counterparts, they still included all the elements of a typical Greco-Roman banquet.[96] The most important birthday banquets celebrated the birthday of one's patron. In Roman society, birthday banquets were considered part of the patronage system.[97] It was a way for a client to bestow honor upon the patron. The Gospel of Mark links the death of John the Baptist to the day "when

93. Taussig, *In the Beginning*, 26.

94. Smith, *From Symposium*, 52.

95. Plutarch, *Quaest. conv.* 717B.

96. Smith, *From Symposium*, 3. See Smith's chart that shows common banquet traditions were adapted to various settings.

97. Ibid., 39.

Herod on his birthday gave a banquet for his courtiers and officers and for the leaders of Galilee" (Mark 6:21).

Like all banquets, birthday celebrations included a full meal, a libation to a deity, and the entertainment.

2.5.3 Nuptials

Weddings celebrations were the most public of banquets. Accompanied by public pronouncements, torches, processions through the streets, an endless guest list, and held over several days, the entire community knew when a wedding was being held. The wedding banquet provided the more affluent an occasion to showcase their status.[98] It could be held in the home of the host or in a sanctuary dining room. Unlike other banquets, women were present for the *deipnon* and symposium.[99] They congregated on their own couches and around their own tables.[100]

2.5.4 Funerals

All funerals during the first-century CE, whether Roman, Greek, or Jewish, concluded with the *perideipnon* or funeral banquet held in the home of the deceased.[101] As mourners returned from the burial or cremation site, they were met by the smell of a freshly cooked meal, which was given in honor of the newly departed. The meal transformed the solemn occasion into a more festive event. The majority of peasants who lived under Roman domination depended on their friends to rally around them and to meet their needs at the death of a loved one.[102] Women played a significant role in funeral meals from making lamentations to composing and delivering eulogies about the deceased.[103]

---

98. Lucian, *A Feast of Lapithae* in *Works of Lucian*, 129.

99. Plutarch, *Conj. praec.* 140A; Dio Chrysostom, *Or. 7.67–7.68*.

100. Smith, *From Symposium*, 39–40.

101. Ibid., 40.

102. Many peasants paid dues to a funerary society or were members of a craft guild, which entitled them to a respectable burial and a nice banquet in their honor upon death. A further discussion of this practice is given later in the chapter (Smith, *From Symposium*, 42).

103. Corley, *Maranatha*, presents the latest research and most insightful analysis of the place of women in meals, particularly ritual feasts associated with funerals.

2.5.5 Hospitality

Extending hospitality to strangers and friends was no light affair, since it involved assembling a two course meal. It involved rules of etiquette and unspoken social obligations on the part of both the host and guest(s). Itinerant sages and philosophers especially depended on the hospitality of villagers for their survival. Traveling evangelists and prophets likely fell into this category. Jesus told his disciples to take no money or supplies on their ministry journeys, but to trust God to open doors of hospitality (Matt 10:5–15; Luke 9:1–6). Saint Paul instructs Philemon to get a room ready for him (Phlm 22). On such occasions, the host might invite friends to a banquet where they could receive instruction from the sage or philosopher. The post-apostolic church established regulations with regard to extending hospitality to traveling ministers (*Did.* 12:1–2).

2.5.6 Farewell Meals

Just as a contemporary family with a son or daughter getting ready to depart for war might invite friends to share in a send-off dinner, so the Romans had similar practices. These meals included times of emotion, instruction, and expressions of affection. In many respects, Jesus' Last Supper might be looked upon as a farewell meal. Likewise, Paul's final meetings with his churches before heading for Jerusalem fit the category of farewell meals (Acts 20:7–16; 17–38; 21:5–6).

2.5.7 Philosophical Banquets

While retaining all the common features of the *deipnon* and customary toasts to the gods, the philosophical banquet devoted the symposium time to uplifting and logical discussions among the diners instead of mere entertainment or revelry.[104] Often a topic of discussion was announced beforehand, possibly as part of the invitation, enabling the guests to ponder the theme before arriving at the banquet. The proverbial questions, "Which came first, the chicken or the egg?" and "How many angels can sit on the head of a pin?" were discussed at these functions.[105]

---

104. Plato, *Symp.* 176E; Lucian, *Feast of Lapithae* in *Works of Lucian*, 128; Plutarch, *Quaest. conv.* 614A–B.

105. Plutarch, *Quaest. conv.* 2.3 [635A].

Many first and second-century CE Jewish and Christian banquets also included lively discussions. In this sense they were like philosophical meals.[106]

2.5.8 Sacrificial Banquets

While all banquets were religious in nature in that they upheld Roman ideology and offered libations to the gods,[107] the sacrificial banquet was more so. It was held usually in one of the many temples located throughout the empire for the specific purpose of worship.

All associations had a patron god or gods that they honored and to whom they sacrificed. At various times members brought animals such as goats and bulls and fowl to a temple, where priests slaughtered the animals at the altar and offered them to the gods as burnt sacrifices. However, the bulk of the offering—mainly the edible portion—was given back to the worshipers for consumption or sold at the public market.

Temples were outfitted with dining rooms where families and friends came together to partake of the sacrificial feast. The festal banquet was part of the sacrificial process.[108] Like all banquets, the event included the meal and symposium. The deity to whom the sacrifice was offered was considered the unseen host who provided the food (since it had been returned to the worshipper) or the guest of honor of the feast.[109] These festive occasions were accompanied by the usual transitional libation, glasses of mixed wine, and stimulating discussions.

The Passover meal was the Jewish version of a sacrificial meal, the locus of which was the Jerusalem Temple until its destruction in 70 CE. The sacrificial lamb was slaughtered at the Jerusalem Temple and portions were returned to the family for their annual feast. Jews originally were instructed to eat the feast in the presence of God who served as the host. By the time of Christ, the meal was eaten in dining rooms in homes scattered

---

106. *Mishnah Abot.* 3.3; Philo, *Contempl. Life* 75–77; Acts 20:7; Sirach 9:14–15.

107. In Greco-Roman culture there was no such thing as a nonreligious meal. Since the empire claimed to exist by the will of the gods, the Roman meal as a social institution supported this view, honoring the pantheon of gods through the raising of libations and the singing of hymns.

108. Dio Chrysostom, *Or.* 3.97, ca. 104 CE.

109. Smith, *From Symposium*, 78, *theoxenia*, lit. "hosting the gods." The deity's presence was acknowledged by setting an empty place at the table and even a portion of food.

throughout the city and beyond.[110] Following the Greco-Roman pattern, the Passover included a lifting of wine glasses, hymns, instructions, and a festive atmosphere. Jesus' last Passover with his disciples likely followed the banquet model and included a *deipnon* and symposium.[111]

2.6 Christian Communal Meals

Christian *ekklesiai* ate together because that is what all groups did in the Roman Empire during the first-century CE, regardless of their religious identity.[112] Believers reclined on couches before low-lying tables to celebrate weddings, to bid farewell to friends and families, to extend hospitality to traveling apostles, evangelists, and prophets, to join the bereaved in a meal after the funeral of a loved one, and so on.[113] "The dining room was the default context for early Christian social formation in the house church."[114]

Christian communal meals performed the same function as all Greco-Roman banquets. They served as venues for social formation, where people not only discovered their place within society, but how to live out their assigned role on a daily basis. The church used the communal meal as an opportunity for believers to discover their identity in Christ and learn what God expected of them as citizens of his kingdom. Here they were able to express openly their alternative social vision and gain strength from each other. As such the Christian banquet was characterized by anti-imperial behavior and beliefs that were subversive and counter to the purposes of the empire. Hence, the very social institution originally designed to promote Roman peace through social stratification, actually served to undermine the ideology of the empire.[115]

From NT accounts one discovers that Christian communal meals followed the same general structure as all other Greco-Roman meals. When

---

110. Fitzmyer, *Luke X–XXIV*, 1377.

111. This will be discussed in chapter 6.

112. Smith, *From Symposium*, 279.

113. The NT refers to Jesus reclining at a table on several occasions (Luke 7:36; 11:37; 17:7; John 13:12). This act of reclining explains how Mary could easily anoint Jesus' feet with her hair at the dinner held in his honor at the home of Mary, Martha, and Lazarus (John 12:3), and how the beloved disciple leaned against Jesus' breast (John 13:23, 25).

114. Smith, "A Review of Hal Taussig's *In the Beginning was the Meal*," 2.

115. Chapter 7 will examine how Christians used the meal to form their own identity and theology.

one considers 1 Corinthians 11–14 as descriptive of a typical evening worship, the pattern becomes clear. The believers came together to: 1) eat a *deipnon*, or first course, 2) share in a cup ritual upon which the meal pivoted, and 3) participate in a symposium, an extended time of drinking, conversation, singing, and other forms of conviviality. Craig Blomberg takes issue with this characterization and states that only "superficial similarities existed between Christian and Greco-Roman meals."[116] While claiming that the differences between Roman and Christian meals far outnumber their similarities, Blomberg offers only three disparities, which when examined carefully fail to make his case.[117] Contrary to Blomberg, this writer stands with the members of SBL "Meals in the Greco-Roman World" Study Group that all meals, Christian or otherwise, followed the two-part Greco-Roman format. While recognizing that Christians had their "own repertoire of inventions to contribute to this second part of the sessions," De Jonge states with assurance, "Structurally, however, their after-supper gathering is the exact equivalent of the after-dinner session which followed the periodical banquet of many clubs and societies in the Graeco-Roman world, both gentile and Jewish."[118]

The remainder of this chapter will establish that Christian communal meals, variously called the Lord's Supper, *Agapé*, the breaking of bread, and the Table of the Lord, were patterned after the Greco-Roman banquet, and contained many of the same features as the pagan counterpart, including the use of identical language.

2.6.1 The Deipnon in the Christian Meal

From the accounts in the Gospels, Acts and the Epistles, it becomes clear that the apostolic churches met regularly in homes to eat a full evening meal. The meal was the locus of worship, not ancillary to it. It was their

---

116. Blomberg, *Contagious Holiness*, 94.

117. Ibid., 94–96. Blomberg mentions that 1) the practice of breaking bread was never used by the Romans to open their meals, 2) Jews would not eat with immoral or impure persons like the Romans, and 3) that people often reclined while eating daily meals, showing that reclining was not exclusive to the banquet. While these points can be conceded, this does not make a case that formal Christian meals were different than any other Roman banquet in format, if not function.

118. Jonge, "Early History," 217, also points to John 13:2–20 which describes a supper proper and to 13:31—17:26 which describes after dinner activities including among other things: prayers, instructions, Q & A, and speeches.

modus operandi of worship.[119] Unlike modern-day evangelicals who attend an hour-long worship service consisting of a sermon and a few congregational hymns, or those of liturgical backgrounds who enter a sanctuary to hear a homily and receive the Eucharist, the early believers gathered around a *triclinium* in Greco-Roman fashion.

119. Among scholars who acknowledge that early Christians gathered for actual community meals, some make a distinction between the two-course Greco-Roman banquet and the Eucharist. They suggest that the first-century church made such a distinction, referring to the meal as the *agapé* or love feast and the Eucharist as the sacramental eating of the symbolic elements over which the "words of institution" were repeated. They also claim that the Eucharist was eaten at the conclusion of the meal. They base this view on Paul's version of the Lord's Supper in 1 Cor 11:17–34, which includes a full meal (v. 21) and a reference to the institution narrative (vv. 23–25). Many scholars believe the two forms eventually were separated as a result of the problems at Corinth.

These same scholars interpret the instructions found in *Did.* 9:1–5 dealing with Eucharistic prayers spoken over the cup and bread after eating a full meal: "And after you are satisfied, thus give thanks" (*Did.* 10:1) as proof that the meal and Eucharist were separate from one another. See Jeremias, *Eucharistic Words*; Dix, *Shape of the Liturgy*; Bradshaw, *Eucharistic Origins*; Marshall, *Last Supper*. While the meal proper was viewed to be a normal secular practice, the Eucharist was deemed to be sacred. Jeremias, Dix, Bradshaw, Marshall, and Fee are among those holding to such a position. The phrase "after you have had enough" (10:1) shows that the early church was still eating a meal. According to LaVerdiere, *Dining in the Kingdom of God*, 140, however, there was no separation. The church was merely following the pattern established by Jesus at the Last Supper. The first historical reference to a division between meal and Eucharist is found in Justin Martyr, *1 Apol.* 67, ca. 150 CE, with the Eucharist celebrated in the morning among the faithful and an *agapé* feast enjoyed in the evening by a wider audience, and seen as a ministry of benevolence to the poor, widowed, orphans, slaves and other needy souls.

Additionally, while scholars may *assume* that the words of Jesus from the institution narratives were liturgically recited over the bread and wine after supper, no record actually exists of such a practice until the third century, where the narrative first appears as a liturgical prayer (Hippolytus, *The Apostolic Tradition*, 4.9).

Only in the past two decades have scholars such as Klinghardt, Dennis Smith, Hal Taussig, and Andrew McGowan offered substantive evidence that the meal in its entirety was the Lord's Supper and developed out of the Greco-Roman banquet as a social institution. All groups, regardless of whether they worshiped the gods of Rome or Yahweh like the Jews and Christians, ate meals together. The institution narratives, rather than being liturgical texts meant to be repeated in perpetuity, provide a "theological" interpretation of the kingdom ideology which served as a foundation for the church's self identity as it reclined at the table. McGowan believes that the institution narratives functioned more as etiological texts than a statement of how the church was to observe the Lord's Supper. There is no compelling reason to think that Paul made a distinction between the real meal and a Eucharistic sacramental meal. See Taussig, *In the Beginning*; McGowan, *Ascetic Eucharists*; and McGowan, "Is There a Liturgical Text in this Gospel?," 73–87.

Scripture support is overwhelming that first-century believers gathered together regularly to eat an entire meal (*deipnon*) as part of their corporate worship experience. When one examines the language used in the NT to describe Christian communal meals, it becomes obvious that they are the same terms associated with Greco-Roman meals.

Support Based on the Phrase "Come Together"

On four occasions in 1 Corinthians 11 Paul uses the phrase "when you come together" to describe corporate worship, which includes a meal. This repetition serves to unite the chapter and identify its theme. Paul first uses "come together" (συνέρχεσθε) in verses 17 and 20, when he reprimands the church for turning what should be a good worship/meal experience into a bad one. He repeats the phrase twice more and adds modifiers: "When you come together *as a church* (ἐν ἐκκλησίᾳ)" (v. 18) and "when you come together *to eat* (φαγεῖν)" (v. 33). These additional usages: 1) show that the gathering is "a church" meeting, and 2) define its purpose for gathering, which is "to eat." When viewed in this manner, one can state that the reason for coming together as the church at Corinth was to eat together.

Support Based on the Use of the Phrase "Lord's Supper"

When describing the communal meal, Paul uses the phrase "Lord's Supper" or κυριακὸν δεῖπνον (1 Cor 11:20). By calling this meal a "supper," Paul intimates that it is a real meal. As shown earlier in the chapter the word *deipnon* refers to a full or entire meal, with a host and invited guests in attendance. By calling it the "Lord's" Supper, he seems to indicate that either Christ is the host or the originator of the Christian communal meal.

Support Based on Paul's References to the Abuses

The nature of the problems surrounding the Lord's Supper at Corinth provides further reason to believe that the Lord's Supper was a complete meal. From the text it appears that some of the wealthier members arrived early to the meal and began eating the food and drinking the wine without waiting for the arrival of the peasants and servants. The result was that the former overindulged and became "drunk," leaving little for latecomers who ended up going "hungry" (1 Cor 11:22). Drunk and hungry are words associated with abundance and a lack thereof, indicating that a full meal was in view and not just a morsel of bread and sip of wine.

Likewise, the Epistle of James devotes much of its teaching to addressing problems related to abuses at mealtime. James particularly condemns his readers for showing partiality by offering the better seats to the wealthier members in attendance (Jas 2:1–7), and calls upon the readers to treat all as equals regardless of their status in society (v. 8). These instructions make perfect sense in the context of a Greco-Roman style banquet.[120]

Support Based on Paul's Reference to the Last Supper

Paul points to Jesus' final supper with the apostles as an example of proper table etiquette for the Lord's Supper (vv. 23–26). In doing so he mentions specifically how Jesus took the cup "*after* supper (μετὰ τὸ δειπνῆσαι)" and interpreted the cup's significance to his disciples (v. 25). The analogy is clear—just as Jesus waited for everyone to finish eating the paschal meal before lifting the cup of wine, so everyone in Corinth should be allowed to eat the Lord's Supper. Paul offers a solution, "So then, my brothers and sisters, when you come together to eat, wait for one another" (v. 34). In this way, everyone will get to eat.[121] These texts show that both the Last Supper and the Lord's Supper were entire meals and followed the form of a Greco-Roman banquet.[122]

---

120. Streett, "Food, Fellowship and Favoritism," makes a strong exegetical case that the instructions found in Jas 2:1–9 apply to a meal setting and not a judicial setting as traditionally understood.

121. While some scholars suggest that in railing against the Corinthian abuses at the Lord's table, Paul is suggesting the real meal should be abandoned, leaving only the symbolic elements of bread and wine, Fee, *Corinthians*, 568, says Paul's instructions to the wealthy, "If you are hungry, eat at home" (1 Cor 11:34), means "if you want to gorge" you should eat at home and is not a cause to abandon the proper use of the meal.

122. The Gospel of Matthew also records, "*While they were eating*, Jesus took a loaf of bread, and after blessing it, he broke it and gave it to the disciples" (Matt 26:26), again indicating that a full meal was in progress. Likewise, Mark's Gospel: "And *as they were eating* . . ." (Mark 14:22). In John's account, Jesus' Thursday night farewell meal is called a *deipnon* (John 13:2, 4).

Support Based on Paul's Reference to Cultic Meals

In 1 Cor 10:14–22, Paul forbids believers from eating both at "the table of demons" and "the table of the Lord." By the former he refers to a sacrificial meal, eaten by worshippers in a pagan temple after the priest has offered the innards to idols. Since the "table of demons" refers to a real meal that is eaten in the presence of the gods, then likewise the "table of the Lord" points to a real meal eaten in the presence of the exalted Lord. Paul then discusses a scenario where an unbeliever invites a follower of Jesus to a banquet, in which food that has been offered to an idol is being served (vv. 23–30). He forbids them to participate. Both 1 Corinthians 10 and 11, therefore, speak of real meals, whether they are called a "Table of the Lord" or a "Lord's Supper" and compares them to other meals served throughout the empire.

Support Based on the Term "To Break Bread"

According to Luke, the first believers in Jerusalem met together in homes much like their Corinthian brethren more than a decade later (Acts 2:42). Luke's use of the phrase "to break bread" is his way of identifying the Christian communal meal, i.e., the Lord's Supper (Acts 2:42, 46; 20:7, 11) as their purpose for congregating.[123] Speaking of the believers at Jerusalem he writes, "They devoted themselves to the apostles' teaching and fellowship, to the breaking of bread and the prayers" (Acts 2:42), the kinds of activities one would expect to find at a typical Greco-Roman banquet. That he mentions "fellowship" (*koinonia*), one of the foundation blocks along with friendship (*philia*) and equality (*isonomia*) of a Roman banquet (see above), places the Christian meal in the same category as all other meals. Luke adds, "They broke bread at home [lit., "from house to house"] and *ate their food* with glad and generous hearts" (vv. 47–48), again describing a real meal. Likewise, the account of Paul's stopover at Troas before departing on his trek toward Jerusalem, gives the reader insight into the purpose of the church's coming together: "On the first day of the week, *when we met to break bread*, Paul was holding a discussion with them" (Acts 20:7). The remainder of the paragraph depicts a prolonged mealtime, most likely because it not only served as a communal meal but also as a farewell meal.

123. Stegemann and Stegemann, *Jesus Movement*, 216–17, 281–84, after examining the phrase "breaking bread" in relationship to the Lord's Supper conclude, "The 'breaking of bread' appears to be the main purpose of the [church's] gathering" (282).

Luke writes that "after he had broken bread and eaten, he continued to converse with them until dawn; then he left" (v. 11). In a sense this was Paul's own last supper or farewell meal with his fictive family at Troas.

Luke uses "breaking bread" language on only a single occasion without reference to the Lord's Supper, and then he still uses it to describe an entire meal (Acts 27:35). Facing a dangerous shipwreck and its horrific consequences, Paul commands the 276-man crew to eat: "Then all of them were encouraged and took food for themselves. . . . [and] *satisfied their hunger*" (vv. 36–38).

Support for a Real Meal Based on the Incident at Antioch

Galatians 2:11–13 is another source that suggests full meals were the locus of Christian worship. Here one discovers a Christian community comprised mainly of Gentile believers who congregate regularly for supper. When Peter visits the thriving church he joins in the festivities without regard to kosher food customs, but when his Jewish brethren arrive from Jerusalem (described as coming "from James"), Peter withdraws from the table of fellowship and sides with the delegation in upholding OT purity laws (2:14). Despite the temptation to examine the passage theologically, this writer desires only to point out that eating together was a regular event and was of "central importance to the identity of the community."[124]

Support for a Real Meal Based on the Concept of an Agapé Meal

The use of the term *agapé*, also referred to as the love feast, is another indication that the Lord's Supper was a full meal along the lines of a Greco-Roman banquet.[125] The Epistle of Jude speaks of "certain intruders"

124. Smith, "Meals and Christian Origins," 2–3.

125. See footnote 119 above for a discussion of those who claim that the early church considered the meal (*agapé*) distinct from the Eucharist. According to Dennis Smith, "It is unclear exactly when or under what circumstance the primary ritual meal in early Christianity became a token meal of bread and wine with an accompanying sacramental theology" (Smith, "Response to Andrew McGowan's Article," 4). While some evidence exists that a separation took place in the second century, it was likely localized. McGowan points out that there is no evidence that the early church ever practiced at the same time both a Eucharist and a meal called the *agapé*. By the mid-second century, a shift took place with the advent of a morning hour in which bread and wine were eaten and the words of institution were spoken over them. In the evening the church gathered to eat a real meal. This artificial separation eventually led to the sixteenth-century debates about the significance of the bread and wine as

who stealthily infiltrate the church and "pervert the grace of our God into licentiousness" (v. 4). This sounds a bit like the uninvited banquet guests who appear in many ancient writings.[126] After likening these invaders to historical figures who "indulged in sexual immorality and pursued unnatural lusts," the writer pronounces upon them divine judgment (vv. 7–11). He describes them as "blemishes on your *love-feasts*, while they *feast with you* without fear, *feeding themselves*" (v. 12). To besmirch a feast one had to act in an unseemly way during the first and/or second table. These intruders do just that. They not only take sexual license, but are "bombastic in speech" (v. 16), an indication that they dominate the meal and leave little opportunity for others to participate.

Jude places the entire discussion in an eschatological perspective: "The Lord comes with ten thousand of his holy ones to execute judgment on all, to convict all who are ungodly among them of all their ungodly deeds (or works)." He closes, "But you beloved . . . keep yourselves in *the love* of God, looking for the mercy of our Lord Jesus Christ unto eternal life" (Jude 21).

Using similar language the writer of 2 Peter describes banquet infiltrators as "reveling in their dissipation *while they feast with you* (ἐντρυφῶντες ἐν ταῖς ἀπάταις αὐτῶν συνευωχούμενοι ὑμῖν)" (2:13); again, it is a reference to the church eating an entire meal when it comes together for worship but with some abusing the privilege ("reveling in their dissipation").

When those at the meal table fail to exhibit love toward the other diners, they cease to eat the "Lord's" Supper, and hence abandon the purpose of the meal as a Christian social institution. This is what happened at Corinth (1 Cor 11:17–22).

Possibly the letters written to the churches of Ephesus and Laodicea in Revelation 2 and 3 touch upon a similar problem. After commending the believers at Ephesus, the exalted Christ declares, "But I have this against you, that you have abandoned the love you had at first. Remember then from what you have fallen; repent, and do the works you did at first" (Rev 2:4–5). Clearly the act of abandoning "the love you had at the first" is equivalent to "the work you did at first," and shows that love is not

---

sacramental elements, which remain a hotly contested topic in ecclesiastical circles until the present day. These debates are the result of studying the Lord's Supper apart from its historical context and then imposing an anachronistic interpretation on the various texts dealing with the subject. For an excellent and comprehensive treatment of the various theories regarding the relationship between *agapé* and Eucharist, see Bradshaw, *Eucharistic Origins*, 29–30.

126. Plato, *Symp.* 212D–213A, 223B; Xenophon, *Symp.* 1.11

some vague feeling, but an action. If this charge is failing to act selflessly at the *agapé* (love) feast where kingdom benevolence is expected, then the problem facing that church is connected to the Lord's Supper. Since it is unlikely that they have abandoned or stopped eating supper, what have they abandoned? The probable answer is they have transformed the communal meal into a time of selfish consumption like their Corinthian brethren years before. The writer of Hebrews similarly admonishes, "And let us consider how to provoke one another *to love* and *good deeds*, not *neglecting to meet together*, as is the habit of some, but encouraging one another and all the more as you see the Day approaching" (Heb 10:24–25). These instructions given in the context of a discussion on sacrifices, and thus sacrificial meals (vv. 1–23), make the same point as Rev 2:5—participation in the life of the kingdom takes place at the meal table. That is where one's sacrificial acts of love and good deeds are practiced. Therefore, do not abandon the meal.

Christ also rebukes believers at Laodicea, the final church on the Lycus Valley circuit, for: 1) their barren works, which are good for nothing, and 2) their elevated opinion of themselves (Rev 3:16–17). Again, he finds little about the congregation that manifests a kingdom ethic. While eating a communal meal, they have transformed its character from a Lord's Supper, where the poor are fed and fellowship is experienced, to one where the rich are satisfied. In the midst of their lack of apparent contrition, Christ seeks one person with whom he can fellowship. He declares, "Listen! I am standing at the door, knocking; if you hear my voice and open the door, I will come in to you and *eat* (δειπνήσω) with you, and you with me" (Rev 3:20).

The verb δειπνέω appears only three times in the NT and each time in the context of the Lord's Supper. The cognate nouns, likewise, appear in the NT in the context of an entire meal, i.e., a Greco-Roman style banquet (Matt 23:6; Mark 6:21; 12:39; Luke 14:12–24; John 12:2; 20:46; 21:20; Rev 19:9, 17) and particularly for the purposes of this argument in the context of the Lord's Supper (Luke 22:20; John 13:2; 1 Cor 11:20, 21, 25).

Support Based on Eschatological Fulfillment

At his last Passover meal with the disciples, Jesus said he would not eat the meal or drink from the cup again until it was fulfilled at the kingdom's arrival (Luke 22:16, 18). After supper Jesus said, "I confer on you a kingdom . . . so that you may eat and drink at my table in my kingdom" (vv. 29–30). The *Last* Supper and the first Lord's Supper (1 Cor 11:25), both real meals, pointed to a day of fulfillment when believers would recline with Messiah at his table. Both Jesus and Paul saw the Christian communal meal as foreshadowing things to come. The Revelator wrote down the angelic beatitude: "Blessed are those who are invited to the wedding feast of the Lamb" (Rev 19:7–9). This language associated with the Greco-Roman banquet is unmistakable. Feasting by invitation only was an important characteristic of formal meals.

Jesus likened the kingdom of God to a feast. He referred to the time when "many will come from the east and the west and will take their places at the feast with Abraham, Isaac, and Jacob in the kingdom of heaven" (Matt 8:11). Although misguided in other matters, a Jewish leader rightly responded, "Blessed is the man who will eat at the feast in the kingdom of God" (Luke 14:15).

Support for a Real Meal Based on the Presence of a Host or Patron

Paul's letters are filled with references to individuals who care for the saints, most plausibly by providing meals. For instance, during his stay in Corinth, Paul pens his Letter to the Romans and sends greetings from "Gaius, who is *host* to me and to the whole church" (Rom 16:23). Paul commends Philemon, in whose house the church gathers, for "your love for all the saints" (Phlm 5), likely referring to his hosting and providing a love feast for the local believers.

Third John is addressed to "beloved Gaius" (v. 1) and focuses entirely on hospitality. The author speaks highly of Gaius who shows love to strangers who come his way (vv. 5–6). Others he mentions in his various letters who might have served as patron/hosts include Erastus, Crispus, Stephanas, plus several well-to-do women, including Nympha, Sapphira, and Lydia, who likely made their houses available for meals.[127]

2.6.2 Greco-Roman Libation versus Christian Cup Ritual (The Transition)

Just as the two courses found in a normal Greco-Roman banquet were connected by a libation, so in the banquet of the Lord they were linked by a ritual involving a cup of wine. Taussig calls this Christian cup ritual a

---

127. Women serving as hosts at communal meals might have been a Christian distinctive.

"libation" and claims the only difference between it and its Greco-Roman counterpart was the god to whom the cup was raised and the wine poured out.[128] He fails, however, to provide any evidence that the early church saw its cup ritual as a libation. It might be that Taussig simply uses the term "libation" incorrectly; but since a libation is properly defined as a poured out sacrifice to a deity, Taussig muddies the waters.[129]

That the church followed the general structure of the meal yet refused to make a libation to Caesar or the gods shows that its meal gatherings included counter-imperial elements. The cup ritual honoring Christ replaced the libation as the link between the *deipnon* and symposium.

Paul makes two seemingly innocuous statements that provide clues into the sequence or order for the Christian meal. The first concerns the start of the meal. He writes, "For when the time comes to eat" (1 Cor 11:21), which signifies that people have arrived at a certain location and hour to share a meal. Hence, there is an opening or time when the meal begins.[130] Second, he mentions that on the night of his betrayal Jesus "took the cup also, *after* supper" (v. 23). This shows that both the Last Supper and subsequently the Lord's Supper followed the Greco-Roman custom linking the two courses by a cup ritual. While Romans made a "libation" to a good deity or to Dionysus following the *deipnon*, the Christians raised a "cup of blessing" ("*to poterion tes eulogia*") in memory of Christ (1 Cor 10:16). Like its pagan counterpart, the Christian cup followed the same sequence as the Greco-Roman banquet, i.e., it came "after supper."[131] In this sense, it marked a transition or shift from meal to symposium, where lively discussions were held.

2.6.3 Symposium in the Christian Meal

Since Paul portrays the Lord's Supper in 1 Corinthians 11 as a full evening meal, followed by the raising of a cup "after supper" (1 Cor 11:25), it should

128. Taussig, *In the Beginning*, 109–12.

129. Unfortunately, Taussig uses the word libation incorrectly in every instance that he applies it to the Lord's Supper, which is quite often throughout his book. The mistake reduces the value of an otherwise excellent book.

130. The act of literally breaking the bread by the host and distributing it to guests may have served as the actual starting point for Christian meals.

131. Fee, *Corinthians*, 468, following Barrett, *Corinthians*, 231, places the cup at the end of the meal, and does not conceive of the Lord's Supper as being patterned after a Greco-Roman banquet but only as an every day of the week type supper, devoid of a symposium.

come as no surprise that he would also discuss the activities typically identified with the symposium or second tables, i.e., the drinking and entertainment section of the banquet. He does this in 1 Corinthians 14.

Symposium Language

The identical phrase that Paul uses in 1 Cor 11:23–25 to describe the gathering for the first course—"come together"—he uses again to describe the gathering for the symposium: "What should be done, my friends? When you *come together* one has a hymn, a lesson, a revelation, a tongue, or an interpretation. Let all things be done for the building up" (1 Cor 14:26). The passage which has become known popularly as the "gifts chapter" is actually placed in the context of a symposium setting.

Symposium Activities

Hymns and teachings were activities ordinarily a part of a normal pagan symposium. In the environment of a Christian symposium—the time when believers collectively expressed worship to God in a vocal manner—songs and doctrine served to unite the church around the truth of the gospel.[132] The churches learned the many hymns and teachings through apostolic letters that circulated among them and through traveling evangelists and teachers who passed through the region.

Revelations, prophetic utterances, tongues, and interpretations were associated with cultic and sacrificial meals. Should one make a random visit to a Roman temple dedicated to Bacchus or one of the mystery cults located throughout the empire in the first century, he or she might have discovered a meal or meals being held in the dining room(s). Filled with much wine and enthusiasm for their faith, the worshippers might break into unintelligible tongues, the language of the gods or receive a prophecy from an anointed oracle in their midst.

Paul identifies the same kind of practices taking place during the Christian symposium, but exhorts his readers to use them to build up one another in the faith (v. 26), showing that he embraces the highest of symposium etiquette, which calls upon diners to manifest fellowship (*koinonia*), friendship (*philia*), and equality (*isonomia*).

132. Chapters 7–8 identify and expound on the Christian symposium.

In the remainder of 1 Corinthians 14, Paul writes about how those participating in symposium activities should conduct themselves (vv. 27–40). He gives particular attention to the necessity of speaking in turn (v. 29), the role of women at a symposium (v. 34),[133] and how "all things should be done decently and in order" (v. 40). The second tables of the Christian banquet was filled with festive joy as was its pagan counterpart, but the entire time was to be characterized by decorum.

—Part 2—
Voluntary Associations and Anti-Imperialism

Roman banquets were not self-existent or self-perpetuating. They involved much effort and planning. Guests had to be selected and invited, food had to be purchased, meals had to be prepared and served, and entertainers had to be secured. A sponsor was usually needed. Individual patrons often served in this capacity, but just as frequently voluntary associations sponsored banquets.[134]

Associations—also referred to as *collegia*—were social organizations, or more specifically, supper clubs with each having its own goals and purposes for existence.[135] There were four types of associations: 1) professional or occupational, 2) religious or sacrificial, 3) funeral or burial, and 4) household or ethnic.[136] The first two needed to obtain official sanction from the local government to operate, while the latter more informal

133. The role of Christian women actively participating in the *deipnon* and symposium will be examined in chapter 7.

134. Jewett, "Tenement Churches and Pauline Love Feasts," 43–58, makes a strong case that many meals, especially Christian communal meals, were not sponsored by an association or hosted by a patron. Some people did not belong to an association or have a benefactor. For many on the lowest economic rung of society living in crowded tenements and without a trade, communal meals were self-sponsored with each person setting aside a small portion of his meager income to support a weekly or monthly supper. Also see Jewett, "Tenement Churches and Communal Meals," 23–43. This issue will be explored in more depth in an upcoming chapter.

135. While the term association was not the term used in the first century to describe societies, guilds and dinner clubs, both Taussig, *In the Beginning*, 88 and Harland, *Associations*, 25, use it as an umbrella term for descriptive purposes. This thesis will follow suit. There were all kinds of associations, ranging from guilds to funeral societies, but all had one thing in common—they were "supper clubs."

136. Jewett, "Tenement Churches and Pauline Love Feasts," 43–58.

groups did not, since their emphasis was mainly on fellowship and be-nevolence.[137] Regardless of their stated purpose, all associations had one thing in common—their meetings revolved around meals.[138]

2.7 Different Kinds of Associations[139]

2.7.1 Those Focused on Occupation

Many associations were related to one's occupation, similar to modern-day labor or trade unions. There were associations for builders, crafts-men, accountants, merchants, carpenters, dyers of fabric, and Corley adds "shopkeepers, weavers, coppersmiths, bakers, purple sellers" to the mix.[140] Nearly all artisans belonged to an association.[141] Jesus himself might have been a member of such a guild. Likewise, Paul may have belonged to an association, since he was a skilled tentmaker (Acts 18:3). When preaching in Ephesus, he found himself in danger when members of the powerful silversmith's guild accused him of hurting business (Acts 19:23–41).

Occupational associations were organized so individuals with com-mon interests or trades, but of low status, could come together and eat in a friendly and orderly atmosphere. Some individuals belonged to more than one kind of association and might attend several guild-sponsored meals throughout the month. One's social ranking was determined by the meal to which one was invited and the seat they were assigned. Through meals members could improve their status. As they moved up in the guild, they were invited to move closer to the head of the table or attend a different banquet.

2.7.2 Those Focused on Religious Practice

Other associations were purely cultic in nature and sought to keep alive the traditions surrounding a particular deity, often a god or goddess con-nected with the members' conquered homeland. Rome was tolerant of any

137. Jeffers, *Greco-Roman World*, 76–77.

138. Kloppenborg and Wilson, *Voluntary Associations*, 43.

139. The best sources for the different kinds of associations are Harland, *Associa-tions*; Taussig, *In the Beginning*; Smith, *From Symposium*; Jeffers, *Greco-Roman World*; Kloppenborg and Wilson, *Voluntary Associations*.

140. Corley, *Maranatha*, 11–12.

141. Cotter, "Collegia and Roman Law," 87.

religions that did not claim exclusiveness or seek to elevate a foreign god above the gods of Rome.[142] Cultic activities took place in temples, where sacrifices were offered by the priests to the gods on behalf of the worshippers and dining rooms were set up for meals. Additionally, many Roman citizens met for cultic banquets to honor the gods of Rome.

2.7.3 Those Focused on Benevolence

Funerary societies were among the most popular associations.[143] Since most peasants could not afford a decent burial, they had limited options. They could: 1) resign themselves to a pauper's burial, which meant their body would be tossed in a community pit, 2) find a patron to cover the cost of a proper burial, or 3) pay an initiation fee and monthly dues to a funeral association that guaranteed them a respectable burial and a memorial meal to follow.[144] While burial societies were not required to be registered with the government, they had to inform the local city officials of their existence before being allowed to meet for monthly banquets.[145]

2.7.4 Those Focused on Ethnic Roots

Some associations existed to maintain solidarity among peoples of a particular ethnic background, just as a contemporary organization like the Saint David's Society seeks to perpetuate the Welsh heritage among its membership who live abroad. When Rome conquered the peoples of the eastern Mediterranean region, "various elements of Hellenistic society . . . threatened the dissolution of [their] ethnic solidarity."[146] These threats included: 1) pressure to be loyal to the empire above one's ethnicity, 2) the scattering of ethnic groups throughout the empire, and 3) the danger of losing one's identity by becoming part of Rome's giant melting pot of

142. By special arrangement, Judaism was the exception to the rule. See chapter 4 for a discussion of this issue.

143. Similar associations still exist. This writer's grandfather, native of Baltimore, MD, was a member of The Improved Order of Red Man, a fraternal organization originally founded in Baltimore in 1834 as a Funeral Society for the expressed purpose of providing burial insurance for its members. Many of the "animal lodges" (Elks, Moose, Eagles, etc.) began as benevolence societies and eating clubs.

144. *Corpus Inscriptionum Latinarum* (*CIL*) XIV, 2112. Harland, *Associations*, 83–86 gives close attention to burial societies, as does Corley, *Maranatha*, 16–17.

145. Jeffers, *Greco-Roman World*, 76.

146. Taussig, *In the Beginning*, 92.

nationalities.[147] In fear of losing all connection to their ancestral, social, and religious roots, and to preserve their ethnic distinctiveness, individuals found themselves forming and joining associations whose membership was drawn from among those with similar backgrounds.

Associational meetings were held regularly throughout the month with the main component of these gatherings being the Greco-Roman banquet.[148] Around the meal table members bonded and supported each other, talked about their common heritage, while at the same time pledging their allegiance to the empire. Rome encouraged membership in societies because they sponsored banquets, which Rome viewed as tools of domination.

2.8 The Roman Banquet as the Heart of the Association Meeting

That the Roman banquet was at the heart of association gatherings[149] is evidenced by Harland's research of art work found in association-owned buildings. Several reliefs graphically portray members reclining at a meal.[150] Harland's documentation also includes proof that an association building in Ostia featured four dining halls with permanent couches.[151]

While wealthy Roman and native elites often hosted non-association banquets in their homes, associations provided peasants and artisans with meals as one of the benefits of membership.[152] Vast numbers of people, even the poorest of the poor, living in the empire belonged to one or more voluntary associations, which ranged in membership from less than a dozen to ten times that amount with the average being somewhere in the

147. Ibid.

148. Ibid., 34. Also see Nerney and Taussig, *Re-Imaging*, 11–12.

149. These include Kloppenborg and Wilson, Klinghardt, Smith, Harland, as well as the members of the SBL study group on "Meals in the Greco-Roman World."

150. Harland, *Associations*, 63.

151. Ibid., 65.

152. The reason so little is written about peasant class associations is that the chroniclers themselves were part of the upper class and therefore focused on their own groups. Peasants were mostly illiterate and left few records of their activities. See Nerney and Taussig, *Re-Imaging*, 12, who give a glimpse into the dynamics of a working class association of the first century. They note that the peasant groups did not abide by many of the restrictions found in elite associations, especially those related to women and slaves.

middle.[153] Depending on the size and financial worth of the association, meetings were held either in homes, rented quarters, a local temple, or a building which the association owned.[154] Usually the members met on a monthly basis. Since some people belonged to more than one association, e.g., one occupational and another ethnic, they attended meals more often.

Rome imposed two obligations upon all associations: 1) They must honor the emperor with a libation at its meals and 2) They could not participate in any political action against the state.[155] Otherwise, associations were free to meet regularly without restraint, collect dues, sponsor banquets, and provide benevolence to their members.

2.9 The Association as a Model for the Local Church

From the start, Rome considered the Jewish followers of Jesus to be part of a movement within Judaism, similar to the way members of the Methodist movement were part of the Church of England at the time of John Wesley. The early Jesus movement did not stand alone as a recognized religion within the empire. Most Jewish disciples attended synagogue on the Sabbath, observed Jewish feasts, and kept the Mosaic law like their non-messianic brethren, but they also held their own meetings and meals with fellow believers.

Just as Rome did not make a distinction initially between Judaism and Christianity, neither did she make a distinction between synagogue and church gatherings. Rome likely viewed both as association meetings, which met for meals.[156] Ascough and Taussig hold that the local church was deliberately modeled after the association, but Jeffers believes that only non-Christians viewed the church to be an association, possibly a funeral or household society.[157] Meeks takes a position contrary to both

153. Harland, *Associations*, 8–62.

154. Roussel and Launey, *Inscriptions de Delos*, 1529.

155. Jeffers, *Greco-Roman World*, 73.

156. See Jeffers, *Greco-Roman World*, 73. The formation of voluntary associations still exists. In many jurisdictions in America, for instance, a group of individuals can voluntarily form an association without going through the process of legal incorporation. Not-for-profit associations often are formed for charitable purposes and can receive tax-deductible donations. Some jurisdictions require that associations be registered to assure against fraud. In the Roman Empire of the first-century CE, both sanctioned and unsanctioned associations existed. Although voluntary associations were not sanctioned, they were still legal. Likely, Rome viewed local gatherings of believers as voluntary associations.

157. Ascough, *Paul's Macedonia Associations*, 190, makes a strong exegetical case

Taussig and Jeffers, and holds that the differences between church and association far exceed the likenesses.[158] Dennis Smith, while acknowledging that the local church fits into the category of being an association, believes that a study of meals within the church is more important than the church's relationship to the association; thus, he devotes only one chapter of his book to associational or club banquets.[159] Smith makes a good point, but it leads to a question: Would the church have been able to carry out Jesus' understanding of kingdom ethics at mealtime with little or no governmental scrutiny had it not functioned as an association?

Corley offers a succinct summary of why the voluntary association is considered "the primary analogue" for understanding the formation of the church, stating that many terms that were common to voluntary associations were used to describe Christian groups and their members, including *ekklesia, adelphoi, episkopos,* and *diakonos.*[160]

Because Rome placed the Jesus movement within the sphere of Judaism, a tolerated religion, *Christianity* was able to flourish. Because Rome additionally viewed the *ekklesia* to be an association, the *local church* was able to meet freely for meals.

2.10 The Potential Anti-Imperial Threat of Associations

Despite its outward support of associations, Rome also realized that they could become potential breeding grounds for organized dissent and insurrection against the empire. Members of household societies whose homelands had been conquered by Rome were especially prone to divided loyalties. Unless checked, this tension could give way to animosity. Since Rome could not regulate or monitor the hundreds of symposia being held throughout the empire on any given day of the month, she was cautiously suspicious of what went on behind closed doors around the *triclinium.*

---

that Paul understands his Macedonian congregations to be associations. Kloppenborg mentions how Tertullian used association language to describe Christian assemblies ("Collegia and Thiasoi" in Kloppenborg and Wilson, *Voluntary Associations,* 18). Also see McGready, "Ekklesia and Voluntary Associations," 69–70; Taussig, *In the Beginning,* 93–95; Jeffers, *Greco-Roman World,* 80.

158. While recognizing a similarity between congregations and associations, Meeks, *First Urban Christians,* 74–83, argues there were too many differences to classify churches as associations. Harland's *Associations,* 210, more exhaustive study takes Meeks to task.

159. Smith, *From Symposium,* 87–131.

160. Corley, *Maranatha,* 12.

One might liken the situation to the British government's distrust of certain Catholic organizations in Northern Ireland that came together for meals in private homes prior to the Belfast Agreement of 1998 and the subsequent voluntary disarmament of the IRA in 2005. In this protected environment, the Irish could speak freely about the "good old days" and "bad-mouth" the Brits. They might even plan some mischief or terrorist action. None of their peers at the dinner party would report them to officials. What went on "behind closed doors," remained hidden.

Another less volatile analogy might be in order. The home school movement is legal in the United States of America. This means that parents, not the government, can take responsibility for educating their children. Parents can serve as teachers, choose curricula, assign research papers and projects, etc. The home serves as the classroom and the dining room table serves as the student's desk. Parents determine how to teach reading, writing, arithmetic, science, history, sociology, economics, civics, and so forth. In states like Texas there are few, if any, regulations. Many professional educators and governmental authorities are suspicious of what goes on "behind the closed doors" of these unmonitored home classrooms. Are parents teaching evolution like state-sponsored schools or theism? Do they promote tolerance toward alternative lifestyles or do they teach a fundamentalist-based Christian morality? While the government recognizes the legality of home schooling, some officials are wary of the project and consider it dangerous.

Likewise, Rome officially viewed associations as legal and allowed them to assemble for meals without interference. But because she could not supervise or control the vast number of groups located throughout the empire, she also looked upon associations as being potentially dangerous.[161] Even associations that had received official status (sacrificial cults and occupational societies) were occasionally held in suspicion. In his letter to Pliny the Younger, the governor of Bithynia in the early second-century CE, Emperor Trajan expresses his concern that, "If people assemble for a common purpose, whatever name we give them and for whatever reason, they soon turn into a political club."[162] Trajan's statement is significant because it is a reply to Pliny's seemingly innocent request to form a volunteer fire department in his city.

161. Cotter, "Collegia and Roman Law," 76–79, notes that as early as 64 BCE the Roman Senate sought to ban any associations whose agenda opposed the policies of the Republic. For the next two centuries Rome sporadically clamped down on voluntary associations based on the whims of the respective emperor.

162. Pliny, *Letters to the Younger Pliny* 10.35, 272.

Rome's misgivings were not entirely without cause. While most members of associations met to enjoy a good meal and support the goals of the empire, the possibility always existed that some could vent anti-imperial sentiment.[163] The threat that private groups had the potential of becoming politically subversive may have led to periodic persecution of the Christian congregations, i.e., associations (Acts 17:7). As Jeffers observes, "This suspicion . . . that private groups, even when formed legally, tend to become politically subversive, could easily have focused on Christian congregations."[164]

First-century churches/associations were anti-imperial because their members' beliefs centered on Jesus' interpretation of the kingdom of God and they conducted their affairs in a nonviolent manner.[165] While believers sought to live under Christ in peaceful coexistence with their neighbors and the government whenever possible (1 Pet 2:13–17), they also knew that Rome's attempt to achieve and maintain peace through coercive means would not succeed. Because their values were informed by their understanding of the reign of Christ, these believers would have spoken out against Roman domination at mealtime. Their combined conversation and activities at the Lord's Supper would by nature be pro-kingdom of God and anti-imperial. Usually these nonviolent but subversive practices went unnoticed and did not draw the attention of the authorities.

2.11 Scenario

The association-like Jesus groups were able to function without great distraction or disruption from the government because on the surface, at least, they looked like any other association participating in a Greco-Roman banquet (Acts 2:41–42; 1 Cor 11:33). This means that if a first-century passerby on her way to the market happened to look in the window of a home where followers of Jesus were eating together she would see a meal that looked like any other Roman meal. She would see the diners reclining on couches at tables, drinking mixed wine, singing and having lively discussions. Nothing would seem out of the ordinary. However, if the

163. Harland, *Associations*, 161–73; 239–64, on the other hand, warns against sweeping generalizations and states that on the whole the vast majority of associations supported the Roman ideology and complied with normative meal practices.

164. Jeffers, *Greco-Roman World*, 73.

165. The thesis that the first-century church was anti-imperial in its outlook and actions will be developed in chapters 4–8.

passerby decided to hide in the bushes for several hours and eavesdrop, she would discover that during the symposium the banquet participants were engaging in subversive practices by refusing to pour a libation to a Roman deity or acknowledge Jupiter and Caesar as their patrons. She would recognize that the banqueters crossed socioeconomic lines, with peasants and landowners around the same table, in defiance of the accepted social structure of the empire. Listening to their hymns, she would be shocked to discover them singing about their allegiance to a new kingdom and a different Lord. And when their teacher stood and renounced Rome's authority and its imperialistic means to bring peace and security to the world, her jaw might drop and her heart skip a beat.

The above scenario, based on historical imagination, presents one with a sense of how an early local church, gathering to recline for its weekly communal meal might have appeared to an outsider.

2.12 Conclusion

The first-century Roman banquet was not only a regular event in which every free man participated, but also a social institution used by the empire to promote its imperial ideology and dominate the masses through social stratification. All persons attending banquets followed certain protocols, such as the pouring out of libations to Caesar and the gods, designed to demonstrate their allegiance to the empire. Not to do so would be considered unpatriotic.

Whether sponsored by an association, temple cult, synagogue, or house church, banquets followed the same outward pattern of meal and symposium. What made Christian gatherings different from other association meetings was not their form, but their refusal to support the Roman social agenda and ideology. Christians declared that Jesus was Lord and pledged their allegiance to his kingdom. Thus, the Lord's Supper served as a "community building" and "boundary securing meal" that was part of "an alternative social movement."[166]

Chapter 3 will examine the Passover meal as a subversive act that, according to the Exodus narrative, Jews ate as they anticipated God's deliverance from Pharaoh's tyrannical rule. The author will trace the Passover celebration from its start until the first-century CE when the Jews again

---

166. Based on correspondence between author and Warren Carter (December 15, 2007).

found themselves under foreign control. As in its past, the Passover became a symbol for hope, taking on an anti-imperial character.

Just as the Roman banquet had a profound influence on the Lord's Supper, so also the Passover meal. While the former provided the Lord's Supper its two-part format, the latter supplied it with anti-imperial ideology.

3

The Passover as an Anti-Imperial Activity

3.1 Introduction

"Early Israel was born as an anti-imperial resistance movement."[1] According to the Exodus narrative, the Hebrew slaves prepared for their escape from Pharaoh's totalitarian regime as they sat to eat their first Passover meal. This hastily eaten family supper was an anti-imperial event that effected, celebrated, and anticipated Israel's emancipation from Egyptian imperial rule. It was during the meal itself that God destroyed the firstborn of Egypt, leading to Israel's release from Egyptian bondage.

The thesis of this chapter is that the Passover meal originated as a subversive act of defiance against Egyptian domination and eventually became a symbol of Israel's liberation. Lest future generations of God's people forget the Exodus event, Yahweh instructed the nation to organize and to observe an annual Passover feast as a reminder of the divine deliverance.

By the time of Christ, the Jews found themselves living again under tyranny. Like Egypt, Rome operated as a domination system that used military might and other oppressive means to control the masses. Each spring when Jews from far and wide congregated in Jerusalem to celebrate the Passover, they not only remembered the original Exodus, but yearned for God to rescue them from the present authoritarian regime. This chapter traces the Jewish Passover meal from Egypt to Rome and

---

1. Gottwald, "Early Israel," 9.

shows how this feast of freedom evolved into an anti-imperial meal and a symbol of apocalyptic and eschatological deliverance. This emphasis provides a basis for interpreting Jesus' Passover meal with his disciples as being an anti-imperial praxis that points to Rome's defeat and the arrival of God's kingdom.[2] In turn, Jesus' final Passover lays the foundation for the Christian communal meal, i.e., the Lord's Supper, as being anti-imperial in character.[3]

3.2 Exodus from Egypt

The Jewish resistance to imperial Roman domination in the first century, which ultimately led to the great revolt in 66–70 CE and the destruction of Jerusalem, did not occur through happenstance. Jewish oppression and resistance have a long history.

According to the Exodus account, the ancient Hebrews lived in Egypt as resident aliens and then as slaves during the age of Egyptian imperialism.[4] Egypt's powerful military successfully conquered territories, captured multitudes of slaves, and amassed great wealth for its kingdom.

Whether one deems the second book of the Hebrew canon to be historically accurate or not, most agree that it is a piece of subversive literature that recounts in epic style how Yahweh liberated his people from a tyrannical regime, called them to remember what it was like to live as slaves, and challenged them to live differently when they enter the land of promise.

Brueggemann characterizes the Exodus event as a critical analysis of dominant ideology from the perspective of the victims.[5] It is the one event Jews were never to forget, and to which they would hearken back whenever they found themselves enslaved or living again under the heavy hand of oppression. The God who delivered them in the first place could do it again. The Exodus spoke of hope and deliverance.

2. The anti-imperial nature of the Last Supper, Jesus' final meal with his disciples, will be discussed in chapter 6.

3. The anti-imperial nature of the Lord's Supper will be examined in chapter 7.

4. Prior to the Exodus, the Hebrew children lived peacefully in Egypt under a succession of Pharaohs, who supported their presence based on historical precedence and Joseph's faithful years of service to the kingdom (Gen 41:41–57; 47:1–6). Pleins, *Social Visions*, 174, concludes, "The contrast between the pharaohs of Genesis and Exodus tells us that there is room for good monarchic, priestly, and tribal hierarchies in the estimation of the various narrators."

5. Brueggemann, *Hope*, 8, 12.

Egyptian Imperialism

The Egyptians, basing their actions on their imperial ideology, claimed the divine right to enslave the Hebrews. God's people, however, refused to accept the imperial arrangement "as normative or deserving of either respect or obedience."[6] Believing Pharaoh's power to be neither ultimate nor legitimate, they retained their identity as God's people, and in the midst of suffering, cried publicly and collectively for Yahweh to deliver them. This public outcry constituted an "irreversible act of civil disobedience."[7] James C. Scott labels such open forms of resistance as "public transcripts."[8] It was the kind of act that could get the culprit killed.

The Scripture recounts, "God heard their groaning, and God remembered his covenant with Abraham, Isaac, and Jacob. God looked upon the Israelites, and God took notice of them" (Exod 2:24–25). Yahweh first paid attention to the cries of the Hebrews because he had made a promise to their forefathers that he would give to their offspring a land and transform them into a great nation through which he would bless the peoples of the earth (Gen 12:2–3; 17:4–8). Second, he responded out of compassion: "I have observed the misery of my people who are in Egypt; I have heard their cry on the account of their taskmaster. Indeed, I knew their sufferings, and I have come down to deliver them from the Egyptians" (Exod 3:7–8).

In a sense, Israel's faith was birthed in the crucible of suffering, and would later be sustained through the same means. Prior to her enslavement, when the Hebrew people had a place of privilege in the empire, they did not depend upon Yahweh for survival. Then "a new king arose over Egypt, who did not know Joseph" (Exod 1:8), their fortunes were reversed and they returned to the God of their fathers. The experience of pain begins the formation of a Jewish counter-society within the empire based on their "alternative perception of reality."[9] This evolves into a new social imagination, i.e., envisioning a preferred future that involves the Hebrew people living under the reign of God (Exod 3:8).[10]

6. Ibid., 12.

7. Ibid., 11.

8. Scott, *Domination*, 2. By public transcripts Scott does not mean a conversation that takes place merely before a group of people, but confrontational communication between persons with power and those who lack power.

9. Brueggemann, *Hope*, 17–18.

10. Ibid., 20–21, Brueggemann explains that the social aspect of the "social imagination" refers to the fact that it is embraced by the greater Hebrew community. It is not a "privatization of imagination" which leads to "abdication and resignation in the public arena" and allows for overall conformity with public policy. Social imagination

In responding to the plea of his people, God commissions Moses to speak on his behalf to Pharaoh. When Moses asks for God to identify himself, he receives the answer, "I AM WHO I AM . . . This is my name forever" (Exod 3:13–14). As Yahweh's ambassador, Moses is told that he will be "like God to Pharaoh" (7:1), i.e., he will be God's authoritative spokesperson. He will speak truth boldly into the face of power. When Pharaoh refuses to grant the Hebrews a reprieve to offer sacrifices to their God, the Lord exhibits his power through miracles and plagues so the "Egyptians shall know that I am the LORD [I am that I AM]" (7:5).

A trio of three plagues are unleashed upon Egypt, followed by a devastating tenth plague—the death of the firstborn among both animals and humans. Each set (plagues 1–3, 4–6, and 7–9) begins with God offering Pharaoh an opportunity to repent before the next judgment falls.[11] The first plague in each set also serves to reveal God's power to Pharaoh (Exod 7:17; 8:22; 9:29). "The miracles and plagues are proofs of God's presence and power with Israel—even in the land of Ham."[12] Despite warnings of further judgment, Pharaoh ignores Yahweh's appeal.

The tenth and final plague, death of all firstborn males is accomplished by a direct act of God without any assistance from Moses, and leads to Israel's exodus from Egypt.

Because of his compassionate covenant promises to their forefathers and the manifested faith by the Hebrew slaves, God announces that death will pass over their firstborn. He instructs them that between 10–14 Nisan they are to get ready for deliverance by preparing and eating a sacrificial meal in anticipation and celebration of imminent liberation (Exod 12:3–8). The meal will not be a mere symbolic act, but will actually effectuate their freedom. Each family is to take a lamb, kill it, smear the blood on the lintels of their houses, roast the lamb and eat it with unleavened bread and bitter herbs.[13] God calls the meal "the Passover of the Lord" (v. 11). When the plague strikes Egypt, death will pass over all homes marked with the

---

is profoundly a community endeavor. In many ways, contemporary Christianity in the West has replaced social imagination with personal imagination that offers hope of heavenly salvation for the individual. The pharaohs of this world encourage privatization of faith because its leaves public affairs intact.

11. Waltke and Yu, *An Old Testament Theology*, 378.

12. Ibid., 379.

13. The word "bitter" first appears in Exod 1:13–14, "The Egyptians became ruthless in imposing tasks on the Israelites, and made their lives bitter with hard service in mortar and brick and in every kind of field labour. They were ruthless in all the tasks that they imposed on them."

blood of the lamb. Without delay, the Jews must be dressed and ready for their escape (vv. 12–13).

The meal functions in two practical ways. First, it serves as the means by which the firstborn are delivered from physical death with the blood from the dinner lamb smeared on the lintel to protect the children. Second, it provides God's people nourishment for the first leg of their wilderness trek.

Before her exit, God instructs Israel to retell continuously the story of her miraculous exodus from bondage by means of "liturgical recital and enactment."[14] This will be accomplished primarily by observing an annual Passover meal: "This day shall be a day of remembrance for you. You shall celebrate it as a festival to the Lord; throughout your generations you shall observe it as a perpetual ordinance" (Exod 12:14).[15] Moses adds, "When you come to the land that the Lord will give you, as he has promised, you shall keep this observance. And when your children ask you, 'What do you mean by this observance?' you shall say, 'It is the Passover sacrifice to the Lord, for he passed over the houses of the Israelites in Egypt, when he struck down the Egyptians but spared our houses'" (vv. 24–27).[16]

3.3 Excursus: The Fourfold Purpose of Memory

According to Miroslav Volf, sacred memory serves four functions.[17] First, it defines the identity of a people. To be a Jew is to remember the Exodus, but it also includes acting in the present. Memory is not a single event. Each succeeding generation must remember in the light of its particular historical and cultural context. God's redemptive action in the Exodus not only formed the ancient Hebrew people into a holy nation, but *informed* their heirs as to how they were to act as Jews. While memory focuses

---

14. Brueggemann, *Hope*, 10.

15. God also included guidelines for celebrating a seven-day Feast of Unleavened Bread, which was to precede the Passover meal (Exod 12:15–20). Whereas the sacrificial Passover meal symbolized escape from *God's judgment* of death upon all firstborn, the Feast of Unleavened Bread signified separation from *Egyptian domination and oppression*: "You shall observe the festival of unleavened bread, for on this very day I brought your companies out of the land of Egypt: you shall observe this day throughout your generations as a perpetual ordinance" (v. 17).

16. Similar instructions are given in Exod 23:4–15; 34:18–25; Lev 23:4–6; Num 9:1–8; 28:16–25; Deut 16:1–8.

17. Volf, *End of Memory*, 97–102.

mainly on the past, it speaks to the contemporary circumstances. Therefore, memory is relevant.

It is the Passover's "commemorative rituals and liturgies" that perpetuate the sacred memory, enabling worshippers to be caught up existentially in the events and their meaning.[18] By eating the future paschal meal "at the precise moment of the exodus, the Israelites embody the memory of their salvation."[19] The food, drink, stories, songs, and symbols that accompany the Seder helps to transport the diners mentally back to Egypt so they participate in the redemption wrought by God through the Exodus. The imagined memory elicited by the meal also allows celebrants who live centuries after the original event to experience the Exodus for themselves as if they were there. The Mishnah declares, "In each and every generation, each person can regard himself as though he has emerged from Egypt."[20] Therefore, every post-Exodus Passover meal reflected in some sense a "realized eschatology."[21]

Second, memory functions to unite a people. Passover was to be a communal rather than a solitary experience. Yahweh entrusted the memory of Exodus to the entire nation (Exod 12:14; 17:24–25; 13:10) to assure it would be kept alive and not fade into oblivion. Memories can be lost if assigned only to a select few individuals. God's plan assured that each person acquired their sacred memories from the larger society—family, community, or nation. Just as each citizen learns about America's history in school and retains these memories through community or national celebrations, so Jews remembered the Exodus by corporate participation in the Passover feast.

Third, sacred memory produces hope. The past is connected to the future. Recollections of former horrors provide a hopeful outlook that God will ultimately set accounts right by vindicating the afflicted and judging the wrongdoers. Even when the evildoers escape justice in this lifetime, they will one day stand at Yahweh's judgment bar and receive recompense for their malicious behavior. Evil will be expunged and God's righteous rule will prevail. Thus, the nation of Israel was instructed to connect the past deliverance with future hope. Redemption was always just over the

18. Ibid., 98.

19. MacDonald, *Not by Bread Alone*, 99. MacDonald's study offers not only a valuable survey of food in the OT, but also acute analysis.

20. *Pesahim* X.5. Pesahim, (פסחים), which literally means "Passovers" is the third section of the *Seder Moed* of the *Mishnah* and discusses post 70 CE rabbinic debates dealing with Passover.

21. Leonhard, *Jewish Pesach*, 426.

horizon. Passover Seders include a place setting at the table for Elijah, the messianic forerunner, who will pave the way for the coming of the Lord. An open window and a door, and a full glass of wine await his arrival.[22] The modern observance, like its ancient counterpart, looks to the future as well as to the past as the faithful anticipate the redemption to come.

Fourth, Israel's Passover memories were actually *"memories of God."*[23] The Exodus was not merely a fortuitous event or an example of human-kind's ability to overcome suffering and evil, but God's loving intervention on behalf of his people—based on his own memory of the covenant he made with Abraham. "In the biblical tradition, remembering is an expression of the experience of liberation given by God."[24] Memory focuses on salvation-history. In history God revealed himself as Israel's mighty champion who fought their wars and secured their freedom (Exod 12:27; 13:8, 14, 16).[25]

3.4 The Eating of the Passover and the March from Egypt

After receiving these instructions about memory, the Israelites consumed the first Passover lamb (v. 28) and "it came to pass at midnight that Yahweh struck down all the firstborn in the land of Egypt, from the firstborn of Pharaoh who sat on his throne to the firstborn of the prisoner who was in the dungeon, and all the firstborn of the livestock" (v. 29).[26]

22. Barth, *Rediscovering the Lord's Supper*, 11–12.

23. Volf, *Memory*, 101.

24. Bieler and Schottroff, *Eucharist*, 158. Based on remembering her own captivity, Israel was expected to be an anti-imperial alternative society. In emulating Yahweh by compassionately exercising her power for redemptive purposes rather than emulating Egypt and her gods for tyrannical purposes, Israel reflects God's merciful nature and blesses the nations.

25. In like fashion, the memory associated with the Lord's Supper will look to the cross as the new turning point in salvation history through which God secures eschatological deliverance for his people.

26. Because death passes over the eldest among Hebrew children or beasts, God claims them as his own. He instructs Moses, "Consecrate to me all the firstborn; whatever is the first to open the womb among the Israelites, of human beings and animals, is mine" (Exod 13:1–2). While all Jewish firstborn belong to God, provisions are made so parents can buy them back from the Lord for five shekels (Exod 13:12–15; 22:29–30). This process is called redemption. The firstborn among clean animals would be sacrificed to God. The firstborn among unclean animals could be redeemed or put to death (Exod 13:13; 34:19–20). Like other practices associated with the Exodus, fathers were required to explain the significance of the redemption system to their children (Exod 13:14–16). The Levites replaced the human firstborn who were redeemed. "Then the

Crushed by the deadly tragedy that befell his land, Pharaoh urged God's people to leave Egypt immediately (vv. 31–33). "By the roundabout way of the wilderness towards the Red Sea" they made their escape (Exod 13:17–18). Gustavo Gutierrez, the Latin American theologian rightly characterizes the "liberation of Israel" as a "political action" that leads ultimately to "the construction of a just and fraternal society."[27] Unfortunately, he erroneously views the Exodus as the result of a successful people's resistance movement that achieves liberation through sacrificial self effort and not God's blessings.[28] In reality, the Scriptures attribute the victory to Yahweh's miraculous intervention alone.

When safely out of harm's way, the throng of liberated slaves sing in unison what traditionally has been labeled the "Song of Moses" (Exod 15:1–18), which concludes with the words, "The Lord will reign forever and ever." In singing this canticle by the sea, Israel acknowledges Yahweh to be the true king whose dominion is everlasting and far superior to the world's most powerful Pharaoh. The women join in "with tambourines and with dancing" as Miriam directed them to, "Sing to the Lord, for he has triumphed gloriously; horse and rider he has thrown into the sea" (vv. 20–21). What is normally characterized to be a victory song, Brueggemann portrays as "a liturgic enactment of a changed social situation"[29] that bespeaks a new political and economic reality wherein Israel rejects Pharaoh as king as they accept and affirm the kingship of God.

The Passover/Exodus is the pivotal point in Israel's history. According to the narrative, it ends four hundred and thirty years under despotic Egyptian rule, marks Israel's birth as a free people, and paves the way for the Mosaic covenant that forms the Hebrew people into a priestly and holy nation, living uniquely under the rule of God as a new political entity (Exod 19:5–6). Harkness denotes, "The concept of the covenant between God and his chosen people . . . underlies [the] concept of kingdom."[30] Gottwald and Mendenhall likewise affirm that when Israel enters the

---

Lord spoke to Moses, saying: 'I hereby accept the Levites from among the Israelites as substitutes for all the firstborn that open the womb among the Israelites. The Levites shall be mine, for all the firstborn are mine; when I killed all the firstborn in the land of Egypt, I consecrated for my own all the firstborn in Israel, both human and animal; they shall be mine. I am the Lord'" (Num 3:11–13).

27. Gutierrez, *Theology of Liberation*, 155.

28. Ibid., 68, 91.

29. Brueggemann, *Hope*, 21.

30. Harkness, *Understanding the Kingdom of God*, 69.

covenant, she pledges her allegiance to the kingdom of God.[31] The giving of the Law thus provides Israel with ethical guidelines to help her live under God's reign. The first commandment, which prohibits the worship of other gods, recognizes Yahweh's superiority over them all (Exod 20:2–3). The Psalmist will later connect Yahweh's power over the pagan gods to his being king: "For the Lord is a great God, and a great *King* above all gods" (Ps 95:3). The Mosaic covenant moves social imagination out of the realm of the theoretical into the sphere of the practical. Hence, imagination becomes social reality.[32]

3.5 Passovers as Liturgical Enactments during the Time of Judges and Monarchy

In describing Israel's origins as a free people, Horsley remarks, "The exodus was clearly a paradigmatic story (later celebrated each year in the Passover festival) identifying their God as the one 'who brought you out of the land of Egypt, out of the house of bondage' (Ex 20:2)."[33] When instructing his people to eat an annual Passover to commemorate the Exodus, God was asking them to participate in a liturgical act. Liturgy involves remembrance and performance. In some sense it is a ritualistic and dramatic reenactment of the past through the use of storytelling and symbols. For the Jews, Passover was a yearly opportunity to praise God for their past liberation and their new political reality. It also served as a reminder that Israel was not to become a domination system that enslaved and marginalized people and as a corrective if she did. As Israel's king, Yahweh expected Israel to live according to his sociopolitical principles as reflected in the Law. As Brueggemann notes, "If the subject of liturgy is kingship [which the Passover liturgy is] . . . then liturgy serves to

31. For Mendenhall, *Law and Covenant*, the Mosaic covenant should be seen as the establishment of an alternative political kingdom. Gottwald, *Tribes of Yahweh*, likewise, believes the covenant should not be seen as forming Israel into a mere spiritual community, but into a new experimental political system based on ethical principles of freedom and justice.

32. In the sight of other nations (dominated by imperial powers which exploit and enslave) Israel, as an alternative society, will live according to the principles of justice, servitude and mercy. The blessings that result from abiding under the active rule of Yahweh will be a testimony of God's goodness. Israel will additionally serve as a "kingdom of priests" to bring their idolatrous neighbors into a relationship with Yahweh. God's election of Israel, therefore, is to spread knowledge of him to the surrounding Gentile nations.

33. Horsley and Hanson, *Bandits, Prophets, and Messiahs*, 5.

authorize, recognize, acknowledge, coronate, legitimate the ruler and the order that belongs to the ruler. The liturgy is a festive act of enthronement and the obedient act of submitting more and more areas of life to that newly wrought sovereignty."[34]

Since the Exodus secures freedom from domination and marks the birth of Israel as a nation, it is the essence of her identity and sets her apart from the other nations on earth.[35] Israelites are a free people and constitute a nation that is not to oppress others. Rather she is to be an advocate for justice and a champion of the downtrodden. The Passover was intended to help Israel remember her past and serve as a reminder of her obligations. If she applies the lessons of the past to the present, she will find favor with God and humankind.

Freed from servitude to the foreigners, the Israelites are on the verge of possessing the land of promise. At God's command Joshua circumcises the males, who had remained uncircumcised throughout four decades of wandering (Josh 5:2), and he calls for a Passover: "While the Israelites were encamped in Gilgal they kept the Passover in the evening on the fourteenth day of the month in the plains of Jericho. On the day after the Passover, on that very day, they ate the produce of the land, unleavened cakes and parched grain (Josh 5:10–11).

Scripture is silent as to whether or not Israel continues keeping a yearly Passover under Joshua's leadership. It does make clear, however, that by the time of Joshua's death Israel is in danger of moving away from God and becoming like the surrounding nations. The "Mosaic covenant functioned like a constitution for early Israel" and called upon the nation to give exclusive allegiance to God as their king.[36] In his farewell speech, Joshua encourages the people to keep the Law and warns them not to fol- low the ways of the heathen nations or to intermarry with their children, lest they fall into a snare and "perish from this good land that the Lord your God has given you" (Josh 23:12–13).

With Joshua's death (Josh 24:29), the nation regresses into patterns of unbelief and idolatry. Instead of influencing her neighbors for the good, Israel succumbs to their sins. An endless series of military rulers, known as judges, lead her on a rollercoaster ride of moral ups and downs, typified by the words, "In those days there was no king in Israel; all people did

34. Brueggemann, *Israel's Praise*, 10.

35. An eating by all, including the disenfranchised, of an annual Passover, marks Israel as a nation that reflects God's attitude toward all his people regardless of status. See MacDonald, *Not by Bread Alone*, 99.

36. Horsley and Hanson, *Bandits*, 5.

what was right in their own eyes" (Judg 21:25). Only once does she make a brief, but fleeting commitment to follow the covenant (Judg 24:19–27).

Rather than being the alternative society that points the nations to Yahweh, and thus fulfilling her social imagination, she desires "to be like all the nations" and demands that the prophet Samuel anoint a king to reign over her (1 Sam 8:5). When told of their request, God says to Samuel, "They have rejected me from being king over them" and charges Israel with being disobedient "from the day I brought them up out of Egypt to this day, forsaking me and serving other gods" (v. 7). He then gives Samuel the task of warning the people what will happen if their wish is granted.

God is not concerned that they ask for a king, but that they want a king so "they can be like the other nations" (v. 5), which they repeat a few verses later: "We are determined to have a king over us, so that we also may be like other nations, and that our king may govern us and go out before us and fight our battles" (vv. 18–19).

God had revealed to the patriarch Jacob his plan to give Israel a king (Gen 49:8, 10), anticipating their desire for a king once they entered the Promised Land (Deut 16:14a). Through Moses he instructed them to select a godly king, one to his liking, who would carry out his mandates, i.e., to uphold justice, show mercy, and enforce the socioeconomic principles outlined in the Law. He warned them against crowning a king "like all the nations" (v. 14b), who would "acquire many horses for himself, or return the people to Egypt in order to acquire more horses" (vv. 15–16). The Lord commanded, "You must never return that way again" (v. 16b). The new king additionally "must not acquire many wives for himself, or else his heart will turn away; also silver and gold he must not acquire in great quantity for himself" (vv. 17–18). Rather, he should be a man with a passion for the Law (vv. 18–19), one who is humble and leaves an example which his royal descendants can follow (v. 20).

Ignoring these long-standing guidelines, Israel does not seek a king who will rule "under God," but covets one like the foreign nations who will rule "instead of God."[37] This was tantamount to abandoning faith in Yahweh and breaking the everlasting covenant.

Although somewhat overstated, Dale Patrick's analysis is correct that in asking for a king Israel "repudiated" the "theocracy which began with Moses and endured through the period of the judges . . ."[38] While, on the one hand, she wants to identify with Yahweh; on the other hand, she

---

37. Roberts, *God's Big Picture*, 80.
38. Patrick, "The Kingdom of God in the Old Testament," 74.

desires to abandon her divine social obligation to be a distinctive society. Her worship of God will become perfunctory and meaningless.

"Yahwehism" was not simply dogmatism, but "was an alternative way of life—social, economic, political, religious. It gave a transcendent dimension to the struggle of diverse, marginalized peoples to overcome the dominant mechanism and ideologies of oppression and to create a new social order in which all would have enough."[39] Driver judges the matter thus: "In asking for a king 'like the other nations,' God's people have actually become like the nations around them."[40]

God grants Israel's request and tells Samuel "to anoint [Saul] to be ruler over my people Israel" (1 Sam 9:16). Saul reigns twenty years (1020–1000 BCE), followed by the successive reigns of David (1000–962), and Solomon (962–922). Under David, Israel expands its borders, conquering all of Palestine and the surrounding Canaanite city-states, and establishes an imperial monarchy with a strong central government. "The previously free tribes are now ruled from the capital in Jerusalem, the 'city of David.'"[41]

Through Solomon, Israel becomes increasingly more like other nations as she embraces idolatry and operates in the manner of a domination system. With King Solomon's new temple, the monarchy takes on the appearance divine legitimacy. According to the biblical narrative, in the course of time, Solomon rose to become the most powerful leader in the Mediterranean. He not only matched the wealth and wit of other rulers, but also "excelled all the kings of the earth in riches and wisdom" (1 Kgs 10:23). Regrettably, the very kind of king God warned against (Deut 16:14–20) was the kind of king Solomon had become.

During the time of the Judges and monarchs the scriptural narrative contains only a single reference to Israel observing the Feast of Unleavened Bread (2 Chr 8:12–13). It is impossible to know if an annual Passover meal was still being celebrated or fell by the wayside. If the former, one can only imagine how the Jewish populace felt as they ate the meal of freedom. Scriptures hint that the peasants did not submit readily to their own oppressive monarchs. At least two major citizenry revolts occurred during the reign of King David (2 Samuel 13–18 led by Absalom and 2 Samuel 20 led by Sheba). In light of the political atmosphere among the masses, one might suspect that the Jews sitting at Passover were not only remembering their past deliverance from Pharaoh, but were hoping for deliverance from

39. Kinsler and Kinsler, *Biblical Jubilee*, 35.
40. Driver, *Images of the Church in Mission*, 29.
41. Horsley and Hanson, *Bandits*, 7.

their own imperial kings. Further evidence of the discontent occurs after Solomon's death and ten tribes split to form the northern kingdom (1 Kgs 11:31–35). Except in rare instances, both kingdoms choose to serve their own interests rather than God's. Both Israel and Judah find themselves making moral compromises and entering into political alliances with their heathen neighbors in order to survive.

3.6 Passover during the Divided Kingdom

In the northern Kingdom the Israelites mistrusted the kings and resisted the call to submit to autocratic rule.[42] One monarch after another emulated the sovereigns of the Gentile nations. They no longer upheld the social vision to be a "holy nation" that included an egalitarian way of life, debt forgiveness, and complete loyalty to Yahweh. They developed visions that supported their own devious plans. As a result, Yahweh commissioned prophets to call the people, especially her leaders, to repent or else face judgment. They denounced unholy alliances with foreign neighbors and condemned bribery, half-hearted worship, oppression and affliction of the poor and disenfranchised, charging of usury, and even pronounced woe on the institution of the monarchy (Amos 2:6–16; 3:9–10; 4:1–13; 5:10, 22; 6:12; Hos 4:1; 6:8; 8:1–4, 14; 10:4; etc.).[43] Along with the message of condemnation, the prophets offered hope if the nation returned to God and his covenant (Hos 14:2). Instead of heeding the prophetic warnings, the leaders persecute the prophets (Amos 2:6–7), and God allows Israel to fall prey to the Assyrians in 722 BCE.

The southern kingdom of Judah fared little better as a succession of kings destroyed the moral fiber of the nation. Only a small remnant of Jews observed sporadically the Passover. As in the north, God sent prophets to the south who condemned the rulers for their inequitable practices and harsh and repressive treatment of the lowly masses (Isa 1:4–5, 15–23, 28–29; 3:13–15; 5:1–7, 24; 6:1–13; 26:21; 30:1–5; Jer 7:1–4; Mic 3:1–2, 9–12).

Scriptures record only two occasions when Judea as a nation joined together to eat a Passover. Both occurred during times of national revival. The first took place when King Hezekiah (ca. 741–740 BCE) ordered the Temple to be cleansed from defilement (2 Chronicles 29) and invited tribes from the north to "come to the house of the Lord at Jerusalem to

42. Ibid.

43. There is no scriptural evidence or extrabiblical record that the northern kingdom of Israel ever observed an annual Passover.

keep the Passover to the Lord the God of Israel. . . . for they had not kept it in great numbers as prescribed" (2 Chr 30:1–2, 5).

Verse 5b ("for they had not kept it in great numbers as prescribed") indicates that before Hezekiah's national decree, few Jews had faithfully kept the feast. Since Passover was a ritual enactment intended to keep alive the memory of the Exodus and to motivate the nation to live according to God's values, verse 5b implies that Judah had abandoned her high calling.

Hezekiah's invitation to the northern tribes to join in a Passover celebration was an effort to bring the northern kingdom to repentance and reunite the people of God (2 Chr 30:6–9). Their overall response was scorn and mockery, with only a few responding favorably (vv. 10–11). Despite Israel's recalcitrant heart, the southern kingdom of Judah joined enthusiastically in the Passover celebration (vv. 12–19). As a result, "The Lord heard Hezekiah, and healed the people. The people of Israel who were present at Jerusalem kept the festival of unleavened bread for seven days with great gladness . . ." (vv. 20–21). The excitement and spiritual renewal poured over into a second week and "the whole assembly agreed together to keep the festival for another seven days; so they kept it for another seven days with gladness" (v. 23).

The Chronicler summarizes the events: "There was great joy in Jerusalem, for since the time of Solomon son of King David of Israel there had been nothing like this in Jerusalem" (v. 26).

When godly Hezekiah's reign ends, his successors abuse their power, forsake the Law and lead Judah back into a spiritual malaise and full-blown idolatry (2 Chr 33; 2 Kgs 21). The people of God, called out of Egypt to create and maintain an alternative sociopolitical reality in contrast to the surrounding nations, once again abandon the annual Passover and thus their identity as a holy nation.

In this setting Jeremiah pronounces judgment on the temple and ruling classes for disregarding the covenant, shedding innocent blood, practicing idolatry and oppressing "the alien, the orphan, and the widow" (Jer 7:1–7). Judah has reverted back to being a domination system. On God's behalf, he asks, "Has this house, which is called by my name become a den of robbers in your sight?" (vv. 8–10).

Passover does not reappear on the pages of holy writ until a second national revival occurs under the reign of King Josiah (641–609 BCE). After the high priest discovers the long lost "book of the Law" in the Temple, the king arranges to have it read publicly to the people (1 Kgs 23:1–3). As Josiah listens to the Word, he falls under conviction of sin and pledges openly his faithfulness to Yahweh. The people follow suit and vow allegiance to God and the covenant that he made with their forefathers.

With a renewed vision that Israel was created to serve as God's alternative political reality to the nations, Josiah orders that the heathen priests and their cultic high places be destroyed (vv. 4–20), and commands the entire nation to "keep *the Passover* to the Lord your God as prescribed in this book of the covenant" (v. 21). According to the account in 2 Chr 35:1–5, the priests prepare for a Passover celebration to be held on 14 Nisan and Josiah and his governing officials, "contributed to the people, as Passover offerings for all that were present, lambs and kids from the flock to the number of thirty thousand, and three thousand bulls; these were from the king's possessions" (vv. 6–9). The text declares: "The people of Israel who were present kept the Passover at that time, and the festival of unleavened bread for seven days. No Passover like it had been kept in Israel since the days of the prophet Samuel; none of the kings of Israel had kept such a Passover as was kept by Josiah, by the priests and the Levites, by all Judah and Israel who were present, and by the inhabitants of Jerusalem. In the eighteenth year of the reign of Josiah this Passover was kept" (vv. 17–19). What does verse 18 mean?—"No Passover like it had been kept in Israel since the days of the prophet Samuel; none of the kings of Israel had kept such a Passover as was kept by Josiah." Pleins believes it to mean that the Passover had never been observed during the monarchy, claiming that the fall festival may have taken precedence over the spring festivals.[44] The chronicler, however, records that the nation celebrated the Passover under kings Solomon (2 Chr 8:12–13) and Hezekiah (2 Chr 30:1), and speaks of the events in positive terms (v. 26). Therefore, verse 18 likely implies the Passover celebration under Josiah was more splendorous and meaningful than those held under the aegis of previous kings.

There is no evidence that the remaining southern rulers promoted faithfulness to the covenant or sponsored annual Passover feasts in Jerusalem What is known is that God raised up prophets like Jeremiah, Habakkuk, Ezekiel, and Obadiah to exhort these rulers for their breaking of the covenant with God and for weakening the southern kingdom, which led the nation into Babylonian captivity in 587 BCE (2 Chr 23–24).

---

44. Pleins, *Social Visions*, 426–27.

3.7 Prophetic Pronouncements of Judgment and Restoration of Passover

As early as 750 BCE, God spoke to the northern kingdom through the prophet Amos of a day when he would "raise up the booth of David that is fallen, and repair its breaches, and raise up its ruins, and rebuild it as in the days of old in order that they may possess . . . all the nations who are called by my name" (Amos 9:11–12). He goes on to proclaim, "The mountains shall drip sweet wine, and all the hills shall flow with it. I will restore the fortunes of my people Israel, and they shall rebuild the ruins and inhabit them; they shall plant vineyards and drink their wine, and shall make gardens and eat their fruit. I will plant them upon the land, and they shall never again be plucked up out of the land I have given them, says the Lord your God" (9:13–15).

Jeremiah, whose prophetic ministry spanned from the thirteenth year of Josiah's reign into the Babylonian captivity, likewise announces judgment upon God's wayward people (Jer 9:1–11; 22:13–19; 23:1–4), but also delivers to the nation a message of hope: "The days are surely coming, says the Lord, when I will raise up for David a righteous Branch, and he shall reign as king and deal wisely, and shall execute justice and righteousness in the land" (Jer 23:5). He then relates this message of hope to the first Passover and Exodus events: "Therefore, the days are surely coming, says the Lord, when it shall no longer be said, 'As the Lord lives who brought the people of Israel up out of the land of Egypt,' but 'As the Lord lives who brought out and led the offspring of the house of Israel out of the land of the north and out of all the lands where he had driven them.' Then they shall live in their own land" (vv. 7–8).

Jeremiah switches the focus away from the Egyptian exodus to a future deliverance when North and South will be reunited and God will establish a "new covenant" (Jer 31:31–34). Jesus likely makes a reference to the "new covenant" in his Last Supper symposium discourse, which Luke characterizes as a Passover meal (Luke 22:20). Likewise, Paul references the covenant in his discussion of abuses at the Lord's Table (1 Cor 11:25). These passages will be examined more critically in forthcoming chapters of this thesis.

Ezekiel connects the future judgment and deliverance specifically to Passover. After pronouncing judgment upon God's people (Ezek 1–24), he offers hope for a new Exodus and a restored nation (Ezek 36:22–28). He speaks of God raising up a new king to rule his people (37:21–22), and describes these future events in eschatological terms: "My servant David shall be king over them; and they shall all have one shepherd. . . . and my servant David shall be their prince for ever" (vv. 24–27). Since King David had been dead for centuries, this reference is to a new king, one who will ultimately fulfill the Abrahamic and Davidic covenants and usher in the kingdom of God.

According to Ezekiel, this golden age will include the reinstitution of the Passover: "In the first month, on the fourteenth day of the month, you shall celebrate the festival of the *Passover*, and for seven days unleavened bread shall be eaten" (Ezek 45:21).

When Isaiah, son of Amoz, speaks for God he too glimpses the destiny of the nation and declares, "He shall judge between the nations, and shall arbitrate for many peoples; they shall beat their swords into ploughshares, and their spears into pruning-hooks; nation shall not lift up sword against nation, neither shall they learn war any more" (Isa 2:4). In another prophecy he speaks of God receiving glory and praise "from the ends of the earth" (24:14–16) and envisions a future utopian kingdom where "the Lord of hosts will make for all peoples a feast of rich food, a feast of well-matured wines, of rich food filled with marrow, of well-matured wines strained clear" (Isa 25:6).

Toward the end of the exile, the writer of Third Isaiah foresees and proclaims good news to the poor and oppressed that economic favor and sociopolitical balance will be restored under the reign of God (Isa 61:1–2). These words hearken back to Lev 25:8–17, 23–55, when God instructed his people, liberated from Egyptian bondage, to celebrate a Jubilee year every half-century,[45] when debts are cancelled, confiscated lands returned, and Jewish slaves emancipated, thus, bringing equality back to the nation.

This arrangement was designed to ensure that the newly formed nation would persevere in her social imagination and her counter-domination posture, and that no Israelite would ever have to live in a perpetual state of bondage or indebtedness. In issuing the edict, God twice reminds the nation: "I am the Lord your God, who brought you out of the land of Egypt, to give you the land of Canaan, to be your God" (Lev 25:38, 42–43).

Both the original edict (Lev 25:10–12) and prophetic announcement (Isa 61:1–2) are reminders of the Passover/Exodus event. Just as Yahweh showered favor on his people and released them from bondage despite their shortcomings, he now calls upon them to act likewise toward one another. Israel is to operate according to a new paradigm: one that eschews

---

45. For an in-depth treatment of Jubilees, especially how it relates to the forming of Israel as a society after the Passover/Exodus, see: Kinsler and Kinsler, *Biblical Jubilee*.

domination. The priestly writer of Isaiah 61 now characterizes the restored eschatological kingdom as a time of continuous Jubilee celebration when everyone experiences social and economic equality under the reign of God.[46] Ironically, some variant of this scheme was God's intention for Israel from the time of the Exodus. The Passover was meant to help Israel remember what it was like to be oppressed and to remind her as a free people not to oppress others.

3.8 Returning Exiles Reinstitute the Passover

After Persia defeated Babylon in 539 BCE, King Cyrus issued a decree by the word of the Lord that all Jews who wished to return to their homeland could do so (2 Chr 36:22–23).[47] Three waves of Jewish exiles returned to Jerusalem between 538 BCE and 444 BCE and formed a functioning civil government under the aegis of the Persian Empire.

At first the returnees may have believed their migration back to Jerusalem fulfilled in some way the eschatological visions proclaimed by the prophets because, after rebuilding the Temple, "the returned exiles *kept the Passover*" (Ezra 6:19). The narrative tells how "the priests and the Levites . . . purified themselves;" then they "killed the Passover lamb for all the returned exiles, for their fellow-priests, and for themselves" (v. 21). All ate "and separated themselves from the pollutions of the nations of the land to worship the Lord, the God of Israel" (v. 22).

Within a short time, however, economic disparity develops with the wealthy taking advantage of the peasantry (Neh 5:1–5). This moves Nehemiah, the governor, to announce a Jubilee, calling upon the wealthy to restore to the oppressed "their fields, their vineyards, their olive orchards, and their houses, and the interest on money, grain, wine, and oil that you have been exacting from them" (Neh 5:11). In response, they agree under oath, "We will restore everything and demand nothing more from them. We will do as you say" (Neh 5:11–12).

The reinstitution of Passover and the attempt to put into practice the Jubilee mandate is temporary and soon it becomes clear that this return to the Promised Land is not the long-awaited restoration of the kingdom of

46. When Jesus announces the arrival of God's kingdom, he uses the language of Jubilees, declaring that the Trito-Isaianic prophecy is now being fulfilled (Luke 4:18–19). Ringe, *Jesus, Liberation*, 88, concludes that for Luke, Jesus links his identity and purpose with Jubilee themes. In Christ the Law and the prophets find their fulfillment.

47. Pritchard, ed., *Ancient Near Eastern Texts*, 316, contains a translation of Cyrus's actual edict.

which the prophets spoke. The people of Israel again abandon their social contract with God and begin serving Yahweh routinely, paying him lip service only, while serving their own selfish desires.[48]

The reconstruction of the Temple opens the way for the establishment of "a ruling priestly aristocracy that owed their position to the imperial regime, and it set up a Temple administration to secure revenues for the imperial court as well as itself."[49] This results in God sending additional prophets, e.g., Micah, Haggai, Zechariah, Malachi, among others, who call one more time for national repentance and tell of God's future plans to gather his people from the four winds and unite them in peace under his kingdom reign (Isa 48:20; 52:7; Hag 2:6–9; Zech 9:9–10; Mal 3:23–24). A small remnant of covenant-keeping Jews hangs onto this hope and passes it down from one generation to the next.

3.9 Hellenization and Passover

The Medo-Persian Empire gave way to the rise of the Greek city-states and the ascendancy of Alexander the Great of Macedon, who conquered Palestine in 333 BCE. Jewish life was altered once again as Hellenization swept the civilized world. Greek troops and teachers crisscrossed the empire conquering and spreading their language and culture. Jerusalem Jews suddenly found themselves living under another regime, no longer as free as they were under Persian self-rule. The priesthood remained unhampered, however, and continued to collect tithes and taxes. They embraced Greek culture and served as surrogates for whichever empire controlled Jerusalem. The result was that an ever-widening gap developed between common Jews and their priestly leaders.

Greek customs such as gathering in festival rooms and eating at a leisurely pace became the preferred way to dine. Formal festivities were elaborate occasions and included the supper proper (the eating course) followed by the symposium (drinking course). Diners reclined on couches throughout the evening as they partook of food and drink. Jews followed suit. According to M. Barth, the Passover meal likewise took on characteristics of a Greek festival meal.[50] In the early second-century BCE, Ben

48. Although their commitment to God was less than enthusiastic, Jews in Jerusalem never returned to the idolatry that brought about their exile in the first place. They strongly embraced monotheism.

49. Horsley, *Jesus in Context*, 25.

50. Barth, *Rediscovering*, 10.

Sirah intimates that Jewish males ate by reclining at the table.[51] Although Bokser points out ways Passover differed from Hellenized meals,[52] he does not adequately deal with the many ways they were the same. The Passover meal would have been viewed by Greeks as a standard sacrificial meal that included an offering, several cups of wine, hymns, instructions, conversation, and encouraged fellowship (*koinonia*), bonding (*philia*), and equality (*isonomia*) among the diners.[53] Leonhard concludes that the Jewish Pesach is "indebted to Greco-Roman sympotic customs."[54]

When eating a Hellenized Passover meal, the Jews reflected on its original meaning. For them the exodus was a metaphor for anti-imperialism.[55] The Passover meal, with its accompanying instructions, kept memory of and desire for freedom alive. Having been dominated by one Gentile kingdom or another since their days in Egypt and ruled by their own tyrannical kings, the Jews began to look for the day when God would liberate them from oppressive regimes and restore his kingdom under a Davidic messiah, who would manifest his rule over the nations.[56]

3.9.1 Resistance to Seleucid Rule

By the third-century BCE, Judea was controlled by Alexander's Ptolemy successors and then came under the heavy hand of the Seleucids. Things reached a critical point for the Jews when Seleucid strong man Antiochus IV (175–164 BCE) recruited willing Jewish collaborators to help with his

51. Sir 9.9 warns, "With a married woman dine not, recline not at the table to drink by her side, lest your heart be drawn to her and you go down in blood to the grave." This quote confirms that it was possible for Jewish men to interact with Jewish women in a banquet setting. Metzger, ed. *Oxford Annotated Apocrypha*, 139–40.

52. Bokser, *Origin of the Seder*, 8, 50–66. By arguing that the Greek banquet did not provide the "impetus for the development of the Passover Seder" (55), Bokser erects a straw man and then knocks it down. The issue is not origin or impetus, but whether or not the Passover meal took on the characteristics of a Hellenistic *symposion*. He additionally argues against the Passover being a Greek "philosophical" meal (51–52). Again, this is not the issue. Not all symposia were philosophical in nature; some were sacrificial banquets. Passover was the latter.

53. See chapter 2, section 2.4, where these issues are discussed.

54. Leonhard, *Jewish Pesach*, 435. "Hellenized Jews who celebrated a 'totally' Hellenistic banquet as Pesach" would be at home in a rabbinic or Hebrew-style banquet, since their structures were not that much different (428).

55. Gottwald, "Early Israel," 15.

56. Harvey, *Jesus and the Constraints of History*, 144–45; Collins, *Scepter and the Star*, 20.

rule of the region (1 Macc 1:20–64). He faced mounting resistance after he proclaimed himself to be "Epiphanes," i.e., god manifest, and plundered the Jerusalem Temple of its treasury, collected excessive taxes, built a gymnasium for the training of prospective young leaders, and encouraged Jewish men to participate in athletic games that were played in the nude (1 Macc 1:13). The penultimate cause for all out revolt occurred when many young Hebrew men, embarrassed over the physical sign of their Jewishness, sought to "remove the marks of circumcision, and abandoned the holy covenant" (1 Macc 1:15). Jews were quickly losing their identity as Jews.

As sociopolitical circumstances worsened, and the extinction of the Jewish religion was a stark possibility, a remnant of Jews mounted a resistance movement in 167 BCE. To resist, however, could end in a martyr's death. Judas Maccabeus, the son of a priestly family, rose to leadership. At the time, a body of apocalyptic literature surfaced from anonymous writers, who claimed to receive revelations about the *eschaton*. The Epistle of Enoch, the Assumption of Moses, The Animal Apocalypse, and Book of Daniel told of God's divine imminent intervention, culminating with arrival of God's universal kingdom over earth (Dan 7:13–14). Inspired by these apocalypses, the freedom fighters fought for national liberation. Those losing their lives in the fight for independence were assured they would not miss out on the kingdom, but would be resurrected (Dan 12:1–3).

Waging full-scale guerilla warfare against Antiochus and his troops involved a prolonged and fearless combat, but the Jewish resistance succeeded in winning their freedom in 164 BCE and ousted their Greek oppressors. They ritually cleansed their sanctuary and began a period of self-rule that lasted until 63 BCE (1 Macc 4:36–59).[57]

3.9.2 Resistance under the Maccabeans

When Simon Maccabeus, Judas' brother, had himself named high priest and leader of the nation, the Jewish masses found themselves living under a new tyrant, only this time, he was one of their own. The priestly Maccabean-Hasmonean family formed a dynasty that "extended the frontiers of the new Jewish state and compelled the neighboring peoples, the Idumaeans in the south and the various foreign clans in and around Galilee,

---

57. Josephus, *Ant.* 14.2.1, 21–28 mentions that the king of Arabia raided Jerusalem during the Passover observance in 65 BCE.

to recognize them as their rulers and embrace Judaism as their religion. This entailed submission to circumcision as far as the male population was concerned."[58] Like many rulers before them, the Maccabees personally amassed great power and wealth, and exploited their own people on the home front.

What should have been a century of freedom for God's people was turned into an era of subjugation for the demoralized masses. As a result, a majority of Palestinian Jews yearned to be delivered from their own leaders. Passover always brought these feelings out in the open as the browbeaten peasants gathered together and cried out for God to usher in the long-anticipated messianic era.

The *Book of Jubilees* (ca. 160–105 BCE)[59] includes a lengthy description of how Passover was to be observed in Palestine at the time. Not only was it to include memory of the first Passover meal and Exodus, but it was to provide instructions to the contemporary readers as to how they were to eat the supper.[60] The meal was still to be eaten on 14 Nisan as a remembrance of delivery from Egyptian domination in the distant past *and* from Persian and Grecian oppression in the immediate past. But unlike the original Exodus exiles who ate in homes and in haste (Exod 12:11), these Hellenized Jews "shall eat it in the sanctuary of your God,"[61] i.e., in the Temple court, and in a more relaxed fashion and with a joyous attitude.[62] *Jubilees* was the first Jewish writing ever to mention the use of wine at the Passover table.[63] Now that Passover was associated with the Temple, it "required a pilgrimage" to Jerusalem "where the sacrifice was held."[64]

The Essenes, believing the Hasmonean priesthood to be illegitimate and dissatisfied with its leadership in Jerusalem, withdrew to the wilderness where they "formed a new covenantal community in strict adherence

---

58. Vermes, *Who's Who*, 16.

59. The oldest manuscript among the Dead Sea Scrolls was *Jubilees*, likely written prior to 100 BCE but after 164 BCE. See VanderKam, *Book of Jubilees*, 18.

60. *Book of Jubilees* 49:1–23.

61. Ibid., 49:17.

62. Ibid., 49:22–23.

63. Ibid., 49:6.

64. Smith, *From Symposium*, 147. Originally, the head of the Jewish household killed a lamb and performed the rituals at a Passover meal held in the home. In the first-century BCE, the father was still responsible for the actual slaughter of the lamb, but needed assistance of a priest to pour the blood on the altar. See Segal, *Hebrew Passover*, 26–29.

to the Torah."[65] They saw themselves as preparing the way for the arrival of God's kingdom. As such they participated in symbolic acts such as eating a communal meal in anticipation of the messianic banquet to come. By nature and design, the meal was an act of resistance that spoke of the demise of the wicked priesthood and the advent of the long-awaited messianic priest.[66]

3.10 Passover under Roman Imperialism

With the Roman conquest of Judea (63 BCE), which will be discussed in the next chapter, the Jews found themselves living under a Roman domination system. Although a conquered people, the Jews were allowed to participate in their religious festivals, including Passover.

3.10.1 The Structure of the Passover Meal

Philo (20 BCE–50CE), an Alexandrian Jew, makes several scattered references to Passover and describes it as being practiced in a Hellenistic manner, i.e., a meal with two courses (*deipnon* and *symposion*) that incorporates traditional Jewish traditions.[67] According to the *m. Pesahim*, which likely reflects back on the Passover meal tradition in the first century, reclining was the proper posture for eating the Seder.[68] This included women participants reclining at the side of their husbands.[69] Hand washing also became part of the ritual.[70]

Philo also links Passover to a sheaf offering that the worshippers gave to the high priest to be laid on the altar.[71] Josephus (ca. 37–100 CE), the Jewish historian, mentions further that the sheaf offering was presented to

---

65. Horsley, *Jesus and the Spiral of Violence*, 18.

66. The Messianic Rule (1QSa=1Q28a) 2.15–20, in Vermes, *Complete Dead Sea Scrolls in English*, 159–60.

67. Philo, *Spec.* 2.144–173.

68. *m. Pesah.* 10:1, concludes, "And even the poorest Israelite should not eat until he reclines at his table." Also see *b. Pesah.* 108a.

69. Corley, *Private Women, Public Meals*, 72.

70. *m. Hag.* 2:5–7.

71. Philo, *Spec.* 2.162.

the priest on Sunday, 16 Nisan,[72] and treated as a firstfruits offering.[73] In time this act took on eschatological significance.

Passover meals had now been moved from the Temple into homes scattered throughout Jerusalem, although lambs were still being purchased and sacrificed at the Temple.[74] By the Roman era, Jews often used the terms "Passover" and "Unleavened Bread" interchangeably; only context determined whether they spoke of the same event or as distinct observances.[75]

Since there are no extant first-century records that describe what actually occurred during a typical Passover meal, it may be impossible to reconstruct a detailed order of events. Green, Jeremias, and Theissen make attempt to do so, basing their imaginative reconstructions on second-century documents.[76] Theissen, representative of the others, divides the Passover Seder into four parts: 1) Pre-meal activities, which include the first cup, hand washing, and the dipping of bitter herbs,[77] 2) Passover *haggadah*, i.e., questions and answers about the features of the meal, along with a song of praise and a second cup, 3) the main banquet and third cup,

72. Josephus, *Ant.* 3.10.5, writes, "On the second day of unleavened bread, that is to say the sixteenth, our people partake of the crops which they have reaped and which have not been touched till then, and esteeming it right first to do homage to God, to whom they owe the abundance of these gifts, they offer to him the first-fruits of the barley in the following way. After parching and crushing the little sheaf of ears and purifying the barley for grinding, they bring to the altar an *assaron* for God, and, having flung a handful thereof on the altar, they leave the rest for the use of the priests. Thereafter all are permitted, publicly or individually, to begin harvest."

73. Segal, *Hebrew Passover*, 26–29.

74. Since the days of King Josiah, the Passover was eaten in the Temple court in Jerusalem on 14 Nisan (2 Chr 35:16–19), but by the first-century CE the great influx of pilgrims to Jerusalem (possibly because of better roads and policing by the Empire) forced the observance to take place in homes within the city limits. See Fitzmyer, *Luke X–XXIV*, 1377 and Josephus, *Ant.* 18.2.2 for a fuller discussion.

75. Passover and the Feast of Unleavened Bread originally were separate observances. See Jeremias, *Eucharistic Words*, 92n4. Passover celebrated Israel's divine liberation from Egypt (Lev 23:5). The Feast of Unleavened Bread immediately followed and was a week-long affair commemorating how the Hebrews ate only unleavened bread on the eve of the Exodus (Lev 23:6–8). By the time of Jesus the two events had merged and the terms Passover and Unleavened Bread were used synonymously (Luke 22:1, 7). See Josephus, *Ant.* 18.19.

76. Green, *Luke*, 757–58; Jeremias, *Eucharistic Words*, 68–71, 84–88, Theissen and Merz, *Historical Jesus*, 424, all base their reconstruction on *m. Pesah.* 10.

77. Athenaeus, *Deipn.* 2.58b–60b. The typical Roman banquet included a pre-meal appetizer course. This is where the Seder ritual dipping lettuce into vinegar would fit into structure.

and 4) Closing, i.e., song of thanksgiving followed by a fourth cup.[78] The *haggadah* may have existed in oral form as far back as the first-century CE.[79] The order of the meal and its outward form fit nicely within the structure of a Roman banquet. It contains hand washings, hors d'oeuvres, conversation, meal, and singing and wine.

3.10.2 Anti-Imperial and Eschatological Nature of the Passover Meal

For many first-century Jews living under Roman oppression, the Passover meal not only celebrated the liberation of their forbearers from the slavery under Pharaoh, but produced a renewed longing for deliverance and the restoration of the nation under the rule of God. According to Wainwright, eschatological expectation ran high, especially during Passover week.[80] Warren Carter believes that Passover "evoke[d] and reenact[ed] the victory of God over . . . Egypt" and served "as a code reference to Rome's downfall."[81] Bokser likewise comments, "The message of Passover remained viable and relevant . . . Within the biblical period the memory of the exodus gave people hope that their imperfect situation would end and a new liberation would occur, a message that also fit the situation of the Jews under Roman domination."[82] He adds, "As reflected in Philo and other sources, this message of thanksgiving and hope for future protection or redemption was often tied to the offering of the paschal sacrifice."[83] Thus, Passover had taken on an eschatological significance.[84]

Temple priests and local merchants in Jerusalem saw Passover as an opportunity to make money for services rendered. The pilgrim travelers, however, viewed such practices as graphic reminders of the oppressive conditions under which they lived. The meal with its symbolism and stories of liberation caused the masses to long for a new exodus from tyrannical gentile rule and the overthrow of their own native rulers. It was an occasion for pious Jews to reaffirm their vision for "a new social order

78. Theissen and Merz, *Historical Jesus*, 424.

79. Leonhard, *Jewish Pesach*, 76.

80. Wainwright, *Eucharist and Eschatology*, 23.

81. Quoted from a letter written by Warren Carter to the author (December 15, 2007).

82. Bokser, *Origins of the Seder*, 9.

83. Ibid.

84. Fitzmyer, *Luke X–XXIV*, 1390.

and natural order" that could and would one day come about.[85] As they eagerly awaited the arrival of God's kingdom, these peasant masses likely remembered the prophetic words of Ezekiel who spoke of a new age and a new Passover under the reign of God's new Davidic king (Ezek 45:21–22).

Jeremias notes that first-century Jews not only interpreted the unleavened bread in the traditional manner, but added *"an eschatological interpretation,"* which pointed to a future abundance of bread in the kingdom of God.[86] They additionally found eschatological meaning in the words of the *Hallel,* which they sang each Passover—"Blessed is he who comes in the name of the Lord" (Ps 118:24). These words sank deep into their consciousnesses as they sought divine deliverance from the heavy hand of Roman Imperial rule. After the destruction of the Temple in 70 CE, Passover protocol included a place at the table for Elijah, the messianic forerunner, who would pave the way for the coming of the Lord. An open window or door, an empty chair, and a full glass of wine awaited his arrival.[87] Joshua ben Hananiah, a rabbinic sage (ca. 90 CE), in his comments on Exodus 12 and 42, says that the night of Israel's *future* redemption would be on the same night of her deliverance from Egypt.[88]

According to James C. Scott, people who live under tyranny have very few outlets to voice opposition, lest they face severe reprisals. Therefore, they choose to express their pent-up feelings and hostilities outside the sight or hearing of the power brokers. These "hidden transcripts" enable them to go undetected while engaging in subversive conversation with others of like mind. For first-century Palestinian Jews the Passover meal became a defiant and subversive act that anticipated the day when God would defeat Rome and deliver his people, just as he had done before.

When Jesus, along with the apostles, ate his final Passover meal, commonly referred to as the "Last Supper," it reflected the same anti-imperial sentiment as other Passover meals being eaten around the city that year.[89] First-century Jews viewed Rome to be as much an oppressor as ancient Egypt and Caesar as much a tyrant as Pharaoh. Like his contemporaries, Jesus linked the present Passover with the future Passover that would find its fulfillment in the restored kingdom (Luke 22:16).

85. Bokser, *Origins of the Seder*, 83.

86. Jeremias, *Eucharistic Words*, 59.

87. Barth, *Rediscovering*, 11–12.

88. Strack and Billerbeck, *Kommentar zum Neuen Testament aus Talmud and Midrash*, 85.

89. Chapter 6 looks at Luke's version of Jesus' final meal as a Passover, and examines its anti-imperial nature.

At times, the repressed emotions and heightened tensions spilled over into the public square. With up to 200,000 sojourners converging on Jerusalem to attend Passover festivities, the atmosphere was like a powder keg ready to explode.[90] According to Josephus, crowds were often provoked to violence with little or no provocation.[91] To guard against "civil unrest," the Roman prefect personally traveled to Jerusalem with extra troops.[92] Stationed along the portico of the Temple, the soldiers were ready "to quell any uprising that might occur,"[93]

Josephus mentions ten disruptions that took place during Passover week from 4 BCE–70CE. The public protests were often aimed at native retainers who did Rome's bidding by imposing heavy taxes upon the Jewish masses.[94] On other occasions, the dissent was directed toward Roman occupation troops. One such outbreak happened when a Roman soldier on the roof of the Temple made lewd gestures toward the pilgrims. A rock throwing riot ensued. Cumanus, procurator of Judea (48–52 CE), brought in additional troops to stop the rebellion. They were successful, but not before many people lost their lives.[95]

3.11 Conclusion

The thesis of this chapter was that Passover served as an anti-imperial meal that effected, celebrated, and anticipated emancipation from Egyptian totalitarian rule. When the Hebrew children gathered on the night of their deliverance and ate the Passover lamb, they participated in a seditious act.

As the pivotal point in Israel's primary history, the Exodus was chiefly a political act of deliverance from tyranny and oppression. God instituted an annual Passover to remind Israel of his compassion toward them as a people and of their obligation to show compassion toward others.

When Israel failed to fulfill her moral mandate and abandoned a perennial Passover celebration, she fell prey to one empire after another.

90. Josephus, *J.W.* 2.14.3; 6.9.3, estimated the number of pilgrims to be ten times that amount, but Wilson, *Our Father Abraham*, 263, voicing the consensus of most scholars, believes the number to be less than 200,000.

91. Josephus, *J.W.* 1:88–89; 2:8–13; 2:223–227.

92. Sanders, *Historical Figure of Jesus*, 249–50.

93. Josephus, *Ant.* 20.106–107.

94. Josephus, *J.W.* 2:10–13; *Ant.* 17.213–218.

95. Josephus, *J.W.* 2.223–246; *Ant.* 103–136. According to Josephus 20,000 to 30,000 people died in a stampede.

By the mouth of prophets God revealed that he would one day draw his people out of the nations and restore the kingdom. Under the leadership of his anointed king, Israel would once again celebrate Passover as a sign of his new covenant with the holy nation.

By the first-century CE, Palestinian Jews were yet again under another domination system. Roman troops occupied the Jewish homeland. Amidst dire circumstances, many pious Jews longed for God to fulfill his prophetic promises. Passover week became an opportunity to raise their voices in protest as they prayed and waited for God to lead them in another Exodus.

The church later adopted the structure of the Roman banquet for its communal meals, but drew its eschatological and anti-imperial nature from the Passover.

Chapter 4 will examine the Roman domination system at the time of Christ. Special attention will be given to the sociopolitical and economic conditions that led to the rise of the Jesus movement.

4

The Jesus Movement in Its
First-Century CE Context

4.1 Introduction

IN ORDER TO UNDERSTAND how and why the Lord's Supper was an anti-imperial praxis, one must examine the Jesus Movement within the historical context of the Roman Empire. Jesus and his followers did not live in a cultural vacuum, but interacted daily with the religious, social, political, and economic world around them. They were not affected only by Rome's claim of a divine right to rule the world, but forthrightly opposed it. Jesus and the nascent church preached and practiced principles that were antithetical to Roman imperialism, and offered an alternative vision for the world; one in which all people were equal and peace was secured through nonviolent means. They called this message "the good news of the kingdom of God."

By necessity, this chapter offers a descriptive analysis of the world into which Jesus and his followers were born. For without this knowledge it is impossible to understand how and why the Lord's Supper was an anti-imperial activity. The Roman Empire and the kingdom of God stood in juxtaposition to each other. Therefore, when believers came together at mealtime they discussed and responded to the prevailing worldview of their day.[1]

---

1. Chapters 5 and 6 will show how Jesus used the meal table to counter Roman imperialism and promote the kingdom of God. Chapters 7 and 8 will show how the church did the same.

4.2 The Jewish Experience of Domination

Israel's century of independent rule (164 BCE–63 BCE) was a tenuous one at best and continually threatened as Rome to the west began flexing her military muscles. In 202 BCE Rome defeated the North African city of Carthage and began her march eastward. Over the next twelve decades she conquered one Greek stronghold after another until the empire finally collapsed in 88 BCE. Led by Pompey, hailed as the greatest military genius of his day, the Roman naval fleet then took on piracy that threatened the Mediterranean coastline and hindered trade. In 64 BCE, he marched into northern Syria and disposed of Antiochus XIII, claiming the Seleucid territory for the Republic and turning it into a Roman province.[2] Pompey then sent Scaurus southward into Judea to represent him and negotiate a settlement.[3] He found the Jews in armed conflict with each other over which of two brothers should serve as high priest and kingly ruler—the eldest but weaker brother Hyrcanus II, who had been driven from Jerusalem, or Aristobulus II, his power hungry junior, who currently controlled the Temple. Disregarding the arguments over who was legitimately qualified to be high priest, Scaurus sided with Aristobulus II and ordered the conflict halted. When Pompey arrived in Damascus in 63 BCE, he was met by three delegations from Jerusalem to the south, one pro-Aristobulus, one pro-Hyrcanus, and one led by the Pharisees, representing the people. They wanted Pompey to weigh their arguments and select a priest. Pompey agreed to do so, but first wanted to march his army into Petra before returning to deliver his verdict. As soon as he departed, Aristobulus's enthusiasts took the opportunity to restart the civil war. Upon hearing the report, Pompey redirected his troops and laid siege to Jerusalem and the Temple where the pro-Aristobulus supporters were barricaded. The battle that ensued lasted three months. Aristobulus II and his family were arrested and "held as trophies for a triumphal celebration Pompey was planning in Rome; they would lead the convoy of Jewish captives taken during the siege of Jerusalem."[4] Pompey appointed Hyrcanus II to be high

2. Josephus, *J.W.* 1.127–158 and *Ant.* 14.46–75, gives two accounts of the entire incident. Sartre, *Middle East*, 40 offers an historian's critical perspective.

3. Although Rome used its military might to expand its holdings, one can see from this incident that Pompey did not conquer a new territory unnecessarily. He would first send a delegation to negotiate Roman rule over a territory. In similar fashion an agreement was reached with Jewish elites who invited Rome to enter Palestine at the first, although some fighting ensued when a group of resisters took control of the Temple.

4. Sartre, *Middle East*, 41.

priest but did not grant him any royal or honorific title. Between 63 and 41 BCE, the Hasmonean state was essentially dissolved,[5] with some of their land becoming part of the newly formed province of Syria, including cities beyond the Jordan River and the Sea of Galilee, along with many other cities along the coastline such as Gaza and Joppa.[6] The former Hasmonean territory was reduced in size to include only Judea, Samaria, southern Galilee, and eastern Idumea. Between 65–41 BCE, known as the Pompeian Era, these regions were divided into a series of city-states, which operated independent of each other, each with its own local government. Groupings of city-states made up a province.[7]

4.3 The Roman Empire as a Domination System

The Republic of Rome acquired and controlled a massive expanse of land that extended from Britain in the west to Turkey in the east to North Africa in the south. Nearly sixty-five million people from various ethnic backgrounds came under her domain.[8]

When the Roman Senate named Julius Caesar ruler for life in 44 BCE, the old republic took its last breath and died as power was transferred to one man. This new political reality met with immediate opposition, resulting in Caesar's assassination. A struggle for power ensued, leading to the formation of a triumvirate, consisting of General Lepedus, Antony (Julius Caesar's brash young lieutenant), and Octavian (Caesar's grand-nephew and adopted son). Antony and Octavian were mortal enemies. Octavian increased his power by building a massive war machine, and in 31 BCE he marched into Actium where he confronted and defeated Antony, who in the intervening years had married and divorced Octavian's sister to begin a love affair with Cleopatra. Octavian won a great victory in the battle of Actium, and Antony and Cleopatra fled to Egypt where they committed suicide. The good news (εὐαγγέλιον) of the victory moved the masses to proclaim Octavian their savior (σωτὴρ), who had single-handedly brought "peace and security" to the kingdom.[9]

---

5. Ibid., 40; Vermes, *Who's Who*, 17. With Pompey's conquest of Jerusalem the Hasmonean state was transformed into a province of Rome.

6. Sartre, *Middle East*, 41–42.

7. Ibid., 42–43.

8. Carter, *Roman Empire and the New Testament*, 3.

9. Rieger, *Christ and Empire*, 26.

4.3.1 The Emperor

In 27 BCE, Octavian succeeded his uncle and took the title Augustus Caesar. Historians generally agree that under Augustus Rome entered a new phase known as "empire." He and all who succeeded him as rulers would take the title emperor.[10]

Claiming to be ordained by the gods to represent them and carry out their will on earth, Augustus exercised enormous, if not ultimate, power throughout the empire.[11] His subjects recognized his face by the coinage that bore his image and the larger than life statues of him placed strategically throughout the empire. He shared the benefits and rewards of his position with those immediately under him, who constituted the ruling class. Augustus was also a visionary leader and builder. By today's standards he was a billionaire and used his wealth for what he deemed to be the common good. In *Res Gestae*,[12] a document he penned between 8 BCE and 6 CE, Augustus chronicles his numerous humanitarian and philanthropic efforts that he hopes will serve as his legacy.[13]

Augustus considered the *Pax Romana* to be his greatest contribution to the empire. *Pax Romana* was the establishment of universal peace among people of different national and ethnic backgrounds under the banner of Rome, and was hailed as one of the most remarkable accomplishments in history.[14] The emperor guaranteed peace and security to

10. Starr, *Emergence of Rome*, 80.

11. Ibid. Despite his great power, Augustus described himself simply as the *Princeps*, meaning "first citizen," and called his new system the *Principate*.

12. Augustus, "Res Gestae," 105–11.

13. Among his accomplishments he includes: 1) building of numerous temples throughout the empire; 2) vast amounts of land he purchased and donated to retired soldiers; 3) millions of *sesterces* he distributed out of the spoils of battle to hundreds of thousands of loyal subjects; 4) massive food distribution programs he initiated; 5) numerous bailouts of the national treasury in the amount of 150,000 *sesterces*; 6) another 200 million more he donated to the soldiers' bonus fund; 7) gladiatorial shows and other forms of public entertainment and exhibits he regularly sponsored; 8) statues, theatres, roads, canals and aqueducts he built; 9) colonies he established for soldiers in Africa, Sicily, Macedonia, Achaia, Asia, Syria, Gaul, Italy, among other locations; 10) many censuses he conducted that measured population growth in the empire and resulted in increased tax income for the empire; 11) his being elected sole guardian of the laws and morality for the empire; 12) many victories at land and sea, which brought great land holdings, human suppliants, and tribute into Roman coffers; 13) vast supply of money [coinage] which he minted that enabled commerce to operate and prosper with confidence; 14) and a host of other accomplishments that fill many more pages.

14. Starr, *Emergence*, 90.

all nations that submitted to his leadership, promising that the Roman military would protect their borders from invaders and maintain concord within their provincial boundaries.[15] Those rejecting his unity plan were conquered militarily and subjected to Roman rule.

The *Pax Romana* was the political goal of Roman domination. It was the good news that Rome offered to the world.[16] The emperor utilized several powerful means besides the military to bring people in line with his will and preserve the peace, including the use of political collaborators, economic policies, Roman banquets, patronage networks, the rule of law, Romanization of the masses, and civil religion.[17]

Luke links Jesus' birth in Bethlehem historically to a census ordered by Augustus (Luke 2:1–7).[18] In complying with the edict, Mary and Joseph traveled from their home in Nazareth to be registered and assessed their share of the tax burden. The registration was an instrument of imperial domination used to keep tabs on its subjects and make sure they did not escape paying taxes. Hence, Jesus is portrayed as part of a people living under the strong hand of Roman domination, where the conquered are expected to comply with the oppressive economic policies of the empire. Ironically, the one born in Bethlehem would one day call upon the emperor's loyal subjects to switch their allegiance from the kingdom of Rome to the kingdom of God!

Next Luke records the words of the angel to the shepherds, "I am bringing you good news of great joy for all the people: to you is born this day in the city of David a Saviour, who is the Messiah, the Lord" (Luke 2:11–12). This announcement is followed by "a multitude of the heavenly host, praising God and saying, 'Glory to God in the highest heaven, and on earth peace among those whom he favours!'" (13–14). Later at the Temple, Simeon declares after looking upon the child, "My eyes have seen your

15. Horace, *Odes* 4.15, 130.

16. Augustus claimed that Rome had a right to rule the world based on divine decree. This was Rome's manifest destiny. Augustus considered himself to be the savior of the world who brought peace through victory as a blessing from the gods. Thus Rome had an imperial ideological or theological basis upon which it operated. Virgil, *Aeneid*, 6.850–853, writes in poetic form of Rome's heavenly entitlement to rule the world and to "conquer and crush" all resistance.

17. For a definitive treatment of the *Pax Romana* see Wengst, *Pax Romana and the Peace of Jesus Christ*. Crossan, "Roman Imperial Theology," 65, remarks, however, that *Pax Romana* could be characterized mainly by the succinct mantra, "*Peace through Victory*" (emphasis in original).

18. See footnote 121 for a discussion of the variance between Luke's account of events and historical records.

salvation, which you have prepared in the presence of all peoples, a light for revelation to the Gentiles and for glory to your people Israel" (2:31–32). In identifying Jesus as both universal "savior" and "Lord" who is a "light to the Gentiles" as well as the Jewish "messiah," i.e., king, the bringer of "peace," Luke's birth narrative asserts that Caesar has a competitor. As Lord, Augustus possessed totalitarian power and authority over the empire. As Savior, he was the empire's deliverer and protector, who brought "peace on earth" and assured Rome's security through military might.

Luke also places the start of Jesus' public ministry "in the fifteenth year of the reign of Emperor Tiberius, when Pontius Pilate was governor of Judea, and Herod was ruler of Galilee, and his brother Philip ruler of the region of Ituraea and Trachonitis, and Lysanias ruler of Abilene, during the high-priesthood of Annas and Caiaphas" (Luke 3:1–2). By doing so, Luke identifies several governmental authorities and native retainers with whom Jesus and his followers will either oppose indirectly or confront openly.

When Christ's followers confessed him to be Lord and Savior, it apparently got the attention of the local Roman officials and their Jewish surrogates. To challenge Caesar's exclusive right to these titles was likely interpreted as treasonous. If Jesus was Lord, then Caesar was not![19]

Augustus and all his successors[20] were variously called "Father of the Fatherland" (*Pater Patriae*) or "Father of the Country,"[21] implying that the empire was a big family over which the emperor stood as a father to protect, discipline, and bless his family members. He thus functioned as benefactor, making certain that their needs were met. It also spoke of the

---

19. Paul actually goes a step farther when he writes that the church waits for the "Savior" to return from heaven to judge the enemies of the cross, vindicate those who were martyred by the present world leaders and subdue all things to himself (Phil 1:15–30; 2:14–18; 3:20–21). Such anti-imperial sentiments not only proclaim Jesus to be Savior, but identify Caesar as opposing God's will. Such political language is what led to Paul's numerous arrests and beatings.

20. Augustus ruled as Rome's first emperor from 31 BCE–14 CE. He was followed by Tiberius Caesar (14–37 CE), who reigned during the lifetimes of John the Baptist and Jesus. Tiberius was succeeded by Caligula (37–41 CE), his twenty-five-year-old grand nephew. A contemporary of Apostle Paul, he persecuted Jews for not acknowledging his divinity and refusing to worship him. The next Roman ruler was Claudius (41–54 CE), who is mentioned twice in the NT (Acts 11:28–30; 18:2). The latter reference speaks of his expelling Jews from Rome. The fifth Roman emperor was Nero (54–68 CE), whose hostility toward Christians is well known. According to Eusebius, *Eccl. Hist.* 2.25, he executed Peter and Paul. In 68 CE, during the Jewish War, Nero committed suicide.

21. Suetonius, *Aug.* 2.58; Carter, *Roman Empire*, 32. Also see Barrow, *Romans*, 81.

emperor's divine right to rule the earth on behalf of Jupiter and to carry out his divine will.[22]

When Jesus called God his "Father" and admonished his disciples to "call no one your father on earth, for you have one Father—the one in heaven" (Matt 6:9; 23:9), he invited people to look to God for their welfare and not Caesar. Paul carried on this tradition when he wrote, "Yet for us there is one God, the Father, from whom are all things and for whom we exist" (1 Cor 8:6). If such bold statements were verbalized and overheard by the authorities, they could be deemed politically subversive and bring down the wrath of Rome on all who subscribed to them.

Additionally, the emperor accepted the title "king of kings," i.e., king over all lesser client kings.[23] By contrast, the Book of Revelation, written long after Paul toward the end of the apostolic era, identifies Jesus as "the ruler of the kings of the earth" (Rev 1:5) and likens the emperor to a powerful "beast" that commits fornication with the kings of earth (17:2, 5, 8), who together "make war with the Lamb . . . for he is Lord of lords and King of kings . . ." (v. 14). But the lamb prevails, defeating the armies of the world with a sword that proceeds from his mouth. He is called "KING OF KINGS AND LORD OF LORDS" (Rev 19:19).

This anti-imperialistic message, which the church circulated throughout Asia Minor and read during their communal meals, pitted the Jesus communities against their imperial dominators.[24]

Years earlier when the Jews brought Jesus to Pilate they charged, "We found this fellow perverting the nation . . . saying that he himself is Christ, a King" (Luke 23:2–3, 25). In the Fourth Gospel, the Jews threaten Pilate with the words, "If you release this man, you are no friend of the emperor. Everyone who claims to be a king sets himself against the emperor" (John 19:12).

That the execution of Jesus was a political act intended to eliminate rivals and maintain the *Pax Romana*, will be shown later in the chapter.

22. Carter, *Roman Empire*, 32.

23. Starr, *Emergence*, 97.

24. Chapter 7 will discuss how the Gospels and Epistles were read aloud during the symposium section of the Christian communal meals, and thus served as anti-imperial hidden transcripts.

4.3.2 The Roman Senate

The emperor and the Senate shared power and collectively ruled the empire. By virtue of being commander-in-chief and "master of land and sea," the emperor controlled the outer provinces of the empire and its military.[25] The Senate governed Italy and other less volatile regions. It also managed the empire's finances, which were dependent on the emperor's personal wealth. Situated in the capital city of Rome and comprised of six hundred wealthy landowners among the top echelon of the aristocracy, this exclusive legislative body represented and protected the interests of the elites by establishing laws and appointing loyal and deserving persons to prominent political, civic, and military posts. Peasants who served the elites were not represented by the Senate or any other political body. In essence, there existed only two classes of people living in the empire: the rulers and the ruled, the dominators and the dominated.

By contrast, Seneca (5 BCE–65 CE), a contemporary of Jesus and Paul, was a famous senator, humanitarian, essayist, and philosopher, who addressed the ethical problems of the noble class.[26] He regularly wrote essays opposing slavery and the bloodthirsty nature of Roman amusements such as gladiatorial shows and contests between beasts and humans, which were used to entertain and thus control the populace.

4.3.3 Social Structure of the Empire

A domination system is a social structure in which a minority of the population known as elites has absolute authority over the great multitude of people and controls all social and governmental structures. Domination and empire building usually go hand in hand. Imperial Rome operated on the principle of domination, using her military might to invade and conquer nations, and then dominate them both politically and economically.[27]

25. Sartre, *Middle East*, 56. In 27 BCE, the provinces were divided between Augustus and the Senate. According to Millar, Syria was the only province of Caesar in the Middle (Near) East, and the only geographical area with a direct Roman presence. Caesar personally appointed the governors who ruled the province on his behalf. They were called *legati*, and chosen from the highest senatorial ranks. Caesar's provinces were military strongholds with legions of soldiers, led by a commander of senatorial rank, also called a *legatus*. In provinces controlled by the Senate, governors were called *proconsules* and were chosen by lot. Their military leaders were chosen from the equestrian ranks. See Millar, *Roman Near East*, 31–33.

26. Starr, *Emergence*, 92–94.

27. Borg, *Jesus: Uncovering the Life*, 79–82, mentions four common features of

A multilevel social hierarchy evolved within Roman society that might be likened to a pyramid, with the emperor at the top and the lowliest peasants at the bottom. An aristocratic or noble class, which accounted for less than 2 percent of the entire population,[28] held in its grasp the collective wealth and power of the empire. As ruling elites, they lived in luxurious palaces and villas and enjoyed the finer things in life.

Power, privilege, and prestige were the qualities that came with being part of the elite class. Property and wealth were only two factors that determined one's social class. The most important was pedigree. Caesar, as son of god, along with his family members, held the most honored positions within the empire. Caesar served as Jupiter's earthly representative, but some considered him a god.[29]

Senators held the next most prestigious slot in the Roman social hierarchy. Each of the 600 members came from a noble family with vast land holdings and a minimum wealth of one million *sesterces*.[30] They were easily identifiable by their "toga with the broad purple stripe (*latus clavus*)."[31] Senatorial seats were inherited, and sons of senators sat in meetings of the Senate with their fathers.[32]

Another elite group was the equestrian order of 20,000 freeborn nobles who were not born into nobility, but gained their wealth from real estate leases or business holdings.[33] To qualify one must possess a net

---

imperial domination systems, all of which characterized the Roman Empire at the time of Christ. First, they are *politically oppressive*. A small minority of the population possesses complete authority over the great masses of people and over all social and governmental structures. Second, they are *economically exploitative*. The rich amass and control the wealth of the empire by levying high taxes on the peasants who are forced to work for low wages or else starve. Third, they are *religiously legitimated*. In a domination system the ruler claims he has a manifest destiny or divine right to control all property and wealth and distribute it as he sees fit. Fourth, all domination systems are characterized by *armed conflict*. To amass greater wealth and more property, the imperial kingdom utilizes her powerful military to invade and conquer weaker nations, and then dominate them in every area of life. Likewise, Crossan, "Roman Imperial Theology," 60–61, identifies these same types of power as characteristics of the Roman domination system.

28. Stegemann and Stegemann, *Jesus Movement*, 14; Carter, *Roman Empire*, 3.

29. Suetonius, *Aug.* 52.

30. Dio Cassius, *Roman History* 56.41.3 tells how Augustus increased the "property requirements" for one to become a Senator. Stegemann and Stegemann, *Jesus Movement*, 72–73, do a good job sorting out the various stratifications of among the elites.

31. Ibid., 73.

32. Ibid.

33. Ibid.

worth of 400,000 *sesterces*.[34] They were recognizable by their gold rings and the narrow purple striped toga they wore.[35] Many lived in Rome and held positions of authority, but the majority held posts in provinces.

Councilors composed the third group of 200,000 aristocrats who served Caesar exclusively in the provinces of the empire.[36] Wealth, Roman citizenship, and leadership qualities and loyalty were the criteria needed to obtain this status. Like other elites, they wore special clothing and were honored with the best seats at banquets, sporting events, and the theater.

All elites pledged their allegiance to the emperor, who shared with them a portion of the tax revenue, appointed them to high political office, and presented them with confiscated lands that had been won in battle. He acted as their benefactor and they in turn helped finance future war efforts, construction projects, the arts, and the erection of monuments honoring the emperor. The more support they gave the emperor and his causes, the more favors, riches and prestige they received. It was an endless cycle. Through this means, their assets continued to grow.[37]

4.3.4 The Military

Believing that paid soldiers were more loyal to their emperor and less likely to support local rebellions, Augustus Caesar dismantled the militias and formed the first permanent full-time army and navy, over which he served as commander-in-chief. He used taxes to pay for this professional army.[38] Military service was a lifetime profession, and it was not uncommon for soldiers to serve stints of twenty-five years or more.[39]

The army consisted of between twenty-five to thirty legions, i.e., about 200,000 infantrymen, composed entirely of Roman citizens.[40] They were assisted by another 200,000 auxiliaries of foot soldiers and cavalry, composed of 500–1000 soldiers each, recruited from non-Roman ranks

34. Ibid.

35. Pliny the Elder, *Nat.* 33.29–36, makes reference to the regulations regarding the wearing of rings by the various elite groups.

36. Stegemann and Stegemann, *Jesus Movement*, 74.

37. Borg, *Jesus*, 81–82.

38. Stegemann and Stegemann, *Jesus Movement*, 48.

39. Starr, *Emergence*, 88.

40. Caesar had four legions stationed in his province of Syria on the northern border of Palestine. See Sartre, *Middle East*, 60.

that were granted Roman citizenship upon discharge. Sons usually followed in their father's footsteps.[41]

Apart from the Praetorian Guard that protected the emperor in Rome, the army was stationed on the frontiers of the empire. It patrolled provinces that had been conquered recently and brought under Roman rule and was charged with maintaining the tenuous *Pax Romana*, by force when necessary. Many far-off regions were still prone to border attacks or internal uprisings by those not yet Romanized, and the army's very presence served as a civilizing influence.[42] Since Palestine was one such distant province, located close to Rome's eastern border with the Parthian Empire, it had a heavy concentration of occupied troops.

Roman soldiers from Caesarea traveled to and bivouacked in Jerusalem during the major Jewish festivals to maintain and control the teeming crowd. Others were stationed permanently at Fort Antonia at the southeast corner of the Temple complex.[43] While Jews in general, including members of the Jesus movement, may not have had daily contact with Roman governors or client kings, they were always conscious of the troops in their midst. On a daily basis they rubbed shoulders with military personnel who patrolled the streets, always ready to quell riots, arrest, humiliate, and flog dissenters. When called upon to do so, they crucified insurrectionists along busy thoroughfares in order to drive fear into others who might have similar thoughts of rebellion. The military represented Rome's absolute power over life and death.

Jesus often referred to soldiers in his parables (e.g., Matt 22:7), his prophetic pronouncements (e.g., Luke 21:10, 20), and in the Sermon on the Mount (e.g., Luke 6:29). He instructed his disciples to go the extra mile when soldiers made demands of them. In doing so they exposed the diabolical and tyrannical nature of coercion.

While all soldiers served Caesar and outwardly pledged to him their allegiance, the NT depicts some as showing favor to the Jesus movement (Mark 8:5–13; Luke 7:1–10) and a few as transferring their allegiance to Jesus (Matt 27:54; Mark 15:39; Acts 10:34–48; 11:13–18).

Like Jesus before him, Paul had several encounters with irate local Jewish leaders who sought to kill him and with Roman soldiers who arrested and at times protected him. (Acts 21:27–33; 22:24–29; 23:23; 27—28:16). When writing to the believers at Philippi he mentions that news of

41. Barrow, *Romans*, 90.
42. Ibid.
43. Josephus, *J.W.* 5.5.8.

his arrest has spread not only to Christian communities, but "throughout the whole imperial guard" (Phil 1:13).

To sustain imperial rule Rome depended on its powerful military to exercise force when needed. In this context, Jesus' message of the kingdom of God, which called upon people to embrace humility, service, sacrifice and nonviolence must be viewed as anti-imperial in nature.

4.3.5 Financing the Empire: Domination through Taxation and Forced Labor

The Roman government heavily taxed its subjects, claiming that funds were needed to provide services. In reality, taxes were used to increase the net worth of the empire with much of it eventually working its way into the hands of the noble class. Rome levied four kinds of taxes on conquered nations: 1) *tributum soli*, a tax assessed on all cultivated land; 2) *capitation*, a head tax assessed based on a census; 3) tolls for using the Roman road system; and 4) *portoria*, a shipping tax.[44] The ruling elites did not accumulate wealth through their own labors but got rich off the backs and taxation of the poor.[45] Since a decrease in or "nonpayment of taxes would mean the collapse of the lifestyle" of the Roman and native elites, peasants were pushed always to work a little harder.[46]

Because economics in the first-century CE was based on agricultural output, Rome sought to increase its land holdings by invading other nations. The emperor shared the spoils of battle with the nobles, who passed down their land holdings from one generation to the next.[47] The conquered peasants were forced to relinquish their land and work as sharecroppers on property they once owned. From the crop production, they were allowed to keep only a small portion (about 30 percent) for themselves. From this amount, they then had to pay high taxes to Rome and rents to their landlords. The remainder of the crops went to the new aristocratic owners, who sold it in the marketplace for profit.

Some peasants, whose lands had been confiscated, were kept on as hired hands without any claim to the crops. As a result, they were forced to purchase from the *agora* the very food they grew or else starve. This practice was based on the principle that if one grows crops or makes clothes

44. Sartre, *Middle East*, 103–4.

45. Borg, *Jesus*, 83.

46. Carter, *Matthew and Empire*, 14–15.

47. Ibid., 13.

for someone else, then she or he must obtain their goods from some other source.[48] The powerful and wealthy had an uncanny sense about how much they could squeeze out of the peasants without starving them.[49] The peasants had little recourse but to go along with the oppressive system. When they did protest publicly or conduct a work stoppage, either they lost their employment and faced starvation or else the army mercilessly beat them into submission. To navigate the economy, peasants resorted to deception, often hiding crops or lying to tax collectors about their production output.[50]

Jewish peasants were somewhat more brazen than their pagan counterparts. Believing the payment of tribute to Rome to be an act of idolatry, they revolted against the practice on numerous occasions.[51] When they did, the native retainers sought to calm them and stabilize the situation. If unsuccessful, the military stepped in to quell the protest in a decisive and brutal fashion.[52]

4.3.6 Emperor Worship

When Octavian was named the new Caesar and the Senate bestowed upon him the title *Augustus*, a new Roman cult was born—the cult of the Emperor, which gained widespread popularity. In times past, Rome recognized and honored her deceased rulers on special days for their moral qualities, but when Octavian became Rome's first emperor, a subtle shift took place. Because the Senate posthumously recognized Julius Caesar as divine (42 BCE) by bestowing upon him the title *Divus Iulious*, Octavian was able to claim for himself the title *Divi filius*, i.e., "Son of God."[53] Some people throughout the empire took this to mean that Augustus was the embodiment of a god, while others viewed him as a representative of the gods.[54] Up until the reign of Augustus, deification was pronounced only

48. Borg, *Jesus*, 88.

49. Ibid., 84.

50. Carter, *Matthew and Empire*, 18.

51. Josephus, *Ant.* 18.23–25; *J.W.* 2:118. According to Bauckham, *Bible in Politics*, 80, "to render tribute to Caesar in his idolatrous coinage was to acknowledge his blasphemous claim to a right which was really God's alone." He adds that the paying of tribute was most likely the basis of popular support for revolt against Rome.

52. Carter, *Matthew and Empire*, 15.

53. Syme, *Roman Revolution*, 202.

54. Barrow, *Romans*, 144.

upon the dead. The poet Horace in his *Epistle to Augustus*, writes, "Upon you, however, while still among us, we already bestow honors, [and] set up altars to swear by in your name . . ."[55] After hailing Augustus as Rome's greatest leader, Virgil pronounces, "This is he . . . Augustus Caesar, son of a god, who shall set up again the Golden Age."[56]

As early as 29 BCE "Augustus supported, or at least permitted, the establishment of a cult in his honor . . . in Bithynia, Pontus, and in Asia."[57] The peoples of the Eastern Mediterranean region, who had attributed divine qualities to their earthly leaders for centuries, had no difficulty accepting Augustus's divine status.[58] An inscription of a decree issued in 9 BCE by the Provincial Assembly in Asia declares Augustus to be "divine," "equal to the Beginning of all things," "sent . . . as a Savior," whose birthday marks the "beginning of good news" for the entire world.[59] A temple of Augustus was built in Pergamum and another one was constructed in Smyrna for Tiberius, his successor.[60] Greeks were among the first to embrace emperor worship. Their cities of Corinth and Ephesus erected temples to Augustus as a living god that were larger and more ornate than their temples to the Greek gods. Shrines and images of Augustus were located in all public areas. Circa 89–90 CE, a provincial temple was built in Ephesus for emperor worship and consecrated to Emperor Vespasian (69–79 CE) and his two sons, who reigned after him, Titus (79–81 CE) and Domitian (81–96 CE).[61] Ceremonies honoring the emperor were modeled closely on traditional ceremonies honoring the Greek gods.[62] Apart from "obstinate

55. *Ep.* 2.1.15–16 in Horace, *Satires, Epistles, and Ars Poetica*.

56. Virgil, *Aen.* 6.793.

57. Sartre, *Middle East*, 58.

58. Ibid., 144–45.

59. *Orientis Graeci Inscriptiones Selectae*, 458, 1.3–30.

60. Wengst, *Pax Romana*, 50–51. Dio Cassius, *Roman History* 51.20.6–8; Suetonius, *Aug*, 52, mention that Caesar Augustus authorized the cities of Pergamum and Nicodemia to build temples dedicated to emperor worship. John the Revelator recalls a believer named Antipas living in Pergamum, "where Satan's throne is" and "where Satan lives" who has been martyred for his faithfulness to Christ (Rev 2:13–14). The reference to Satan's throne and dwelling place likely refers to the temple.

61. Kraybill, *Apocalypse and Allegiance*, 60. Crossan, "Roman Imperial Theology," 61, notes that the Arch of Titus in Rome was dedicated to the "divine Titus Vespasian Augustus, the son of the divine Vespasian." Kahl, "Acts of the Apostles," 149, adds, "A panel at the very top of the Arch of Titus portrays the emperor going up into heaven on the back of an eagle . . ."

62. Horsley, *Paul and Empire*, 20.

Jews and Christians," the majority living in the Mediterranean region of the empire "worshipped at the feet of the emperor."[63]

The citizens of Italy and its capital of Rome, however, saw the emperor more as their benefactor, who provided them with goods and services on behalf of the gods, rather than as a god himself, although some of their poets wrote lyrically of the emperor as a divine being.[64] Italians reverenced the emperor only to the degree that he exhibited high virtues of kindness, generosity, and justice. At his death in 14 CE, the Senate pronounced that Augustus had ascended into heaven to take his honored placed among the pantheon of Roman gods.[65]

Tiberius, successor to Augustus as emperor, also carried the divine title until his death in 37 CE.[66] He was followed by Gaius, also known as Caligua (37–41 CE), who claimed divinity for himself, and when appearing in public, dressed "in symbolic garb traditionally associated with various deities."[67] Philo tells how Caligua "transformed himself into Apollo, crowning his head with garlands" and on another occasion how he "assumed the disguise" of Bacchus and had choruses sing "paeans" and "Bacchic hymns" to him in his honor.[68] Likewise, Nero (54–68 CE) and Domitian (81–96 CE) followed their predecessors in accepting divine accolades. Domitian wanted to be addressed as *Dominus et Deus noster*, i.e., "my Lord and my god."[69] The emperor cult was the common denominator that drew the kingdom together and provided a basis for patriotism, regardless of whether one accepted the emperor's divinity. In reality, it became an imperial or civil religion and was the "unifying bond of the *imperium*, the symbol of the loyalty of all citizens to emperor and state."[70]

An imperial theology soon developed. Colleges and associations were formed, whose members pledged their honor and allegiance to both

63. Kraybill, *Apocalypse and Allegiance*, 20.

64. Ibid.

65. Borg and Crossan, *Last Week*, 3.

66. Others who kept the title included Nero and Domitian.

67. Thatcher, *Greater than Caesar*, 24. Philo (ca. 30 BCE–50 CE) in *On the Embassy to Gaius*, 349–67 writes of Alexandrian Jews who opposed the reign of emperor Caligua because he claimed to be a god, but were unwilling to voice their opposition openly without being arrested and charged with treason.

68. Philo, *Embassy*, 95–96.

69. Suetonius, *Dom.* 13.2. This is the same phrase found in John 20:28 and Rev 4:11.

70. Wengst, *Pax Romana*, 49.

the emperor and empire.[71] The cult infiltrated all aspects of life and culture. Public events became opportunities to pay homage to religion and state. Special days were set aside to honor imperial Rome and her leader. The emperor's birthday, which marked the Roman New Year, was such an occasion. Others included anniversaries of great victories at sea and on land, celebrations to remember deceased rulers, heroes, or significant historical events. Sporting events, national feasts days, and even ordinary meals eaten in the name of Caesar were times when people expressed piety (eusebia) and devotion, and renewed their commitment to the emperor and Rome.[72]

"In Lyons there is an altar dedicated to the goddess Roma and Augustus, which formed the focal point of the imperial cult in Gaul."[73] Similar structures were located throughout the empire that paid homage to both the emperor and the goddess Roma, the national deity of the empire.[74] In a real sense, imperial theology was the *zeitgeist* or spirit of the age that dominated and shaped the Roman Empire. All sectors of society— the social, intellectual, political, economic, spiritual and ethical—were touched and shaped by the imperial cult. It was more than a religion or philosophy; it was the actual foundation upon which the empire stood. Crossan and Reed call it the "superglue" that held the entire empire together.[75]

The imperial cult engendered patriotism and a sense of moral obligation to the empire and its benefactors. It was the common denominator that united peoples of various ethnic backgrounds who lived throughout the empire. In a real sense, it may have been more powerful in controlling the masses than the strong arm of the army.

Horsley rightly assesses, "The Spirit of the Empire ran deep and wide."[76] With the emperor as its religio-political head, the cult provided benefits to rulers and the ruled, and the groups in power had much to gain by sustaining the emperor cult.[77]

71. Barrow, *Romans*, 145.

72. Horsley, *Paul and Empire*, 20–21.

73. Wengst, *Pax Romana*, 49.

74. Rieger, *Christ and Empire*, 26.

75. Crossan and Reed, *In Search of Paul*, 142.

76. Horsley, *Paul and Empire*, 13.

77. Rieger, *Christ and Empire*, 27.

4.3.7 Religious Syncretism

As the empire expanded its borders, it not only acquired the lands and resources of the conquered people, but also their native religions. Rome did not tolerate religious competitors, since it held that its religious beliefs were superior to all others. However, it willingly Romanized those foreign religions that were compatible with its basic cultic system. Many pagan religions had common characteristics, making syncretism possible.[78] On this basis, Rome granted official status to many non-Roman religions, which enabled the conquered masses to continue practicing their respective faiths, attending their own temples, and observing their own festivals. In addition, each foreign religion had to pass a threefold test, which included: 1) showing respect for the central role of the imperial cult throughout the empire; 2) fostering political stability and support for Rome; and 3) discouraging immoral behavior, as defined by the emperor.[79]

Rome did not grant Judaism official status of *religio licita*. Judaism was uniquely monotheistic, and by nature, non-syncretistic. The idea that the emperor was a god or that humans should bow down to his image was abhorrent to Jews. Despite the differences, however, Rome granted Jews permission to worship God exclusively and to observe their annual feasts of Passover, Pentecost and Tabernacles, so long as they paid their tribute to Rome, prayed for and offered sacrifices to their God on behalf of the emperor,[80] and did not seek to proselytize non-Jewish neighbors. Their Temple leaders assured Rome that such would be the case. This arrangement was unique to Israel and would eventually lead to conflict between Jewish purists and their compromising leaders, as well as between Jews and their imperial dominators, often leading to civil unrest. As early as 53 BCE Cicero recognized that the religions of the Romans and Jews were irreconcilable.[81]

Despite this arrangement, most Jews were not supportive of the compromise, and longed for the day when God would deliver them from the heavy hand of Roman domination. These hopes were based upon the writings of ancient prophets, who foretold how God would free his people from bondage and restore their land. Whenever they gathered in Jerusalem to

78. Thus, the Greek god Zeus became known by his Roman name Jupiter, Artemis was recognized as Diana, and so on.

79. Barrow, *Romans*, 144.

80. According to Josephus, *Ant.* 20.409, when Eleazar, son of the high priest, ordered this sacrifice to be ceased in 66 CE, it set the stage for the war with Rome.

81. Cicero, *Flac.* 69.

celebrate the annual Passover Feast—a commemoration that marked their liberation from Egyptian oppression—emotions ran high and it was not uncommon for Jews to publicly cry out to God to send another deliverer like Moses. Some identified Jesus as that prophet.

4.4 The Administration of Palestine

When Rome gained control of Palestine in 63 BCE, she turned to Israel's priestly families and wealthy aristocrats to help keep the Jewish population in line with the empire's goals. If these leaders could not fulfill their obligations, they were replaced.

Preserving order throughout Palestine was not easy. Since the Hasmonean era, a fervent nationalism filled the hearts of the Jewish people. They despised Gentiles ruling over them, and thus dissent and unrest were always in the air.

4.4.1 Palestinian Client Kings

When a number of the Jewish leaders started competing with each other for power, Augustus Caesar intervened and appointed Herod as vassal king over them. Herod the Great[82] (40/37–4 BCE) immediately and forcefully began putting an end to these struggles for power by swiftly executing the troublemakers. It took him "three years to subdue the peoples he was appointed to rule."[83] He replaced their former leaders with new rulers who owed their positions to him and thus their loyalty.[84]

Hoping to gain legitimacy with the Jewish people, Herod married Mariamne, the granddaughter of high priest Hyrcanus II, but this caused only more animosity. Judea never ceased being a hotbed for unrest in the eastern part of the empire.[85] A majority of Jews wanted independence and

82. Initially Herod was appointed king of Judea in 41 BCE, but it was not until 37 BCE that he actually gained control of his kingdom. Millar notes that in the early years of the empire "Rome possessed no more than a beachhead in the Near East." See Millar, *Roman Near East*, 27–30. In the first years of his reign, Herod was kept busy stopping a Parthian invasion.

83. Horsley, "Jesus and Empire," 79.

84. Borg and Crossan, *Last Week*, 13; Sartre, *Middle East*, 89.

85. Sartre, *Middle East*, 89; Vermes, *Who's Who*, 19. Despite his love for Mariamne, Herod had her executed, along with two sons by her, her brother and high priest Aristobulus III, her mother, grandfather, and sundry other relatives over a perceived struggle for power. See Josephus, *Ant.* 15.237–239 for the account of her death.

would settle for nothing less.[86] Since Herod worked for Rome, he was not viewed as their friend.

In the face of opposition, Herod used his administrative prowess, backed by military might, to strengthen his hold on power and establish a legacy. Ruling from Jerusalem, he built for himself a lavish mansion and took special interest in the city's affairs. Herod personally appointed high priests, whom he chose on the basis of loyalty, regardless of their qualifications. They were his puppets, whom he used as instruments for civil authority.[87]

In 20 BCE, he began the reconstruction of Zerubbabel's Temple, turning it into a magnificent structure situated on forty-five acres of prime real estate, which popularly became known as "Herod's Temple." This brought initial favor with Pharisees, who were strict observers of the Law and supporters of the Temple, but when he demanded that all citizens of his kingdom take an oath of loyalty to Rome and himself, the Pharisees refused. He executed many of them.[88] Josephus writes that prior to his death, Herod also had placed a golden eagle above the "Great Gate" of the Temple, a flagrant violation of Jewish Law (Exod 20:4–6) that caused a riot and led to the slaughter of many Jewish young men.[89] For Herod, the eagle represented the Roman "great tradition" that all subjugated peoples must acknowledge. Even the native retainers refused to support Herod's dictum and stood instead with the protestors.[90]

Herod had an insatiable penchant for building projects. He designed and constructed a new seaport city, which he called Caesarea to honor Caesar Augustus. He additionally financed several construction works, including an amphitheater in Jerusalem which rankled Jewish sensitivities. In Caesarea, Samaria, and Panias, he built pagan temples to honor Augustus, which were used for cultic sacrifices and worship.[91] Moreover, he sponsored athletic contests, including the Actiac games and Olympics, which featured nude contestants.[92] While the emperor and Roman

86. This would eventually lead to the Jewish War against Rome from 66–70 CE, resulting in the destruction of the city and Temple and the dispersal of the Jews.

87. Sartre, *Middle East*, 92, 105.

88. Josephus, *Ant.* 17.41–45.

89. Ibid., 17.149–167; Josephus, *J.W.* 1.650.

90. Two well-respected rabbis, Matthias and Judas, were among the leaders who encouraged the protest and stirred up forty youths to destroy the eagle. It costs them their lives (Josephus, *J.W.* 1.651–65).

91. Sartre, *Middle East*, 92.

92. Millar, *Roman Near East*, 355; Sartre, *Middle East*, 91; Josephus, *Ant.* 16.149.

aristocrats held Herod in high esteem, Jews despised his sponsorship of these projects.

To pay for his building ventures and his own extravagant standard of living, Herod used resources from his land holdings as well as contributions from the native elites, mainly from Sadducees, who received his patronage. He also levied "a heavy burden of taxation on his subjects, which they met with only the greatest difficulty."[93] Udoh argues, however, that Herod did not overburden his citizens with excessive taxes.[94] He reaches this conclusion based on two occasions when Herod reduced taxes by one-third and by one-fourth in 20 BCE and 14 BCE, respectively.[95] The truth of the matter probably lies somewhere in between. Like most perceptive politicians, he likely knew when he could raise taxes and get away with it and when to lower them.

Herod undertook seriously his responsibilities as king. He erected fortresses to protect his subjects and his holdings, and brought relative stability to Palestine.[96] When a famine struck the region in 25 BCE, he melted down gold and silver items from his palace in order to purchase wheat from Egypt that his people might eat.[97]

On the other hand, Herod was ruthless when it came to keeping his throne and suppressing attempts at insurrection. He ordered his wife Mariamne and several children killed when he suspected that they were attempting a coup.

Herod was a complex individual. At times he sought the welfare of his subjects, but at all times he was more concerned about his own survival. In the eyes of most Jews, Herod was nothing more than a client-king who upheld the Roman domination system, which existed solely for the benefit of the ruling class.

At his death in 4 BCE, people throughout Israel celebrated in the streets, and riots "erupted in every major district of his realm, Galilee, Judea, and the TransJordan,"[98] indicating how unpopular his regime was viewed. In response, Rome dispatched the military to control the outburst. The troops marched on Sepphoris to recapture the capital city of Galilee, leaving destruction and carnage in their wake. At Jerusalem to the

---

93. Horsley and Silberman, *Message and the Kingdom*, 17.

94. Udoh, *To Caesar What is Caesar's*, 113–206, 286.

95. Josephus, *Ant.* 16.64.

96. Sartre, *Middle East*, 93.

97. Ibid., 93.

98. Horsley, "Jesus and Empire," 81.

south, two thousand rioters were crucified in public view to deter further rebellion.[99]

4.4.2 Herod's Successors

Upon Herod's death, after determining which one of Herod's last wills and testaments was binding, Augustus Caesar divided the kingdom among Herod's three sons.[100]

Philip received southern Syria and Lebanon, the northern region of Herod's kingdom, and was given the royal title of tetrarch.[101] He ruled successfully until his death during the winter of 33–34 CE. His lands were annexed briefly to Syria[102] before they were given in 37 CE, along with his royal title, to his nephew Agrippa I.

Nineteen-year-old Archelaus inherited Samaria, Idumea, and Judea (the latter included the capital city of Jerusalem), but he received the lesser title of ethnarch. According to Josephus, Archelaus eliminated taxes levied by his father on "public purchases and sales."[103] This initially endeared him to his subjects. However, when he refused to appoint a new high priest to the Jews' liking, he soon fell out of favor.[104] Archelaus reigned for less than ten years before Rome exiled him to Vienna in Gaul.[105] In 6 CE, his land was annexed to Syria and a Roman prefect was appointed to administer it from a base of operations in Caesarea.[106]

Seventeen-year-old Herod Antipas was appointed ethnarch over Perea and Galilee, a position he held during the ministries of John the Baptist and Jesus and the first years of the church (Luke 3:1). He reigned with an iron fist and handled anti-imperial resistance swiftly and harshly. This was the Herod who arrested and executed John the Baptist (Luke 3:19–20) after being excoriated by him for divorcing and marrying his

---

99. Borg, *Jesus*, 89; Vermes, *Who's Who*, 21.

100. Sartre, *Middle East*, 94.

101. A tetrarch ruled over a "little kingdom" (Sartre, *Middle East*, 70–71).

102. Millar, *Roman Near East*, 54.

103. Josephus, *Ant.* 17.204–205.

104. Ibid.

105. Sartre, *Middle East*, 94. Archelaus was unpopular with the people, and they continually lodged complaints against him to Rome.

106. Ibid., 103. A prefect was part of the equestrian class and functioned in a military capacity. Appointed directly by the emperor, the prefect served as commander of the Roman troops stationed in Caesarea.

brother Philip's wife.[107] When he heard that Jesus' popularity was growing because of his miracles, Antipas became anxious and wanted to meet with him (Luke 9:7–9). According to Luke, when Pilate learned that Jesus was a Galilean, he paraded him before Herod Antipas, who was delighted to finally meet Jesus. When Jesus refused Herod Antipas's request for a miracle, he was turned over to soldiers who mocked and ridiculed him (Luke 23:6–12).

Antipas was eventually replaced by Agrippa I with the territory of Judea being upgraded to that of a province.[108] Agrippa I reigned as King of Judea from 39–44 CE, during the ministry of the Apostle Paul. As a direct descendant of the Herodians and the Hasmoneans, Claudius Caesar thought he would be the perfect candidate to reestablish Palestine as a single kingdom and bring some semblance of order to the land. Caesar expanded the size of Agrippa's holding, "nearly re-creating the kingdom as it had been under Herod."[109]

Seeking favor with the Jewish native elites, Agrippa persecuted the church (Acts 12:1) and attempted to kill its leaders. He executed James, the brother of John, (v. 2) and arrested Peter, who escaped before facing trial and sure death (vv. 3–19). When Agrippa learned of the successful getaway, he blamed the prison guards and put them to death. Luke's account tells how the people of Tyre and Sidon hailed Herod Agrippa I as a god, and when he welcomed the accolades "an angel of the Lord" struck him with a fatal disease (vv. 20–24), showing God's displeasure with the worship of a human ruler.[110]

Like his grandfather, Agrippa I was a visionary who built baths, theaters, and amphitheaters. He sponsored gladiator fights and other sporting events. He gave his brother Herod the territory of Chalics. When Agrippa I died in 44 CE, his kingdom was added to the province of Syria.[111] A procurator, rather than a prefect, was appointed to run the administrative affairs of Judea.[112] Agrippa's brother Herod of Chalics assumed authority for the Temple, treasury, and the appointment of the high priests until his own death in 48 CE.[113]

107. Ibid., 97.
108. Millar, *Roman Near East*, 46.
109. Sartre, *Middle East*, 100.
110. Carter, *Roman Empire*, 36.
111. Sartre, *Middle East*, 100.
112. This marked a major shift of policy.
113. Sartre, *Middle East*, 100–101.

Claudius Caesar eventually named Agrippa II, son of King Agrippa I, to be ruler over eastern Galilee, Lebanon and southern Syria, and Chalics, which he inherited from his uncle. He reigned from 53 to ca. 95, and in the latter portion changed the name of his capital city Caesarea Philippi to Neronias in honor of the new emperor.[114] He steps onto the pages of Scripture in Acts 25 when he, along with his entourage, travels to Caesarea to welcome Festus as the new governor of Judea. At the time Paul was incarcerated, and Agrippa II asked Paul to appear before him and present a defense (v. 22). After patiently listening to Paul's testimony and impassioned plea, Agrippa II declared, "You almost persuaded me to become a Christian" (26:28). From this statement alone, it is difficult to know if Luke is portraying Agrippa II as even-handed and somewhat sympathetic to Paul's cause or as a sarcastic ruler with little or no concern for Paul's plight.

In some ways, the Jewish client-kings were between a rock and a hard place, attempting on the one hand to satisfy the demands of their Roman superiors, and on the other, attempting to keep order among the irascible Jews. Since the main responsibility of kings was "to uphold the elite-dominated status quo," they stood opposed to the Jesus movement which called upon people to give their allegiance to a new kingdom and another king (Luke 23:2; Acts 17:5).[115]

4.4.3 Palestinian Prefects or Governors

Provincial prefects were Roman citizens and part of the ruling class who governed in occupied territories. As appointees of the emperor, prefects wielded tremendous power and authority as they administered the affairs of Rome within their prescribed provinces. Like client-kings, they were responsible for collecting taxes, maintaining the peace, dispensing political favors, adjudicating legal matters, and using Roman troops stationed in the area when civil outbursts occurred. They served as the strong arm of the law in maintaining peace. They were also charged with protecting the high priestly robes when they were not being worn. These practices upset particularly the Pharisees, whose strict observance of purity laws forbade contact with Gentiles.[116]

Many Roman prefects showed little respect for Jewish practices or beliefs, and used force when their authority was challenged. In Jerusalem,

114. Ibid.
115. Carter, *Roman Empire*, 36.
116. Josephus, *Ant.* 15.403–6; 20.7.

prefects were regularly called upon to marshal their troops when public protests and small-scale riots got out of hand.

Pilate served in this office from 26 to 37 CE, and is pictured in the NT as a hard-nosed, self-serving politician who was not afraid to use coercion to carry out the duties of his office. The task of maintaining law and order without provoking riots took a great deal of political skill, which very few governors were able to master.

Pilate never quite understood the Jewish people, and like most Roman aristocrats, judged their religion to be far inferior to Rome's. This indifference to Jewish beliefs hindered his effective governance of Judea. On one occasion he siphoned off Temple funds to build an aqueduct, which led to a violent protest and scores of Jews being slain by Roman troops.[117] Luke writes that Pilate slaughtered a group of Galileans, and mixed their blood with the Temple sacrifices (Luke 13:1–2). Marshall believes this event took place during the Passover festival.[118] Philo, in his letter to the emperor, describes Pilate as a man prone to taking bribes, practicing wanton cruelty, and regularly executing suspects without a trial.[119] He was eventually removed from office because of his unauthorized actions.[120]

Other Roman provincial leaders mentioned by Luke included: Sergius Paulus, Governor of Cyprus (Acts 13:4–12) who was converted when Paul preached the gospel; Gallio, governor of Achaia, before whom Paul was charged with "persuading people to worship God in ways that are contrary to the law" (Acts 18:12–15); Felix (52–60 CE), the crafty people-pleasing governor of Judea, who kept Paul incarcerated for two years (Acts 24:1–22); and Festus (60–62 CE), who like his predecessor sought favor with the Jewish leaders and ordered Paul to Rome to stand trial (Acts 25:1–27:1).[121]

117. Josephus, *Ant.* 18.60–62; *J.W.* 2.175–177.

118. Marshall, *Gospel of Luke*, 553.

119. Philo, *Embassy*, 302.

120. Josephus, *Ant.* 18.88.

121. The historical nature and value of Luke's two-volume work is a matter of debate, since some of his events and dates cannot be reconciled with secular records. How precisely or loosely does Luke handle the facts? For an overview of the issue, see Soards, *Speeches in Acts*, 1–17, who presents the various scholarly opinions over the last century. For example, M. Schneckenburger departing from F. C. Baur understood Acts to be mainly a reliable historical work, while E. Zeller sees Acts "as wholly unreliable, although some bare historical facts and legends may lie behind Luke's creative composed account" (3–4). Luke certainly professes that his writings are factually reliable (Luke 1:1–4), and his opening statement places the events contained in his gospel in a historical context (v. 5; 2:1–2). The scholarly consensus is that Luke followed more

According to Acts, the Roman ruling elites often demonstrated hostility toward the leaders of the Jesus movement. As a result, many were arrested and beaten, and the apostle Paul spent several years in prison or under house arrest because the governing officials failed to administer justice.

The political hostility toward leaders in the Jesus movement was not without cause. Had Jesus and his followers been preaching about a heavenly salvation, Rome would have cared less. It was their denunciation of Roman imperialism and their annunciation of the coming kingdom of God that got Rome's attention.

In Matthew's gospel, Jesus forewarned his disciples in that because of their allegiance to him, they would be brought before governors and kings (Matt 10:17–18). He explicitly instructed them not to fret about preparing a defense, but to trust the Spirit of God to give them words to speak (vv. 19–20). Jesus never offered any assurance that they would escape mistreatment or punishment. To the contrary, he said that since disciples were not above their master (v. 24), they could expect persecution and possible death (vv. 21–23). Still they were not to fear their persecutors, but God only (vv. 19, 26, 28, 31). Regardless of the immediate outcome, they could expect deliverance at the end of the age (v. 22).

4.4.4 Retainers or Native Elites

As Rome acquired more territory, it recruited and relied on native leaders to help administer the affairs of state. It reasoned that conquered peoples would more readily follow their own leaders, if left intact, than foreign occupiers.

Native elites, comprising about 8 percent of the entire population of the Roman Empire, served as part of Rome's provincial bureaucracy.[122]

---

in the tradition of Greek historians, whose research methods included "personal observation (*autopsia*) and participation in events, travel, inquiry, the consultation of eyewitnesses" than Roman historians who "were often satisfied to stay at home and consult documents and records." See Witherington, *Acts*, 27; Cadbury, *Making of Luke-Acts*, 184–93. Unlike Greek historians Thucydides or Polybius, who chronicled political or military history, Luke devotes his attention to a social history of the church within the empire. He writes of events that happened "among us" (Luke 1:1). Aune, *New Testament*, 88, categorizes this as "general history." For a fuller discussion see 77–153. The Gospel of Luke and Acts do not offer a detailed narrative that includes all the Roman provincial rulers and their specific dates, but rather mention rulers only as they fit into the story of the progression of the Jesus movement.

122. Borg, *Jesus*, 83; Carter, *Matthew and Empire*, 17.

Also known as "retainers," they helped the Roman ruling class govern in the outlying provinces of the empire. To handle its affairs of Palestine, especially in its capital city of Jerusalem, Rome chose retainers from among those leaders associated with the Temple, the dominant political-economic institution in Judean society throughout the Second Temple period.[123]

The Sanhedrin was the supreme council located in Jerusalem that adjudicated matters throughout Judea. It consisted of seventy-two members, mainly priests, scribes, and respected elders associated with the Pharisees or Sadducees, the two most influential religious/political parties in the land.[124]

Pharisees were possibly the most important and influential members of Jewish society.[125] They were part of the ruling aristocracy who aligned themselves with Rome out of necessity to retain their positions of power and influence. According to Josephus, these wealthy laymen saw themselves as the defenders of the Torah and trustees of the oral law, which was to be transmitted from one generation to another.[126] As a socioreligious movement and a political interest group, in particular, they sought to reform society and influence Judean policy makers, according to their understanding of biblical tradition.[127] Some Pharisees were rulers of synagogues. Others likely served as judges, bureaucrats, and educators.[128] In the Synoptics, Pharisees are closely linked to Galilee, while the Gospel of John places them within Jerusalem.[129] In the Gospel of Luke, Jesus says they are lovers of money (Luke 16:14) who seek the best seats at banquets (Luke 11:43), placing them among the elites in Jewish society.

Sadducees were more conservative than the Pharisees because they embraced only the written Law, i.e., the five books of Moses. Whatever the Torah did not specifically forbid was permissible. Therefore, the Sadducees were more likely to be Hellenized than the Pharisees.[130] As part

123. Borg and Crossan, *Last Week*, 15.

124. Sartre, *Middle East*, 105. At the town and village level, local town councils, consisting of elders handled all decisions.

125. Ibid., 109.

126. Josephus, *Ant.* 17.42.

127. Saldarini, *Pharisees, Scribes and Sadducees*, 280–82, 288.

128. Ibid., 284.

129. Ibid., 291–97. Saldarini presents several scenarios of why Pharisees might have been in Galilee, including that they represented the Jerusalem authorities in the area.

130. This is a contested theory. Since Greek culture influenced the entire Roman world, it is likely that Pharisees were Hellenized as well (see Saldarini, *Pharisees,*

of the aristocratic priesthood,[131] Sadducees collaborated with the Romans and promoted their political agenda. Whereas most Jews desired to be free from Roman domination, the Sadducees were ready and willing to compromise in order to maintain their elite status. As such, they opposed Jesus and the early messianic movements (Acts 4:1; 5:17).

The high priests and chief priests were members of a few aristocratic families who controlled Temple affairs, offered sacrifices for the people, and "were responsible for collection of the tribute to Rome."[132] The Temple in Judea served "as an instrument of political domination and economic extraction."[133] Initially appointed by King Herod and upon his death by Roman prefects, the high priests also served as native retainers of Rome.[134] Because of their position on the council, the priests assured that Rome's policies would be represented and carried out. There was no area where Caesar's tentacles did not reach. Because priests derived their wealth and status by doing Rome's bidding, ordinary Jews feared them, but few respected them.

Scribes are first mentioned in Judg 5:14. By the time of the divided kingdom, they had reached a status of a high cabinet office (2 Kgs 22:2–20). Baruch is listed as a scribe during the time of Jeremiah the prophet (Jer 36:10, 32). In comparing 2 Kings and Jeremiah 36, it seems a connection can be made between the two, and that the office of scribe was passed from one generation to the next through family line. The best known scribe in the OT is Ezra, described as "a skilled scribe in the Law of Moses," who asks permission of the king of Persia to lead a remnant of Jews back to their homeland (Ezra 7:6). In Neh 8:1–6 he is found reading and explaining the Law to the assembled people.

In the NT scribes appear only in the Synoptic Gospels "as an organized social group, where they are associated with both the Pharisees and high priests as opponents of Jesus."[135] Because of their alignment with the

---

302–3). However, it seems to this writer that, as protectors of Jewish purity, Pharisees would resist Hellenization as much as possible. Paul, while identifying himself as a Pharisee, also adds that he was reared a "Hebrew of the Hebrews" (Phil 3:5), a likely reference to his retaining the Hebrew language and other aspects of his culture.

131. Sartre, *Middle East*, 111.

132. Horsley, *Jesus in Context*, 9.

133. Ibid., 128.

134. Vermes, *Who's Who*, 22; Sartre, *Middle East*, 105. Valerius Gratus (15–26 CE), who served as prefect immediately prior to Pilate, named three high priests in three years before appointing Caiaphas who held the post from 18–37 CE.

135. Saldarini, *Pharisees*, 241.

priests and Pharisees, they were part of the Jewish ruling class and "representatives of the temple-state."[136] Scribes functioned as copyists, teachers, and interpreters of the Law.[137]

Elders were wealthy Jewish laymen who often owned large amounts of agricultural property. Since every Jewish family supposedly owned land in perpetuity according to the Law of Moses, the only way elders could expand their property holdings was to confiscate ancestral lands of the peasants, contrary to the Law, in exchange for debt relief. In such cases, the peasants were either forced off the family farm or allowed "to stay on the land as tenant farmers . . . sharecroppers or day laborers."[138] As a result of their faithful service to the empire, rich Jews received additional land as gifts from their Roman benefactors, who had confiscated Jewish property in like manner.[139]

Together these native elites set guidelines for what it meant to be a Jew living in Palestine under Roman rule. It was a difficult and thankless task. Although they may have felt a moral obligation to care for the people under their charge, their legal duty was to Rome, whom they served in exchange for privileges not enjoyed by the general Jewish population. It was to their advantage that local governmental affairs ran smoothly.[140]

As a result, Jewish peasants had a love/hate relationship with their leaders, and occasionally demonstrated against unjust and oppressive policies. To assure these protests did not accelerate and turn into full scale riots, Jewish leaders often chose to act heavy-handedly against their own people. This did not sit well with the populace, who viewed their leaders as Roman collaborators. When native retainers could not restore order, they called upon Roman occupation troops for help. If matters got out of hand too often, Rome replaced a retainer with someone who could meet his obligation to the state. This may explain why Rome appointed eighteen different high priests between 6 CE and 66 CE, although the Law of Moses mandated that a priest hold the office for life. Rome did not feel bound by such parochial statutes.

The typical high priest in the first-century CE held office for less than two years. Caiaphas was one of three exceptions, and served eighteen

136. Horsley, *Jesus in Context*, 9.

137. Ibid.

138. Borg and Crossan, *Last Week*, 15.

139. Carter, *Matthew and Empire*, 17.

140. In similar fashion, German Lutheran and Roman Catholic religious leaders cooperated with the Third Reich in WWII, not because they necessarily embraced Nazism, but in order to maintain their positions of authority among the people.

years from 18 CE to 36 CE, which leads Borg and Crossan to conclude that he was "in the back pocket" of Rome.[141] Bond, offers other reasons for his longevity, but concedes that all are based on "speculation."[142]

Jesus regularly confronted the Jewish native elites, especially those who used the Temple as their base of operation. The Temple had become as much a house of Caesar as it was the House of God, since it was used as an economic clearinghouse through which Jewish taxes as well as tithes flowed.[143] The priesthood collected both, and the amounts were based on the peasants' income from crops grown and wages earned. The tribute was received, stored, and sent on to Rome, and the tithes went into the priests' coffers. Elaborate and accurate records were kept to account for every denarius.

Jesus likely viewed Jewish authorities as puppets of Rome. His numerous confrontations with Pharisees and priests, therefore, should be interpreted as conflicts with Imperial Rome as much as with the recalcitrant leadership of the Jewish nation.

When Jesus overturned the money tables in the Temple, he was making as much a political statement as a religious one. His words and actions in the Temple courtyard were meant to be an enacted prophecy. He announced the destruction of the Temple and railed against the Jewish native elites who used God's house to support the government of Rome rather than as a place of prayer (Mark 13:1–2; 14:58; Luke 19:45–46). These retainers revealed where their allegiance lay when, after arresting and delivering Jesus to Pilate, they charged, "If you release this man, you are no friend of Caesar" (John 19:12). Then they announced of themselves, "We have no king, but Caesar" (John 19:15). Whether or not this statement expressed an inner reality, it showed clearly the extent of their public commitment.

4.4.5 Agrarian Peasants, Urban Artisans, and Slaves

Mediterranean society was mainly agrarian in nature. Nearly 90 percent of the population, mostly peasants, lived in the country and earned their living by agriculture.[144] Referencing Ben-David, Stegemann notes that at the time of Herod the Great, Israel consisted of 2,500,000 acres of which

141. Borg and Crossan, *Last Week*, 19–20.

142. Bond, *Caiaphas*, 43.

143. Stevens, *Temples, Tithes, and Taxes*, 169.

144. Stegemann and Stegemann, *Jesus Movement*, 7.

1,700,000 acres were usable for farming.[145] The peasants worked the land and produced great wealth for the empire, but rarely received any benefit from it for themselves.[146] Most peasants were poor, but all were not at the same level of poverty. Some were "dirt" poor, earning only two hundred denarii per year, about one-half the amount needed to subsist. Many depended on the well-organized Jewish charity system to make ends meet.[147]

In the urban centers, poor persons worked also as artisans, making pottery, textiles, and handcrafted items; while others were manual laborers, toiling on such construction projects as temples, bridges, aqueducts and roads; some were bakers, cobblers, tanners, carpenters, fishermen, and barbers; a few were merchants, shop keepers, and wholesalers; but in all cases they were poor, barely making a livable wage.[148] Collectively they produced goods and services for the Roman aristocracy and native elites. They paid excessive and oppressive taxes, which kept them in poverty but sustained the lifestyle of the rich and famous.[149]

A large slave population worked at occupations ranging from menial labor to management. Some held positions of responsibility as secretaries and administrators within the empire.[150] Free labor was a major economic reason for the empire's wealth. Individuals became slaves in one of three possible ways. They were either: 1) captured as prisoners of war and sold to finance the military, 2) born into slavery, or 3) submitted to or sold themselves into slavery to improve their lot in life.[151] The latter might be the means of paying off debt, escaping tax obligations, or securing an executive position in a wealthy household, which would eventually lead to wealth, freedom and citizenship.[152] Josephus identified Felix, Governor of Judea, as a freedman of Claudius Caesar, who had gone on to obtain a high station in life.[153]

The lowest of the low on the social pyramid were the expendables, people with no skills or resources to contribute to Rome's economic growth. Many were beggars, social outcasts, the handicapped, sickly, and prisoners.

145. Ibid., 42.

146. Stevens, *Temples, Tithes and Taxes*, 169.

147. Stegemann and Stegemann, *Jesus Movement*, 90.

148. Ibid., 30–33.

149. Stevens, *Temples, Tithes and Taxes*, 18.

150. Lyall, *Slaves, Citizens, Sons*, 27.

151. Ibid., 28–34.

152. Winter, *Seek the Welfare of the City*, 154–55.

153. Josephus, *Ant.* 20.7.

4.5 Jewish Resistance to Domination

Since their captivity to Babylon, Jews had awaited the "Day of the Lord" when God would intervene on their behalf, establish his promised new covenant, and restore the kingdom to Israel (Jer 31:31–34; Ezek 36:24–27; Hosea 2–3). At such time, the divided and exiled nation would be reunited under the reign of another King David (Ezek 37:15–28). Starting in the second-century BCE, popular apocalyptic and eschatological literature began circulating, raising expectations of God's people. Some Jews expected the appearance of a new High Priest, who would purify the Temple and free the nation from enslavement. Others looked for an anointed emissary from God, a Messiah, like Moses, who would triumph over their enemies. The Essenes, a group of purists similar to the Pharisees, withdrew to the Judean desert and formed a community at Qumran under the leadership of a "Teacher of Righteousness," where they awaited the arrival of the Messiah, who would lead a victorious end-time battle against the forces of darkness.[154] Many variations of the same theme circulated among the masses.

With the appointment of Herod as king of the Jews (37 BCE) and with their own native leaders collaborating with Rome,[155] it must have seemed to average Jews that God had forgotten the nation. As a result, pockets of resistance soon developed in and around Galilee, a northern hotbed of unrest.[156] Charismatic leaders like Ezechias "the robber," who roamed the Galilean hills with his bandits, led an unsuccessful revolt against Herod. He was swiftly defeated and along with his marauders was executed.[157] Scott views such open acts of rebellion as the natural outcome of oppression. When the marginalized and disenfranchised reach the point of hopelessness, some among their number eventually reach a breaking point and attack their oppressors either verbally or violently.[158] Scott's reasoning, as previously mentioned in chapter 1, offers a sociological and anthropological basis for the various organized and spontaneous Jewish resistance movements that followed.

---

154. 4Q171; 1QH XIII.

155. The Pharisees were certainly an exception. They despised unclean Gentiles ruling over them, defiling their land. However, they saw no realistic way to freedom, except for divine intervention.

156. Sartre, *Middle East*, 113.

157. Josephus, *Ant.* 14.159, 167.

158. Scott, *Domination*, 213–15.

According to Josephus, a zealot movement arose that he called the "Fourth Philosophy,"[159] whose members thought they could hasten the end of the age and the coming of the Messiah. Like Robin Hood, they stole from the rich and gave to the poor. This gave them legitimacy among the common folk. While most scholars feel the Zealots as a movement did not actually develop until the 60s CE, many zealous insurrectionists and revolutionaries had been wreaking havoc for decades; among them the *sicarii*, a group of assassins who infiltrated crowds at festivals and plunged their *sicos* or curved daggers into the bodies of their unsuspecting victims, usually a Roman officer or compromising Jewish official.[160]

Upon Herod's death, many revolutionary leaders claimed the title of king for themselves. One, Athronges, "was an obscure poor shepherd of remarkable stature and physical strength, who in the company of four equally powerful brothers started an uprising in the political chaos that followed the death of Herod the Great in 4 BCE."[161] They fought valiantly, but unsuccessfully. Another, Judas of Galilee, son of Ezechias, mentioned in Acts 5:37 recruited a small army and seized the arsenals at Sepphoris in 4 BCE, while the Herodian army was away facing a different enemy. Varus, the governor of Syria came to the rescue and squashed the rebellion. He restored order by publicly crucifying the remaining 2,000 Jewish insurrectionists.[162] Judas's sons were charged and crucified a generation later (46–48 CE) for banditry by Tiberius Caesar.[163] A year prior to their arrest and death, Theudas, claiming to be a miracle worker,[164] called upon his disciples to follow him in a new Exodus out to the desert. The Roman governor Crispus Fadus (44–46 CE) arrested and executed Theudas as his followers scattered.[165] In Acts, Gamaliel mentions Theudas as an example of a revolutionary whose efforts were brought to naught (Acts 5:36). On another occasion the Apostle Paul is mistaken by a Roman commander as being an insurrectionist known simply as "the Egyptian," who "some time ago stirred up a rebellion and led four thousand assassins out into the

---

159. The other three philosophies would be the Sadducees, Pharisees, and Essenes. While the Zealot movement did not begin until 66 CE, many were zealous for independence throughout the first century. Their resistance eventually morphed into a full-scale movement.

160. Sartre, *Middle East*, 115.

161. Vermes, *Who's Who*, 55; Josephus, *J.W.* 2.60–65; *Ant.* 17.278–84.

162. Sartre, *Middle East*, 114. Vermes, *Who's Who*, 165–66.

163. Sartre, *Middle East*, 115.

164. Josephus, *Ant.* 20.97–78 called him a sorcerer and imposter.

165. Ibid.

wilderness" (Acts 21:38). According to Josephus, the Egyptian ascended the Mount of Olives and told his followers, like Joshua of old, that at his command the walls of Jerusalem would fall and as Israel's new prophetic leader, he would defeat the Roman troops stationed in the city.[166] Governor Felix (52–60 CE), anticipating his strategy, preemptively attacked the insurgents, slaughtering and/or capturing six hundred of them. Somehow, "the Egyptian" escaped.

Sometimes protests were spontaneous as when Augustus Caesar visited Syria in 20 BCE, and the people of Gadara rushed forward to accuse Herod of stealing from Rome and destroying temples, in the hope of "gaining liberation from his kingdom."[167] They were unsuccessful. On another occasion a riot broke out when the prefect Pontius Pilate strategically placed throughout Jerusalem military ensigns, which bore the image and divine title of Caesar.[168] It caused an uproar. Masses of Jews trekked to Caesarea to lodge a protest in front of Pilate's palace. On the sixth day with no signs of the protest abating, Pilate ordered his soldiers to ready themselves for action. He demanded the Jews return home, but they refused and lay bare their necks, saying they would rather die than break God's Law. Impressed by their bravery and convictions, Pilate acquiesced and had the ensigns removed.[169] These bold "public transcripts" by the politically oppressed were rare, but show the extent they were willing to go to protect some vestiges of their "little tradition." Philo writes of another Pilate-related incident that took place in 26 CE, when Pilate entered Jerusalem by night carrying golden imperial shields and planted them in public sight.[170] This resulted in another prolonged Jewish protest, which ended only after word reached Tiberius Caesar and he ordered Pilate to remove the shields.[171]

When Caligula Caesar disregarded the Jewish law prohibiting idolatry and "ordered a colossal statue of himself be erected in the holy of holies" in the Temple in 40–41 CE, the Jews were grieved to the core.[172] Their sadness soon turned to anger and they marched *en masse* to protest

---

166. Josephus, *Ant.* 20.171. In *J.W.* 2.261, Josephus places the deluded Egyptian's defeated troops at 30,000.

167. Millar, *Roman Near East*, 39.

168. Josephus, *Ant.* 18.55–59.

169. Ibid.

170. Philo, *Embassy*, 299–306.

171. Ibid.

172. Philo, *Embassy*, 774.

the decree.[173] Since Rome had little tolerance for any public displays of rebellion, troops were often called to break up the crowds and arrest the troublemakers. The native Jewish retainers intervened whenever possible to stay judgment.

Riots were numerous throughout Judea and rumors of revolution filled the air. Between self-proclaimed prophets, messiahs, bandits, charlatans, agitators, and gangs of assassins, something was always astir.[174]

When John the Baptist and Jesus stepped onto the public stage (ca. 30 CE), claiming to speak for God and calling upon people to prepare for the imminent arrival of God's kingdom, both Roman and Jewish authorities viewed them as agitators. In commanding the masses to purify themselves by submitting to baptism, the two eschatological heralds were asking people to align themselves with the radical margins of Judaism. When the pious Pharisees, who considered themselves the guardians of the kingdom, discovered Jesus had little respect for traditions they held high, they turned against him, with few exceptions.

As the multitudes began identifying Jesus with the coming Davidic king, his fate was sealed. The powerful ruling elites likely looked upon him as another charlatan or revolutionary who threatened the stability of the region. He had to be stopped.

4.6 Jesus as a Political Prophet

Some NT commentators view Jesus predominantly as a religious figure with little or no concern about the politics and culture of his day. Such an interpretation results when one anachronistically presupposes that the idea of separation between church and state existed during NT times. The first-century Roman world had no such concept or custom. Religion and politics, whether Roman or Jewish, were interwoven into a single fabric.

A failure to define Jesus and his movement in historical context leads to spiritualizing Jesus' life and ministry. Beavis's position is a case in point. Accepting the false dichotomy between church and state, she argues, albeit unconvincingly, that Jesus preached a nonpolitical, spiritual, and utopian kingdom.[175] She agrees that the early church used vocabulary particular to the empire and participated in activities patterned after those in the

173. Josephus, *Ant.* 18.271–272; Sartre, *Middle East*, 115.

174. For a contemporary treatment of the resistance movements of the first-century CE, the reader is referred to Horsley and Hanson, *Bandits*.

175. Beavis, *Jesus and Utopia*, 94–98.

empire, yet she does not attribute any political significance to them, recognize how they challenged the social structure of the empire, or served as Christian alternatives to similar imperial practices.[176] For her, Jesus was mainly a spiritual savior.

Kim is another recent NT scholar to categorize Jesus' ministry and message exclusively in spiritual terms without any tinge of anti-imperial content or political purpose.[177] Like Beavis, Kim makes a distinction between realms of Caesar (secular) and Jesus (spiritual). He claims that Jesus came to liberate Israel and the world from spiritual, not political oppression.[178] Hence, Kim rejects that Jesus' messianic reign will be "a literal restoration of the Davidic kingship" that results in the "political subjugation of the nations."[179] By discarding a political interpretation, Kim presents no logic for Jesus' crucifixion other than a theological one.[180] For him, the gospel is "politically innocuous."[181] Obviously, titles like Savior and Lord carried political overtones for those living in the empire; yet, Kim strips them of such connotations when applied to Jesus.

Kim holds that the empire-wide *Pax Romana* allowed for safe preaching of the gospel and offered a positive environment in which the Jesus movement could advance.[182] For Kim the Roman world seems to be nothing more than the setting in which Jesus ministered. With a clearer understanding of the matter, Ehrensperger explains that "the context of the Roman Empire far from providing the mere background of events resulting in the emergence of the early Christ movement is the ever-present foreground the early Christ followers and Jewish communities had to relate to and in which they had to interact."[183]

Kim points out that Jesus encouraged people to pay their taxes, and that Paul, likewise, commanded them to submit to the government. In making this case, Kim ironically fails to see that the very act of submitting to Caesar would be as much a political practice as resisting, just different

176. Ibid., see chaps. 4–5.
177. Kim, *Christ and Caesar*, 76, 147.
178. Ibid., 94–113.
179. Ibid., 15.
180. Ibid., 23. Like many within the Reformed camp, Kim views the cross primarily as a place where forensic justification was secured for the believer.
181. Ibid., 77.
182. Ibid., 174.
183. Ehrensperger, *Paul*, 10.

in nature.[184] Just as disturbing is Kim's failure to consider seriously the alternative interpretation that Jesus' statement about paying taxes to Caesar is not made in support of paying taxes, but is actually intended to have the opposite force.[185] Since, "The earth is the Lord's and the fullness thereof" (Ps 24:1), all belongs to God and nothing belongs to Caesar. Thus, it is an anti-imperial hidden transcript.

While it is understandable that twenty-first century Westerners would view Jesus as a spiritual king and Caesar as a secular king, one would be hard pressed to find the early church making such a distinction. Politics and religion were conjoined twins. They were intertwined and could not be separated.

Roman imperial ideology combined religion and politics. As *pontifex maximus*, the emperor served as both chief priest and king.[186] Romans believed that the gods created the empire and ordained Rome to rule the world. In like manner, the NT writers portray Jesus as both priest and king.

Jews, like Romans, made no distinction between secular and spiritual. All their past and present rulers were viewed as religio-political leaders. From Genesis onward the Hebrew Scriptures tell how God ruled earth through representative leaders; from his commission of Adam and Eve to take dominion over the earth; to his promises to Abraham that he would raise from his loins a succession of kings; to his covenant with David that a royal line would continue indefinitely; and finally the promises he gives through the prophets of a coming messiah. God selected rulers to serve in a religio-political capacity. Even the high priest, elders, scribes, and others associated with the Temple were a combination of religious and political leaders. A division between the two was foreign to both the Hebrew and Gentile mindset.

Old Testament writers rarely, if ever, speak of salvation in spiritual terms alone. For them, salvation was just as much a geopolitical deliverance as it was religious. Since their days in Egyptian slavery, Jews were dominated by one empire or another. From Moses onward prophets declared that one day God would intervene, deliver his people from tyranny, judge their oppressors, and ultimately vindicate their martyrs at the resurrection, thus, completing their salvation. Jews understood the goal of history to be the destruction of the world's kingdoms and the establishment

184. Warren Carter makes this point in his review of Kim's book (Carter, Review of *Christ and Caesar*).

185. Herzog, "On Stage and Off Stage with Jesus," 41–60.

186. Suetonius, *Aug.* 2.31.

of God's kingdom on earth. For them, "salvation" was synonymous with deliverance, and it carried the idea of earthly not heavenly liberation.

To suggest that his early followers saw Jesus as the king of heaven, who concerned himself with people's spiritual needs and otherworldly salvation only, ignores the historical context in which they lived. From its inception, the Jesus movement was a combined religious and political movement. Jesus was a man of his times. His preaching of the good news of the kingdom to the poor spoke of how God would restore social, economic, and political justice to those who had been marginalized. In his kingdom prayer, Jesus speaks of a day when debts are cancelled and food abounds for all (Matt 6:11–12). The Beatitudes deal with economics. The Jews, whether followers of Jesus or not, looked for a salvation that was essentially sociopolitical, when God's government displaced the rule of tyrants.

Luke uses Palestinian political markers to set the context for the life and ministry of both John the Baptist and Jesus.[187] He places their births "in the days of king Herod" (Luke 1:5). He then compares John to the prophet Elijah who stood up to a tyrant king (1:17). Of Jesus, he records, "He will be great, and will be called the Son of the Most High, and the Lord God will give to him the throne of his ancestor David. He will reign over the house of Jacob for ever, and of his kingdom there will be no end" (1:32–33). Herod was known as "great." He was king of the Jews! If Jesus is to reign, then Herod must be removed.

As a prophet, Jesus emerges from the baptismal waters announcing the imminent arrival of God's kingdom. This political message "challenged Rome's imperial power"[188] and its claim of manifest destiny. It did not go unnoticed but got the attention of the Jewish ruling elites and the Roman prefects. It was this message that eventually got Jesus arrested, scourged, and executed and subsequently many of his followers as well. Jesus was not stoned as a blasphemer for founding a new religion which pointed people to a heavenly salvation but for being an insurrectionist. Crucifixion was a political act. It demonstrated graphically Rome's power and the extent to which she was willing to go to eliminate any threat against the state. Scott notes that Rome used crucifixion as a ritual of ridicule and scorn.[189] The victims were dehumanized in order to drive terror into the hearts of the

187. As prophets, both John and Jesus speak to political issues and both will die at the hands of politicians (see Luke 3:12–14; 9:7–9; 20:21–22; 22:25; 22:30; 23:2; 23:6–12; 23:13–38).

188. Ehrensperger, *Paul*, 11.

189. Scott, *Domination*, 23.

masses lest they consider a similar act of rebellion.[190] By proclaiming the good news, i.e., the triumph of God's kingdom, Jesus inferred that Rome's days were numbered. Jesus suffered precisely because religion and politics were not separated but intricately intertwined.

4.7 The Dove and the Donkey: Jesus as God's Anti-Imperial Caesar

4.7.1 The Dove

Jesus' public ministry commenced with his baptism in the Jordan and served as the defining event when God inaugurated Jesus as Israel's eschatological king. This interpretation is based in part on the accompanying words from heaven: "This is my beloved son in whom I am well pleased" (Luke 3:22b), a quote from Psalm 2, in which God declares David to be his son or earthly king with power to speak and act on his behalf (Ps 2:6–7).

While recognizing the link between his baptism and inauguration as king, biblical scholars, with rare exception, have not interpreted Jesus' baptism as a hidden transcript that carries anti-imperial implications. This is due to their failure: 1) to examine the baptism in its Greco-Roman context and 2) to give a plausible and satisfactory explanation of why the Holy Spirit descends "in bodily form" as a dove (Luke 3:22a) and lights upon Jesus' shoulder.[191] When these two components are considered, one discovers that Luke desires for his readers to interpret the baptism as antithetical to the inauguration of the Roman emperor.

In his unpublished dissertation dealing with the British monarchy, William Karlson traces the coronation of English kings back to ancient Rome and shows how Romans used augury, i.e., the study of the flight

---

190. Thatcher, *Greater than Caesar*, 93–94, identifies crucifixion as a "*commemorative* ritual" and a "symbolic reenactment" signifying "Rome's conquest of the victim's nation." He explains, "In this drama, the officiating soldiers played the role of the conquering Roman legions, while the person on the cross represented his entire people group, beaten, broken, and subjugated. In Palestine particularly, every crucifixion reenacted Pompey's conquest of the region in 63 B.C.E., reminding both Rome and the Jews of exactly how things came to be the way they are. Every Jewish cross was planted in a master commemorative narrative that both rationalized Roman power and discouraged future attempts at innovation in view of past failures."

191. Nolland, *Luke*, 35A, 161. Also see Keck, "The Spirit and the Dove," 41–67, who offers a brief summary of various interpretations, all of which lack biblical support or logical coherence.

of birds, to choose their kings.[192] The term "augur" has Latin roots and etymologically means "to consecrate by augury." Thus, one finds it imbedded in the English word in*augur*ation, meaning the coronation of a king.

Roman Augury and King-Making

Cicero (106–46 BCE) writes that Romulus, the legendary founder of Rome and its first king, attributed his ascent to the throne to avian signs.[193] This myth then became the basis for historical precedence. During the three periods of Roman history, augury was the standard method for choosing a ruler. Numa Pompilius, whose reign began in 715 BCE, became king by an accompanying sign of augury. In turn, he instituted the office of the *augurate* and organized the augural college, both of which continued until the late fourth-century CE.[194]

Referencing Pliny, Karlson notes that whenever a royal family line or dynasty came to an end, Romans turned to augury for the selection of its next king.[195] Augury confirmed whom, among the challengers, the gods had chosen.

Avian omens or signs accompanied the selection and confirmation of all rulers but one from Augustus to Domitian. Interestingly, when the Roman senate confirmed Octavian as emperor in 27 CE, it also bestowed upon him the title Augustus, which Suetonius links etymologically to augury.[196]

The Flight of the Eagle

Romans gave additional significance to those avian omens which involved eagles, believing the eagle to be connected to Jupiter. Just as Jupiter was the king of the gods, so the eagle was the king of the birds. It was stronger, flew higher, and preyed on other species, both celestial and terrestrial. Pliny the Elder said, "Of the birds known to us [Romans] the eagle is the most

192. Karlson, "Syncretism."
193. Cicero, *Div.* 1.48.
194. Livy, *History of Rome*, 1.18.
195. Ibid., 1.34; cf. Dionysius of Halicarnassus, *Ant. rom.* 3.47.3.
196. Suetonius, *Aug.* 7.2.

honorable and also the strongest."[197] As a result, "the eagle became the bird of emperors," that the gods sent to authenticate their choice as ruler.[198]

During the NT era each emperor who claimed the throne based on avian signs could point to the descent of an eagle as divine confirmation. Tiberius (14–37 CE), successor to Augustus, for example could confidently wear his crown because an eagle had landed on the roof of his house.[199]

The Flight of the Dove

For Luke's readers, the descent of the Holy Spirit upon Jesus "in bodily form" at his baptism would be seen as an avian sign that God had chosen him to be Israel's king, just as the gods used the flight of birds to confirm their choice of the Roman emperor.[200] As such, this text should be viewed as a hidden transcript, containing a veiled message directed to those within the Jesus movement.

This question remains: "In what way was the baptism of Jesus anti-imperial or antithetical to Roman inauguration? The answer lies in the kind of bird that accompanied the baptism.[201] Jewish, Christian, and Greco-Roman literature extant in the first-century CE identifies the dove as antithetical to the eagle. In the Hebrew Scriptures the dove is associated with tranquility and tenderness (Gen 8:8–12; Cant 2:14; 5:2; 6:9; Nahum 2:7). Homer portrays the dove as powerless, serving as prey for other

---

197. Pliny the Elder, *Nat.* 10.6–15.

198. Woolf, *Ancient Civilizations*, 38.

199. Suetonius, *Tib.* 14.2–3.

200. Although the early church rejected augury as an art or the augurate as an office, it believed that God occasionally and sovereignly used signs to reveal his will. In the *Protevangelium of James*, paragraphs 8–9, the temple priest asks God to indicate by a sign who is to be the Virgin Mary's husband. When a dove lands on Joseph's head, it is taken as an avian sign that he is God's choice. Eusebius mentions in *Eccl. Hist.* 6.29 the descent of a dove upon the head of Fabianus convinced the people in 236 CE that God had chosen him to be the new bishop of Rome.

201. Keck, "The Spirit and the Dove," 63–67, points out that in the Gospels of Matthew, Mark, and John the adverbial phrase "as a dove" is used to describe the motion of the Spirit's descent. But Luke adds the words "in bodily form" to "as a dove" transforming it into an adjectival phrase.

Not only did the Spirit arrive like a bird, but came in dove-like form or appearance. Luke's Hellenistic audience not only would have interpreted the descent of the Spirit as an avian sign of inauguration, but in this researcher's opinion, they would have seen it as the inauguration of a different kind of king; one confirmed by a dove, not an eagle.

birds, particularly the eagle.[202] Plutarch saw the dove as a gentle domesticated creature that loves and nurtures its own and refuses to harm other living things, unlike an eagle that devours and destroys even its own.[203] Greeks and Romans associated the dove to the goddess of love, rather than the powerful Zeus/Jupiter. Philo, a Hellenistic Jew, describes the dove (περιστερά, same word used in gospels) as "the gentlest of those whose nature is tame and gregarious."[204] Likewise, the Roman author and equestrian, Pliny the Elder also contrasted the aggressive actions of the eagle with the gentle behavior of the dove.[205] Jesus admonished his disciples to be "as wise as serpents and harmless as doves" (Matt 10:16).

Why would Luke want his audience to know that God publicly confirmed Jesus to be king through the flight of a dove, when the normative avian sign was the flight of an eagle? The dove narrative likely functioned in the same manner as the account of Jesus riding into Jerusalem on a donkey. Each depicts Jesus' kingship in contradistinction to imperial expectations. The flight of the dove is a confirming sign that Jesus is God's king, whose rule stands contrary to the Roman notion of power as confirmed by an eagle. Throughout his gospel, Luke consistently portrays God's kingdom as the antithesis of the Roman Empire (Luke 6:20; 13:29–30; 18:16; 22:25–27). Jesus is a different kind of king than Caesar. He is a king who brings peace not at the expense and suffering of others but through his own service and suffering. This is symbolized by the descent of a dove rather than an eagle, the national emblem of Rome.

This anti-imperial understanding of Jesus' baptism based on the dove is strengthened when the accompanying voice also quotes from Isa 42:1, "Behold *my servant* whom I uphold; my chosen one in whom my soul delights. I have put my Spirit upon him, and he will bring justice to the nations." By combining Ps 2:7 and Isa 42:1, the heavenly voice creates an oxymoron—a king who serves. Kings do not serve, they rule. Others serve them. Thus, Jesus is inaugurated to be a king of a different stripe—a humble king.

In like fashion, chapters 7 and 8 will present the Lord's Supper as both a hidden transcript and an anti-imperial activity.

202. Homer, *Od.* 3.525–534.
203. Plutarch, *Is. Os.* 379-D.
204. Philo, *Spec.* 1.163.
205. Pliny, *Nat.* 10.10.

4.7.2 The Donkey

Jesus' triumphal entry into Jerusalem serves as another example of a hidden transcript/anti-imperial action. Why does Jesus ride on a donkey and not on a horse or in a chariot? Why do the crowds which line the streets welcome him with branches? By comparing Jesus' entry with Solomon's entry right before he was installed as Israel's new monarch, one finds an answer:

> King David said, "Take with you the servants of your lord, and have my son Solomon ride on my own mule, and bring him down to Gihon. There let the priest Zadok and the prophet Nathan anoint him king over Israel; then blow the trumpet, and say, 'Long live King Solomon!' You shall go up following him. Let him enter and sit on my throne; he shall be king in my place; for I have appointed him to be ruler over Israel and over Judah" (1 Kgs 1:33–35).

> So the priest Zadok, the prophet Nathan, and Benaiah son of Jehoiada, and the Cherethites and the Pelethites, went down and had Solomon ride on King David's mule, and led him to Gihon. There the priest Zadok took the horn of oil from the tent and anointed Solomon. Then they blew the trumpet, and all the people said, "Long live King Solomon!" (1 Kgs 1:38–39).

Gihon was the spring alongside the Temple mount where Solomon was anointed before making his grand entry to the cheers of the crowd and his installation as king. These parallels are obvious. As Solomon was anointed with oil at the site of water, so Jesus was anointed with the Holy Spirit at the Jordan, both events foreshadowing their triumphal entry and enthronement.

One stark difference should be noted. Solomon's ride on a lowly animal signifies that he is succeeding his father David as God's servant-king. Unfortunately, he eventually departs from that role and becomes an imperial king. By contrast, Jesus' ride into Jerusalem can be interpreted as a hidden transcript that exposes Caesar's imperial rule. Jesus is replacing David as God's eschatological king, but unlike Solomon his reign will be characterized consistently by servanthood.

Zechariah writes prophetically of a coming king who makes a triumphal entry, but describes his entry in terms that are self-effacing. "Rejoice greatly, O daughter of Zion! Shout aloud, O daughter of Jerusalem! Lo, *your king comes to you*; triumphant and victorious is he, *humble and riding on an ass*, on a colt, the foal of an ass" (Zech 9:9). According to the prophet, Yahweh will install a different kind of king ("triumphant" yet "humble and riding on an ass"). Like the dove, the donkey points to a countercultural leader, an anti-imperial monarch, who serves in humility rather than ruling by force.

Yahweh then indicates that he will use the newly installed king to end war and reunite his people through the means of a new covenant: "I will cut off the chariot from Ephraim and the war horse from Jerusalem; and the battle bow shall be cut off, and he shall command peace to the nations; his dominion shall be from sea to sea, and from the River to the ends of the earth. As for you also, because of the blood of my covenant with you, I will set your captives free from the waterless pit. Return to your stronghold, O prisoners of hope . . ." (Zech 9:10–11). The eschatological king riding on a donkey also brings peace ("the battle bow shall be cut off, and he shall command peace") and institutes a universal reign ("he shall command the nations . . . his dominion shall be . . . to the ends of the earth"). He will end the exile ("I will set your captives free") and reunite the nation ("return to your stronghold"). God declares this "hope" is based on "the blood of my covenant" with his people.

The Gospel writers likely see Jesus' triumphal entry as a partial fulfillment of Zechariah's prophecy. According to Luke, as Jesus enters the city the throngs that line the wayside make a similar connection. They cry out:

> Blessed is the king
> > who comes in the name of the Lord!
> Peace in heaven,
> > and glory in the highest heaven! (Luke 19:38)

Then Luke records Jesus' response: "As he came near and saw the city, he wept over it, saying, 'If you, even you, had only recognized on this day *the things that make for peace!* But now they are hidden from your eyes'" (Luke 19:41–42). While the crowd rightly interprets the royal symbolism of Jesus' triumphal entry, they fail to grasp the means by which he will secure their peace. They expect him to overthrow Rome through the use of force and set up God's kingdom in Jerusalem. Jesus has a different peace plan.

Had he done as they anticipated, his rule would have been no different than Caesar's reign, but Jesus' peace initiative was based on nonviolent resistance and suffering.

Borg and Crossan, using historical imagination, compare and contrast the *Pax Christa* to the *Pax Romana* by describing two simultaneous processions that took place on Sunday of that Passover week.[206] The one, commandeered by Governor Pilate atop a charger, consisted of a column of six thousand foot soldiers. The other, led by Jesus mounted on a donkey, consisted of peasant pilgrims who entered the city from the opposite direction. Pilate's grand entrance was designed to drive the fear of Caesar into all who might be contemplating a violent demonstration. The sheer display of physical force could deter even the bravest insurgent from shattering the *Pax Romana*. By contrast, Jesus' entrance on a donkey, prearranged and orchestrated to coincide with, mock, and mimic the governor's arrival, was intended to be an anti-imperial subversive act, an enacted parable of sorts.

The two processions represented two opposing kingdoms. The one, personified by Pilate, was built on brute strength and maintained at all cost. The other, typified by Jesus on a beast of burden, offered an alternative vision of the kingdom of God, built on humility, sacrifice, and servitude (Zech 9:9–11). By the end of the week the kingdoms had clashed, and men and women were forced to align themselves with one or the other.

Jesus' parabolic ride into the city ended at the Temple mount, where he challenged the Jewish elites. Built originally to serve as a house of prayer for all people and as a holy space where priests served as intermediaries between God and his people, the Temple had long lost its purpose (Luke 19:46). The priesthood now served as functionaries of the empire and oppressed God's people.

According to the Synoptic Gospels, Jesus not only upsets the tables of the moneychangers on Palm Sunday, but throughout the week excoriates the Jewish leadership from the portico of the Temple for their role in serving themselves at the expense of God's people (Matt 21–23; Mark 11–12; Luke 20–22). Hidden transcripts—thoughts normally voiced only in private settings and behind closed doors—suddenly became open and brazen public denunciations against Rome and her native retainers (public transcripts). From the perspective of the Jewish retainers, Jesus' actions galvanized in their minds that he was a subversive agitator who had to be stopped at any cost, lest his disciples follow suit, resulting in a full-scale revolt.

In reality, while Jesus rode the wave of Jewish nationalism, he never encouraged his disciples to use violence in overthrowing Rome or displacing the Jewish leadership. To the contrary, he always encouraged them to avoid physical conflict. That very week he had foretold of a day when

206. Borg and Crossan, *Last Week*, 2–6.

Jerusalem would be surrounded by armies. He said when it happened, his followers should flee the area rather than participate in a brutal revolution (Luke 21:20–24).[207]

When Jesus was brought before Pilate, the Jewish authorities charged, "We found this man perverting our nation . . . saying that he himself is the Messiah, a king" (Luke 23:2). In John's gospel the accusation stands that Jesus "υἱὸν θεοῦ ἑαυτὸν ἐποίησεν," i.e., "made himself the Son of God" (John 19:7). The allegation that Jesus claimed the title "Son of God" had profound political ramifications for both Jews and Romans. For the Jewish elites, the title was a messianic designation. The fact that they charged Jesus with claiming the title for himself shows they personally do not believe him to be messiah. For the Romans, "Son of God" was viewed as a challenge to Caesar's exclusive claim to the title. Both Jews and Romans deemed the charge worthy of death. Pilate had no choice but to execute him as a political revolutionary against the state. By applying Rome's ultimate weapon of domination—crucifixion—Pilate likely hoped to end swiftly any further Passover attempts to resist imperial rule.

4.8 Jesus as God's Caesar

There is no way of knowing exactly when Jesus came to realize that he would die as a martyr for God's kingdom. According to Matthew, he spoke of his death in response to Peter's declaration that Jesus is the kingly messiah. During this conversation Jesus informed the apostles that he planned to form an ἐκκλησία and give them the keys to the kingdom (Matt 16:13–20). The unexpected announcement of his impending death and resurrection, and his charge that they were to carry on his work, caught the disciples off guard. He then spoke of the possibility of their martyrdom, but promised that the gates of death, i.e., hades, would not prevail against them any more than it did against him.[208] His challenge was all encompassing: "Then Jesus told his disciples, 'If any want to become my

---

207. The prediction became a reality in 66 CE. The Jewish resistance movement proclaimed itself independent of Roman control. Its fighters stripped Palestine of imperial images and took its final stand at Masada. According to Eusebius, *Eccl. Hist.* 3.5, over one million Jews were killed and nearly one hundred thousand taken prisoner in 70 CE. As Titus ransacked Jerusalem and destroyed the Temple, the Christians crossed the Jordan and escaped into Pella.

208. On two other occasions Jesus announced his impending death (Mark 9:31; 10:32–34) and further revealed that he would be rejected by the Jewish retainers and executed by the Romans (Luke 9:21–22).

followers, let them deny themselves and take up their cross and follow me. For those who want to save their life will lose it, and those who lose their life for my sake will find it. For what will it profit them if they gain the whole world but forfeit their life? Or what will they give in return for their life?'"(Matt 16: 24–26). This must have been confusing to the Twelve who were expecting Rome's imminent defeat and the commencement of God's kingdom on earth.

Jesus and his disciples headed toward Jerusalem, where his expectations would be fulfilled. After his entry into the city and several days of teaching in the Temple, Jesus ate his last supper with his disciples before retiring to Gethsemane where he faced doubts about his call and God's promise. Had Jesus misinterpreted his mission? Were the words of God circulating in his head only figments of his imagination? Had God really spoken to him? What if he were mistaken or delusional? Would all be for naught?

After an agonizing "dark night of the soul" in Gethsemane, Jesus emerged victorious and assured that God had authentically spoken. When arrested and facing the executioner's cross, he exhibited unequivocal faith, trusting that God would raise him on the third day. Ironically, in his weakest and most vulnerable moment, Jesus defeated mighty Rome without lifting a finger in his defense. God honored Jesus' faith and vindicated him by raising Jesus from the dead.

The resurrection was a sign to the disciples that God and not the earthly rulers controlled the affairs of humankind. The empire's most powerful weapon—death—could not deter God's plan. Jesus rose victorious over the grave. He was given ultimate authority over creation (Matt 28:18–20) and declared to be the "Son of God with power" (Rom 1:4). To the Romans living in the heartland of the empire Paul declared that "to this end Christ died and rose and lived again, that he might be Lord of both the dead and the living" (Rom 14:9).

4.9 The Church Preaches an Anti-Imperial Message

The heralds of the Jesus movement headquartered in, and sent out from, Jerusalem proclaimed Jesus to be the Jewish messianic king and also the Lord and Savior of the world (Acts 2:25–26, 39; 5:31; 10:34–36; 11:18). From the holy city on the periphery of the empire, the movement spread westward in various forms until it reached Rome, the center and imperial capital of the empire (Acts 25:11–12; Acts 28:11–31).[209] The itinerant spokespersons delivered a common message: Yahweh, the creator and rightful ruler of the universe, has appointed the crucified and risen Jesus to reign in his stead until all usurpers and power brokers, earthly and heavenly, are defeated, at which time Christ will deliver the kingdom to his Father so that God may be all in all (Acts 2:29–39; 1 Cor 15:20–28; Heb 1:13). This anti-imperial message got the attention both of native retainers and Roman officials. Wherever the heralds of God's kingdom preached they faced opposition from those who had the most to lose politically and economically should the message be embraced by the masses. Angry councils, mobs, merchants, magistrates, governors, and client-kings sought to stop their anti-Roman propaganda by threatening them, driving them out of town, arresting and hauling them into court, hiring false witnesses to testify against them, legally punishing them by stripes or execution, stoning them in the marketplace, and even conspiring to assassinate them (Acts 4:1–18; 5:17–40; 6:8–15; 7:54–60; 8:1–4; 9:23–25; 12:1–19; 13:45–50; 14:19–20; 16:16–24; 17:5–9; 19:21–41; 21:16–36; Acts 22–28).

At the start, the Jesus movement in Jerusalem viewed itself as a renewal movement within Judaism. God's promise to renew his covenant with his people and establish his kingdom was now being fulfilled within the messianic communities. They in turn were inviting others to join them, including the Gentiles (Acts 10–11; Acts 13–28).

The church's mission was to take the good news of God's kingdom to τὰ ἔθνη or the nations (Acts 13:46)—which in the Roman context meant the very peoples whom the empire had conquered—and to offer them hope of ultimate deliverance from domination.[210] From a Roman perspective, this activity would not be seen as harmless "pie in the sky" preaching, but as an attempt to subvert Rome's imperial rule over her subjects.[211]

---

209. Kahl, "Acts of the Apostles," 150, observes astutely, "Acts starts with a programmatic demonstration of two counter-imperial moves: from earth to heaven and from Jerusalem (not Rome) to 'the ends of the earth,' thus displacing Rome from the center to the periphery and thus reversing the imperial dynamics profoundly subverting the Roman mastery of the *oikoumene*."

210. Ibid., 154–55.

211. Ibid., 155–56, Kahl believes that Luke places the Jesus movement within the context of Judaism, the source of its main opponents. She views Christianity, therefore, as "politically innocuous" to Rome. This begs the question: What about Paul's opponents who are not Jewish? Why were they so upset? Acts 16 and 17 are cases in point. It seems more likely that while the Jesus movement stirred up much local concern, it was able to stay under the national radar until the mid-60s, when persecution from Rome became more prevalent. Peter and Paul were not executed for preaching a politically

When Christ's followers formed associations or *ekklesiai* through-out the empire, whose members proclaimed Jesus as Lord and pledged their allegiance to him via baptism (Acts 2:36; 10:36; Rom 10:9; Eph 4:5), their actions challenged Rome's claim of manifest destiny, and could be construed as nothing less than seditious. Believers established their own social institutions and observed rites which were similar in fashion to their imperial Roman counterparts, but based on kingdom principles. The communal banquet was one such example. Disciples invited friends and neighbors to participate in these "Christian" alternatives which honored the *cultus Christou.*

By joining one of the local Christian associations, believers became part of a political resistance movement. Most resistance, however, did not take the form of public transcripts, i.e., open confrontations but fell more often under the category of hidden transcripts. Hence, church members did not universally experience persecution. Rather, they resisted nonvio-lently. In public, they lived according to kingdom principles and values, returning love for hate and kindness for cruelty. In private they gathered in homes for weekly meals where their sacred writings were read and dis-cussed. These Gospels and Epistles contained anti-imperial exhortations and instructions, would be labeled subversive if they fell into the hands of Roman authorities. Therefore, the believers often used coded or cryptic language, whose meanings were known only to those who had been initi-ated into the group through baptism. Terms like "Babylon," "beast," and "harlot" eventually gained meaning for insiders, but had no significance to outsiders (1 Pet 5:13; Rev 17:1–5; 18:1–9).

The early church assigned to Jesus titles normally reserved for the emperor alone and, in doing so, committed acts of "calculated treason."[212] It additionally borrowed familiar political terms of the day, imbuing them with Christian meaning. Church (ἐκκλησία) referred to a civic gather-ing of Roman citizens or an association of like-minded people. Good news (εὐαγγέλιον) was the announcement of an imperial victory. Peace (εἰρήνη) referred to the *Pax Romana* wrought by Augustus. Lord (κύριος)

---

innocuous gospel. The Apocalypse, above all NT writings, identifies imperial Rome as a tyrannical beast and calls upon believers, despite the threat of death, to give their allegiance to the exalted Lord, knowing that the kingdom of Christ will soon replace on earth the kingdom of Caesar.

212. Crossan and Reed, *In Search of Paul*, 11. For another perspective, see Kim, *Gospel and the Roman Empire*, 44, who says that the political titles assigned to Jesus, while appearing at first glance to be political terms associated with Roman ideology, are traceable actually to the Hebrew Scriptures, and thus they mean something quite different than Crossan and Reed claim.

was the title bestowed upon all Caesars from the time of Augustus. Faith (πίστις) spoke of faithfulness that existed between rulers and the people. Savior (σωτήρ) was Caesar's official title and described him as the protector of the nation.[213] No first-century reader of the Gospels or other early Christian writings could have read these "Christianized" terms without relating them to politics. Paul saw himself as an ἀπόστολος or diplomatic envoy who represented the kingdom of God and announced the triumph of its king. As Neil Elliott remarks, "We do not hear of other itinerant philosophers or moralists on Paul's landscape using such politically provocative language."[214]

Although the Jesus movement adopted the language of the empire, it did not embrace its "top down" or "power over" model of governance. It was qualitatively a different model. The kingdom of God, an alternative to Roman imperialism, operated on an upside-down model of power.[215] Following the example of its king, the church was characterized by servanthood.

The church's leaders, many of whom were itinerants, carried their message to other locales, and thus fulfilled Christ's command to reach the masses with the good news of the kingdom. They preached the gospel in all kinds of public venues in full view of opponents, at times leading to arrest and/or punishment (Acts 4:1–3; 5:17–19; 7:54–59; 8:1–4; 9:23–24; 12:1–3; 13:50; 14:19; 16:19–35; 17:5–9; 18:12–17; 19:23–29; 21:28–31; 23:12–14, etc.). With persecution, they scattered and established *ekklesiai* beyond the borders of Jerusalem (Acts 8:1–4).

Paul's *ekklesiai*, which he established among Gentiles as well as Hellenized Jews, served as alternatives to sanctioned Greco-Roman societies where people came together to praise politicians, discuss common social concerns, debate issues, plan community events, uphold the *Pax Romana*, promote patronage and endorse Roman imperial theology and values. "Christian" societies or associations were havens where followers of Jesus congregated to engage in kingdom affairs. They were counter-distinctive to Roman assemblies in that they were inclusive, recruiting people from all segments of society regardless of gender, race, or class, yet exclusive in that they refused to participate in "imperial society, whether civil courts or temple banquets."[216] Each assembly served as a local expression of the

213. Reiger, *Christ and Empire*, 30.

214. Elliott, "The Apostle Paul and Empire," 99.

215. Reiger, *Christ and Empire*, 40.

216. Horsley, *Paul and Empire*, 8.

kingdom of God and as an alternative to Roman imperial order with its enforced *Pax Romana*. Wright calls them "colonial outposts" of God's kingdom, scattered throughout the empire.[217]

Christ's followers claimed that God had already judged and defeated Rome and had installed Jesus as universal Lord by virtue of his resurrection. They also held that at the παρουσία he would replace the world domination system with God's peaceful kingdom, which was being manifested already in part through the church. Ehrensperger asserts that such a claim was an affront and "an implicit threat to Roman imperial order."[218] From Rome's perspective, this affirmation was nothing less than a declaration of war. They did not view such teaching as harmless or amusing, but as subversive, since it challenged Caesar's right of ultimate authority.[219] The charge leveled against the Christians at Thessalonica was: "They are all acting contrary to the decrees of the emperor, saying that there is another king named Jesus" (Acts 17:7).[220]

Paul locates the kingdom's appearance in the context of Rome's presumptuous assurances: "When they say, 'Peace and security!' then sudden destruction shall come upon them." He remarks that the elitist rulers and their collaborators "shall not escape" (1 Thess 5:3). And then comforts the Thessalonians with these words, "But you brethren are not in darkness that this day should overtake you . . . For God did not appoint us to wrath, but to obtain salvation through our Lord Jesus Christ" (1 Thess 5:4, 9). Believers will survive the Day of Judgment and inherit the kingdom of God.

217. Wright, "Paul's Gospel and Caesar," 182.

218. Ehrensperger, *Paul*, 116.

219. Ibid., 97.

220. Rowe, *World Upside Down*, counters Kahl's skewed argument and calls for a reading of Acts that presents a Jesus movement that is simultaneously politically innocuous and dangerous. The perspective, he avers, depends on who within the historical context evaluates the movement. From the point of view of Roman provincial rulers, pagan merchants, and native retainers, the Jesus movement might well be seen as seditious and politically destabilizing. From the church's perspective, however, its mission is to proclaim and live in accordance with a new way of life under the Lordship of Christ, and not to mount a political coup to overthrow the empire. While living under the reign of Christ might not be technically seditious, it is certainly anti-imperial and demonstrates in the present what society in the future kingdom will look like. From Rome's perspective, the message and activities of the Jesus movement could be seen as a threat to social order and a political nuisance. When this happened, local rulers took action against the church and its leaders. For a discussion and interview with Rowe on this topic, see Michael Bird's blog, *Euangelion*, August 15, 2009: http://euangelizomai.blogspot.com/2009/08/interview-with-kavin-rowe-on-luke-acts.html.

4.10 Conclusion

This chapter provided a descriptive analysis of the first-century Roman world, which is essential to understanding how and why the Lord's Supper was anti-imperial in nature. As Rome dominated the masses through political, social, and military means, Jesus offered a counter-imperial vision for society, which he identified as the kingdom of God. Using Scott's terminology, Rome's worldview was the "Great Tradition"[221] accepted by the elites and forced upon the masses, while Christ's vision was a "Little Tradition"[222] and embraced willingly by his followers.

Chapter 5 will analyze how Jesus, according to the Gospel of Luke, used the symposium setting to resist Roman imperialism and the stratification practices of the Jewish elites. It will also show how he called upon his hearers to invite people of all social classes to the meal table, and thus reflect the ethics of the kingdom of God. Egalitarian table fellowship mirrors the eschatological banquet at the end of the age when people from all walks of life will sit at the table with Abraham in the kingdom. Jesus' symposium teachings and deeds also served as the basis for his disciples' observance of post-resurrection anti-imperial meals.

221. Scott, *Domination*, 50.
222. Ibid., 42.

5

Jesus' Lukan Meals as a Venue to Proclaim His Anti-Imperial Gospel of the Kingdom

5.1 Introduction

FROM THE ERA OF Alexander the Great to the early days of the Jesus movement, the symposium was portrayed in literature as the setting where men could pontificate on numerous topics of interest. Plato's *Symposium*,[1] Plutarch's *Table Talk*,[2] and the Jewish *Letter of Aristeas*[3] are examples where banqueting is described and discussed. Jewish banquets at the time of Christ and the apostles were similar in format to Greco-Roman banquets, apart from the excessive drinking during the symposium.[4]

This chapter examines Jesus' meal practices in the Gospel of Luke. Of the four Gospel writers, Luke gives the most attention to meals. He chronicles ten occasions when Jesus reclines, beginning with the banquet hosted by Levi (Luke 5:27–39) and ending with his post-resurrection meal with the apostles (24:36–49).[5] Markus Barth estimates that meals account for nearly one-fifth of all verses found in the Gospel of Luke

---

1. Plato, *Symposium on Love* or *The Banquet*.
2. Plutarch, "Table-Talk, Books 1–6."
3. Aristeas, "The Letter of Aristeas."
4. Johnson, *Luke*, 225.
5. LaVerdiere, *Dining in the Kingdom of God*, 10.

and Acts.[6] According to Koenig, "eating and drinking" serve as the organizing motif of Luke's gospel narrative.[7] Karris, likewise, believes Jesus' meals are central to Luke's gospel.[8] Unique among the Gospel writers, Luke places more of Jesus' teaching about the kingdom of God within the context of a meal setting.[9]

While Luke uses Mark as a source,[10] when it comes to his understanding of Jesus' meals, which reach their apex with the Last Supper, he draws more upon Paul's writings, particularly 1 Corinthians, than upon Mark's. Wenham notes, "From 9:51 through into chapter 18 we have a major section of Luke's Gospel that has no parallel in Mark."[11] In this block of material Luke includes information on Jesus' anti-imperial deeds and teachings done around meal tables as he journeys to Jerusalem, which are not contained in other Gospel accounts.

Just as Rome employed the banquet as a vehicle to promote its imperial ideology and control the masses of people through patronage and stratification, Luke portrays Jesus as using the venue as an opportunity to call upon Jewish elites to switch their loyalties, i.e., to stop paying homage to Rome and its domination system. These bold table talks challenged the premise of Roman imperialism and Jewish utilitarianism. Because Jesus' symposium diatribes were delivered behind closed doors, and at times in parabolic fashion, they can be characterized as hidden transcripts and acts of resistance against the empire and her collaborators.

In Luke, meals are occasions when Jesus breaks down ethnic and sectarian boundaries, and calls for a more inclusive table fellowship, one

---

6. Barth, *Rediscovering*, 71.

7. Koenig, *Feast of the World's Redemption*, 181.

8. Karris, *Luke: Artist and Theologian*, 47–78. Karris also observes that "the theme of food occurs in every chapter of Luke's Gospel" (5–6).

9. Other Gospel writers position the same teachings in different social contexts. This reveals something about the nature and structure of Luke's gospel. In his account of Jesus' mealtime encounters, Luke is not attempting to reconstruct an historical record of the events as if he were an eye witness to them. Rather, he gleans his information from various written and oral sources, and only selects certain of Jesus' words and deeds at the meal table that he feels will be relevant to his contemporary audience (ca. 85 CE). He freely rearranges and modifies the materials as needed. This allows him to use the materials for his own purposes. One might classify Luke's gospel as Midrash Pesher, i.e., an interpretative commentary. See Ellis, *Luke*, 6–9, for the relationship between history and interpretation in the Gospel of Luke.

10. Johnson, "Book of Luke-Acts," 406.

11. Wenham, "Purpose of Luke-Acts," 89.

which reflects God's social vision for his kingdom.[12] Luke likely includes these discussions to address similar social and political struggles facing his Christian community as it comes together for table-fellowship.[13]

Since the structure of the Roman banquet allowed for lively discussion and debate, Jesus' teachings were often questioned, challenged, and even rejected by respected Jews in attendance whose loyalties were divided between pleasing God and Rome. Only as native retainers succeeded somewhat at both were they able to protect their positions of privilege and maintain a semblance of order within the Jewish community, thus providing it with leadership. Jesus challenged Jewish elitists to "get off the fence." While most Jewish power brokers considered his words and actions to be subversive and a hindrance to the fragile peace in Palestine, many among the Palestinian poor and disenfranchised embraced his words as prophetic. Emboldened by his table talks, they joined the eschatological revolution espoused by Jesus.

Jesus not only encouraged diners to practice kingdom ethics and discard their imperialistic principles, but he also practiced what he preached. He ate with sinners and outcasts. By inviting those without any status in either Roman or Jewish cultures to dine, Jesus demonstrated in real time what God's kingdom was like. It was all inclusive; women, children, slaves, and even expendables were invited to partake of God's table.

Jesus transformed meals into enacted parables to illustrate graphically that God's offer of forgiveness is extended to everyone. Like a loving Father, God invites all prodigals to recline at his table and dine.

The stated thesis of chapter 5 is that, according to Luke, Jesus used the meal as an opportunity to condemn imperialistic practices and exhort God's people to embrace his kingdom agenda; while, at the same time, he modeled kingdom ethics at the meal table for all to see.[14]

---

12. Esler, *Community and Gospel in Luke-Acts*, 22, 45.

13. Ibid., 71–109. Esler devotes the entirety of chapter 4 to Luke's treatment of table fellowship in Luke-Acts, especially how the early church handled Jewish opposition to Jews and Gentiles eating together.

14. As Jesus used the banquet for his counter-imperial table talks, the early church used its communal meals as safe places where it could express its hopes and voice its concerns in the form of hidden transcripts. This will be discussed in chapter 7.

5.2 Eating with Saints and Sinners:
A Picture of the Kingdom

In his monograph *Eucharist and Eschatology* Geoffrey Wainwright makes a convincing case that Yahweh instituted communal meals among his OT people to demonstrate their relationship with him and to experience his blessings for them.[15] Many of Israel's significant events were celebrated and remembered with feasting: Passover, Yom Kippur, Purim, Succoth, Pentecost, Sabbath meals, and a host of lesser occasions when God's people offered animal and grain sacrifices to God and ate a portion of the food in his presence. Eating was a reminder that God was their deliverer and sustainer and always in their midst. Meals connected the Jewish people to their past and gave them hope for the future.

As the nation moved away from God and embraced the lifestyles of the surrounding nations, eventually resulting in captivity, eating in God's presence dropped by the wayside.[16] As the exilic and postexilic prophets called the nation to repent or face judgment, they also announced God's intention to restore the kingdom to Israel under his reign. In doing so, they described the kingdom in terms of joyful feasting.[17] The following is representative of this prophetic vision:

> On this mountain the Lord of hosts will make for all peoples
> a feast of rich food, a feast of well-matured wines,
> of rich food filled with marrow, of well-matured wines strained clear.
> And he will destroy on this mountain
> the shroud that is cast over all peoples,
> the sheet that is spread over all nations;
> he will swallow up death for ever.
> Then the Lord God will wipe away the tears from all faces,

15. Wainwright, *Eucharist and Eschatology*, 19–21, places OT meals under four headings, each will contribute to the development of the Lord's Supper in the NT: 1) Meals associated with covenant making as found in Exodus 24, which included drinking from a symbolic cup; 2) meals eaten in the presence of God at the place where the sacrifice is offered (Gen 31:34; Exod 18:12; Deut 12:5–7; 14:23–26; 15:20); 3) meals found in Wisdom literature which express divine blessing, i.e., "he prepares a table for me" (Ps 23:5) and "Come eat my bread and drink the wine that I mixed" (Prov 9:6); and 4) meals that point to future salvation and depict life in the restored kingdom of God (Isa 25:6–9; 34:2–31; 55:1–5; Zech 9:17, among others).

16. The matter of ancient Israel's disobedience and subsequent abandonment of eating an annual Passover was discussed in chapter 3.

17. Chapter 3 discussed how the prophets envisioned the restored kingdom in terms of a renewed Passover meal celebration. Jesus does likewise in Luke 22:16.

and the disgrace of his people he will take away from all the
earth,
for the Lord has spoken.
It will be said on that day,
Lo, this is our God; we have waited for him, so that he might
save us.
This is the Lord for whom we have waited;
let us be glad and rejoice in his salvation (Isa 25: 6–9).

5.3 Meals in Luke: Eating with Saints and Sinners

Jesus ate meals in light of his understanding of the kingdom, calling sinners to recline with him at the table. His meal practices and teachings
demonstrated that the kingdom of God was at hand.[18] In Luke's gospel
most of Jesus' symposium discussions are held with or precipitated by the
Pharisees, whose members constitute a Jewish "lay brotherhood" who
"claim authority in religious matters."[19] They were part of a reform movement within Judaism and, as such, seemed genuinely interested in hearing
Jesus' message on the kingdom of God and his call for moral change. This
is likely the reason they asked Jesus to be their dinner guest. These occasions allowed Jesus an opportunity to expound on his concept of kingdom
ethics and revealed the main difference between him and the Pharisees.
While having much in common, Jesus described the kingdom in inclusive
terms and demonstrated it by eating with those on the margins, people
whom the Pharisees excluded from the table. In doing so, Jesus challenged
the Pharisees' understanding of holiness and the way they structured
relationships in order to "fulfill their holiness codes."[20] This remained a
bone of contention between Jesus and these pious laymen according to the
Gospel of Luke. In the end, the vast majority of the Pharisees severed their
relationship with him.

18. This explains why after feeding the five thousand the crowds sought to make
him king (John 6:15). The Lukan version mentions that immediately prior to feeding
the masses, Jesus "spoke to them about the kingdom of God" (Luke 9:11).

19. Tannehill, *Narrative Unity of Luke–Acts*, 169.

20. Crosby, *Prayer*, 71.

5.3.1 Eating with Levi (Luke 5:27–39)

Luke's first meal scene occurs when Levi, "a tax collector," abandons all to follow Jesus (Luke 5:27–28) and decides to host a "banquet" in his honor: "Then Levi gave a great banquet for him in his house; and there was a large crowd of tax-collectors and others sitting at the table [κατακείμενοι, literally "reclining"] with them" (v. 29). Levi's guest list not only includes Jesus and the disciples, but many of Levi's associates. Marshall sees the meal as a means for Levi to introduce his colleagues to Jesus.[21] This causes a stir. "The Pharisees and their scribes were complaining to his [Jesus'] disciples, saying, 'Why do you eat and drink with tax-collectors and sinners?'" (v. 30). This question focuses on a single issue—reclining at a feast made up of unsavory characters—but, involves two basic concerns. First, it seeks to understand the reason "why" Jesus would dare cross the lines of social protocol to eat with "sinners." According to Evans, the designation of sinner "refers to those who could not or would not observe the Law of Moses, particularly the oral laws and traditions of the scribes and Pharisees."[22] Fuellenbach agrees: "The Law defined the boundaries of the People of God; breaking the Law meant living outside th[at] boundary . . ."[23] As such, Gentiles were also categorized as sinners as much as rebellious Jews who chose not to obey the Law. Sinners were those who did not keep the Sabbath, practice ritual purity, pay their tithes, and so on. The worst sinners were called "outcasts" i.e., prostitutes, murderers, extortionists, etc., and those of certain occupations such as tax collectors and shepherds.[24] The righteous, on the other hand, was an observer of the Law. In light of this definition, Jesus' announcement, "I have not come to call the righteous, but sinners" takes on the meaning that his ministry is to be directed toward the disenfranchised. That both pious Pharisees and their scribal hermeneutists question Jesus indicates that he is breaking with their recognized and accepted interpretations of the Law.

Despite their ability to accumulate wealth, mainly through dishonest means (Luke 3:12–13), tax collectors were considered persons of low social and moral status. Rome used them to perform an unpopular task and pious Jews despised them for collaborating with the oppressor. They were not the kind of people with whom any respectable person would

---

21. Marshall, *Luke*, 217.
22. Evans, *Luke*, 97.
23. Fuellenbach, *Kingdom of God*, 145.
24. Ibid.

naturally recline. Green remarks, "the presence of Jesus at the table with social outcasts begs for rationalization, given that shared meals symbolized shared lives—intimacy, kinship, unity—throughout the Mediterranean world."[25] The boundary lines have been transgressed. This leads to the second concern.

Second, the Pharisees' inquiry is "concerned with the nature of this 'kingdom' proclaimed by Jesus."[26] Based on erroneous application of OT purity passages, some Pharisees of Jesus' day believed that redemption was reserved exclusively for those who separated from sinners. As Evans comments, "The Pharisees regarded these people as having no hope for participation in the kingdom of God or resurrection of the righteous."[27] Therefore, they must have pondered, "What kind of teacher or prophet announces the arrival of God's kingdom and, at the same time, dines with tax-collectors and sinners?"

In the narratives immediately preceding the banquet scene, Luke has already offered his readers the answers to the queries by: 1) identifying Peter as a "sinful man" whom Jesus befriends (5:8) when separation is the expected norm; 2) having Jesus heal an unclean leper (vv. 12–16); and 3) exercising authority to forgive sin (vv. 17–26), which is restricted to God and his earthly representatives. From the context, Luke lets his readers know that Jesus operates outside the present system and views the kingdom as restorative or redemptive in character. He not only forgives sinners, he welcomes them into his social sphere.[28]

It is difficult to tell if the Pharisees and scribes are diners or onlookers. Marshall places them in the latter category, since these respectful persons would not likely recline at the same table with sinners.[29] A banquet of this size might have been held in a semi-public location where outsiders had some access to the event. In either case, the question sets the stage for Jesus' symposium teaching, which covers verses 31–39. Despite the question being asked of the disciples, it is Jesus who responds, "Those who are well have no need of a physician, but those who are sick; I have come to call not the righteous but sinners to repentance" (vv. 31–32).

---

25. Green, *Luke*, 246.

26. Johnson, *Luke*, 99.

27. Evans, *Luke*, 97.

28. Ellis, *Luke*, 166; Marshall, *Luke*, 217.

29. Marshall, *Luke*, 219–20. It is just as textually possible to view the Pharisees as diners rather than spectators, based on the phrases "in his house" and "there was a large crowd of tax collectors and *others* sitting at the table."

By using medical terminology, Jesus reframes the discussion and depicts his participation at the table as an opportunity to restore these outcasts to a proper relationship with God. A physician is one who, by virtue of his profession, regularly crosses boundaries. For health to be restored, the physician must have contact with the physically ill.[30] Rather than being a place of exclusion, Jesus defines the table as a place of transformation.

It is precisely at this point that Jesus' teaching is anti-imperial. Since stratification was the expected norm, everyone attended Roman banquets with only those of their own class. Palestinian Jews knew the rules and followed them. By objecting to Jesus eating with sinners, they intimate that he is violating both Roman and Jewish social protocol.

In his response, Jesus represents himself as a host who summons outcasts to be his dinner guests. By describing the banquet invitation as a "call" (καλέσαι), Luke chooses a word that earlier in his Gospel he linked to evangelistic appeals for sinners to repent, i.e., an invitation to a changed life, and includes abandoning unrighteous practices (3:13) and following Jesus (5:11). Those responding to Jesus' invitation are accepted as full members into God's new eschatological community, represented by the fellowship experienced in the banquet. The inclusive meal, therefore, might be seen as a sign that God is restoring Israel and forming it into a new alternative society where compassion and mercy are manifest.

In saying that he calls "not the righteous but sinners to repentance," Jesus implies that the kingdom is a place of acceptance, where the filthy are cleansed and invited to eat at the Lord's Table, while those who view themselves as righteous or clean are excluded. Marshall concludes, "The whole point of the story is that Jesus was prepared to eat with sinners in order to lead them to repentance."[31] To the Pharisees and scribes who observe the meal, such a practice is anathema, and to be avoided at all costs. They would rather accept the status quo than adopt Jesus' kingdom agenda.

Jesus' unconventional answer leads to another question: "Then they said to him, 'John's disciples, like the disciples of the Pharisees, frequently fast and pray, but your disciples eat and drink'" (v. 33). Because the speakers ("they") are not clearly identifiable, and the reference to "the disciples of the Pharisees" is in the third person, it is not likely that the Pharisees ask the question but one of the other diners. As Green comments, "In a symposium it is not at all unexpected that others will participate in discourse,

---

30. Green, *Luke*, 248.

31. Marshall, *Luke*, 221.

and there is no reason not to imagine that the question of fasting is raised more generally at the table."[32]

The query probes the reason why Jesus' followers do not accompany their prayers with fasting. After all, Luke's gospel indicates that John's disciples fasted frequently (Luke 7:33) and the Pharisees' disciples abstained twice a week (Luke 18:12), most commonly on Monday and Thursday (*Did.* 8:1). Fasting had many purposes, but in all cases it spoke of hope for the future. Evans notes, "Fasting was regarded as essential in preparing for Israel's long awaited deliverance."[33] Since both John and the Pharisees fasted as they waited for the arrival of God's kingdom, it must have seemed strange to the inquirer that Jesus' disciples did not.

Jesus answers by asking a rhetorical question, using metaphorical language: "You cannot make wedding-guests fast while the bridegroom is with them, can you?" The answer is obvious. As long as the groom is present at the feast, it would be unimaginable to ask the guests to abstain from eating. Then Jesus adds, "The days will come when the bridegroom will be taken away from them, and then they will fast in those days" (vv. 34–35). Using an analogy, Jesus likens Levi's banquet to a wedding feast with Jesus serving as the groom, and his disciples as the guests.[34] What makes the illustration so engaging is that the bridegroom does not simply depart but is "taken away." Looking in hindsight, Luke's audience would likely interpret Jesus' words as a reference to his death or exaltation.

Kümmel observes that "the impossibility of fasting in the present is contrasted with the necessity for the disciples to fast at a later time."[35] The question begs to be asked, "When does the fasting begin and end?" Does it commence at his death ("when . . . taken away") and end with his resurrection/exaltation? Or does it begin with his death and end with the *parousia*? If the latter, as most commentators believe, Luke's record of the incident provides his readers, two generations removed from the actual events, with a basis for their current practice of fasting (Acts 9:9; 13:2; 14:23; 2 Cor 11:27).

If, on the other hand, fasting is limited to the short period between the crucifixion and resurrection, this accounts for the times Jesus is again found eating with the disciples on the road to Emmaus (Luke 24:30), back

32. Green, *Luke*, 248.

33. Evans, *Luke*, 97.

34. Johnson, *Luke*, 98, remarks that the OT prophets likened "the image of a bridegroom . . . to the relationship of Yahweh to Israel (see Isa 61:10; 62:5; Hos 2:16–23; Jer 16:9)." See also Marshall, *Luke*, 225.

35. Kümmel, *Promise and Fulfilment*, 57.

in Jerusalem (Luke 24:41–43), by the seashore (John 21:12); and referenced by Peter (Acts 10:41). It also sets the stage for the post-ascension accounts when the growing number of disciples gather regularly for the "breaking of bread" (Acts 2:42, 46; 6:1–3; 20:7), referred to variously as the Lord's Supper (1 Cor 11:23–25) and love feast (Jude 12). Even the exalted Lord expresses his desire to participate in a meal with believers at Laodicea (Rev 3:20). The church is found mostly feasting rather than fasting after the Lord's ascension, the second option might offer the best explanation of Jesus' words.[36]

Kümmel points out that since Jesus uses the terms "bridegroom" and "wedding" metaphorically in his parables about the kingdom, it is likely he uses them here in similar fashion.[37] If such is the case, then Levi's banquet with its open table, along with the post-ascension meals that follow, may be viewed as proleptic kingdom meals.

So while the disciples of both John and the Pharisees fast as they wait for the kingdom's arrival and the accompanying eschatological wedding feast, Jesus implies that in some sense the kingdom has come already.[38] Since the bridegroom is with them, feasting not fasting is in order.

If Jesus uses metaphorical language to imply, however vaguely, that he is the eschatological bridegroom, his answer must shock his listeners for it connotes that Rome's days of domination are coming to an end. Those who side with Rome will be disposed of as well.

To fast or feast reveals whether a person awaits the kingdom or participates in it already. To illustrate the stark difference between the two and their incompatibility, Jesus proceeds to offer a parable: "He also told them a parable: 'No one tears a piece from a new garment and sews it on an old garment; otherwise the new will be torn, and the piece from the new will

36. Fasting is mentioned only four times after the exaltation of Jesus. None of the references indicate that the church fasted because it was mournful over the departure of the "bridegroom." In fact, the church can be found eating joyously. With the giving of the eschatological Spirit, the Christian community participates in the "already" aspect of the kingdom by eating as a community in the presence of Christ.

37. Kümmel, *Promise and Fulfilment*, 71.

38. For Luke, the beginning of the kingdom has arrived in some aspect with the giving of the eschatological Spirit at Jesus' baptism (Luke 3:21–22). Jesus confirmed its presence on many occasions through his words and deeds, e.g., his announcement in the Capernaum synagogue, "Today this scripture has been fulfilled in your hearing" (Luke 4:21), his response to John the Baptist that the "lepers are cleansed, the blind see, the lame walk" (7:18–23) is a clear reference to Isa 35:5, and his assurance that "if it is by the finger of God ['Spirit of God'–Matt 11:28] that I cast out the demons, then the kingdom of God has come to you" (11:20). Therefore, feasting, not fasting is in order.

not match the old. And no one puts new wine into old wineskins; otherwise the new wine will burst the skins and will be spilled, and the skins will be destroyed. But new wine must be put into fresh wineskins'" (Luke 5:36–38). The parable conveys the dichotomy between the way John and the Pharisees view the kingdom on the one hand, and Jesus on the other. These two approaches cannot be reconciled. Just as new and old garments and new and "old wineskins" are incompatible, so are fasting and feasting. One group fasts as it anticipates the age to come, while the other feasts because it already has come.

Fuellenbach explains, "Meals were Jesus' favorite means to demonstrate the future of the kingdom having already arrived with him."[39] He adds further, "Jesus saw his practice of table fellowship in the light of the end-time. For him the meals already mirrored the character of the festive banquet of the new age (Mk 2:18–19; Lk 14:12–24) . . . using imagery which contemporaries would relate primarily to the hoped-for future (as in Is 25:6–9)."[40]

5.3.2 Eating with a Pharisee (Luke 7:36–50)

Luke's account opens with the words, "One of the Pharisees asked Jesus to eat with him, and he went into the Pharisee's house and took his place at the table" (Luke 7:36). The verb κατεκλίθη is translated "to eat with" by the NRSV, but means to recline at a table and thus marks the event as a traditional banquet.[41] In this venue, which includes both meal and symposium, standard procedures are to be followed and accompanied by expected decorum.[42] As they recline at the table and eat, they are interrupted by a person identified as "a woman in the city, who was a sinner" a designation that likely means she is a known prostitute.[43]

To understand Luke's second meal narrative, context is essential. Prior to reclining at the Pharisee's table, Jesus arrives in Nain, compares his ministry with that of John the Baptist, and declares that tax collectors gladly accept God's invitation to enter the kingdom, while many self-righteous Pharisees and lawyers reject it by their refusal to be baptized

---

39. Fuellenbach, *Kingdom*, 95.
40. Ibid.
41. Green, *Luke*, 308; Johnson, *Luke*, 127; Marshall, *Luke*, 308.
42. Green, *Luke*, 306.
43. Corley, *Private Women*, 92, 121–30; Marshall, *Luke*, 308. The issue may not have been so much purity as propriety.

(7:20–30). Using their own words against them, Jesus reveals that some of the Pharisees oppose God's messengers: "For John the Baptist has come eating no bread and drinking no wine [fasting], and you say, 'He has a demon'; the Son of Man has come eating and drinking [feasting], and you say, 'Look, a glutton and a drunkard, a friend of tax-collectors and sinners!' Nevertheless, wisdom is vindicated by all her children" (vv. 33–35).

The woman who interrupts is likely one of these "sinners."[44] Deemed marginal by Rome and unclean by the Jews, this uninvited guest brings "an alabaster jar of ointment" into the Pharisee's house where the respectable have assembled for the *deipnon* (v. 37).[45] Her actions are provocative and suggestive. The text reads, "She stood behind him at his feet, weeping, and began to bathe his feet with her tears and to dry them with her hair. Then she continued kissing his feet and anointing them with the ointment" (v. 38). Green acutely observes, "She goes behind Jesus because of the placement of the people around the U-shape table" and notes, "reclining on his left side, his legs would have stretched out behind the person to his right, giving her ready access to his feet."[46] Based on her ignoble reputation, her actions are perceived to be lewd and erotic. She then lets her hair down, the mark of a loose woman, and proceeds to fondle and rub Jesus' feet with perfume, which she possibly purchased from ill-gotten gain.

When Jesus does not protest but welcomes the fragrant and soothing massage, the respectable host is taken aback, and thinks to himself, "If this man were a prophet, he would have known who and what kind of woman this is who is touching him—that she is a sinner" (v. 39).[47] Prior to this unexpected scenario, the host had thought of Jesus as a prophet or holy man, who naturally would not want to be defiled.[48] But his opinion changes

44. Talbert, *Reading Luke*, 85, sees the inclusion of this meal narrative as Luke's way of illustrating that Jesus is a friend of sinners.

45. Since the Gospel of Luke does not have the account of Jesus being anointed during Passion Week (Matt 26:6–13; Mark 14:3–9; John 12:18), Fitzmyer, *Luke I–IX*, 684–85, suggests that this is Luke's rendition placed in another time frame to serve his didactic purposes. Johnson, *Luke*, 128–29, shows however, that of the twenty-three possible points of contact in all four accounts, Luke's account agrees with the other Gospels in three details only.

46. Green, *Luke*, 309–10. See also Johnson, *Luke*, 127.

47. Johnson, *Luke*, 127, believes that she is enough of a public figure that the host knows her by reputation, if not personally. Her reputation precedes her.

48. Evans, *Luke*, 122. Johnson, *Luke*, 127, considers the phrase, "If this man were a prophet, he would have known . . ." to be axiomatic.

quickly.[49] If Jesus does not have enough "prophetic insight" to discern the woman's character and occupation, he must not be a legitimate prophet.

Despite actions not apparent otherwise, Jesus possesses acute prophetic powers and accurately knows the hearts of both the woman and the host![50] The host's nonverbal judgment moves Jesus to tell a parable during the symposium (v. 40). He starts by addressing his host by name, "Simon," and proceeds to ask him a rhetorical question, "A certain creditor had two debtors; one owed five hundred denarii, and the other fifty. When they could not pay, he cancelled the debts for both of them. Now which of them will love him more?" (vv. 40–42).[51]

Simon knows the answer. In the Roman domination system when a creditor cancelled a client's debt, he became the client's patron or benefactor. In return, the debtor became ethically obligated to serve the benefactor. The patron-client system pervaded all of society and was one with which the Pharisee not only was familiar, but had embraced. It was in his capacity as a patron that he sponsored and hosted this very banquet, which placed all his dinner guests under obligation to him.

To Jesus' question, the Pharisee answers, "I suppose the one for whom he cancelled the greater debt" (v. 43). Marshall suggests that Simon realizes he has been caught in a trap and therefore offers a correct but reluctant ("I suppose") answer.[52] However, Marshall reads too much into the words, "I suppose." There is no indication the host is apprehensive in his response, but simply gives an honest evaluation. Jesus agrees with his answer and "then turning towards the woman," but speaking to Simon, he says, "Simon, Do you see this woman?" (v. 44a). Jesus directs Simon to see this woman in a new light: "I entered your house; you gave me no water for my feet, but she has bathed my feet with her tears and dried them with her hair. You gave me no kiss, but from the time I came in she has not stopped kissing my feet. You did not anoint my head with oil, but she has anointed my feet with ointment. Therefore, I tell you, her sins, which were many, have been forgiven; hence she has shown great love. But the one to whom

49. Green, *Luke*, 307.

50. Jesus saw this woman not as a recalcitrant sinner, but as one touched by grace. On another occasion, when the scribes and Pharisees question his authority to teach in the Temple, Jesus scolded them for their lack of belief (Matt 21:23–30) and then said, "Truly I tell you, the tax-collectors and the prostitutes are going into the kingdom of God ahead of you" (Matt 21:31). Jesus did not judge on the basis of status or gender.

51. A denarius was one day's wage; thus, the one person's debt was fifty times more than the other. (Johnson, *Luke*, 127).

52. Marshall, *Luke*, 311.

little is forgiven, loves little. Then he said to her, 'Your sins are forgiven'" (vv. 44b–48). Jesus no longer views her as a sinner, but one whose debt has been cancelled. As a result, she now expresses her love through selfless actions. That the woman is moved to tears as she ministers to Jesus might indicate overwhelming gratitude or brokenness and repentance, both of which have scriptural bases.

Simon has sorely misjudged the woman's actions, while conveniently overlooking his own shortcomings. She expressed her gratitude for forgiveness by her extravagant and costly actions. Simon, on the other hand, has failed to extend even the most basic forms of hospitality to Jesus (his guest of honor), which included water and towel for his feet, a kiss of greeting on his neck or hand, and anointing oil for his head.[53] What does this say about Simon?

The other table guests are stunned at Jesus' words, and inquire among themselves, "Who is this who even forgives sins?" (v. 49). This query implies that Jesus is usurping the role of the Temple priests who alone are authorized to speak on God's behalf to forgive sin (cf. 5:21). Jesus boldly responds by turning to the woman and saying, "Your faith has saved you; go in peace," suggesting that faith makes salvation/forgiveness possible, and leads to peace (v. 50). This is the first time in Luke's gospel where faith and salvation are explicitly joined.[54]

Luke does not inform his readers when the woman actually experienced forgiveness. Was it during or prior to the meal? When he calls attention to the woman's thoughtful actions (vv. 44–47), Jesus speaks of her in the third person, which according to Green and Evans, indicates that her actions are the result of being forgiven previously.[55] If this is the case, Jesus' next words, "Your sins are forgiven" (v. 48) spoken directly to her are simply words of assurance. However, the other guests' question, "Who is this who even forgives sins?" naturally places the timing of her forgiveness within the context of the symposium itself. What Jesus says about the woman (vv. 44–47), he now says to the woman. In this scenario, the woman's acts are demonstrative of repentance, and the encounter is similar to the one that takes place at Zacchaeus's dinner table, in which Zacchaeus finds salvation (Luke 19). If such is the case, Simon's banquet like Levi's banquet, is transformed into an evangelistic milieu and becomes a venue where sinners find forgiveness.

53. Green, *Luke*, 313.
54. Johnson, *Luke*, 128.
55. Green, *Luke*, 313; also Evans, *Luke*, 122.

The woman, considered an untouchable by the Jewish community and a person on the margins of Roman society, accepts Jesus as a true prophet and demonstrates it by her actions, characteristic of repentance; but, Simon and his guests show no such propensity.

Several conclusions can be drawn from this second Lukan meal account. First, Jesus broke with both Roman and Jewish banquet protocol. He offered a counter vision of society, based on his understanding of God's kingdom ethics and opposition to Roman ideology. Thus his message was anti-imperial. Unlike the vast majority living under Roman domination, he was not an exclusivist, nor was he a separatist like the Pharisees, but was comfortable mixing with people from all levels of society. Second, but related, Jesus used the symposium as an occasion for evangelism, where sinners are embraced, forgiven and delivered from their present condition. For Jesus, forgiveness on the basis of faith, apart from Temple sacrifice, was an eschatological sign of the kingdom's arrival. Without having obtained priestly sanction he claimed authority as God's envoy to forgive sins. His message and actions, which were done out of public site during a meal setting, confronted popular but erroneous Jewish understandings of the kingdom and challenged Roman domination practices, offering an alternative to both. By Scott's definition, Jesus' mealtime symposium acts fall into the category of a hidden transcript that challenges the great traditions of the day.[56]

5.3.3 Jesus Engages the Dinner Guests at the Home of a Pharisee (Luke 11:37–54)

The third Lukan meal takes place after the return of the seventy, and as Jesus and the disciples move from city to city where he teaches privately and publicly about the kingdom of God (11:1–36). This section includes his teaching on the Lord's Prayer (vv. 1–4), the story of the importune friend (vv. 6–13), the assertion that his casting out of demons by the "finger of God" is a sign of the kingdom's arrival (vv. 14 26), that one greater than Jonah has arrived (vv. 27–32), and the importance of people being filled with light and not darkness (vv. 33–36). In this context Luke places the third meal narrative, where one finds Jesus condemning in the strongest terms his host and dinner companions.

The story begins, "While he was speaking, a Pharisee invited him to dine with him; so he went in and took his place at the table," i.e., reclined

---

56. Scott, *Domination*, 4.

at the table (Luke 11:37). Since the meal includes "invited" guests it can be identified clearly as a formal banquet. When held on weekdays, such meals usually took place in late afternoon.[57] Set in the home of a Pharisee, this third meal scene is evocative of the one immediately preceding it (Luke 7:36–50). In similar fashion this host, identified as "a Pharisee" and thus a stickler for purity, is caught off guard by Jesus' apparent lack of concern for following dining protocol. Luke writes, "The Pharisee was amazed to see that he did not first wash before dinner" (v. 39). Green claims that handwashing likely served as a boundary marker of Judaism, and to ignore it placed one outside the community.[58] Since handwashing was not a requirement under OT Law, however, Green overstates the case. Nevertheless, the issue was a matter of debate among various Sadducees and Pharisees, hence, the raised eyebrows.[59] According to Josephus, the Essenes actually required ritual washing of the entire body before each meal.[60] The point Luke makes is simply that this group of Pharisees noticed when Jesus did not wash his hands—for whatever the reason. At the least, it was either an insult to this particular host or to those dinner guests who held this ritualistic practice to be important.

Jesus may have reclined without washing his hands intentionally in order to elicit a response. Although the host remains silent, his countenance speaks louder than words. Jesus uses the occasion to excoriate the Pharisees for giving attention to trivialities, while ignoring the weightier matters of the Law: "Then the Lord said to him, 'Now you Pharisees clean the outside of the cup and of the dish, but inside you are full of greed and wickedness. You fools! Did not the one who made the outside make the inside also?'" (vv. 39–40). These mealtime comments open the door for a lively discussion. Jesus' accusation is not directed toward his host alone but to all Pharisees who embrace erroneous views on purity. Going on the offensive he addresses them as "You fools." Luke Timothy Johnson points out that "fools" is an epithet and has its "roots in the biblical tradition, referring to those who resist the wisdom that comes from God (see e.g.,

---

57. Marshall, *Luke*, 493–94. The main difference between a weekday banquet and one held on the Sabbath was the time they began. Sabbath meals served as the locus of the synagogue gathering, which often met in the home of the president or other prominent member. The meal proper was followed by the symposium, when ministry and teaching took place.

58. Green, *Luke*, 470.

59. *Yad.* 4:6–8 in Schiffman, *Texts and Tradition*, 269–71.

60. Josephus, *J.W.* 2.8.5.

Prov 1:22 and Ps 13:1 [LXX]) . . ."[61] Lacking wisdom, the Pharisees place emphasis on the wrong thing. By judging another for failing to wash outwardly, they cannot see the log in their own eye, i.e., the filthiness of their own hearts, which are filled with greed and wickedness.[62]

Here one sees Jesus speaking "truth to power,"[63] i.e., to those possessing power, which is by Scott's definition not only an act of resistance, but one of the strongest forms of hidden transcript.[64] By using the title "the Lord" (ὁ κύριος), Luke identifies Jesus as the one who rightfully speaks for God.[65] As such Jesus' declaration that God is more concerned with the inner than the outer life carries weight.

Jesus then issues a command that, if followed, can remedy their condition: "So give for alms those things that are within; and see, everything will be clean for you" (v. 41). If the command is "an accusative of respect," which Bock favors, it means, "Give alms with respect to inside things" i.e., in accordance with a pure character.[66] If, on the other hand, it is "an adverbial accusative," which Marshall prefers, it means give alms from the heart.[67] Either way, when the heart is clean, outer cleansing is not necessary. In light of the story of Jonah which immediately precedes the banquet scene (11:29–32), Jesus may be identifying the Pharisees as part of an "evil generation" which stands condemned apart from repentance.[68] If this is the case the order "give for alms" (δότε ἐλεημοσύνην), an aorist imperative, should be seen as a command, which, if followed, will express a repentant heart and cleansing from sin.

Jesus then launches into a triad of "woes" against some Pharisees for giving attention to trivial pursuits while ignoring the ethical requirements of the Law: "But woe to you Pharisees! For you tithe mint and rue and herbs of all kinds, and neglect justice and the love of God; it is these you ought to have practised, without neglecting the others" (v. 42). While commending their faithfulness for keeping part of the Mosaic law, Jesus

61. Johnson, *Luke*, 189.

62. Marshall, *Luke*, 491.

63. Horsley, *Hidden Transcripts*, 11.

64. Scott, *Domination*, 206; Horsley, *Jesus in Context*, 177.

65. For Luke's readers (ca. 85 CE) Jesus is already Lord by virtue of his death and exaltation. They understand the term in its truest meaning. He is not only Israel's Lord, but Lord over humankind. Jesus, not Caesar, is the rightful ruler of earth.

66. Bock, *Luke 9:51—24:53*, 1114.

67. Nat Turner, *Grammatical Insights into the New Testament* quoted in Marshall, *Luke*, 495.

68. Bock, *Luke*, 1115.

condemns them for forsaking the ethical values that were the unmistakable identity markers that distinguished Israel from her neighbors. Israel no longer acts compassionately toward others as God did toward her in the Exodus. She has abandoned justice and mercy. Israel must forsake her oppressive ways or face the same judgment that will come upon the other oppressive nations.

Jesus' next two pronouncements of "woe" focus on those Pharisees who desire public recognition and preferential treatment: "Woe to you Pharisees! For you love to have the seat of honour in the synagogues and to be greeted with respect in the market-places. Woe to you! For you are like unmarked graves, and people walk over them without realizing it" (vv. 43–44).

Verses 42 and 43 contrast the "love of God," which the Pharisees lack with their insatiable "love to have seats of honour." Since synagogue meetings focused on meals like all other association and cultic meetings, "the seat of honour" refers to the position at the right hand of the host or president.[69] Whether in a semi-private banquet room or in the public square, the Pharisees, according to Luke, love being the center of attention rather than showing love toward the needy. Jewish elites have adopted a Roman hierarchical structure at mealtime. For embracing Rome's imperialistic ways, rather than treating all Jews as equals, Israel will be judged.

By applying the metaphor "unmarked graves," Jesus deems these Pharisees and those like them to be impure. In saying that people inadvertently traipse or "walk over them," Jesus suggests the Pharisees "are like graves that have become overgrown and so are able to hide their corruption from people."[70] Fitzmyer remarks, "Because they are unmarked, people do not recognize them for what they are, and so unwittingly come in contact with them."[71] Thus, the unsuspecting people are defiled by the Pharisees!

Jesus' use of "graves" to describe these Pharisees also implies they do not possess life. They are dead and corrupt already. They must be reborn. Likewise, all within the nation who do not long for salvation must follow the same course. The kingdom and eternal life go hand in hand.

Jesus' accusations do not go unchallenged. An unnamed expert of the Torah and dinner guest is highly offended by what he hears and

---

69. Vetta, "The Culture of the Symposium," 100. By mistakenly placing the seats in a Temple setting rather than a meal setting, Bock, *Luke*, 1117, believes the seats "to be a row of seats near the ark."

70. Evans, *Luke*, 189.

71. Fitzmyer, *Luke X–XXIV*, 949.

rebukes Jesus: "Teacher, when you say these things, you insult us too" (v. 45), i.e., we interpreters of the Law. In using the term ὑβρίζεις, translated "you insult," the lawyer chooses the strongest possible word to describe the reproach he feels. The tone indicates that he believes Jesus' charges to be baseless and shameful. In return, Jesus pronounces God's judgment on them: "And he said, 'Woe also to you lawyers! For you load people with burdens hard to bear, and you yourselves do not lift a finger to ease them'" (v. 46). These "burdens" likely refer to extrabiblical obligations that the lawyers added to the Law itself.[72] Lacking God-like compassion toward the heavy laden, they ignore their plight. Again, Jesus is pointing out that Israel's leaders have become oppressors rather than liberators.

Luke includes two more woes that Jesus levels against these esteemed legal scholars. The second woe is aimed at their complicity in persecuting the prophets:

> Woe to you! For you build the tombs of the prophets whom your ancestors killed. So you are witnesses and approve of the deeds of your ancestors; for they killed them, and you build their tombs. Therefore also the Wisdom of God said, "I will send them prophets and apostles, some of whom they will kill and persecute," so that this generation may be charged with the blood of all the prophets shed since the foundation of the world, from the blood of Abel to the blood of Zechariah, who perished between the altar and the sanctuary. Yes, I tell you, it will be charged against this generation (Luke 11:47–51).

By accusing them of building tombs to the martyred prophets, Jesus claims the lawyers are complicit with their forefathers in the death of the prophets. Erecting a tomb for someone is ordinarily a sign of honor or respect for the dead, but in this case it must mean otherwise.[73] Rather than building tombs for the prophets, the lawyers should obey their message. By using the "Wisdom of God"[74] to condemn "this generation," Jesus shows that the lawyers, rather than representing God's wisdom, stand guilty of violating it. He says God will send to them "prophets and apostles," whom they

---

72. Ibid.

73. Marshall, *Luke*, 500. Referencing Manson, *Sayings of Jesus*, 101, Marshall interprets the statement ironically: "Your fathers killed the prophets, and you make sure that they stay dead; you simply complete what your fathers did."

74. Ellis, *Luke*, 171–72 and Marshall, *Luke*, 501–2, discuss the various ways the "Wisdom of God" can be understood. Regardless of its exact meaning, the phrase likely conveys the idea that God has spoken in some way (1 Cor 1:24–30; 2:7; Col 2:3), either through the OT prophets, the Law, or his Son.

will kill (v. 49), not unlike their forefathers. By including apostles among these "martyrs-to-be," Jesus counts his disciples among the contemporary emissaries who will be persecuted. From start to finish God's messengers stand in harm's way as they proclaim God's judgment against this evil generation. Again, Jesus is pronouncing judgment on his people for forsaking their mission and refusing to get back on the right track when warned by God's authorized messengers.

His final woe calls attention to the worst offense: "Woe to you lawyers! For you have taken away the key of knowledge; you did not enter yourselves, and you hindered those who were entering" (v. 52). If a parallel with Matt 23:13, then "the key of knowledge" refers to information one must possess to enter the kingdom of God. In their concern for minutia, the leaders have withheld the essentials of the Law. The result is both they and their charges were locked out of the kingdom.

Jesus' table talk produces a reaction that is not at all unexpected: "When he went outside, the scribes and the Pharisees began to be very hostile towards him and to cross-examine him about many things, lying in wait for him, to catch him in something he might say" (vv. 53–54).

Green believes that this mealtime account in Luke's gospel is intended to show that the Pharisees and scribes have a marked change of attitude toward Jesus from this point onward.[75] This is evidenced by the active participle "lying in wait" (ἐνεδρεύοντες) coupled with the active aorist "to catch" (θηρεῦσαί), both hunting terms, which signify an aggressive effort to entrap Jesus. Throughout the remainder of Luke's narrative, the Pharisees are portrayed as viewing Jesus in a negative light and seeking to ensnare him (14:1; 15:2). As Jesus moves toward Jerusalem, he will face ever increasing opposition.

There may be a tendency for the exegete to interpret the Lukan meals in too narrow a fashion as applying only to the principals reclining at the table. If Jesus' meals are viewed as enacted parables, however, their import far exceeds the individual diners. His message is directed to the entire nation and the leaders whom the dinner guests represent.

For Luke's original audience living decades after these events, who heard this Gospel read for the first time while they themselves were reclining at a communal Lord's Table, the message provided them with insights into why Jesus was executed by his own people. Her leaders could not tolerate Jesus' anti-imperial hidden transcripts. Since the Jewish elites dominated and oppressed God's people, acting little different than Roman

75. Green, *Luke*, 476.

authorities, then judgment would be their lot. In context, the pronouncement of eschatological woe was intended to bring the dinner guests and the nation to repentance. While "shared meals with Jesus do not necessarily constitute a guarantee of salvation (13:26–27), nevertheless, they do signal the possibility of salvation."[76]

This and other meals also provide Luke's "Christian" readers with a model for conducting the Lord's Supper. Their communal meals are to be times of speaking out against the Roman domination system and opportunities for believers to examine their own actions in light of the kingdom of God. Are they truly living as an alternative society, and outpost of heaven, in the midst of the empire?

5.3.4 A Sabbath Meal at the Home of a Pharisee (Luke 14:1–24)[77]

The fourth Lukan banquet that Jesus attends also takes place at "the house of a leader of the Pharisees . . . on a Sabbath" (Luke 14:1). This means to avoid violating the fourth commandment, the meal was prepared the previous day. By noting that the dinner guests "were watching him closely" (v. 2), Luke may intend to show that the tide is turning against Jesus.

According to the immediate context, Jesus has healed a crippled woman on the Sabbath (Luke 13:10–14) and has called the ruler of a synagogue a hypocrite for objecting (vv. 15–17). Jesus also has announced that many who think they will enter the kingdom of God will be left out (vv. 18–30). In addition, Luke tells of a group of kindly Pharisees that warn Jesus to avoid murderous Herod, which indicates that some Pharisees wished Jesus no harm. He responds by saying that the Jewish leaders in Jerusalem are more dangerous to him than Herod. These events placed prior to the meal narrative portray Israel and her rulers as missing the real meaning of what it means to be the people of God. When a synagogue ruler shows little concern for a sick woman and cannot rejoice over her healing, then Israel no longer reflects the kind of compassion God exhibited when he liberated her from physical bondage.[78] This was the basis for Sabbath keeping in the first place.

76. Ibid., 473.

77. Ellis, *Luke*, 192, maintains that it is unlikely that the events associated with this dinner actually took place on a single Sabbath, but is a "Lukan 'symposium' that summarizes Jesus' teachings at a number of such dinner parties." Even if Ellis is correct in his assumption, Luke 14 is indicative of a meal setting and therefore pertinent to this study.

78. Kinsler and Kinsler, *Biblical Jubilee*, 10–11, astutely observe that the theological

As the fourth banquet scene opens, the reader is informed that the host holds a prominent position within the Pharisee party. This likely puts him "among the socially elite, the powerful for whom the good news generally involves loss of status."[79] Marshall contends that the term "leader" (ἀρχόντων) or ruler might identify this man as a member of the Sanhedrin.[80] Whether a council member or not, it is safe to assume that the invited guests are people of an elevated status. Jesus is probably invited because he is a teacher/prophet, and may have spoken at the synagogue earlier in the day. That Jesus reclines at the table of a Pharisee is additional evidence that, according to Luke, there are still some Pharisees who have not turned antagonistic toward Jesus.[81]

Since Lukan meals often include the arrival of an uninvited guest, the reader is not entirely surprised to read, "Just then, in front of him, there was a man who had dropsy" (v. 2). The NRSV erroneously translates καὶ ἰδοὺ as "Just then" (instead of "Behold," or "See"), which might be taken to signify the time of the man's arrival. The point is that his presence is surprising. The phrase "in front of him" (ἔμπροσθεν αὐτοῦ) carries the idea "that Jesus could not help noticing the man."[82] Most likely he is not a welcomed guest, but arrives unannounced during the symposium portion of the meal (v. 2).[83] To the Pharisees, who place a premium on purity, this must have been disconcerting.[84] The intruder provides Jesus with an

foundation of the Sabbath commandment (Exod 20:8–11) was memory of the Exodus: "I am the Lord your God, who brought you out of the land of Egypt, out of the house of slavery" (20:2). The same statement is given again (Deut 5:6) as the basis for the commandments (5:12–15). This means that the Law was "the cornerstone for the fulfillment of the process of liberation from Egypt and the establishment of God's people as an alternative social reality" (*Biblical Jubilee*, 12).

79. Green, *Luke*, 545.

80. Marshall, *Luke*, 578; Ellis, *Luke*, 192. This may be the case. If so, Jesus and his traveling companions must be near Jerusalem. The text, however, offers no hint to the location of this Sabbath meal. Fitzmyer, *Luke X–XXIV*, 1040, notes that there is "not a shred of evidence to suggest that . . . the setting for the meal is in Jerusalem . . ."

81. Green, *Luke*, 537–38. Marshall, *Luke*, 578, contends to the contrary that "the general theme" of this entire chapter "is criticism of the Pharisees."

82. Marshall, *Luke*, 579.

83. As discussed in chapter 2, the arrival of an unexpected guest was a common literary device found in symposium literature.

84. Johnson, *Luke*, 223, describes dropsy as a "condition of swelling due to an excess of fluid, now more commonly called edema." According to Marshall, *Luke*, 579, some third-century rabbis believed that dropsy was the consequence of an immoral lifestyle, hence, a judgment. Fitzmyer, *Luke X–XXIV*, 1041, mentions that another feature of dropsy was "distention" of the stomach. Also see Bock, *Luke*, 1256.

opportunity to ask a question and get discussion going: "Jesus asked the lawyers and Pharisees, 'Is it lawful to cure people on the Sabbath, or not?' But they were silent" (vv. 3–4a).[85] According to Bock, the verb "asked" (ἀποκριθεὶς) conveys the idea of a reply, "indicating that [Jesus] is in dialogue with their suspicion."[86] At their refusal to respond, "Jesus took him and healed him, and sent him away" (v. 4b). That the man with dropsy is dismissed after being healed indicates he is not one of the invited guests.[87]

By healing on the Sabbath, Jesus gives the Pharisees potential ammunition to condemn him as a renegade prophet and healer who does not adhere to the Law. Therefore, Jesus takes the initiative and asks a rhetorical question about "the legitimacy"[88] of his actions: "'If one of you has a child or an ox that has fallen into a well, will you not immediately pull it out on a sabbath day?' And they could not reply to this" (vv. 5–6).[89] Obviously, any such rescue attempt would involve far more effort than expended by Jesus to heal the man. If a dumb ox and a precious son can be rescued, could not a person with a chronic illness be healed?[90] The question is not designed to challenge the Law *per se*, but to show the shortsightedness of their interpretation of it. By keeping their silence, the Pharisees are unable to trap Jesus in a Sabbath mishap.

Green believes that banquet settings provide Jesus with opportunities to conduct himself as if "the transformation of the world had already occurred."[91] Good news and healing are offered to the marginalized and the sinners (Luke 4:18–19). For Jesus, the Sabbath points to an eschatological Jubilee where the helpless and oppressed are released from their burdens. In some sense, that day has already arrived ("Today," 4:21).

Having spoken with authority and uncanny insight, to which the diners cannot respond, Jesus then addresses two more important issues that

85. In legal matters to remain silent is a sign of agreement. See Fitzmyer, *Luke X–XXIV*, 1041.

86. Bock, *Luke*, 1257.

87. Evans, *Luke*, 218; Ellis, *Luke*, 193.

88. Marshall, *Luke*, 579.

89. The difference in response between being "silent" (v. 4) and "could not reply" (v. 6) is noticeable. According to Fitzmyer, *Luke X–XXIV*, 1042, the latter signifies that they could not find an adequate answer to the question.

90. That the scribes remained silent is not unusual, since there was much ambiguity on this matter. The Babylonian Talmud, (*b. Shab.* 117b) did not offer precise instructions about what to do if an animal and its young fall into a ditch on the Sabbath. Thus, a controversy existed over the issue. The Qumran "Community Document" (CD 11:13–14) clearly forbids the rescue of a trapped animal on the Sabbath.

91. Green, *Luke*, 546.

serve as the pillars of the entire social structure of the Roman Empire, not just Jewish meals. First, he deals with seating arrangements at a banquet table or social stratification (vv. 7–11), and second, the issue of reciprocity or whom one should invite to a banquet (vv. 12–24).

Seating Arrangements

As explained in an earlier chapter, where one reclined at a meal in relation to the host was an open acknowledgement to all present of one's social status. Seating arrangement could fluctuate with each meal. A person could move up in status, for example, if he performed some public act that brought recognition or honor to the host. The seats closest to the host were the seats of honor. Most guests knew their assigned seats but occasionally an early arrival might claim the seat of another in an attempt to move up the social ladder. Such might have been the case at this banquet. This portion of the text deals with Jesus' parabolic teaching on social stratification:

> When he noticed how the guests chose the places of honour, he told them a parable. "When you are invited by someone to a wedding banquet, do not sit down at the place of honour, in case someone more distinguished than you has been invited by your host; and the host who invited both of you may come and say to you, 'Give this person your place,' and then in disgrace you would start to take the lowest place. But when you are invited, go and sit down at the lowest place, so that when your host comes, he may say to you, 'Friend, move up higher'; then you will be honoured in the presence of all who sit at the table with you. For all who exalt themselves will be humbled, and those who humble themselves will be exalted" (Luke 14:7–11).

To seek a "place of honor," i.e., the chief place of reclining (πρωτοκλισίαν) for oneself at a banquet, only to be moved to a lower seat, brings shame on oneself.[92] By the use of a parable Jesus does not seek to make an obvious point but an opaque one that will be understood only by those with ears to hear. Rather than teaching the diners how to navigate the Roman system of honor and shame, he is presenting in parabolic fashion a contrast between God's kingdom values and Rome's. This is an anti-imperial hidden transcript in which Jesus offers an alternative or counter proposal

---

92. Green, *Luke*, 550. To take a seat of honor without being invited to do so was likely an effort to advance one's status. Such an action was risky and could result in humiliation.

to Roman stratification and patronage that, if implemented, would deal a death blow to social boundaries and reciprocity. Just as Jesus overturns the tables at the Temple, so he attempts to overturn self-serving table practices embraced by Roman and Jewish elites.

Jesus concludes his story with this maxim, "For all who exalt themselves will be humbled, and those who humble themselves will be exalted" (v. 11). The way one acts at the meal table now will result in either reward or judgment. Jesus connects the two meals; the one eaten in the present and the messianic meal/wedding feast to be eaten at the consummation of the age (Rev 19:9). At the latter meal, God will serve as host. The invited guests are those humbled in this lifetime, i.e., elitists who have chosen to humble themselves and the marginalized that have been shamed and victimized. God will honor those who ignore class and rank and befriend the poor. These are the ones he invites to his feast and calls "friend."[93]

The parabolic lesson is clear: exchange imperial values based on status for kingdom values based on equality.

Reciprocity

The social climate of the Roman Empire was built also upon reciprocity. Those who were invited to a banquet were expected to repay in kind. Gifts were never free, but came with strings attached. Therefore, one invited to his banquet only those who could reciprocate. In this way, one's social status was maintained. A person of wealth or status would never consider inviting a peasant to such an affair, else his own status would be diminished. Thus, careful attention was given to the guest list. The banquet as a social institution perpetuated social stratification and hence reciprocity. It was a means of maintaining the status quo. By challenging this concept, Jesus acts subversively and undermines traditional Roman values, which most Jewish elitists have observed: "He said also to the one who had invited him, 'When you give a luncheon or a dinner, do not invite your friends or your brothers or your relatives or rich neighbours, in case they may invite you in return, and you would be repaid. But when you give a banquet, invite the poor, the crippled, the lame, and the blind. And you will be blessed, because they cannot repay you, for you will be repaid at the resurrection of the righteous'" (vv. 12–14). Addressing his host specifically ("the one who had invited him"), Jesus gives instructions on the right and wrong way of compiling a guest list for a formal dinner

93. Evans, *Luke*, 222.

party. By using the negative imperative μὴ φώνει ("do not invite") Jesus offers a corrective to the customary Roman meal practices, which by design excluded the impoverished. One's social status was never advanced by inviting the disenfranchised to one's banquet; they could only defile and bring a host down a notch in the social order.[94] Jesus calls upon the host to stop following social protocol. Fellowship among God's people should have no social boundaries.[95] In fact, those with high status because of birth or circumstance "should seek to do good to those who are so needy that they cannot do anything in return and leave the whole recompense to God."[96] To invite the poor to the banquet transforms it into an economic meal where the needy are provided a good meal. This is the Jubilee agenda that God wished for Israel throughout her history and which she failed to implement.

God's people, as an alternative society, should not play by the world's rules. Reciprocity should not be factored in when making a guest list. If one follows God's kingdom ethics, he will invite "the poor, the crippled, the lame, and the blind" (v. 13). These very ones Jesus mentions in his Jubilee sermon (Luke 4:18); the ones who cannot repay. Jesus calls upon the host to start implementing the principle immediately. This teaching, echoing the sentiment of Isa 35:3–7, expresses God's love for all his people. To those who do likewise, Jesus says God will reciprocate "at the resurrection of the righteous." As he often does Jesus relates the "meal practices in the present to divine compensation at the eschaton."[97] Since the Pharisee embraced a belief in resurrection, this message touches a positive chord.

The word "resurrection" triggers a response from an unnamed guest: "Blessed is anyone who will eat bread in the kingdom of God!" (v. 15). Elsewhere in Luke the phrase "eat bread" refers to the eating of a full meal, i.e., a two-course *deipnon* (see 7:33; 14:1). The placing of the meal in the future "kingdom of God" shows that the man connects divine reciprocity at the "resurrection of the righteous" (v. 14) with reclining at the messianic banquet, a relationship mentioned several times in the Hebrew Scriptures (Isa 25:6–8; 55:1–2; 65:13–14; Zeph 1:7). Divine blessing is described in terms of eschatological feasting. This man may have heard Jesus speak earlier about people coming from the four corners of the earth who will

94. Qumran went even further than the Pharisees by excluding the poor, lame, and marginalized from being a part of their community (1Q 28a).

95. Bock, *Luke*, 1266.

96. Marshall, *Luke*, 583.

97. Green, *Luke*, 558.

recline with Abraham at the kingdom feast,[98] when he said, "There will be weeping and gnashing of teeth when you see Abraham and Isaac and Jacob and all the prophets in the kingdom of God, and you yourselves thrown out. Then people will come from east and west, from north and south, and will eat in the kingdom of God. Indeed, some are last who will be first, and some are first who will be last" (Luke 13:28–30). Evans believes the man's comment "strikes at the very heart of the question with which he is most concerned: 'Who really are those who will be included in the kingdom of God?'"[99] To the invited guests, the answer seems obvious: as children of Abraham, *they* will be the ones to gain entrance. However, in his next parable Jesus suggests that the uninvited guests—those rejected by the Pharisees and lawyers—actually will be the ones that God allows into his kingdom.

> Then Jesus said to him, "Someone gave a great dinner and invited many. At the time for the dinner he sent his slave to say to those who had been invited, 'Come; for everything is ready now.' But they all alike began to make excuses. The first said to him, 'I have bought a piece of land, and I must go out and see it; please accept my apologies.' Another said, 'I have bought five yoke of oxen, and I am going to try them out; please accept my apologies.' Another said, 'I have just been married, and therefore I cannot come.' So the slave returned and reported this to his master. Then the owner of the house became angry and said to his slave, 'Go out at once into the streets and lanes of the town and bring in the poor, the crippled, the blind, and the lame.' And the slave said, 'Sir, what you ordered has been done, and there is still room.' Then the master said to the slave, 'Go out into the roads and lanes, and compel people to come in, so that my house may be filled. For I tell you, none of those who were invited will taste my dinner'" (Luke 14:16–24).

This parable serves as another hidden transcript, and it will take interpretive insight to understand its message. The man who hosts a dinner represents God.[100] The "dinner" (δεῖπνον) refers to the kingdom of God, often portrayed as an eschatological feast.[101] The "invited" guests who

98. Fitzmyer, *Luke X–XXIV*, 1054.

99. Evans, *Luke*, 223.

100. Nolland, "The Role of Money," 182.

101. Green, *Luke*, 557–58, points out, "At Qumran meals the normal cycle of meals anticipated the messianic banquet and in the Lukan narrative Jesus himself has repeatedly acted as though the kingdom were proleptically present in his meals." Jesus often

"make excuses" and decline the invitation are people like the Pharisees and scribes, those with social rank who consider themselves righteous according to the Law. It is not that they are disinterested in the kingdom, but their attention is drawn to temporal matters.[102] Since social standing was affirmed by peer approval, the host is knocked down a notch when his invitation is rejected by those whom he deemed his social equals. Those on his "A List" have socially vilified the host by placing other concerns above his banquet.[103] Jesus depicts the host as "angry." Repudiating the need for approval, he extends an invitation to all regardless of station in life. He first sends his couriers into "streets and lanes of the town," which serve as the "location of the dwellings of those of low status."[104] The "poor, the crippled, the blind, and the lame," mentioned here and in verse 13 are also the ones to whom Jesus came to preach the good news (Luke 4:18–21).[105] With room to spare for more guests, the host gives further instructions to "go out into the roads and lanes, and compel people to come in." Such entails exiting the city gates and traveling the ὁδοὺς (roads) and φραγμοὺς (lanes), i.e., the hedgerows or walls "along which beggars might rest for protection."[106] The first group is not merely invited or called, but brought or led (εἰσάγαγε) to the banquet (v. 21), and the latter must be compelled or persuaded (ἀνάγκασον) (v. 23), indicating a reluctance on their part to attend the banquet, likely because they know they cannot reciprocate. To attend means they must step beyond their restricted social barrier.[107] The host, however, has stepped outside his comfort zone as well. By humbling himself and associating with the utterly destitute, he has nothing to gain, and expects no repayment. His "great tradition" has been totally transformed.[108] Life will never again be the same for him. Through his actions,

---

uses meals as an "occasion for discourse on the kingdom banquet."

102. Evans, *Luke*, 224. Green, *Luke*, 560, adds the invited guests are engaged in "priorities that should be subordinated to the demands of the kingdom."

103. Green, *Luke*, 560.

104. Ibid., 561.

105. According to Lev 21:16–22 the lame, blemished or disfigured could not "offer the bread" or "eat the bread" of God. Qumran writings excluded such persons from full membership of the people of God in the Qumran community (1QSa 2:5–6). Pharisees believed these marginalized individuals would not be allowed to participate in the eschatological meal. Hence they were not invited to meals connected with the people of God. See Green, *Luke*, 561.

106. Marshall, *Luke*, 590.

107. Green, *Luke*, 562.

108. Ibid., 563. Green comments, "His transformation is without qualification. No longer will his social relationships be governed by the old system."

"He initiates a new community grounded in gracious and uncalculated hospitality."[109] The end result finds the host declaring, "none of those who were invited will taste my dinner" (v. 24).[110]

It must be remembered, that Jesus tells the above parable in response to the unnamed guest's comment, "Blessed is anyone who will eat bread in the kingdom of God!" (v. 15). This means the main characters in the parable should be viewed from a kingdom perspective. Jesus uses κυρίῳ (v. 21) and κύριος (v. 23) to describe the host, who obviously represents God. Those who reject the host's invitation are the ones who will not recline at the eschatological banquet, which represents the kingdom of God. On the other hand, the marginalized of society who accept the invitation, will be "blessed" and "eat bread in the kingdom of God."

As a hidden transcript and an act of resistance, Jesus' parable stands opposed to the traditional and prevailing views among Jews of his day. He "subverts conventional mealtime practices related to seating arrangements and invitations."[111] For Jesus, the kingdom is characterized as a banquet where everyone is welcomed regardless of status. The "poor, the cripple, the lame, the blind" of this life (v. 13) will participate, and like the man with dropsy, they will be totally healed, since the kingdom feast will take place at the resurrection when all things are made new (v. 14). Corley suggests that the invitation in the parable "portrays the kingdom of God as a large inclusive meal to which people from all levels of society are invited, including women."[112] Jesus challenges the banquet guests to embrace egalitarian kingdom ethics, not Roman ethics or the ethics of the Pharisees, which was based on their noble desire to build a protective hedge around the Law.

If the Pharisees implement his instructions, their meals will become love feasts where the poor are honored and receive a bountiful blessing, and thus be transformed into proleptic kingdom meals that serve as an alternative paradigm to the Roman meals that reflect patron-client relationships based on the domination system.

109. Ibid., 562.

110. Evans, *Luke*, 227, points out Luke's wordplay. The term "invited" rightly can be translated "chosen" or "elected," showing that the parable deals with more than inviting people to dinner. Rather it refers to the *chosen* or *elect* people of God. He explains, "Seen in this way the irony of the parable is enhanced. The apparent elect, chosen to enter the kingdom, failed to heed the summons, and so the apparent non-elect (the poor, crippled, etc.) enter instead."

111. Green, *Luke*, 550.

112. Corley, *Maranatha*, 67.

As a prophet, Jesus speaks for God and uses the parable to invite his hearers to take the necessary action to enter the kingdom of God.[113] Failure to reorient their lives in accordance with God's values, which have been proclaimed by prophets throughout the age, shows they are not true children of Abraham and will not recline with him (Luke 13:18–30). Thus, refusal to accept Christ's call now is tantamount to rejecting God's invitation to the eschatological banquet.[114] If they miss the kingdom meal, it will not be for lack of an invitation, since they were the first to be summoned.[115] The eschatological feast will be held on schedule and all seats will be filled by somebody.

Manson draws two lessons from the symposium teaching: 1) No one "can enter the kingdom without the invitation of God" and 2) No one "can remain outside it but by his own deliberate choice."[116] The question then remains, "How do the Pharisees respond?" While no answer is given, one thing stands out. Like the other Lukan meal narratives, this banquet is the venue for evangelism and a locus of redemption.

In each Lukan banquet in which Jesus eats with the Pharisees, his inclusive table fellowship reflects the ethics of God's kingdom, while theirs reflect ethics more in line with the empire's value system. The lesson for the audience who reads Luke's gospel nearly sixty years after the fact is that they must conduct their own communal meals in accordance with Jesus' instructions. Since the Christian banquet is a sign and a foretaste of the messianic banquet, what kind of people should be invited to their table? Will their symposia provide opportunities for forgiveness?

5.3.5 A Banquet Celebration upon the Prodigal's Return (Luke 15:11–32)

Jesus' parable of the prodigal son, dubbed "the pearl among parables,"[117] contains an informative account of "a great feast." The immediate context sets the stage for the parable: "Now all the tax-collectors and sinners were coming near to listen to him. And the Pharisees and the scribes were

---

113. Nolland, "Role of Money," 182.

114. Fitzmyer, *Luke X–XXIV*, 1053.

115. Bock, *Luke*, 1278.

116. Manson, *Sayings of Jesus*, 130, adds, "Man cannot save himself; but he can damn himself."

117. Hunter, *Parables*, 59.

grumbling and saying, 'This fellow welcomes sinners and eats with them'" (Luke 15:1–2).

As the Gospel of Luke unfolds, the Pharisees and scribes have evolved into Jesus' nemeses. Their charge is that he not only eats with riffraff, but "welcomes" (προσδέχεται) or receives them warmly.[118] Such egregious acts stand as evidence that he departs from both Roman and Jewish mealtime protocol. The accusation motivates Jesus to tell three parables of the lost sheep (vv. 3–7), lost coin (vv. 8–10), and lost son (vv. 11–32). The parables serve to vindicate Jesus' relationship with people who do not observe the Law of Moses.[119]

The parables have three things in common. First, they all deal with something that has been "lost" (vv. 4, 8, 32). Second, they deal with repentance (vv. 7, 10, 18). Third, when that which is lost is restored, the main character[120] invites "friends" and "neighbors" to celebrate the occasion at a feast (vv. 6, 9, 32).

The location of these parables is significant because they are bracketed between a chapter on table etiquette (14:1–35) and the story of the rich man who "feasted sumptuously" and Lazarus "who longed to satisfy his hunger with what fell from the rich man's table" (16:20–21), both of which teach that: 1) God accepts into his kingdom both the socially respectable and the socially abhorrent who reorient their lives toward his kingdom ethic, 2) Jesus is God's spokesperson who invites people into the kingdom, and 3) feasting follows reconciliation.

Of the three parables in Luke 15, the writer will limit his examination to the parable of the prodigal son. The story opens with the words, "There was a man who had two sons" (v. 11). This parable can be divided into two acts.[121] Act One (vv. 11–24) contains the account of the younger son who demands from his father his portion of the family inheritance (v. 12), goes to a far country and squanders the entirety of his resources on fleshly pleasures (vv. 13–16), comes to his senses and returns home to beg his father's

---

118. Green, *Luke*, 571, states that the term προσδέχεται means "to extend hospitality" and is analogous to δέχομαι in 9:53; 10:8, 10; 16:4, 9. In other words, Jesus practiced what he preached. He told others to invite to meals those outside their circle of friends and social class (14:12–14).

119. Scott, *Hear Then the Parables*, 101.

120. Jeremias, *Rediscovering*, 101, correctly identifies the father and not the younger son as the main character in this parable. Thielicke, *Waiting Father*, includes a sermon on this parable entitled "The Waiting Father."

121. Scott, *Parables*, 109.

forgiveness (vv. 17–20a), and receives an unexpected response from his father that includes forgiveness and a joyous celebration (vv. 20b–24).

Act Two (vv. 25–32) covers the elder son's livid response upon learning of his brother's return and his father's willingness to accept him with open arms.

Act One (The Younger Son)

When the prodigal resolves to go back home, he also decides what he will say to his father: "I am no longer worthy to be called your son; treat me like one of your hired hands" (v. 19). He hopes his father will grant his plea and give him a servant's job on the farm. In telling the story, Jesus adds an unexpected twist, "But while he was still far off, his father saw him and was filled with compassion; he ran and put his arms around him and kissed him" (v. 20).[122] Amidst this surprising reception, the young man starts to deliver his brief, but pre-rehearsed speech (v. 21) when the father interrupts him in mid-sentence and calls out to the servants: "'Quickly, bring out a robe—the best one—and put it on him; put a ring on his finger and sandals on his feet. And get the fatted calf and kill it, and let us eat and celebrate; for this son of mine was dead and is alive again; he was lost and is found!' And they began to celebrate" (vv. 22–25).

The son who had brought so much shame upon the father is received lavishly as an honored guest. The father's "compassion"[123] is demonstrated by his humility and acceptance of the prodigal as a full and privileged member in the family.[124] The "best" robe, literally the first robe, may be a veiled allusion to Isa 61:10 ("the robe of righteousness"), giving the robe eschatological significance.[125] By ordering "a ring" (likely a signet) to be placed on the prodigal's "finger and sandals on his feet," the father restores his son to his former status. He will not be treated as a slave but as a free

---

122. Blomberg, *Interpreting the Parables*, 176, sees the father's unexpected response as a pivot in the story, since no honorable Palestinian patriarch in Jesus' day would run out in public view to greet a rebellious son in this fashion. It is upon this compassionate and humbling action that the story finds its meaning.

123. Johnson, *Luke*, 237, notes that in describing the father's compassion, "Luke uses the same verb (σπλαγχνίζομαι) as was attributed to Jesus in 7:13 and the good Samaritan in 10:33."

124. Scott, *Parables*, 117, remarks, "The father goes overboard, and his behavior is out of character for an eastern master/patron, for it violates his honor."

125. Hendrickx, *Parables of Jesus*, 156.

man, and the servants will respect him as their master.[126] All the rights and privileges of the son of a wealthy and powerful man will be his. The declaration, "this son of mine was dead" is ironic; since the son for all practical purposes had pronounced his father dead when he asked for his inheritance.[127]

The father spares no expense in preparing an elaborate feast to honor his son's return home. Roasting and eating a "fatted calf," i.e., grain-fed calf, was reserved for only the rarest and most special of occasions. The son who faced famine will now feast. The reason for the celebration is given: "for this son of mine was . . . lost but is found!" (v. 24). The term "lost" probably refers to being a stranger in an unfamiliar country and working for a foreigner, and connects this parable with the previous two in the chapter. The sheep, coin, and son are all missing and in a foreign place; thus, they are lost.

Act Two (The Elder Son)

> Now his elder son was in the field; and when he came and ap-
> proached the house, he heard music and dancing. He called one
> of the slaves and asked what was going on. He replied, "Your
> brother has come, and your father has killed the fatted calf,
> because he has got him back safe and sound." Then he became
> angry and refused to go in. His father came out and began to
> plead with him (Luke 15:25–28).

Jesus now switches the emphasis in the parable to the elder brother, who returns from "the field" to find a spitted calf, the band playing (συμφωνίας), wine flowing and dancing in the courtyard (v. 25). When he "asked" (ἐπυνθάνετο, imperfect, i.e., "kept asking him") the reason for the celebration, he finally discovers that the feast is being held to honor his brother's homecoming; this elder sibling becomes "angry" and chooses not to participate in the festivities. In refusing, he humiliates his father before servants and guests.

Just as he had done for his younger son, the "father came out" of the house "and began to plead" with the elder son to come inside (vv. 25–28), but he refuses and gives the reason: "For all these years I have been work-ing like a slave for you, and I have never disobeyed your command; yet

126. Ibid., 156; Scott, *Parables*, 118.

127. Scott, *Parables*, 111, notes, "Disposition of property assumes his [father's] death."

you have never given me even a young goat so that I might celebrate with my friends. But when this son of yours came back, who has devoured your property with prostitutes, you killed the fatted calf for him!" (vv. 29–30). According to common logic and the social protocols of the day, his argument seems sound. By refusing to join in the banquet, "the elder son has social propriety on his side."[128] The father is the one acting outside the traditional Jewish value system. The prodigal, not the other son, has brought embarrassment and shame upon the family; he should be shunned and not rewarded. With the statement, "you have never given me even a young goat" the elder son charges the father with showing favoritism to the prodigal. In comparison to his younger brother, the elder is the morally responsible one, who serves his father faithfully, albeit out of obligation rather than love.

Not persuaded by the elder son's argument, the father replies, "Son, you are always with me, and all that is mine is yours. But we had to celebrate and rejoice, because this brother of yours was dead and has come to life; he was lost and has been found" (vv. 31–32).

The break between the elder son and the father is not much different than the break between the prodigal and the father at the beginning of the parable.[129]

One is drawn immediately to the contrast between the responses of the father and the elder son. First, the father shows "compassion" (v. 20); the son is "angry" (v. 28). The father embraces ("puts his arms around") the prodigal (v. 20); the son distances himself from his brother. The father addresses his eldest as "Son," i.e., child (τέκνον), an endearing term (v. 30); but the son does not call his father πάτερ,[130] nor does he see himself as a privileged son, but as one who works "like a slave" (v. 29). When speaking to his father about the prodigal, the elder brother calls him "this son of yours" (v. 30);[131] but the father says, "this brother of yours" (v. 32), indicating that the elder son should have the same affection as the father.

---

128. Green, *Luke*, 585.

129. Hendrickx, *Parables*, 158. Both were outside the house, in the field, and return home. "Just as the father went out to meet the younger son, so he now comes out and entreats the elder son to join the celebration, thus repeating the same gesture of love."

130. The prodigal however uses the term Πάτερ in verses 18 and 20 to address his father.

131. Ellis, *Luke*, 237, remarks, "By calling his brother 'this son of yours,' instead of 'my brother,' the older son reveals his contempt for his brother. Likely, it reflects the idea that such a disloyal son had been regarded as 'dead' to the family (see vv. 24, 33) and so the older brother, would have said that he had no brother."

The elder son accuses the father of "never" treating him royally (v. 29); the father replies that his wealth has "always" had been at the elder son's disposal (v. 31).[132]

The father contends that the prodigal's return demands a joyous celebration. He says, "We had to celebrate and rejoice" (εὐφρανθῆναι δὲ καὶ χαρῆναι ἔδει). The use of imperfect ἔδει, literally, "it is necessary" coupled with the infinitives, carries the meaning that the action is required.[133] The reason given is "because" (ὅτι) "this brother of yours was dead and has come to life" (ὁ ἀδελφός σου οὗτος νεκρὸς ἦν καὶ ἔζησεν). Such a circumstance necessitates a celebratory response.

Jesus leaves his listeners in the dark regarding the outcome of the parable. Although the father repeatedly invites the elder son into the feast, signified by the imperfect verb παρεκάλει ("began to plead"), one never learns if he is persuaded.[134] Does he eventually join the celebration or continue in his stubborn refusal? The story ends with the elder son left standing outside. To remain alienated from his younger sibling, the elder brother will also be alienated from his father.

What lesson does Jesus intend for the grumbling scribes and Pharisees to learn from this parable? To Jeremias, the narrative "describes with the most impressive simplicity what God is like—his goodness, his grace, his great mercy, his abounding love."[135] God is like the father who reaches out and welcomes his wayward son into his presence as a full member of his family. And like the father, "God loves the sinner while he is still a sinner, before he repents."[136] Tax collectors and sinners are like the prodigal who comes to his senses and returns to the father, crying out, "I have sinned against heaven and before you" (v. 18). Thus the parable portrays a sinner who turns to his heavenly father. The Pharisees and scribes are like the elder brother, a person of respect and social status who obediently keeps God's Law, but who becomes angry when his father welcomes

132. Scott, *Parables*, 121, insightfully observes, "The elder fails to recognize that the father is always on his side and he need not earn his father's approval. He has made himself a slave for something that was already his."

133. Fitzmyer, *Luke X–XXIV*, 1091. Johnson, *Luke*, 239, observes, "The same construction is used in 13:16 for the need to liberate the daughter of Abraham who was bound by Satan."

134. Talbert, *Reading Luke*, 151.

135. Jeremias, *Rediscovering*, 103.

136. Fitzmyer, *Luke X–XXIV*, 1086. The father runs out to meet his son while he is far off, embraces and kisses him, even before the son can ask his father's forgiveness. "This detail expresses the father's initiative, his basic and prevenient love for the son who left him" (1089).

with open arms his errant but repentant brother. Instead of emulating his father's compassion, he chooses to remain aloof.

Does Jeremias do justice to the parable? Is it mainly about individual forgiveness and reconciliation or is there something deeper and hidden? Wright thinks so. He interprets the parable in light of "the story of Israel, in particular exile and restoration."[137] He notes, "The Exodus itself is the ultimate backdrop."[138] Just as the son goes off in disgrace to a far country, serving foreign masters, and returns home, only to be challenged by another son who has stayed put, so Israel goes into exile because of her disobedience and returns in repentance, is restored by a loving father, but opposed by her own leaders, represented by the elder brother and pointing to the Pharisees and other rulers, who remain outside the kingdom.[139] "Israel's history is turning its long awaited corner; this is happening in the ministry of Jesus himself; and those who oppose it are the enemies of the true people of God."[140]

In this writer's estimation, both Jeremias and Wright miss the single point of the parable. One must remember that Jesus tells the story of the prodigal to answer his critics' charge that he associates with the wrong kind of people—"he welcomes sinners and eats with them" (v. 2). Thus, the "grumbling" of the scribes and Pharisees is contrasted with the repeated call "rejoice with me" and "celebrate" (vv. 6, 9, 23, 32).[141] In Luke, Jesus' other parabolic stories speak cryptically of the kingdom of God as a banquet or feast. As with other Lukan meal narratives that feature Pharisees, this one carries a similar theme and lesson. Those who put status aside and follow Jesus' kingdom agenda—by reclining with the poor, oppressed, and marginal of society—will also be invited to recline with God at the eschatological banquet. The father in the parable, representative of God, invites both sons to dine together.

Jesus uses a mealtime context to challenge the Jewish establishment's flawed understanding and assumptions about the kingdom. By reissuing the message of the Hebrew prophets he corrected erroneous beliefs and practices that had crept into Israel's daily life and had supplanted the covenant identity markers meant to set Israel apart from other nations. Jesus

137. Wright, *Jesus and the Victory*, 126.
138. Ibid.
139. Ibid., 127.
140. Ibid.
141. Hendrickx, *Parables*, 168.

calls for the nation to repent and reorder its priorities in accordance with kingdom ethics.

In telling the parable, Jesus insinuates that his mission and actions represent God's agenda. Those who join him at the open table, depicting redemption and reconciliation, will experience kingdom life here and now. To refuse to join God's people at the table is a sign that one is alienated from God. Hence, eating with God's people, regardless of status, is to participate in the life of the kingdom "already," which in turn points to the "not yet" kingdom to come.

Dodd asks, "Do the Pharisees and scribes (vv. 1–2) reorient their lives and accept Jesus' invitation to join in the celebration?"[142] While Luke's readers may not know if these individuals sought repentance, they are certain that the nation as a whole did not. To the contrary, their leaders executed the one who told the parable rather than accepting his message. The one whom they rejected, God vindicated by raising him from the dead. For Luke's Christian community, the father's parabolic declaration "This son of mine was dead and is alive again" was a symbolic or hidden reference to resurrection (v. 24). To them, Jesus is reigning Lord and "present in their community, where his stories are narrated over and over again."[143]

The most important question for Luke's readers is, "Will they welcome repentant sinners into their communal meals or become like lukewarm Israel and adopt the ways of the world?"

5.4 Excursus: A Brief Word about the Other Meals in the Gospel of Luke

Two other meals in Luke's gospel—the feeding of the five thousand (Luke 9:10–17) and eating with Zacchaeus (19:1–10)—have not been discussed in this chapter because they do not fit the definition of a formal Roman-style banquet.[144] Each, however, provides insight on how Jesus used private

---

142. Dodd, *Parables*, 92, wisely cautions, "We need not ask whether Jesus Himself, or God, is thought of as the Seeker of the lost. In the ministry of Jesus the Kingdom of God came; and one of the features of its coming was this unprecedented concern for the 'lost.'" Since Jesus is God's prophetic voice, his invitation and God's are the same.

143. Hendrickx, *Parables*, 169.

144. Standhartinger, "Rethinking the Eucharistic Origins," 1, distinguishes between the Lukan meals Jesus shared with Pharisees, tax collectors, and others, and those which he hosted like the feeding of the five thousand and the Last Supper. She feels the latter actually reflect post-Easter practices of the church.

meals, out of public view, to propagate his pro-kingdom, anti-imperial message.

Rather than exegete each passage, the writer will make only a few pertinent observations about each.

5.4.1 Feeding of the Five Thousand (Luke 9:10–17)

Upon the triumphant return of the Twelve from their mission (v. 10), Jesus leads them to Bethsaida where he plans for them to spend some private time together. When the multitudes follow, Jesus uses the occasion to teach. Luke writes, "He welcomed them, and *spoke to them about the kingdom of God*, and healed those who needed to be cured" (v. 11). As the sun starts to set, "the twelve came to him and said, 'Send the crowd away, so that they may go into the surrounding villages and countryside, to lodge and get provisions; for we are here in a deserted place'" (v. 12). Instead, Jesus instructs the Twelve to have the people recline (κλισίας) in rows of fifty (v. 14). Luke tells of their compliance: "They did so and made them all sit down (κατέκλιναν)," i.e., recline in banquet-like fashion (v. 15). Jesus then feeds the people by multiplying the five loaves and two fish (vv. 16–17).

According to the Johannine account, the crowd interprets the miraculous feeding as evidence that the kingdom has dawned and that Jesus is the new Moses (John 6:14) who will free the nation from oppression and poverty. "When Jesus realized that they were about to come and take him by force to make him king, he withdrew again to the mountain by himself" (v. 15). The phrase "take Him by force," translated from ἁρπάζειν, indicates they seek to seize or draft him to lead a revolution and shows the profound impact the miracle has on the crowd. The same word used in Matt 11:12: "And from the days of John the Baptist until now the kingdom of God suffers violence, and violent men *take it by force*." Jesus had no intention of using armed conflict to usher in the kingdom.

There are noticeable parallels between the feeding of the five thousand and the Last Supper (Luke 22:14–22), which make this account an important one. First, Jesus serves as the host at both meals. Second, he takes the bread, blesses it, breaks it, and distributes it. Third, his teaching centers on the kingdom of God. Fourth, the twelve apostles are present and eat. Fifth, Jesus likewise eats and communes with his dinner guests. Sixth, both meals are interpreted by the diners as eschatological meals, i.e., connected to a future messianic banquet where there is abundance and the needs of all will be "satisfied" (Luke 9:17). Finally, in neither incident will

Jesus bring in the kingdom in the way they anticipate. Rather, he uses the banquet as an enacted parable to demonstrate and teach what the kingdom will be like. It will be a time of abundance, healing, and equality for all, just the opposite of what the masses experience at the hands of the Roman and Jewish elites.

5.4.2 Eating with Zacchaeus (Luke 19:1–10)

When Jesus looks up in the sycamore tree and spots Zacchaeus, a chief tax gatherer who has become wealthy by cheating his fellow citizens, he invites himself to Zacchaeus's home (vv. 1–5). While a meal is not specifically mentioned, hospitality is implied by Jesus' desire to "*stay at your house*" and Zacchaeus's eagerness "to welcome him" (v. 6). Green notes, "This signifies from Jesus' point of view that he hopes, in the context of a shared meal, to forge a relationship with Zacchaeus."[145] Zacchaeus scurries down the tree and leads Jesus to his opulent abode. The reaction from the onlookers is typical of the Pharisees as seen in the five meals discussed in the main body of this chapter: "They all began to grumble, saying, 'He has gone to be the guest of a man who is a sinner'" (v. 7). Although the Twelve are not mentioned, they likely accompany Jesus to the home of Zacchaeus.

Luke does not reveal what Jesus says to Zacchaeus as they recline together, but it evidently deals with the kingdom of God for it has a profound impact on the host who interrupts Jesus and declares, "Behold, Lord, half of my possessions I will give to the poor, and if I have defrauded anyone or anything, I will give back four times as much" (v. 8). Zacchaeus's response indicates an immediate change of attitude toward his accumulated wealth, his moral responsibility toward the poor, and his voluntary willingness to compensate fourfold his victims for past wrongs. These actions, which come under the category of "fruits of repentance" (Luke 3:10–14), lead Jesus to say, "Today salvation has come to this house, because he, too, is a son of Abraham" (v. 9). The one dubbed a "sinner" by the self-righteous crowd has become a man of faith. This statement made to a third party (possibly to the disciples) points back to Jesus' first use of the eschatological "Today" to speak of the kingdom's arrival (Luke 4:18–21). Paul speaks in a similar fashion: "Behold, now is the accepted time; behold, now is the day of salvation" (2 Cor 6:2), which is a clear reference to Isa 49:8, where God promises to restore the kingdom to Israel. The restoration is beginning.

145. Green, *Luke*, 670.

LaVerdiere points out that the table conversation between Jesus and Zacchaeus focuses on "justice, concern for the poor and salvation," all of which are associated with the arrival of the kingdom.[146] Zacchaeus shifts his allegiance from serving self and Rome to the kingdom of God. In the midst of table fellowship Zacchaeus gains eschatological salvation and secures a place at the table with Abraham at the consummation of the age (Luke 13:30).

5.5 Conclusion

The thesis of this chapter was that Jesus used the meal setting as an opportunity to condemn imperialistic practices and to encourage people to adopt egalitarian meal practices that reflected the ethics of God's kingdom. This was demonstrated by examining five meals in Luke's gospel where Jesus challenges his Jewish eating companions to abandon ill-conceived policies designed to exclude undesirables from the table. These hidden transcripts and acts of resistance caused quite a stir and would contribute to his eventual execution.

For the church members reading Luke's gospel, Jesus' table talks inform them how they should eat their communal meals. Christian meals, according to Luke, are the place where God invites sinners into his kingdom and offers them a foretaste of its joys. They serve as a bridge to the great messianic banquet at the consummation of the age, when all oppressing kingdoms will be destroyed and God's reign will be recognized on earth.

The next chapter examines the "Last Supper" in the Gospel of Luke and shows how it serves as a link between the original Passover meal and the Lord's Supper. The Passover finds its fulfillment in the messianic banquet, while the Lord's Supper functions as an interim meal between the two. Those eating at the Lord's Table participate in the kingdom of God already and proleptically, and in doing so embrace an alternative social vision of the future.

146. LaVerdiere, *Dining in the Kingdom*, 171.

6

The Last Supper as an Anti-Imperial Banquet

THE LAST SUPPER STANDS as the final in a series of meal scenes in the Gospel of Luke and contains some of the same themes, e. g., status, benefaction, betrayal, and service. For Luke's audience reading the gospel as they gather around the Lord's Table, these mealtime teachings inform them how to conduct their own meals. Since most of Jesus' instruction and example carry anti-imperial overtones, they serve as valuable lessons for the churches as they struggle to live amidst Roman domination.[1]

6.1 Introduction

The four Gospels agree that Jesus traveled to Jerusalem to celebrate Passover week and that he died on Friday.[2] It is therefore no surprise that the Synoptic Gospels characterize Jesus' final meal with his disciples as a Passover Supper (Matt 26:17; Mark 14:12, 26; Luke 22:1–20)[3] in the tradition

1. Wenham, "How Jesus Understood the Last Supper," 12, suggests that the Last Supper must be studied in the context of Jesus' teaching about the kingdom of God because it was central to the ministry of Jesus. This message, which the Gospel writers called "good news," was an announcement that the reign of God, predicted by the OT prophets, was about to begin. The disciples, along with many others, likely thought Jesus would overthrow Rome and set up God's government. So the events that transpire at the Last Supper must have been filled with both excitement and confusion (13).

2. Theissen and Merz, *Historical Jesus*, 157.

3. The Gospel of John does not identify Jesus' Last Supper as a Passover meal *per se* (John 13:1, 27; 18:28; 19:14, 31, 36, 42). There have been many attempts to explain the apparent discrepancies between the Fourth Gospel and the Synoptics. According to

of a typical Greco-Roman banquet. The Lukan account identifies the "Last Supper"[4] as a Passover on six different occasions (vv. 1, 7, 8, 11, 13, and 15). Luke begins to unfurl the events surrounding the meal in a progressive manner. The narrative opens, "Now the Feast of Unleavened Bread, which is called the Passover, *was approaching*." At this point Luke tells how the chief priests and officers secure Judas Iscariot to betray Jesus (vv. 2–6).

He advances the storyline, "*Then came* the first day of Unleavened Bread on which the Passover lamb had to be sacrificed" (v. 7). Luke relates how Jesus sends Peter and John out to prepare for the feast (vv. 8–13), which includes arranging for a dining room, and purchasing of the lamb and other supplies for the evening meal.

Luke then concentrates on the meal itself: "*When the hour had come, he* [Jesus] reclined at the table, and the apostles with him. And he said to them, 'I have earnestly desired to eat this Passover (paschal) with you before I suffer . . .'" (vv. 14–15).[5] The mention here of eating a paschal/lamb, along with Matthew's and Mark's reference to Jesus dipping his food in condiments, gives further weight that this meal is a Passover meal. Luke's inclusion of a cup after supper, a likely reference to the third cup (v. 20), a mainstay of a typical paschal feast, is another sign that Luke characterizes the meal in terms of the Passover.[6] Additionally, according to the Gospel

---

Sanders, *Historical Figure of Jesus*, 72, "The reason is that the author wanted to depict Jesus as the Passover lamb, which was sacrificed on the fourteenth." Some evangelicals in an attempt to support both John and the Synoptics believe the Gospel writers used different calendars. No theory is without its difficulties. Regardless of the exact date, all Gospel writers place the Last Supper within a Passover setting. Since this book looks predominately at Luke's account of the Last Supper, it will seek to understand his perspective. For a discussion of the controversy, see Barrett, *Gospel According to St. John*, 48–51.

4. Fitzmyer, *Luke X–XXIV*, 1378, observes that the term "Last Supper" is not found in the NT but is more a description than title, and derives from the allusion to Jesus dining with his apostles on the night of his betrayal (1 Cor 11:23–25; John 13:1–2). Therefore, one might more accurately say that Jesus' final dining experience with the disciples was a Passover meal, which served partly the basis for the Lord's Supper, both of which can be viewed as anti-imperial meals. Despite the imprecise nomenclature, this writer will continue to use the phrase "Last Supper."

5. While the original Passover meal was eaten in haste as the Jews readied themselves for the Exodus, according to the *Book of Jubilees*, 49:22–23, by the first-century BCE it was eaten in a more leisurely fashion, similar to a Greco-Roman banquet, showing how Jewish customs had been influenced by elements of Hellenism.

6. For helpful discussions regarding the date and nature of the meal, see Wilson, *Our Father Abraham*, 245–46; Marshall, *Last Supper*, 57–75; Barth, *Rediscovering*, 15; and Higgins, *Lord's Supper*, 13–22. Each examines the evidence, pro and con, of the Last Supper being a Passover meal.

of Mark, the disciples close the meal by singing a hymn, most likely the latter part of the *Hallel* (Psalms 115–118), a typical feature of the Passover observance (Mark 14:26).

The thesis of this chapter is that Jesus' reinterpretation of the Passover and his exhortations to his disciples during his Last Supper provide the theological foundation for viewing the Lord's Supper as an anti-imperial activity. According to the Exodus narrative, the Hebrew slaves sat to eat the first Passover as they were preparing to escape from Egypt's totalitarian regime. Hence, the meal should be understood as a subversive act of defiance against the domination system of their day. Egypt's tyrannical control of the world and its imperial grip around the necks of the Jewish people led them to cry out to Yahweh for help, who answered and delivered them from oppression. To enable them and their descendants to remember the Exodus event throughout the centuries, God instituted a memorial feast that they were to observe annually.

At the time of Jesus, the Roman Empire used its imperial powers to dominate the masses. Since Luke depicts Jesus' Last Supper with his disciples as a Passover meal, his readers living a half-century after the event would naturally view Jesus' final meal as part of the ongoing Passover tradition that had originated with the Exodus. But another reality would also grab their attention. Just as the Hebrew children ate the original Passover under Pharaoh on the night before fleeing Egypt, so Jesus and his inner circle ate a clandestine meal under the unsuspecting eye of Caesar whose tyrannical regime sought to kill him.

During the meal Jesus interpreted the Passover from a new perspective. He spoke of another Exodus, eschatological in nature that would be precipitated by his impending death[7] and lead to the restoration of God's kingdom. He said that this Last Supper would have a significant part in the deliverance. Such table talk was subversive and anti-imperial, especially since it implied the decline and defeat of Rome.

After Jesus' death and resurrection, the early Christians gathered regularly in homes to eat a communal meal as they awaited God's intervention on their behalf. The regularly scheduled meal, which Paul called "The Lord's Supper," took the outward appearance of a Roman banquet, i.e., *deipnon* and symposium (see chapter 2), but gleaned its theological

---

7. On the Mount of Transfiguration, Jesus discusses with Moses and Elijah his impending "departure" (NRSV) or "decease" (NKJV) in Jerusalem, a term which is rendered in the LXX as exodoV (exodus). See Exod 19:1; Num 33:38; Ps 104:38. If Jesus' death is seen as an exodus of sorts, then the meal associated with it, likely has overtones of a Passover feast.

significance and meaning from Jesus' subversive table talks, and especially from his teaching during the Last Supper (1 Cor 11:23).

6.2 The Last Supper as a Passover Meal

After entering Jerusalem on "Palm Sunday" to the shouts of "Blessed is the king who comes in the name of the Lord! Peace in heaven, and glory in the highest heaven!" (Luke 19:36–40), Jesus weeps over the city for its leaders' failure to welcome eschatological "peace" (εἰρήνη) or to "recognize the . . . visitation from God" that was unfolding before their eyes (Luke 19:42–44b). This reference to "visitation" has a likely link to Zechariah's prophetic song, which speaks of God's future intervention when he raises up a "mighty saviour" to redeem his people (Luke 1:68–69).[8] Divine visitation, however, cuts two ways. It not only speaks of deliverance for God's faithful remnant, but also of judgment on God's enemies, including unbelieving Jews who align with these enemies (Luke 1:71–74). By choosing to embrace *Pax Romana*, rather than God's salvific peace, they continue to oppress the people of God.

While the vast throng of peasants display their public resistance to Roman domination by waving palm branches and crying out to Jesus, "Save us now," their leaders plot his demise. Jesus, sensing his hour had come,[9] anticipates their efforts to kill him.[10]

Jesus spends a large portion of Passion Week ministering in the Temple, where he expresses anti-imperial sentiment. As he enters the court of the Gentiles, he begins to "drive out" the merchandisers (Luke 19:45),

8. Luke also mentions how after Jesus raised from the dead the widow's son the crowds glorified God and declared, "A great prophet has arisen among us!" and "God has *visited* His people!" (7:16). They interpreted the miracle to be a sign that God was working through Christ in some eschatological way.

9. Luke reveals midway through his gospel that Jesus is aware that he must suffer at the hands of the political authorities (9:22, 43–45). With this understanding "he set his face to go to Jerusalem" (9:51) and pronounces woe upon all those cities that reject his message of the kingdom (10:10–16) and rails against the hypocrisy of the Jewish collaborators with Rome and oppressors of God's people (11:37–54; 12:1–2, 13–21). In his parables he speaks cryptically against those who trust in themselves rather than God, kill the prophets, oppress the lowly, exalt themselves to positions of honor, and refuse to repent even in the face of the kingdom's imminent arrival. Many of his parables are spoken to or about Pharisees and include warnings and pronouncements of judgment (Luke 14–18). He prophesies his death and resurrection a third time and adds that the Gentiles [Romans] will be involved in the execution as well as the native retainers (18:31–34).

10. Green, *Luke*, 690.

declaring, "It is written, 'My house shall be a house of prayer but you have made it a den of robbers'" (v. 46). The phrase "den of robbers" is a likely reference to Jer 7:11, where the prophet excoriates the priests for utilizing the Temple to rob widows and oppress children, yet continue to call it the "temple of the Lord." Josephus likens the misuse of the Temple to a hideout or a cave where robbers run for refuge to escape the sheriff.[11]

Then in a demonstrative prophetic act, Jesus casts out the money changers, just as he expelled or cast out (ἐκβάλλω) demons (Luke 9:40, 49; 11:14–20; 13:32), who likewise sought to control and oppress the people.

Jesus' actions are meant to expose graphically that the Jewish leaders are compromisers and agents of Satan and thus to evoke resistance against them. Once Jesus disrupts the Temple formalities, his fate is sealed. As Geza Vermes suggests, "Had he not been responsible for a fracas in the Temple of Jerusalem at Passover time . . . very likely Jesus would have escaped with his life."[12]

Throughout the week, the Jewish leaders unsuccessfully seek to arrest Jesus (Luke 20:1, 19, 20–26, 27–40), but his popularity hinders them: "Every day he was teaching in the temple. The chief priests, the scribes, and the leaders of the people kept looking for a way to kill him; but they did not find anything they could do, for all the people were spellbound by what they heard" (Luke 19:47–48).

Jesus' anti-imperial message of divine liberation has the city of King David in a state of excitement. With hopes of deliverance swirling in everyone's minds and on everyone's lips what better time than Passover to usher in God's kingdom?

Jesus' counter-imperial entry into the city and his cleansing of the Temple[13] put the military on high alert, causing great consternation for the native elites. Things were about to get out of hand.

It is in this volatile political setting that Jesus eats his "Last Supper" with the Twelve.

6.3 A Pre-Supper Plot to Kill Jesus

Passover was near. The chief priests and the scribes were looking for a way to put Jesus to death, for they were afraid of the people.

11. Josephus, *Ant.* 14.15.4–5.

12. Vermes, *Changing Faces*, 262.

13. Sanders, *Historical Figure*, 252–64, designates these two events as historical and verifiable.

> Then Satan entered into Judas called Iscariot, who was one of the twelve; he went away and conferred with the chief priests and officers of the temple police about how he might betray him to them. They were greatly pleased and agreed to give him money. So he consented and began to look for an opportunity to betray him to them when no crowd was present (Luke 22:1–6).

By stating that Satan enters Judas immediately after the Jewish leaders plot to kill Jesus, Luke informs his readers that *Satan* is orchestrating the events. According to Luke, Satan sought to divert Jesus from his mission at the start, but failed. He then departed to wait "for a more opportune time" (4:13). He now resurfaces at the end of Jesus' ministry in another attempt to derail Jesus' mission "by subverting his followers."[14] Judas and the Jewish leadership secretly arrange for Jesus' arrest and crucifixion.[15] The moment of betrayal will take place later in the week in a secluded garden area away from public view. The opposition, comprised of chief priests, Temple police officers, Jewish elders, and a lynch mob of unsympathetic Jews will confront Jesus in overwhelming numbers (22:47–52) and arrest him under the guise of darkness. The only thing that stands in the way of Jesus being arrested earlier in the week is the support of those Jewish pilgrims who suspect that he might be the messiah. To avoid arrest until "his hour had come," Jesus limits his public outings to teaching venues, especially the Temple courts and porticos, where he is surrounded by large numbers of the curious and committed (Luke 21:38).

Against the sobering realization that his days are numbered, Luke recalls how Jesus prepares to celebrate his last Passover with his disciples.

6.4 Arranging and Preparing the Passover

> Then came the day of Unleavened Bread, on which the Passover lamb had to be sacrificed. So Jesus sent Peter and John, saying, "Go and prepare the Passover meal for us that we may eat it." They asked him, "Where do you want us to make preparations for it?" "Listen," he said to them, "when you have entered the city, a man carrying a jar of water will meet you; follow him into the house he enters and say to the owner of the house, 'The teacher asks you, Where is the guest room, where I may eat the

---

14. Evans, *Luke*, 321.

15. Luke's mention of Satan leaves his readers wondering if the Jewish leaders cooperated knowingly or unwittingly with Satan's plan to destroy Jesus.

Passover with my disciples?' He will show you a large room upstairs, already furnished. Make preparations for us there." So they went and found everything as he had told them; and they prepared the Passover meal (Luke 22:7–13).

Luke places the "Last Supper" in a Passover setting, specifically the "day . . . on which the Passover lamb had to be sacrificed" (vv. 7–8). According to Exod 12:6, the head of the household or his representative slaughters the lamb at twilight, roughly 2:30–5:30 p.m. in the courtyard of the priests.[16] That Luke pays unusual attention to the Passover preparation is evidenced by his use of terms related to "preparation" on four occasions within seven verses (vv. 8, 9, 12, 13). The dialogue between Jesus and his two disciples shows the extent of the preparation (vv. 8–12), with Peter and John specifically asking, "Where do you want us to make preparations for it?" Typical preparations had to be completed by sundown and involved great attention to details, including the purchase, sacrificing, and roasting of a ritually acceptable lamb, the securing of other necessary foodstuffs, e.g., matzo, bitter herbs, vinegar, wine, the arranging of couches, setting the table, and so forth.[17]

Contrary to tradition, however, preparations for this meal were to be done in secret.[18] Jesus gives Peter and John cryptic instructions, which includes signs and code words. The two disciples look for a "man carrying a jar"[19] who will lead them to a house and to its owner. When requesting of the owner the use of a room, they must not refer to Jesus by name but only say, "The teacher asks you, 'Where is the guest room, where I may eat the Passover with my disciples?'" The mysterious unknown owner will understand their request—evidently by their use of the title "the teacher"—and will take them to an upper chamber "already furnished" for the occasion.[20] Identities and locations must be concealed.

---

16. Fitzmyer, *Luke X–XXIV*, 1382. Also see Bock, *Luke*, 1710.

17. Ellis, *Luke*, 252, Marshall, *Luke*, 791.

18. Ibid., 791.

19. While *anthropos* is typically a generic term for "human being," Jesus probably means a male, since the instruction seems to be a sign. As Marshall, *Luke*, 791, notes, "This would be an unusual sight since men normally carried leather bottles . . . and women carried jars or pitchers."

20. The furnishings probably refer to couches upon which to recline during the Passover meal. Ellis, *Luke*, 252, remarks that during the Paschal meal, even slaves and the poor normally consigned to sitting at tables to eat, got to recline on couches. "This signified the freedom obtained by the deliverance from Egypt."

These "cloak and dagger" arrangements must have intrigued the other disciples. None knew beforehand where the meal would be eaten. Peter and John learn only as they carry out orders, and there is no evidence that they return to tell the others. They most likely wait until Jesus arrives with the other ten members.

Why the secrecy? First, this prearrangement strategy assures complete privacy and an uninterrupted evening with the Twelve. By this time, Jesus may have sensed his death was imminent. If so, the meal served as a farewell banquet as well as a Passover, and provided an opportunity to speak of the crucial mission that lay before his disciples. Second, the meticulous planning guaranteed that Jesus could avoid arrest until after he eats his final Passover meal with his closest disciples (see Luke 22:15).[21] Knowledge of his whereabouts must be kept from those who seek to destroy him. Because Judas is unaware of the location beforehand, he cannot tip off the officials.[22]

Since Jesus gives Peter and John specific instructions to carry out, the reader assumes that he had arranged beforehand for the Passover meal. Luke mentions, "So they went and found everything as he had told them." The incident is reminiscent of the way Jesus preplanned and orchestrated the use of the colt for his grand entry into the city (Luke 19:28–37).[23] Secrecy was important.

Jesus' preparations for his last Passover meal also evoke memories of Moses' careful instructions when preparing for the first Passover meal on the eve of the Exodus. It was designed by God to deliver his people from Pharaoh's tyrannical reign and the Egyptian domination system, and to give birth to Israel as a free nation. Likewise, as God prepares to rescue his people from Roman subjugation and inaugurate a new kingdom age, Jesus follows suit.

6.5 Jesus' Final Passover: Opening Remarks

When the hour came, he took his place at the table, and the apostles with him. He said to them, "I have eagerly desired to eat this Passover with you before I suffer; for I tell you, I will not

---

21. Nolland, *Luke 18:35—24:53*, 1032. Also see Marshall, *Luke*, 789; Fitzmyer, *Luke X–XXIV*, 1378.

22. Fitzmyer, *Luke X–XXIV*, 1378.

23. Johnson, *Luke*, 333.

eat it [again] until it is fulfilled in the kingdom of God" (Luke 22:14–16).

"When the hour came" likely refers to the subscribed time to eat the Passover and completes the sequence that began with the words, "the Passover was approaching" in verse 1.[24] The NRSV translation of ἀνέπεσεν ("he took his place") unfortunately does not express the precise meaning of the word, which is to lie back or recline at a table (cf. Luke 11:37; 14:10; 17:7), a common position of eating in the Hellenistic world, even among Jews. "The practice of standing at the Passover meal, ready for a hasty departure (see Exod 12:11), had long since been given up."[25] Jesus takes the position at the head of the table ("his place"), which is most likely configured as a horseshoe. The apostles recline on their elbows to his left or right. In identifying the Twelve as "the apostles" Luke places these men in the role of representatives; hence, the instructions Jesus will give later in the discourse become applicable to all his disciples.

Jesus initially expresses his intense longing ("I have eagerly desired")[26] to eat this meal ("Passover"),[27] knowing it will be his last ("before I suffer").[28] These words seem to indicate that Jesus recognizes his end is near. Given in the context of the eating of the paschal lamb, the announcement sets the stage for Jesus to reinterpret the Passover meal. Since Luke 9:51, the gospel writer has portrayed Jesus as setting his face toward Jerusalem, even knowing the outcome of his journey will likely spell his violent death.[29] Although he has mentioned his death to the disciples on at least three occasions, there is no evidence they ever comprehended the full impact of such statements. Their presuppositions about Messiah's

24. "Most [Passover] meals were eaten in late afternoon" (Bock, *Luke*, 1718).

25. Fitzmyer, *Luke X–XXIV*, 1384.

26. The construction ἐπιθυμία ἐπεθύμησα, which can be rendered "I have desired with desire" is also found in the LXX (Gen 31:30; Num 11:4) and signifies a deep longing or craving. See Johnson, *Luke*, 337.

27. This verse is further evidence that Luke views the paschal lamb as part of this meal (Ellis, *Luke*, 254).

28. While suffering can refer to various human struggles, it is used by Luke specifically as a reference to Jesus' death in Luke 24:46; Acts 1:3; 3:18; 17:3, in addition to here and verse 18.

29. This does not mean Jesus desired to die or had given up all hope, however slim, of escaping death. Even in Gethsemane he makes a final appeal to God for deliverance. But his discussion at the Last Supper indicates he senses his death is imminent and he casts it in eschatological terms.

mission as that of a military conquistador blind their eyes to Jesus' actual nonviolent mission.

In his use of "for" (γὰρ) Jesus gives the reason he desires to eat this final Passover with the apostles: "for I will not eat it [again] until it is fulfilled in the kingdom of God" (v. 16). That he will not eat another Passover with them again until the arrival of the messianic age implies that he will die before the next annual Passover rolls around. Yet, he views himself eating it again "in the kingdom of God." When he does, the meal will not be simply another Passover, but an eschatological Passover feast.[30] By stating that the Passover will be "fulfilled in the kingdom of God," he implies that in its present form the Passover is a type which prefigures or foreshadows something greater to come.[31]

The use of "it is fulfilled" should remind the apostles of OT prophets who cast the kingdom age in terms of a future eschatological meal, even as a Passover meal (Isa 25:6; Ezek 45:21–22). The Hallel Psalms, which were sung at the close of the Passover meal, also look forward to an eschatological deliverance. According to Bock, "Passover looks beyond the first Exodus to the last."[32] It points toward the kingdom of God in its fullness, when God's people are freed from the domination of the state and come under the absolute rule of God. This gives Jesus' interpretation an anti-imperial perspective. God will intervene and deliver his people from all foreign powers and their gods. Jesus, however, does not promote triumphalism. God's kingdom does not commence through human acts of violence; it will be God's doing. For Jesus Passover looks far beyond past liberation from Egypt and forward to ultimate eschatological deliverance, a final exodus, when "salvation history" reaches its goal.[33] Like OT prophets, Jesus links Passover to the anticipated messianic banquet in the

30. Fitzmyer, *Luke X–XXIV*, 1397, "Jesus thus gives a new eschatological dimension to the Passover meal . . ."

31. Ibid.

32. Bock, *Luke*, 1720.

33. Some like Dodd, *Parables of the Kingdom*, 35, hold to a completely realized eschatology and believe that the kingdom arrived with Jesus and is being actualized through the church. In this scenario, the messianic banquet finds its fulfillment in the post-resurrection meals Jesus eats with the apostles (Luke 24:30, 42; Acts 10:41; Rev 3:20–21). This writer believes that the church is a present manifestation of the kingdom to the world and can proleptically experience some of its benefits, but that the consummation of the kingdom is connected to Christ's *parousia*. Therefore, when the apostles eat the Passover meal [and subsequently the Lord's Supper] they participate in the "already" aspect of the kingdom of God while anticipating the "not yet" which is to come.

new age, of which he had already spoken twice before at mealtime (see Luke 13:29; 14:15–24).[34]

In Luke's gospel the Last Supper does not stand alone, but is the last in a series of meals that the human Jesus ate with his followers (5:29–32; 7:36–50; 9:12–17; 10:38–42; 11:37–44; 14:1–24), the penultimate meal that points to the eschatological feast in the kingdom of God.[35]

While Jesus' talk of the coming kingdom and messianic banquet must have thrilled his table companions, his mention of suffering must have confused and even surprised them. He not only spoke with certainty of his own participation in the future messianic meal but implied he must first suffer. What did he mean by this? Did he mean the kingdom would be delayed? Or that he would share in the kingdom blessings like all other faithful Jews at the resurrection? Would someone else carry on the kingdom project in his absence? It all must have seemed very bewildering until Sunday morning they would slowly begin to grasp the magnitude of his teaching.

Such a conversation should have caused Judas great pause and consternation. Did Jesus know about Judas's part in the plot? If God's kingdom prevailed in the end and Jesus expected to be part of it, where did that leave Judas and his fellow conspirators?

To recapitulate, Jesus' opening words at the Last Supper implied several things: 1) he would face death at the imperial hands of the state; 2) he would be vindicated at the resurrection and share in an eschatological Passover meal; and 3) at the kingdom's arrival God would reign over the kingdoms of the world. These anti-imperial statements in the context of a Roman-style banquet meet all the qualifications of being hidden transcripts.

The use of the passive optative verb πληρωθῇ ("it is fulfilled") in a conditional clause "makes a qualitative distinction between a time when something is unfulfilled and a future time when it will be fulfilled."[36] In saying he will not eat the Passover again with his disciples "until it is fulfilled in the kingdom of God," the question begs to be asked, "When does this fulfillment take place?" Does the Passover find its completion in the Lord's Supper or in the messianic banquet at the *parousia*? Does a relationship somehow exist between the original Passover, Jesus' final Passover, the Lord's Supper, and the Messianic banquet at the end of the age? If

34. Johnson, *Luke*, 337.

35. Meier, *A Marginal Jew*, 303.

36. Brumberg-Krause, *Memorable Meals*, chap. 4, p. 36.

answered in the affirmative, what is that relationship? On the one hand, Nolland finds little or no connection;[37] while on the other hand Bock sees several parallels between the meals.[38] This issue will be examined later in this chapter.

6.6 The First Cup

> Then he took a cup, and after giving thanks he said, "Take this and divide it among yourselves; for I tell you that from now on I will not drink of the fruit of the vine until the kingdom of God comes" (Luke 22: 17–18).

Following tradition, Jesus gives "thanks" (εὐχαριστήσας) over the cup.[39] The prayer is likely the customary *berakah* or praise/blessing spoken at meals: "Blessed are you, Lord our God, king of the universe, who has created the fruit of the vine" (*m. Bek.* 6:1). It is from this opening prayer of thanksgiving that the church derives the term "Eucharist" to describe the Lord's Supper. Jesus then passes the single cup around the table and instructs the disciples to "divide it among yourselves." The significance of this action can be understood at various levels.[40] Only two relate directly to the thesis that Jesus and the church used meals as an opportunity to promote anti-imperial and pro-kingdom sentiments. First, the single cup

37. Nolland, *Luke*, 1050.

38. Bock, *Luke*, 1721.

39. This writer is aware of the controversy surrounding the identity of this cup among the four cups drunk at Passover. See Nolland, *Luke*, 1051, for a discussion of the number, identity and sequence of the cups. It is not necessary to precisely identify this cup to make anti-imperial observations about the Passover meal or the Lord's Supper.

40. The single cup can also signify the sharing of authority. For Luke's audience, living on the other side of Christ's resurrection and viewing him as exalted king, to share in his cup might signify shared authority. The Twelve were given authority to carry out the master's mission after his departure (Luke 24:47; Acts 1:5–8). A shared cup might also imply shared suffering with Jesus. In his Temple teachings the day before, Jesus speaks of his suffering and the kingdom to follow when the son of man comes in great glory and power (Luke 21:28–31). On a previous occasion, when the apostles were discussing kingdom affairs, Jesus asks them if they are able to drink from the cup which he was about to drink. They say, "We are able." He assures them they will indeed drink from it (Mark 10:36). Now each is commanded to drink equally from a single cup, a possible allusion to the cup of suffering. In doing so, they partake symbolically of the cup of suffering or affliction, which they will be called upon to experience in reality (Acts 5:41). But the suffering and death which many will face is not the end.

unites all in intimate table fellowship with each other and their master. This will be the final occasion they can have such an experience with Jesus. It is like a family eating together one last time before sending the child off to war and not expecting his return.

Second, Jesus relates the cup to the kingdom of God. The phrase "fruit of the vine" recalls its use in Isa 32:12 (LXX), a chapter that opens with the words, "See, a king will reign in righteousness, and princes will rule with justice" (Isa 32:1) and goes on to describe judgment followed by a glorious kingdom where the desert blooms and justice prevails over the land (vv. 2–20).

Verse 18 explains why they are to divide the cup among themselves: "For (γὰρ) I tell you from now on, I will not drink of the cup until the kingdom of God comes." These words have led some like Jeremias to conclude Jesus himself actually ate or drank nothing during his last Passover meal; he only taught.[41] However, this seems like a strained interpretation, given that Jesus earlier announced in the strongest possible language, "I have eagerly desired (Ἐπιθυμίᾳ ἐπεθύμησα) to eat this Passover with you before I suffer" (v. 15). The most likely explanation is the one that makes the plainest sense: this is his last meal. His next meal will be in the kingdom. This again shows that Jesus expects to suffer at the hands of Rome and her retainers, but victory will follow.[42] He looks forward to that day. This opening volley carries anti-imperial implications, since it spells the ultimate demise of Roman power.

6.7 Reinterpreting the Passover Meal

> Then he took a loaf of bread, and when he had given thanks, he broke it and gave it to them, saying, "This is my body, which is given for you. Do this in remembrance of me." And he did the same with the cup after supper, saying, "This cup that is poured out for you is the new covenant in my blood" (Luke 22:19–20).

Luke's narrative has Jesus breaking the unleavened bread *before* the actual meal and passing around another cup *following* the meal ("after supper"), along with his reinterpretation of these two Passover foods.[43] This

41. See Jeremias, *Eucharistic Words*, 207–18; Danker, *Jesus and the New Age*, 388.

42. Bock, *Luke*, 1724.

43. How Jesus reinterprets the meal is based on whether verses 19b–20 ("'Do this in remembrance of me.' And he did the same with the cup after supper, saying, 'This cup that is poured out for you is the new covenant in my blood'") are part of the

description shows the Last Supper to be a formal evening meal in the Roman banquet tradition, complete with a first course (*deipnon*) and a second course (*symposium*). In structure, therefore, the Last Supper was a Hellenized version of Passover, which included washing of feet, reclining, serving of wine and the meal, singing, lively teaching, and discussion.

6.7.1 The Body

Jesus follows standard Passover procedure by blessing, breaking, and distributing the unleavened bread, which is called the "bread of affliction" in Deut 16:3. Jesus next departs from tradition[44] by connecting the bread with his person: "This is my body." That he speaks metaphorically is evident, since his actual body is reclining on the couch. In this sense the verb "is" indicates representation, not identification.[45] Does Jesus see himself as taking the affliction which is meted out by the forces of tyranny? In executing God's eschatological spokesperson, Roman and Jewish authorities stand opposed to God's kingdom agenda.

Then Jesus adds the explicatory words, "which is given for you." Luke uses the term "given" (δίδωμι) elsewhere to connote a sacrificial offering (Luke 2:24) and other writers use it similarly (see Mark 10:45; John 6:51; 2 Cor 8:5; Gal 1:4). The phrase "for you" (ὑπὲρ ὑμῶν) likely means for your sake or on your behalf, and likely has vicarious implications. Since this was not the ordinary meaning assigned to unleavened bread at Passover,[46] the new explanation must have caught the apostles off guard. Although confused they may have associated it with the messianic woes. Whatever the case, Jesus' affliction would somehow work out to their benefit.

---

original text. The Codex Bezae omits these words, while the vast majority of texts include them. Since the discovery of P75—the Bodmer papyrus dating from ca. 200 CE—a scholarly consensus has emerged that accepts the longer text as valid. This writer will follow the longer text tradition. For a discussion of this textual matter, see Nolland, *Luke*, 1035, 1042; and Metzger, *A Textual Commentary on the Greek New Testament*, 173–77.

44. Wilson, *Our Father Abraham*, 237.

45. Ellis, *Luke*, 256.

46. A typical haggadic explanation of the unleavened bread during early second-century CE, but whose origins go back into the mid-first-century CE, was that this is "the bread of haste eaten when our fathers were redeemed from Egypt."

6.7.2 The Memory and Practice

When Jesus uses the present imperative, "Do this in remembrance of me" (v. 20) he moves from the present, i.e., his desire to eat with them (v. 15), to the future when they will be eating in his absence. The statement suggests that when they recline at upcoming Passover feasts they should begin to reflect differently on the Exodus. Jesus, not Moses, is to be the central figure in the ongoing narrative. By giving the Passover meal a new perspective, Jesus transforms its focus. The disciples will not celebrate Passover as they did in the past. The meal should now be eaten as a sign that a new Exodus is taking place. God is delivering his people in an eschatological way and reestablishing his rule.[47]

Likely, Jesus adopts the images of bread and remembrance from Moses' initial Passover instructions: "You must not eat with it anything leavened. For seven days you shall eat unleavened bread with it—the bread of affliction—because you came out of the land of Egypt in great haste, so that all the days of your life you may remember the day of your departure from the land of Egypt" (Deut 16:3). Just as all Jews were to remember the Exodus, so all followers of Jesus were to remember his affliction that opened the door to a final Exodus.

As mentioned in chapter 3, remembrance in the OT involved more than a set of mere recollections. Memory and activity went hand in hand. Israel remembered by taking action, e.g., by eating an annual meal together and by living as an alternative society under the reign of Yahweh. Memory included a mental conjuring of past events so that they had an impact on the present and/or future.[48] To remember God or the poor, for example, implies a call for action, i.e., worship God and feed the poor. It carries the idea that through the means of memory events of the past can be reexperienced in a tangible way. As the story is retold, each succeeding generation can participate in the event through imaginative memory.[49]

Given the fact that Luke views the Last Supper as a Seder, the memory of the Passion makes sense both theologically and historically as the memory of the Exodus. The Last Supper is the initial meal of the new Exodus and the forming of a new holy nation. It points to deliverance and redemption from the same demonic powers that controlled Egypt of old.

47. Fee, *Corinthians*, 55.

48. Green, *Luke*, 762.

49. Thiselton, *Corinthians*, 879.

Jeremias holds that *remembrance* is more vertical than horizontal. By that he means Jesus commands his disciples to call upon God (vertical) to remember Jesus' death on their behalf and grant them mercy and forgiveness.[50] While such an idea of God-ward remembrance is found on five occasions in the OT (LXX),[51] Jesus does not make it explicitly clear he has this in mind. This writer therefore stands with Conzelmann who, after carefully examining Jeremias's arguments for a God-ward remembrance, concludes that such an understanding "contradicts the plain wording" of the phrase "in remembrance of me."[52]

What exactly are they to remember about Jesus? The context seems to be his death.[53] Since the context of the meal, according to Luke, is "the day . . . on which the Passover lamb had to be sacrificed" (v. 7), the reader may be expected to understand that Jesus is relating his death in some way to the paschal sacrifice; although, he likens his body with the broken bread, connecting it to "the bread of affliction" (Deut 16:3). It is here that the anti-imperial nature of his teaching again appears because the one they are to remember is the man whom the Jewish leaders deemed to be a false messiah and Romans treated as an insurrectionist. By commanding his apostles and, by extension, Luke's readers to eat in remembrance of him, Jesus was issuing anti-imperial orders and encouraging anti-imperial action on their part in the future. That his own people and the government authorities collaborated in his death, lest he disrupt the fragile *Pax Romana*, was a scathing indictment against him. From Rome's perspective, he was a criminal who broke the law and faced the consequences. Public crucifixion was designed to drive the fear of Caesar into even the bravest soul. It silently shouted, "Don't step out of line, lest you too writhe on a cross in humiliation." Yet, this is exactly what Jesus was asking his followers to do. They were to honor him in their memory and form an alternative society based on his ethical teachings, which were contrary to Rome's.

---

50. Jeremias, *Eucharistic Words*, 248.

51. Lev 24:7; Num 10:10; Ps 37 (in the proscription); Ps 69 (in the title); Wis 16:6.

52. Conzelmann, *First Corinthians*, 198–99.

53. The idea of messiah dying, especially by crucifixion as an enemy of the state, was a problem for the Jews. The messiah was not supposed to die. Since the Gospel of Luke was written ca. 85 CE, Theophilus and the wider audience read it with an understanding that Jesus has been raised from the dead. However, when Jesus first speaks these words of remembrance to the Twelve, they do not have such a post-resurrection perspective.

6.7.3 The Cup

Just as Jesus distributed the bread before the meal, "he did the same with the cup after supper" (μετὰ τὸ δειπνῆσαι) and announced, "This cup is . . . the new covenant in my blood poured out for you." To those at the table with Jesus and to Luke's readers the metaphorical use of a cup of blood being "poured out" likely brought to mind an OT animal sacrifice or a Hebrew or Roman libation/drink offering. In his letter to Timothy, the writer uses the identical metaphor to describe his impending death (2 Tim 4:6).

By his use of the prepositional phrase "for you," Jesus identifies the beneficiaries of "the new covenant" which will be established through his death as the same ones who drink from the single cup. These words may be an allusion to Isa 53:12 where Yahweh declares:

> Therefore I will allot him a portion with the great,
>> and he shall divide the spoil with the strong;
>> because he poured out himself to death,
> and was numbered with the transgressors;
>> yet he bore the sin of many,
>> and made intercession for the transgressors.

The "with *you*" (Luke 22:15) and the "for *you*" (vv. 19, 20) are the same ones, i.e., the apostles, who represent the new people for whom the new covenant is being established. Paul will later speak of the church as being created "through his blood" (Acts 20:28).

What is the nature of this "new covenant"? A covenant is generally an agreement into which two parties enter that establishes a bond or relationship between them. In this case the two parties are God and his people. Such an agreement usually involves the spilling or shedding of blood (Gen 15:18; 17:2–21), hence, the familiar phrase "cutting a covenant." Scripture clearly states that when the people of God groaned under slavery, God was moved with compassion because he "remembered his covenant with Abraham, Isaac, and Jacob. God looked upon the Israelites, and God took notice of them" (Exod 2:24 25).

a. Many scholars trace Jesus' use of "covenant" back to Exod 24:8, when after bringing the Jews out of Egypt Moses ratifies God's covenant with Israel and forms them into a holy nation: "Then Moses went up to God; the Lord called to him from the mountain, saying, 'Thus you shall say to the house of Jacob, and tell the Israelites: You have seen what I did to the Egyptians, and how I bore you on eagles' wings and brought you to myself. Now therefore, if you obey my voice and keep my *covenant*, you shall be for me a priestly kingdom and a holy nation'" (Exod 19:3–5).

After Moses receives and delivers the ten covenant commands from God, (Exod 19:6—24:2), the people respond with one voice, "All the words that the Lord has spoken we will do." (Exod 24:3). On the basis of this positive reply Moses reads "the book of the covenant" aloud to the people who reaffirm their commitment to obedience (v. 7). He then splashes sacrificial blood upon the people and says, "See the blood of the covenant that the Lord has made with you in accordance with all these words" (v. 8).

If Jesus' actions at his final Passover mirror the events on Sinai, he likely sees himself as a prophet like Moses who ratifies a "new covenant" with God's people. Just as the old covenant was sealed with a meal, so also the new; thus, the Exodus account can be viewed as an appropriate backdrop for the Last Supper. Through his death Jesus leads a new exodus and forms the people of God into a renewed priestly kingdom and holy nation.

b. Other scholars interpret the "new covenant" in light of Jer 31:31–34. Since Jer 31:31 is the only place in the Hebrew Scriptures where the exact phrase "new covenant" appears, it should be given consideration when interpreting Jesus' Passover instruction in Luke 22. With these words the prophet describes a day when Yahweh will establish a new covenant with his people, "beyond Sinai in which he will bestow forgiveness and bring inner renewal."[54]

Jeremiah 31 focuses on Israel's future restoration and describes how Yahweh responds to the cries, "Save, O Lord, your people, the remnant of Israel" (v. 7) with a promise:

> See, I am going to bring them from the land of the north,
> and gather them from the farthest parts of the earth,
> among them the blind and the lame,
> those with child and those in labour, together;
> a great company, they shall return here.
> With weeping they shall come,
> and with consolations [supplications] I will lead them back,
> I will let them walk by brooks of water,
> in a straight path in which they shall not stumble;
> for I have become a father to Israel,
> and Ephraim is my firstborn (Jer 31:8–9).

54. Nolland, *Luke*, 1054.

In Jer 31:31–32, this ingathering is described in terms of a "new covenant" and contrasted with the covenant made on Mount Sinai: "The days are surely coming, says the Lord, when I will make a new covenant with the house of Israel and the house of Judah. It will not be like the covenant that I made with their ancestors when I took them by the hand to bring them out of the land of Egypt—a covenant that they broke, though I was their husband, says the Lord." The new covenant was actually a covenant of re-newal made with the house of Israel and the house of Judah, and implied a return to the Lord in repentance and a reuniting of the tribes: "But this is the covenant that I will make with the house of Israel after those days, says the Lord: I will put my law within them, and I will write it on their hearts; and I will be their God, and they shall be my people. No longer shall they teach one another, or say to each other, 'Know the Lord,' for they shall all know me, from the least of them to the greatest, says the Lord; for I will forgive their iniquity, and remember their sin no more" (Jer 31:33–34).

Jesus may view his impending death as the means by which God ful-fills his eschatological promise to Israel. Since Jer 31:31 says the covenant is to be made with the united nation, commentators see the twelve apostles as representative of the nation as a whole, the firstfruits of God's newly re-stored Israel.[55] Wright comments: "The very existence of the twelve speaks, of course, of the reconstitution of Israel; Israel had not had twelve visible tribes since the Assyrian invasion in 734 BC, and for Jesus to give twelve followers a place of prominence . . . indicates pretty clearly that he was thinking in terms of the eschatological restoration of Israel."[56] The new covenant is therefore connected with Israel's future hopes of restoration.[57]

According to the prophets, the new covenant was to be the ba-sis for God ushering in his kingdom. It spoke of a "new, eschatological beginning."[58] The prophet Ezekiel spoke of the eschatological Spirit who would bring rebirth to the nation (36:36). Thus, the kingdom age was to be the age of the Spirit. Bock characterizes the Spirit as the heart of the new covenant and the divine means by which the benefits of the kingdom are distributed to God's people.[59]

---

55. Sanders, *Jesus and Judaism*, 98–106; Fredriksen, *Jesus of Nazareth*, 98; and Meier, *Marginal Jew*, 148–54.

56. Wright, *Jesus and the Victory of God*, 300.

57. For a scholarly discussion of Jesus' teaching about restoration, see Sanders, *Jesus and Judaism* and McKnight, *A New Vision for Israel*.

58. Marshall, *Luke*, 806.

59. Bock, *Luke*, 1727.

During the Last Supper when Jesus explains his death in new covenant terms, the apostles likely assume God is about to overthrow Rome and restore the Land back to Israel. Hence, when Jesus makes a post-resurrection appearance, they ask, "Lord, is this the time when you will restore the kingdom to Israel?" (Acts 1:4).

Since Jesus says that both the *bread* is broken and the *cup* is poured out "for you," some scholars, like Luke Timothy Johnson, interpret this to mean that the Messiah's "sacrifice is vicarious."[60] This would fall in line with Paul's use of ὑπὲρ ἡμῶν in 1 Cor 15:3 and 2 Cor 5:15, 21. Even so, it is unlikely that the apostles construe Jesus' impending death as a substitutionary *atonement*, at least not while they are sitting at the table.

In the Matthaean version of Luke 22:20, the words are added, "for the forgiveness of sins" (Matt 26:28). Carter notes this is not a reference to forgiving personal or individual sins.[61] The term ἄφεσιν ("forgiveness" or "release") is the same word as used in Leviticus 25 (LXX) where it is translated fourteen times as "a Jubilee" and "year of Jubilee," and refers to a "massive social and economic restructuring (return of land; freeing of slaves . . . remission of debt, etc.)."[62] Seen from this perspective, Jesus' impending death establishes a new covenant in which those under sin (i.e., under a world ruled by the oppressors) will be set free in a restructured world where God, not the elites, will rule.[63]

In similar fashion, Ehrensperger equates Paul's "for all are under sin" (Rom 3:9) with living under the oppressive hand of imperial "power structures [that] permeated all aspects of life so that no one could escape . . . [its] influence."[64] In such a state, people could either choose to "collaborate with the imperial power and thus collaborate with the power of sin" or they "could submit and be driven into poverty or even slavery" or they may choose to "react violently by joining armed resistance groups."[65] Jesus taught his disciples to follow another route—one of nonviolent resistance.

60. Johnson, *Luke*, 339.

61. Carter, *Matthew and Empire*, 88.

62. Quoted from Warren Carter in correspondence to author (December 15, 2007). Also see Carter, *Matthew and Empire*, 88.

63. Carter, *Matthew and Empire*, 88.

64. Ehrensperger, *Paul*, 115.

65. Ibid.

6.8 Aligning with the Imperial Powers

After speaking of his demise and the new covenant through his blood, Jesus hints at how his arrest and death will be accomplished: "'But see, the one who betrays me is with me, and his hand is on the table. For the Son of Man is going as it has been determined, but woe to that one by whom he is betrayed!' Then they began to ask one another which one of them it could be who would do this" (Luke 22:21–23). With the words "But see" (πλὴν ἰδοὺ) Jesus contrasts his selfless act of sacrifice ("poured out for you") with one who commits a traitorous act of betrayal. While the faithful will eat with him at the future messianic table, the betrayer will face judgment ("woe"). That one of their own would deliver him to the executors is shocking enough, but the announcement, "and his hand is at the table" is absolutely chilling. Jesus may be thinking and applying Ps 41:9 to his own circumstances, in which King David announces, "Even my bosom friend in whom I trusted, who ate of my bread, has lifted the heel against me." A chosen apostle will be the betrayer. He is a turncoat and now serves as a fifth column within the select group. By using the present participle, τοῦ παραδιδόντος, (lit. "the one betraying"), Luke suggests the betrayal is already underway.

Earlier that week in the Temple Jesus charged, "You will be betrayed even by parents and brothers, by relatives and friends; and they will put some of you to death" (Luke 21:16). While they expect to face such a fate themselves, they may not have anticipated that Jesus would be the first of their number to experience familial disloyalty and death, and that the betrayal would occur so soon.

Luke Timothy Johnson notes that "hand" (χεὶρ) in the Gospel of Luke often carries the connotation of power.[66] Following the parable of the wicked vinedressers, Luke reports, "And the chief priests and scribes sought that very hour to lay hands on him" (Luke 20:19; cf. 21:12; 24:7). Green amplifies this idea by showing that χεὶρ in the context of Luke is associated directly with those individuals who seek to destroy Jesus by force.[67] For example, shortly after coming down from the Mount of Transfiguration Jesus declares, "Let these words sink into your ears: 'The Son of Man is going to be betrayed into human hands.' But they did not understand this saying; its meaning was concealed from them, so that they could not perceive it. And they were afraid to ask him about this saying'" (Luke

66. Ibid., 340.
67. Green, *Luke*, 765.

9:44–45). That Jesus would be betrayed was not entirely new information. But now they discover the betrayer is one of them!

The phrase ἐπὶ τῆς τραπέζης ("at the table") will appear again in verse 30 in relationship to the messianic feast: "You are those who have stood by me in my trials; and I confer on you, just as my Father has conferred on me, a kingdom, so that you may eat and drink at my table in my kingdom . . ." (vv. 28–30), and connects the final Passover to the messianic banquet. For Luke's readers, the Last Supper and all future suppers are likely viewed as proleptic eschatological meals.[68]

Luke next has Jesus speak of his death as a "going" or a personal exodus which is divinely predestined: "For the Son of Man is going as it has been determined" (v. 22). Although part of God's foreordained plan, it involves human culpability. Judas is a willing participant and collaborator in the plot. Jesus pronounces judgment ("Woe") on Judas as he had done earlier on those who choose self-gratification over suffering on behalf of the Son of Man (Luke 6:22–26) and upon the cities that reject the Messiah and his message (Luke 10:13–15). Luke uses the title "Son of Man," to identify Jesus, which he uses twenty-three other times in his gospel.[69] In the immediate context it will come again from Jesus' lips when he confronts Judas (Luke 22:47–48).

With the alarming announcement of betrayal and subsequent judgment, the disciples "began to ask one another which one of them it could be who would do this" (v. 23). The thought that one among them—a "family" member—will betray the master is unthinkable; yet, the implication was even more distressful. It meant that one who had been called to provide leadership in the kingdom of God chose instead to cast his lot with the Jewish power brokers and the rulers of the domination system. In doing so, he surrenders control to Satan, the hidden power behind imperial Rome and its cohorts (v. 3).

Luke's original audience may have shuddered when this account was read to them as they gathered at their own communal meal and symposium. If one handpicked by Jesus could betray the master, who among them might defect? The lesson was clear: participation at the Lord's Table "is no guarantee that a disciple will not betray his Lord."[70] The threat and temptation to deny Christ and align with the imperial powers loomed as ever present. Switching allegiance from God's peaceful kingdom to

68. Nolland, *Luke*, 1059.
69. Evans, *Luke*, 92.
70. Fitzmyer, *Luke X–XXIV*, 1409.

Caesar's domination system is a sobering possibility. The meal which was meant to be a venue where kingdom life was manifested and hidden transcripts uttered might not be so safe after all. Who among the reclining Christians might also be part of Satan's fifth column?

6.9 Anti-Imperial Instructions

No sooner had the apostles questioned their own loyalty than they switched focus and ironically began debating among themselves about "which one of them was to be regarded as the greatest" (v. 24). This concern over rank and status, based on societal standards, leads Jesus to interject a comment into their lively symposium discussion and challenge their premise: "But he said to them, 'The kings of the Gentiles lord it over them; and those in authority over them are called benefactors. But not so with you; rather the greatest among you must become like the youngest, and the leader like one who serves. For who is greater, the one who is at the table or the one who serves? Is it not the one at the table? But I am among you as one who serves'" (Luke 22:25–27). In using the words "But he said to them" Luke shows that Jesus contradicts their understanding of greatness, which is akin to the "patron/client system of benediction and honors."[71] Jesus compares the apostles' desire for greatness to the way "kings" and elitist "benefactors" (v. 25) used a banquet setting to "lord it over" others, and thus to elevate and maintain their own status. A well-to-do benefactor/patron sponsored banquets and invited his clients to recline at his right and left hand. In exchange for benefaction, the clients heaped their praise upon and gave their loyalty to him. The patron-client relationship was part of the Roman domination system which assured that power resided with a select few—the king being the ultimate benefactor.

Jesus declares, "But not so with you" (v. 26), and avers the greatest at the table is "the one that serves" (v. 27), thus relating greatness to the role of slaves rather than to the role of "kings" or "benefactors." By Gentile standards, the greatest are the ones who recline. The lowest are the slaves who have no place at the table but serve at the table. As seen in the previous chapter, Pharisaic banquets followed suit and were forums of exclusivity.

In his answer, Jesus does not expect these status-based relationships to abate anytime soon. In fact, he does not condemn benefaction, *per se*, only the way it is practiced in the empire. He does call, however, on those who are part of God's new society to practice a different ethic.

71. Brumberg-Krause, *Memorable Meals*, chap. 4, p. 13.

Rather than using the authority they might possess through family ties or circumstances for selfish purposes, they are to serve the least among them. When this alternative behavior is embraced and implemented, the watching world will perceive the stark contrast between the social and economic foundation of the empire and the kingdom of God.

Jesus offers himself as the prime example: "I am among you as one who serves" (v. 27).[72] As the one who provided the meal, Jesus is their benefactor, but unlike most patrons/benefactors who normally ate only with clients who had been loyal to them, Jesus reclines with ones who have failed him repeatedly and will continue to fail him, and then takes it one step further by serving the tables. For Luke's audience the lesson is clear—they should imitate Jesus and his meal practices and abandon the practices of the status-conscious Gentiles.

6.10 The Giving of a Kingdom

Luke includes Jesus' final symposium statement to the Twelve that deals with eschatological matters: "You are those who have stood by me in my trials; and I confer on you, just as my Father has conferred on me, a kingdom, so that you may eat and drink at my table in my kingdom, and you will sit on thrones judging the twelve tribes of Israel" (Luke 22:28–30). With these words, Christ offers certain hope to his disciples. He bequeaths to them "a kingdom" (v. 29) that he identifies as "my kingdom" (v. 30).[73] This statement must have been difficult for them to understand when uttered, but even more so after his death the next day! They may have thought Jesus was speaking about the eschatological kingdom that would

72. In John's gospel account of the Last Supper, Jesus makes the same point by taking on the role of a slave and washing the disciples' feet; thus, leaving them an example to emulate (John 13:1–17). After a lengthy symposium discussion dealing with the theological meaning of washing, Jesus concludes, "If I then, your Lord and teacher, have washed your feet, you ought to wash one another's feet" (v. 14). The emphatic position of second person plural pronoun "you" along with the "ought," which conveys obligation, indicates they in particular are to wash feet at mealtime and not expect slaves to do the job. In other words, they are to be servants. His instructions, if carried out, will replace stratification at future meals held by his disciples.

73. Beasley-Murray, *Jesus and the Kingdom*, 276, points out that the verb διατίθεμαι ("confer") in verse 29 comes from the same root as the noun διαθήκη ("covenant") in verse 20, and offers a clue into how the kingdom is conferred. The words are linked in the LXX as well. Beasley-Murray concludes, "The covenant mentioned in the distribution of the cup in verse 20 is clearly participation in the kingdom of God." Otto, *Kingdom of God*, 292, renders verse 29, "I appoint the kingdom to you by covenant, as my Father appointed me a kingdom."

arrive at the general resurrection. After all, he had indicated earlier in the evening that he would eat the Passover again when it was fulfilled in the kingdom (vv. 16, 18).

His use of ἵνα ("so that"—v. 30) provides a twofold purpose or result of receiving the kingdom. First, they will share in a kingdom meal which Jesus dubs "my table" (v. 30). Since Jesus spoke of a future meal back in verses 16 and 18 as a fulfillment of the Passover, this meal likely should be interpreted in that context. By designating the kingdom as "my kingdom" and the future meal as "my table" he sees himself as a central figure in the eschatological fulfillment of the Passover. Second, they "will sit on thrones judging . . . Israel." For their loyalty to Christ in this age, these faithful ones will receive positions of authority in the age to come.

6.11 From Last Supper to Lord's Supper

After Jesus' exaltation, did the apostles and the early Jewish church celebrate an annual Passover? If so, in what manner? If not, why not? There are several ways to answer these questions. First, it is possible that Jewish believers "in Christ" gathered together each year to eat a Passover meal with a new covenant understanding. If this is the case, Jesus' words, "This is my body, which is given for you. Do this in remembrance of me" was taken as a command to eat an annual Passover with this fresh teaching in mind.

Second, the Jewish followers of Jesus may have joined their non-messianic friends and family to celebrate a traditional Passover. In doing so, these believers would reflect inwardly upon the words of Christ. The Book of Acts contains only two fleeting references to the feast of Passover or Unleavened Bread (12:3; 20:6) and neither offers insight into if or how Jewish believers in Jesus related to Passover.

That Scriptures are silent on the matter may indicate that Passover played less than a significant role in the life of believing Jewish disciples. On the other hand, Scriptures do speak of the apostles praying daily at the Jerusalem Temple (Acts 4), and later of Paul scheduling his trips to Jerusalem around Jewish feasts. Since there are no extant first-century writings which offer answers, one can only speculate.[74]

A third option offered by Nolland is that the believers in the Jerusalem church initially celebrated an annual Passover but in time abandoned

---

74. Fitzmyer, *Luke X–XXIV*, 1395.

it, replacing it with the Lord's Supper.[75] Such a casting off of Passover could have occurred after the divide between messianic and non-messianic Jews following the Jewish War (66–70 CE). This scenario would explain why the Lord's Supper is given prominence in Luke's gospel (ca. 85 CE).

Fourth, it is conceivable that the embryonic church may have abandoned the Passover immediately, replacing it with the regularly scheduled Christian communal meal. Yoder asserts that Jesus' instructions to eat in memory of him referred to "common" or "ordinary" meals that the believers ate to sustain their physical bodies.[76] He points to the post-resurrection and post-Pentecost meals as evidence that this is the way they took his words at the Last Supper.[77]

Fitzmyer likewise makes a connection between Jesus' final teaching at Passover and the Lord's Supper celebrated by the church:

> Just as the Passover meal was for Palestinian Jews a yearly anamnesis, so too Jesus now gives a directive to repeat such a meal with bread and wine as a mode of representing to themselves their experience with him (especially at the Last Supper). The backward thrust of the Passover meal would take on a new referent in this reinterpretation. Thus Jesus gives himself, his "body" and his "blood" as a new mode of celebrating Israel's feast of deliverance. His own body and blood will replace the Passover lamb as the sign of the way God's kingdom will be realized from now on, even though its fullness will not be achieved until the eschaton.[78]

When examining the validity of Yoder's and Fitzmyer's theories, the logical question to ask is: how did the apostles interpret Jesus' instructions when he gave them at the Last Supper and especially, what did they take them to mean after his glorification? While no definitive conclusion can be drawn, the following case might be made. Most likely, the apostles expected the soon arrival of the kingdom of God and a general resurrection at which time they would be reunited with Jesus at a messianic feast. They clearly were not expecting a long delay. To their surprise, God raised

75. Nolland, *Luke*, 1048.

76. Yoder, *Body Politics*, 16.

77. Ibid., 16–17.

78. Fitzmyer, *Luke X–XXIV*, 1391–92. Also see, Wilson, *Our Father Abraham*, 238, who believes that the Lord's Supper immediately supplanted the Passover.

Jesus "individually" prior to the general resurrection and to the end of the world.[79] This changed everything!

According to Luke, Jesus' followers first encountered the crucified and risen Lord on the Emmaus Road, but were unaware of his identity until "he was *at the table* with them" (Luke 24:30a). Luke adds that "he took bread, blessed and broke it, and gave it to them. Then their eyes were opened, and they recognized him; and he vanished from their sight" (vv. 30b–31).

For Wright, these four actions "cannot be mistaken" since Luke presents them "in such a way as to echo deliberately the Eucharistic action described not only in the Last Supper texts, but also by . . . Paul in 1 Corinthians."[80] In the second Lukan post-resurrection account, Jesus asks, "'Have you anything here to eat?' They gave him a piece of broiled fish, and he took it and ate in their presence" (Luke 24:41–43).[81] These food-related encounters must have caused the disciples to ask if this was what Jesus meant when he said, "I will not eat . . . . I will not drink until the kingdom of God comes" (Luke 22:16, 18)? He is now eating with them, but where was the kingdom? Had they misunderstood its nature? They must have been confused.

Luke opens Acts with the words, "After his suffering he presented himself alive to them by many convincing proofs" (Acts 1:3a). Table fellowship with the disciples certainly fits the category of a proof. Luke will also include Peter's conversation with Cornelius about how God raised Jesus from the grave and "allowed him to appear, not to all the people but to us who were chosen by God as witnesses, and who *ate and drank with him after he rose from the dead*" (Acts 10:40–41). In fact, the apostles broke bread together with the resurrected Jesus nearly a full year before the next Passover.

Then after his exaltation, the nascent church gathered regularly to eat in Greco-Roman style, and likely incorporated into their meals certain features of the Last Supper, e.g., remembering his anti-imperial exhortation against patronage, his discourses on kingdom ethics, the need to serve one another, etc. (Acts 2:42, 46; 4:32; 6:1–3; 10:48; 11:3; 16:15; 16:34; etc.).

79. Perry, *Exploring*, 30.

80. Wright, *Resurrection*, 660.

81. The Gospel of John records another post-resurrection meal encounter with Jesus: "Jesus said to them, 'Come and have breakfast.' Now none of the disciples dared to ask him, 'Who are you?' because they knew it was the Lord. Jesus came and took the bread and gave it to them, and did the same with the fish. This was now the third time that Jesus appeared to the disciples after he was raised from the dead" (John 21:12–14).

If the apostles believed that the resurrection/exaltation of Christ constituted in some way the arrival of the kingdom, then they may have seen their communal meals as a fulfillment of Jesus' words given at the Last Supper. According to Luke's account of Pentecost, this may indeed have been the case. In his sermon Peter declares:

> Fellow Israelites, I may say to you confidently of our ancestor David that he both died and was buried, and his tomb is with us to this day. Since he was a prophet, he knew that God had sworn with an oath to him that he would put one of his descendants *on his throne*. Foreseeing this, *David spoke of the resurrection of the Messiah*, saying,
>
> "He was not abandoned to Hades, nor did his flesh experience corruption."
>
> *This Jesus God raised up,* and of that all of us are witnesses. Being therefore *exalted at the right hand of God*, and having received from the Father the promise of the Holy Spirit, he has poured out this that you both see and hear. For David did not ascend into the heavens, but he himself says,
>
> > "The Lord said to my Lord,
> > 'Sit at my right hand,
> > until I make your enemies your footstool.'"
>
> Therefore let the entire house of Israel know with certainty that God has made him both Lord and Messiah (Christ), this Jesus whom you crucified (Acts 2:30–36).

Likewise, Paul states, "Christ has been *raised from the dead*, the first fruits of those who have died." He then goes on to say, "For *he must reign* until he has put all his enemies under his feet. The last enemy to be destroyed is death" (1 Cor 15:20, 26).

Pannenberg states, "The title of King (Christ) thus designates the position that is due to Jesus because of his resurrection, first of all with regard to the eschatological future, but then also as a present reality in heaven."[82] As exalted Lord, Christ now exercises God's authority over earth through the church, but "will come again as an eschatological ruler."[83] Embracing an "already, but not yet" understanding of the kingdom possibly enabled the church to view the kingdom as having arrived already in Christ and

---

82. Pannenberg, *Jesus*, 241.
83. Ibid.

manifested presently and proleptically through his body the church, while it continued to hold that the fullness of the kingdom lay in the future.

If the church held that the kingdom was inaugurated with the exaltation of Jesus to the throne of God, then it likely saw the Lord's Supper, i.e., the church's communal meal, as a fulfillment in some way of the eschatological banquet. Is it possible also that the first believers might have equated Jesus' reference to "my table" (Luke 22:30) with their own weekly communal meal, which Paul, Luke's mentor, called variously "the Lord's Supper" (1 Cor 11:20) and "the table of the Lord" (1 Cor 10:21)?

According to Nolland these communal meals "developed out of the Last Supper."[84] Waltke holds that the *Lord's* Supper derives its meaning from Jesus' interpretive words and actions on the night he was betrayed.[85] Fee characterizes it as "a continuation of the Last Supper Jesus ate with his own disciples . . . at which he reinterpreted the bread and wine in terms of his body and blood soon to be given over in death on the cross."[86] Garland concludes similarly: "The Lord's Supper was a conscious imitation of Jesus' Last Supper."[87] Horsley likewise observes, "For Paul and the tradition in which he stood, this celebration was regarded as a continuing observance of the Last Supper . . ."[88]

While the Passover and the Christian communal meal were not identical, they were related. As Yoder observes, "Some of the particular usages, such as the term *cup of blessing* (1 Cor 10:16) may reflect the Passover celebration."[89] Paul also connects the Passover to the communal meal when he says of the latter: "For I received from the Lord that which I also delivered to you" (1 Cor 11:23a); and then relates it back to Jesus' final Passover meal: "On the night he was betrayed" (11:23b). Next, he shows that the Lord's Supper mimics at least partially the Passover Jesus ate with his disciples: "[He] took bread . . . He took the cup" (11:23c, 25). Additionally, Paul links the Christian meal to eschatology just as Jesus did of the Passover: "For as often as you eat this bread and drink the cup, you proclaim the Lord's death until he comes" (11:26). Finally, he twice exhorts the Corinthians to conduct themselves at the Lord's Table in a manner

---

84. Nolland, *Luke*, 1048.

85. Waltke with Yu, *Old Testament Theology*, 462.

86. Fee, *Corinthians*, 549.

87. Garland, *Corinthians*, 547.

88. Horsley, *Corinthians*, 160.

89. Yoder, *Body Politics*, 19.

corresponding to the way Jesus at the Last Supper exhorted the apostles to conduct themselves (vv. 27, 33).

Earlier in the letter Paul reminds his readers that "our paschal lamb (Passover), Christ, has been sacrificed" (1 Cor 5:7), and in doing so, opened the door for the Lord's Supper in chapter 11 to be interpreted in like vein.

Wenham connects the two meals by strongly suggesting that the Last Supper served as "an acted parable" in which Jesus dramatically acted out in symbolic fashion "what he was about to do on the cross before his gathered disciples. And he did not just act it out before them: he involved them personally, in a terribly vivid way."[90] These actions were designed to quicken their memory of the event and that which it pointed to—his death—whenever they gathered in the future to break bread and drink wine at mealtime. They would remember and thus experience the event afresh, just as successive generations of Jews experienced the Exodus for themselves when eating their own Passover.

Just as the original Passover meal pointed to Israel's deliverance from tyranny, so the Lord's Supper speaks of an ultimate liberation to come, hence, Paul's instructions, "For as often as you eat this bread and drink the cup, you proclaim the Lord's death until he comes" (1 Cor 11:25). For Paul, the Lord's Supper stood in some way as an interim meal between the Passover and its fulfillment in the age to come. Leithart says the "feast *is* the kingdom in its present form."[91]

6.12 Conclusion

The thesis of this chapter was that while Jesus ate his last meal with his disciples he gave a countercultural reinterpretation of the Passover, signifying that it was his physical death that would open the way for a new eschatological exodus. He taught that the Passover pointed to something beyond itself, namely to the arrival of the kingdom of God. This symposium teaching provided a theological basis for the *Lord's* Supper being an anti-imperial activity.

Jesus also exhorted the disciples to reject Roman table ethics, based on stratification, patronage, and power politics, and to conduct their future communal meals in accordance with egalitarian kingdom ethics. As

90. Wenham, "How Jesus Understood the Last Supper," 14.

91. Leithart, *Kingdom and the Power*, 188 (emphasis in the original).

such, Jesus spoke subversively against the Roman domination system and the state's social agenda.

The *Last* Supper stands between the original Passover eaten by Israel and the *Lord's* Supper eaten by the church, stretching forth its theological arms in both directions.

Passover meal ——— Jesus' Last [Passover] Supper ——— Lord's Supper

Both the Passover and the *Last* Supper were subversive, anti-imperial meals—the one looking back to the first exodus and the other pointing forward to the eschatological exodus—and thus were integral in the theological formation of the Lord's Supper being an anti-imperial praxis as well.

Chapter 7 will establish that when the Jesus communities gathered to eat the Lord's Supper they participated in nonviolent political acts of resistance as they reflected and taught on God's intervention in Christ and waited for the consummation of the age when the kingdoms of the world submit to the authority of God and his Christ.

7

The Anti-Imperial Nature of Christian Meals

MEMBERS OF THE NASCENT Jesus movement carried out the mandate to preach the gospel of the kingdom, i.e., the reign of God. They saw themselves as citizens of this kingdom and their *ekklesiai* as kingdom outposts spread throughout the empire. If anyone wanted to know what the kingdom of God was like, all they had to do was attend a Christian communal banquet. There they would encounter an alternative way of life, where all people, regardless of the status assigned to them by Rome, participated fully as equals in the meal. Around the meal table believers forged a new social identity as being "in Christ." As such, they were now being fashioned into a new body politic, which represented the kingdom of God.

The thesis of this chapter is that whenever the church gathered to eat, its members participated in the kingdom of God. In doing so, they upheld the ethics of God's kingdom and opposed the ideology of the empire. Hence the meal was an anti-imperial praxis. Being a private affair, the meal also took on the character of a hidden transcript.

The banquet was a refuge, an oasis, and a town hall all wrapped up into one. It offered a time for believers to eat, pray, sing, laugh, teach, express fears and hope, have their spiritual and physical needs met, and experience God's presence in their midst through the ministry of Spirit-empowered gifts. As followers of Christ united under one roof they expressed their love for God and each other.

7.1 An Anti-Imperial Interpretation of 1 Cor 11:23–26

> For I received from the Lord what I also handed on to you, that
> the Lord Jesus on the night when he was betrayed took a loaf of
> bread, and when he had given thanks, he broke it and said, "This
> is my body that is for you. Do this in remembrance of me." In the
> same way he took the cup also, after supper, saying, "This cup is
> the new covenant in my blood. Do this, as often as you drink it,
> in remembrance of me." For as often as you eat this bread and
> drink the cup, you proclaim the Lord's death until he comes (1
> Cor 11:23–26).

Part 1 of this chapter will not give a typical exegesis of 1 Cor 11:23–26,
which can be found in many critical commentaries, but will provide a
fresh reading of the text in light of its historical context and offer an anti-
imperial interpretation.

7.1.1 The Reason for Paul's Instructions

When approaching this pericope one notices immediately the term "for"
(γὰρ), linking it to the preceding paragraph where Paul condemns certain
Corinthian members for eating before all other members have arrived (vv.
17–19), which has resulted in the latecomers going hungry and the early
birds gorging themselves and getting drunk (vv. 18–22). This violated the
egalitarian ethics of the kingdom as taught and practiced by Jesus according to the Lukan meal narratives and practiced by the early Judean churches (Luke 9:1–4; 10:4; 15:1–2; 22:24–27). Jesus called for his disciples to
practice inclusiveness at meals. They were to be "community building, and
boundary securing, which valued sacrificial service to humankind above
structures such as patronage" that mainly benefited the elites.[1]

When describing how the early church gathered for meals, Luke
writes, "They devoted themselves to the apostles' teaching and fellowship,
to the breaking of bread and the prayers" (Acts 2:42). Although similar
in form to all Roman banquets, the Christian practice of people from all
social strata eating together with everyone getting the same amount and

---

1. Based on email correspondence between Warren Carter and the author (December 15, 2007). There is some evidence that some Christian meals were sponsored
by wealthy patrons (see chap. 2), but they were not based on the principles of honor
and shame where the patron was looked upon as a superior with the clients kowtowing
to the patron. The Lord's Supper at Corinth may have been patron-sponsored. Even so,
Paul called for egalitarianism to rule the evening.

quality of food "challenged the imperial assumptions of rigid [societal] stratification."[2] Such a practice would be seen as reactionary at best and subversive at worst. In this sense, Christian meals were counter-imperial. Luke goes on to say, "All who believed were together and had all things in common; they would sell their possessions and goods and distribute the proceeds to all, as any had need. Day by day, as they spent much time together in the temple, they broke bread at home and ate their food with glad and generous hearts" (vv. 44–46). Yoder translates the last phrase, "They shared their food gladly and generously."[3] In breaking bread together they did not perform a mere symbolic act, but literally shared their food with each other. The meal had economic ramifications and challenged Rome's economic policy of abundance for the elites and mere subsistence for all others.

The problem at Corinth is that those with societal status and wealth bring their worldly philosophy and practices into the church (1 Cor 11:22). Instead of implementing a classless table, the upper class strives to maintain their honor in the church gathering, but in doing so they bring shame on the less fortunate. Paul admonishes them for failing to follow the pattern set by Jesus.

When interpreting 1 Cor 11:23–26 one must keep in mind that it is part of a wider discussion dealing with meal-related problems. Some Corinthians have been participating in meals honoring both the Lord Jesus and the gods of Rome (1 Cor 10:14–22).

Cultic banquets, especially those associated with the emperor worship, were held at prominent temple sites throughout the empire where participants made food sacrifices to the gods on behalf of Caesar. Meals were as much an integral part of the Emperor Cult as they were of the Jesus Movement. Paul may be including such meals honoring Caesar under the broader category of "table of demons." Believers must refrain from idolatrous meals because they produce bonding or fellowship between the diner and demons, and such actions provoke the Lord to jealousy (10:22).

By identifying pagan gods as demons, Paul views them as the real but hidden powers behind the empire, which seek to move it in a satanic direction. He commands the Corinthians to stop attending temple banquets where sacrifices are offered to demons, ordering them to "Flee idolatry!" (10:14).

2. Quoted from an email correspondence between Reta Finger and author (December 14, 2007).

3. Yoder, *Body Politics*, 16.

The political implications of Paul's letter and its subversive language would not go unnoticed by his readers, since he intimates the emperor cult is demonic and characterizes eating at Roman temples as "fellowship with demons" (10:20).

Many voluntary associations also sponsored cultic-type meals, and Corley believes it is feasible that Christians belonged to these groups as well as to an *ekklesia* that honored Jesus. She points to Erastus, the treasurer of Corinth as a likely candidate.[4] That Paul is troubled over the matter is an understatement.

Roman cultic banquets were eaten typically at home and consisted of food purchased from markets after it had been first offered to gods.[5] These meals included libations to the gods after dinner and before the symposium. Imperial imagery could be found on frescoes in most Roman dining rooms. Balch notes the recent discovery of a fresco in a Pompeian house of the goddess Venus caring for wounded Aeneas, which according to art historians reflects the house owner's reverence for the story of Rome's origins.[6] Balch believes this was "typical" of frescoes hanging in living rooms "in other Roman colonies like Corinth."[7] Some of the more wealthy followers of Christ likely owned homes where similar murals graced their walls. Now they were telling different stories about Christ and the origin of his kingdom.[8] This transformation from being a supporter of Roman imperialism to a supporter of God's kingdom was a radical shift and not without its difficulties.

7.1.2 Paul's Instructions as Authoritative

The first person pronoun "I" (Eγὼ) is emphasized and stands apart from the verb as the first word in the sentence. As such Paul stresses his own

4. Corley, *Maranatha*, 15, believes that "Paul does not disallow the practice but seems to affirm it." First Corinthians 10:20 appears to indicate otherwise.

5. Willis, *Idol Meat in Corinth*, treats in-depth the controversial practice of Christians at Corinth eating meat offered to idols. This work constitutes his PhD dissertation from Southern Methodist University (Dallas, TX) and was published originally under the same title by SBL, Atlanta, 1985. He concludes that the Corinthians were called to follow the pattern of love and service to others as established by Christ and not seek to please themselves (296).

6. David Balch, email correspondence with author (December 14, 2007). Also see Balch, "Zeus, Vengeful Protector," 67–95.

7. Ibid.

8. Ibid.

Subversive Meals

authority to address the issue, explaining that his knowledge was "received" (παρέλαβον), a word both Jews and Greeks used commonly to describe that which is handed down; hence, it is tradition.[9] Whether this wisdom comes "from the Lord" (ἀπὸ τοῦ κυρίου) directly by revelation or by natural transmission, it stands as authoritative. He then identifies this received knowledge as "what I also handed on to you" (ὃ καὶ παρέδωκα ὑμῖν), showing that Paul takes care to pass it on to the Corinthians, since it is intended to correct their errant meal practices.

This tradition concerns Jesus' final meal with his disciples "on the night that he was betrayed" (παρεδίδετο), i.e., the evening when he was handed over to be crucified.[10] With these words, Paul establishes a connection, at least a theological one, between the *Last* Supper—a Passover meal which Jesus reinterpreted afresh—and the Lord's Supper. Paul's concern is that the Corinthians have abandoned traditions that are rooted in the Last Supper.[11]

By mentioning that Jesus "was betrayed," Paul may desire for his readers to see the potential ramifications of their own disobedience during the communal meal. The danger of falling from grace and embracing the ways of the world is ever before Christ's disciples. The Table, therefore, must be a place where church members individually ask of themselves, "Could I be next to betray him?"

7.1.3 The Call to Mealtime Remembrance

Their actions fall short of Jesus' instructions, "Do this in remembrance of me" by focusing their attention on themselves instead of Jesus. Twice within these two verses Paul mentions Jesus' exhortation to remember him (vv. 24, 25). This dual significance is not found in the Synoptic accounts; therefore, Paul must feel his audience needs to hear it repeated. Hays observes, "The most striking feature of Paul's re-narration of the tradition

9. Barrett, *Corinthians*, 264–65. Also see Fee, *Corinthians*, 548.

10. For an excellent treatment of the verb παραδίδωμι used twice in verse 23 and translated "handed on" and "betrayed" (NRSV), see Hays, *Corinthians*, 198. Hays makes a substantial case that the term should not be translated "betrayed" in its second instance but as "handed over" thus referring to God handing Jesus over to death on our behalf. He bases this argument on similar usage in Rom 4:25; 8:32, and in Isa 53:6, 12b (LXX). Paul will again use this verb when describing how he "handed over" or passed on the gospel (15:3).

11. Keener, *Corinthians*, 95–96.

206

is the emphasis he places upon memory."[12] This leads to the question, In what manner are the reclining Corinthians to remember Christ?

The concept of "remembrance" (*anamnesis*) can be understood from either a Hellenistic or Hebrew perspective, especially when it relates to meals. The Romans held commemorative meals for dead heroes.[13] These would be similar to Memorial Day celebrations in the United States that honor soldiers who gave their lives in past wars. Is Jesus asking his disciples to remember his death in this way? Quite possibly, and this leads Dewey to exclaim, "This is a curious remembrance of a Roman criminal, whose memory [at least according to Roman standards] should be damned not raised to the heavens."[14] After all, real heroes die fighting for Rome, not in resisting Rome. The act of eating a secret meal in honor of an insurrectionist would be considered a subversive act and draw suspicion to the participants.

From a Hebrew perspective, especially as exemplified by the Passover, remembrance involved an existential reenactment of the Exodus (see chap. 3). For Paul's audience, the meal served as a venue where food and drink, stories about Jesus, and the songs and symbols helped diners to be transported back to Golgotha so they might participate in the deliverance wrought by God through the Christ event. The imagined memory elicited by the meal was meant to enable those present to experience the crucifixion and resurrection for themselves even though they were not eyewitnesses to the events. Through memory, his story becomes their story.

7.1.4 The Application of Memory

After reviewing how Jesus handled the bread and cup at the Last Supper, Paul applies the actions to his own audience: "For as often *as you* eat this bread and drink the cup, *you proclaim* the Lord's death until he comes" (v. 25).[15] With this statement, Paul links remembrance to proclamation.

Remembrance produces action, i.e., action based on the memory. The call of modern worldwide Jewry to "remember the Holocaust, lest

---

12. Hays, *Corinthians*, 198.

13. Jeremias, *Eucharistic Words*, 82. Also see Horsley, *Corinthians*, 161.

14. Statement made by Art Dewey to author in correspondence of December 12, 2007.

15. Neither Jesus nor Paul instructs their disciples to repeat so-called "words of institution." That the reference "Do this" is a call *to eat the meal* in remembrance of Christ becomes clear in 1 Cor 11:25.

we forget" implies a committed effort on the part of Jews to make people aware of the dangers of anti-Semitism. Likewise, to remember Christ's death was a challenge for the church to make people aware of the menace of tyranny and unrestrained power. When the church "proclaims his death" at mealtime, it exposes the Roman domination system for what it really is: a vessel of death and destruction.

To remember and proclaim Christ's death is, by implication, a call to oppose all domination systems—state, social, religious—that seek to rule by force, coercion, and aggression. Bieler and Schottroff characterize the Lord's Supper "as a counter-liturgy to violent state politics that deny the dignity of the human body."[16] Yet, it was not characterized by violent public demonstrations or unethical scheming. Rather these subversive protests took place at the meal table. To join in a common meal that memorialized a perceived enemy of Rome was to identify with the enemy and his mission. Such an observance, if brought out into the open, might bring down the wrath of Rome upon one's head. It implies facing suffering and oppression in the same way as Jesus, i.e., a nonviolent way.

7.1.5 Paul's Use of "Proclaim"

How does one "proclaim" (καταγγέλλετε) Christ's death? By using a present passive indicative verb, Paul seems to imply that the very act of eating the meal together constitutes proclamation, i.e., the meal which honors a criminal of the state speaks loudly in its own right.

Hays agrees and affirms, "the community's sharing in the broken bread and the outpoured wine is itself an act of proclamation, an enacted parable that figures forth the death of Jesus 'for us' and the community's common participation in the benefits of that death."[17] The errant way the Corinthians eat the meal, showing no regard for the least of the brethren, but adopting an arrogant attitude is more in line with Roman table manners than kingdom ethics. Garland observes that "Paul contrasts Jesus' self-sacrifice at the Last Supper with the Corinthians selfishness at their supper."[18] While they may refer to their meal as a "Lord's Supper," they do not eat it in accordance with Jesus' instructions on humility and servanthood. Right words and wrong practices are contradictory, and send an

---

16. Bieler and Schottroff, *Eucharist*, 13.

17. While Hays, *Corinthians*, 199–200, recognizes the meal itself as the proclamation, he does not relate it to subversion.

18. Garland, *Corinthians*, 547.

unclear message. Hays states, "The problem is not that they are failing to say the right words but that their enactment of the word is deficient: their self-serving actions obscure the meaning of the Supper so thoroughly that it no longer points to Christ's death."[19]

Jeremias, Bornkamm, Barrett, and Fee, however, opine that proclamation relates to a verbal presentation of the gospel.[20] Paul uses the same verb (καταγγέλλω) on other occasions when referring to verbal proclamation (1 Cor 9:14; Acts 4:2; 13:5). If the Passover meal serves as an example, in which Jews over the centuries rehearsed aloud about how Pharaoh oppressed them, of their cries for deliverance, of divine plagues, the slaughtering of the lamb, the original Passover meal and God's miraculous intervention and deliverance, then proclamation at the Lord's Table might involve a verbal presentation of some kind as well, possibly a narrative of Roman oppression and the new Exodus wrought by the Christ event.

The debate over the nature of proclamation cannot be relegated to an either/or proposition but includes both the act of eating and possibly a vocal *kerygmatic* message. In this Corinthian meal and symposium context, Paul also encourages the congregation to utilize Spirit-inspired utterance, e.g., prophecy (1 Cor 14:3). He offers a hypothetical scenario of an "unbeliever" who enters the symposium and hears a prophetic message, whereupon he is "reproved by all and called to account." With "the secrets of the unbeliever's heart . . . disclosed," he bows before God and worships him, declaring, "God is really among you" (1 Cor 14:24–25).

7.1.6 Frequency, Perspective and Duration

Three other aspects of Paul's application of the Last Supper need to be discussed. First, the Corinthians are called upon to remember and proclaim Christ's death "as often" as they eat together. In using this phrase, Paul distinguished the Lord's Supper from Passover, since the former is not an annual feast but a regular and oft-repeated meal, which honors Jesus.[21] While the Lord's Supper was not a traditional Passover meal,[22] nor "a new

---

19. Hays, *Corinthians*, 200.

20. Jeremias, *Eucharistic Words*, 106–7; Bornkamm, *Jesus of Nazareth*, 141; Barrett, *Corinthians*, 270; Fee, *Corinthians*, 556.

21. Fee, *Corinthians*, 555.

22. For instance, there is no reference to a paschal lamb included in Paul's instructions on the Lord's Supper.

Passover,"[23] it clearly evolved out of the Last Supper/Passover tradition. Both find their meaning in relationship to salvation history, with the Passover finding its fulfillment at the consummation of the age, and the Lord's Supper serving as an interim meal.

Second, it must be remembered that both Luke's and Paul's intended audiences were reading the narratives of the Last Supper and Lord's Supper from a post-resurrection perspective. While they remembered that Christ died by the hands of the powerbrokers, they also know that God raised him from the dead. "In celebrating their fellowship around the table, the early Christians testified that the messianic age, often pictured as a banquet, had begun."[24] To participate in the meal was to participate in the "already" aspect of the kingdom. The dawning of a new kingdom posed "an implicit threat to Roman imperial order,"[25] proving that the method of nonviolent resistance and kingdom humility ultimately wins over the dominating forces of evil.

Third, the church is called to remember and repeat the story of Christ's passion with an eye toward the *parousia* ("until he comes"). This eschatological memory, combining a backward look ("proclaim his death") and a forward look ("until he comes"), "mingles memory and hope, recalling his death and waiting his coming again."[26] At the supper table, the community recalls Christ's death "in the interval between the cross and the *parousia*."[27]

Just as Paul opened his letter asking God to strengthen the Corinthians as they "wait for the revealing of our Lord Jesus Christ" (1:7), so he closes it with "Maranatha," i.e., "Come, Lord Jesus" (16:21), showing that the church was to approach the Lord's Table in anticipation of the Lord's return.[28] This is confirmed by the same use of *Maranatha* at the end of the Eucharistic instructions in the *Didache*, the manual of the early church.[29]

23. Horsley, *Corinthians*, 161.

24. Yoder, *Body Politics*, 18.

25. Ehrensperger, *Paul*, 116.

26. Hays, *Corinthians*, 199. Barrett, *Corinthians*, 271, likewise affirms, "The church as it met round the supper table would form a living link between the beginning and end of the interim between the two comings of the Lord."

27. Hays, *Corinthians*, 199.

28. Ibid., 292. By using the Aramaic *Marana tha*, rather than the Greek rendering of the word, Paul addresses the exalted Lord and cries out for him to return and usher in the kingdom which he mentions in 15:20–28.

29. *Did.* 10:5–6 where the Lord's Supper is related to the kingdom of God.

Stendahl writes, "The Eucharist is primarily the banquet. It is the banquet on the way toward the consummation and toward fulfillment."[30]

Despite his ignoble execution, Jesus was raised as Lord and would return as Judge. Past memories provide future hope, and this should affect how the church lives in the interim. Those facing poverty, slavery, persecution, and all that the powers throw at them would be vindicated just like their Lord. The eating of this proleptic kingdom meal provided all participants with a foretaste of the powers of the world to come, knowing that resurrection and victory lay in the future for those who suffer under the restrictions of Rome. Their fortunes would be reversed just like the Lord's.

7.1.7 The Bread and Cup and Forgiveness

Paul mentions how Jesus opened his last meal in typical Jewish fashion by taking and praying over "a loaf of bread" (v. 23), but then surprisingly calls it his "body . . . for you" (v. 24). Since the metaphorical nature of the body was discussed in chapter 6, suffice it to say the body represented Christ's physical being, i.e., his person.[31]

Paul next paraphrased Jesus' words, "the cup is the new covenant in my blood." The covenant that God ratified through the death of Christ (v. 25) now is being "visibly articulated in the Lord's Supper."[32]

The one whom Rome crucified as a scoundrel was the Messiah who now reigns by virtue of the resurrection. The church likewise faces tribulation at the hands of the same imperial powers that killed Christ, but it does so without despair, knowing that God established the new covenant by means of Christ's death. Just as God vindicated him through resurrection, so will he vindicate all those who identify with Christ in his weakness and humility, and refuse to turn their backs on God's kingdom regardless of the cost. As the recipients of the covenant, they must carry out the kingdom mandate as Christ had done. This includes inviting all to the communal table including sinners, the poor, and the disenfranchised, accepting them as equals in the kingdom of God. Unfortunately, the Corinthians are acting more like people of the present evil age who seek to maintain stratification. While professing allegiance to the kingdom of God, they practice Roman table ethics. Yoder avers that there is a "social meaning of the cross

---

30. Stendahl, "New Testament for the Doctrine of the Sacraments," 56.

31. Thiselton, *Corinthians*, 878.

32. Ibid., 885.

in relation to enmity and power. Servanthood replaces dominion, forgiveness absorbs hostility."[33]

To be bound with others in a covenant relationship with God includes obligations and responsibilities to the community, including individual and corporate faithfulness to God. By eating the communal meal in a disrespectful manner, the Corinthians have violated the covenant. They are suffering from amnesia by forgetting the night on which Jesus was betrayed; thus, Paul's twofold emphasis on remembrance.

Paul concludes that if the Corinthians' mealtime actions are status-related as defined by the state and not egalitarian as defined by the kingdom, the erring brethren are "celebrating their own condemnation" (1 Cor 11:29).[34]

7.2 Other Ways the Christian Meal can Be Viewed as Anti-Imperial Praxis

Part 2 of this chapter deals with other anti-imperial aspects of the Christian meal and shows that those activities which Christians have associated traditionally with worship actually took place within a meal setting and carried anti-imperial overtones.

7.2.1 The Lord's Supper and Reclining Women

Although aristocratic women in the empire were beginning to attend some Roman banquet functions with their husbands, they rarely reclined.[35] The Christian communal meal opened the way for women to participate and to exercise leadership at mealtime. This countercultural practice was likely a shock for all concerned, causing no little discomfort. In likening the eschatological banquet to a wedding feast, a meal in which all women not only attended but took significant responsibility, Jesus implies women can be active participants in the proleptic kingdom meal.

Luke tells of Mary "who sat at the Lord's feet" (παρακαθεσθεῖσα πρὸς τοὺς πόδας τοῦ κυρίου) as he taught and "listened to what he said" (ἤκουεν τὸν λόγον αὐτοῦ), while her sister Martha stayed in the kitchen

---

33. Yoder, *Politics of Jesus*, 134.

34. Yoder, *Body Politics*, 18.

35. This was the case even into the second-century CE. Lucian, *Symposium*, 8–9, describes sitting rather than reclining as "womanish."

fulfilling the traditional role of women at mealtime in Roman and Jewish culture (Luke 10:38–42). In the "preferred reading" παρακαθεσθεῖσα is a reflexive aorist passive participle, which can be rendered, "having seated herself beside" or "toward his feet" (πρὸς τοὺς πόδας).[36] Fitzmyer understands Luke as portraying women in a new role as disciples, whom Jesus welcomes by his side, a position not available to them in Judaism.[37] When Martha complains that her sister is not helping with the "many tasks" (v. 40), Jesus answers, "Martha, Martha, you are worried and distracted by many things (πολλά); there is need of only one thing. Mary has chosen the better part (τὴν ἀγαθὴν μερίδα), which will not be taken away from her" (vv. 41–42). With this mild rebuke Jesus makes three points. First, he labels Martha's activities as distractions. Second, he praises Mary's preoccupation as "the better part." Third, he will not instruct Mary to leave her position that she may assist Martha.

According to Corley, the "setting" for this exchange "is clearly that of a meal."[38] Not only is Martha preparing food, but Jesus uses puns that normally are associated with meals, such as Mary choosing τὴν ἀγαθὴν μερίδα ("the better part" or "portion"), a term "used to describe a dish at a meal."[39]

The text does not reveal whether this conversation takes place before, during or after the meal. Nor does it reveal if Mary is sitting at Jesus' feet in front of the table or reclining on the couch at his feet. In either situation, according to Luke, Jesus refuses to allow social norms to diminish Mary's role as a disciple.[40] The Lukan readers would likely turn to this narrative to validate female leadership in their community.

Paul locates women at the meal and encourages them to exercise their spiritual gifts during the symposium, to which they comply enthusiastically (1 Cor 11:5; 12:4–11).[41] The role of women at the Christian banquet is more than ancillary. Still, the picture is sketchy. Did the women get to recline at the *triclinium*, or did they sit in chairs along the outer wall of the *andron* separated from their spouses? Unless the church met in the home of a wealthy member with an extra large dining room or upper room,

36. Fitzmyer, *Luke X–XXIV*, 893.

37. Ibid., 892–93.

38. Corley, *Private Women*, 137.

39. Ibid., 137–38.

40. In the Gospel of John, Martha is depicted as serving while Mary is again portrayed at his feet anointing him with expensive oil (12:1–3).

41. Chapter 8 deals comprehensively with the gift of prophecy during mealtime.

reclining would be limited likely to a few. This might offer an explanation as to why women were having to ask their husbands questions about what was being said, leading to Paul's instructions, "If there is anything they desire to know, let them ask their husbands at home" (1 Cor 14:35). Nevertheless, Paul's exhortation for women to be silent did not extend to their use of prophecy.

To allow all to recline equally regardless of worldly status was a cultural paradigm shift that flew in the face of the Roman domination system as well as the traditional practice of Judaism, and should be seen as an act of resistance.

7.2.2 The Lord's Supper and Reclining Slaves

Slaves played an intricate but subservient role in Roman banquets, carrying out duties ranging from preparation of the meal to serving it.[42] They also delivered invitations, rounded up guests at the appointed time, washed their feet upon arrival, brought food and wine to the table, and occasionally removed party crashers from the dining hall (Matt 22:13). They did not recline at the table or share in the festive joy of table fellowship. If they ate at all, they did so in another room, sitting rather than reclining.

At the Lord's Table, however, Christian slaves were to have equal status with all diners and not be relegated to menial tasks. As seen in chapter 5, Jesus called for an egalitarian meal table. At his Last Supper he spoke against the imperial practice of leaders lording over their subjects and presented an alternative model of servant leadership, using himself as an example of the latter. He said, "I am among you as one who serves." In the early church, the apostles and then deacons waited on tables (Acts 6:1–6).

In John's gospel account, Jesus takes on the role of a slave by washing the disciples' feet, leaving them an example to emulate (John 13:3). His uniquely placed symposium action caused quite a discussion (vv. 4–13).[43] Then he applies the lesson, "If I then, your Lord and teacher, have washed your feet, you ought to wash one another's feet" (v. 14). The emphatic position of second person plural pronoun "you" along with the "ought" which conveys obligation indicates they in particular are to follow suit and not expect slaves to wash their feet at mealtime.[44]

---

42. See Larsen, "Early Christian Meals and Slavery," 5–6.

43. Feet were usually washed before a meal not in the middle of it. By waiting to perform this action, Jesus draws particular attention to it.

44. Plato, *Symposium*, 9. In this scene Agathon greets Aristodemus, a latecomer

Since foot washing in the first century was not a symbolic act but a real life necessity, these instructions would have been taken most naturally as literal. The immediate context also lends itself to such an interpretation. In verse 16, Jesus says, "For I have set you an example that you also should do as I have done to you. Very truly, I tell you, servants are not greater than their master, nor are messengers greater than the one who sent them. If you know these things, you are blessed if you do them" (John 13:16–17). That the church took these instructions seriously is evidenced in Paul's list of qualifications for widows to receive living assistance. He includes as a prerequisite that she "washed the saints' feet" (1 Tim 5:10).

According to John's gospel, Jesus' foot washing comments at the Last Supper were intended to teach that all people are to be treated as equals. The greatest must take on the role of a slave and serve. Slaves must be treated as brothers and sisters and invited to recline at the dinner table.

The *Therapeutae*, a first-century Jewish semi-monastic movement, likewise practiced a form of egalitarianism by requiring its members to perform in servant roles toward dinner guests.[45] It did not use slaves at meals. The difference between the *Therapeutae* and the *ekklesiai*, however, was the latter not only refused to cast slaves as table waiters but treated them as equals "in Christ" and thus invited them to recline next to the wealthiest members.

As stated in chapter 2, since Roman meals were a social institution used to maintain stratification, the Christian practices, reflecting kingdom ethics, went against societal norms and can be seen as acts of resistance.

While Jesus called his disciples to embrace and live by a kingdom ethic, rarely did they succeed. D'Arms claims that even at Christian meals slaves cooked and served the food, and went virtually unnoticed despite their presence.[46] Evidence also shows that there were slave owners even among elite converts.[47] This is borne out by Paul's exhortation that Christian slaves should obey their "*believing* masters" (1 Tim 6:1–2).

In his letter of exhortation to a Christian slaveholder Paul admonishes Philemon to receive back as a free man, Onesimus, his runaway

---

to his banquet, and bids "a slave [to] wash his feet that he might recline." This was the accepted and expected custom. Slaves washed guests' feet. Thus, the "who" as well as the "when" of washing feet was significant. Jesus was now asking his disciples to perform as slaves.

45. Philo, *Contempl. Life* 9.70–72.

46. D'Arms, "Slaves at Roman Convivia," 171–83.

47. For a comprehensive examination of slavery in the early church see Glancy, *Slavery*.

slave: "Perhaps this is the reason he was separated from you for a while, so that you might have him back for ever, no longer as a slave but as more than a slave, a beloved brother—especially to me but how much more to you, both in the flesh and in the Lord. So if you consider me your partner, welcome him as you would welcome me" (Phlm 15–17). It seems that Paul expects Philemon to receive Onesimus as a reclining member at the Lord's Table. Remember, this is a letter sent not only to Philemon, but "to the church in your house" (v. 1), indicating it was to be read aloud to all at mealtime! If Onesimus was the courier of the epistle, the believers may have made room on the *triclinium* for him immediately.

Despite the inconsistency, some Christians owned slaves in the empire. Slavery was tied to the economy, and stratification was so entrenched that wealthy believers may have had a difficult time making the transition to egalitarianism. One might liken the situation to post-Civil War days in the United States. Despite President Lincoln's Emancipation Proclamation in1863, Southern slaveholders, including Christians, were reluctant to show respect to the freed slaves. Only a century later with the election of Barack Obama, its first African American president, has America begun to exorcise its demons.

Paul and other apostolic leaders were realists. While they preached the ideal, they did not expect to eliminate slavery within the empire. That would not occur until the kingdom of God arrived in its fullness at the *parousia*. Hence their instructions for slaves were to "remain in the condition" in which they were called and serve their masters without violence (1 Cor 7:17–24); yet if possible they were to obtain freedom. Apostles, however, expected all disciples to treat everyone equally at the Lord's Supper regardless of the status assigned to them by Rome and to acknowledge, "There is no longer Jew or Greek, there is no longer slave or free, there is no longer male and female; for all of you are one in Christ Jesus" (Gal 3:27–28; also see Col 3:11). At the table they experienced freedom for a short time and got a foretaste of the age to come when they would be free from Roman domination.

In his parable about the unexpected arrival of the kingdom, Jesus uses slavery as a backdrop: "Be dressed for action and have your lamps lit; be like those who are waiting for their master to return from the wedding banquet, so that they may open the door for him as soon as he comes and knocks. Blessed are those slaves whom the master finds alert when he comes; truly I tell you, he will fasten his belt and have them sit down to eat, and he will come and serve them. If he comes during the middle of the night, or near dawn, and finds them so, blessed are those slaves" (Luke 12:35–38). In this parable Jesus not only assigns favored status to the obedient slaves, but reverses the roles between master and slave, with the former now serving the latter. This teaching, which speaks of the kingdom's delay and arrival, portrays a future in which social status is no longer observed and slaves eat at the master's table. In like manner, Jesus' disciples were expected to practice this kingdom ethic now. Unfortunately, as seen in 1 Cor 11:17–34, their attempts were not without difficulty or contention. Pure equality is not obtainable in the "already" kingdom, but will become a reality at the messianic banquet.

7.2.3 The Reading of Anti-Imperial Letters during the Symposium

The early church read aloud texts and letters when their members congregated for worship. In this sense they followed traditions established in the OT.[48] In the past decade, Greco-Roman meal scholars have located these readings within the context of the reclining banquet. The symposium or second tables offered the best opportunity to read letters that had arrived from traveling apostles, prophets, and evangelists, or those ministering permanently in another city. Nearly all the Epistles, prior to their inclusion in the NT canon, were addressed specifically to a local *ekklesia* or group of *ekklesiai* to be read openly before the entire gathering (see Rom 1:7; 1 Cor 1:2; 2 Cor 1:2; Gal 1:2; Eph 1:1; Phil 1:1; Col 1:1; 1 Thess 1:1; 2 Thess 1:1; Phlm 2; 2 John 1; 3 John 9; Rev 1:4).

To the assembly at Colossae Paul writes: "Give my greetings to the brothers and sisters in Laodicea, and to Nympha and the church in her house. And when this letter has been *read among you*, have it *read also in the church of the Laodiceans*; and *see that you read also the letter from Laodicea*" (Col 4:15–16). Likewise, he exhorts the believers at Thessalonica, "Greet all the brothers and sisters with a holy kiss. *I solemnly command you by the Lord that this letter be read to all of them*" (1 Thess 5:26–27).

---

48. The public reading of the Scriptures traces its origins back to Moses, when he "took the book of the covenant, and read it in the hearing of the people" (see Exod 24:4–8) He then instructed subsequent generations to follow suit: "you shall read this law before all Israel in their hearing" (see Deut 31:9–13). The following references contain a few instances when the Scriptures were read aloud to the assembled people (Josh 8:30–35; 2 Kgs 23:1–3; Neh 7:73—8:3, 8; 13:1–3; 2 Chr 34:24; Jer 36:8).

Some were circular letters and intended to be distributed and read in several churches. In addition to letters, "Gospels were read, and stories told and composed."[49]

These gospels, texts, and letters addressed the many issues facing the churches as they attempted to represent the kingdom of God within an empire that claimed the right of manifest destiny, i.e., the divine authority of the gods to rule the earth on their behalf. According to Carter, the apostles and others wrote these letters to "dispute Rome's claims, asserting over against them that God's purposes will eventually hold sway."[50] These were bold Christian communiqués offering ethical instruction that opposed Rome's claim over and vision for the world. Regarding the Gospel of John, for example, Thatcher asserts, "writing a gospel can itself be understood as one of the many hidden transcripts that operated within the Johannine community along with other forms of covert resistance."[51]

The early church also read aloud from the Hebrew Scriptures. This is confirmed by the reminder to Timothy, serving as leader at Ephesus: "give attention to the public reading of scripture" (1 Tim 4:13).[52] Since the sections of the OT that would be of particular interest to Christians included the Psalms and prophecies that foretold of God's coming restoration, they too, would have been anti-imperial in substance.

7.2.4 Praying during the Symposium

Luke's first entry after telling of the three thousand converts on Pentecost is, "They devoted themselves to the apostles' teaching and fellowship, to the breaking of bread and the prayers" (Acts 2:42). This verse is descriptive of a "christianized" Roman banquet (see chap. 2), with prayer as one of the symposium components.

49. Standhartinger, "Response to Hal Taussig's *In the Beginning*," 2.

50. Carter, *Roman Empire*, 99.

51. Thatcher, *Greater than Caesar*, 29. The act of writing a counter gospel that challenged the empire's good news agenda was nothing less than subversive and traitorous (31).

52. Unlike modern times, very few copies of the Hebrew Scriptures were privately owned. Scripture portions were rare and costly, and since most people in the first century were peasants, only wealthy individuals, if so inclined owned copies. Therefore, the typical followers of Christ were only exposed to Scripture when they gathered at the Lord's Table. How the church obtained its copies of the OT is unclear.

If prayer as taught by Jesus in Luke 11:2–4 is a model for Christian prayer ("Lord teach us to pray"), then it becomes clear why prayer is antithetical to Roman ideology.

> He said to them, "When you pray, say:
> Our Father in heaven, hallowed be your name.
> Your kingdom come, your will be done on earth as it is in heaven
> Give us each day our daily bread
> And forgive us our sins,
> for we ourselves forgive everyone indebted to us.
> And do not bring us to the time of trial, but deliver us from the evil one."

Prayer addressed to the God of Israel as "Father" (a father other than Jupiter) in the name of Jesus—an executed criminal against the state—would be considered anti-imperial and subversive. To ask the living God that his will be done on earth is a political request that seeks to replace Jupiter's reign and Rome's divine claim for manifest destiny. Thus, prayer can be seen as a covert act of resistance or defiance, i.e., a hidden transcript, toward the prevailing government. These prayers were not said in public, but in private at mealtime.

The call for God to provide bread for the day was a direct rejection of the Roman system of patronage. As Crosby notes, "Rome's patron/client dynamics undergird every level of political economy of the empire. The political patron/client relations in the daily life of the empire mirrored the patron/client relationship among the religion's gods and goddesses all the way to Zeus or Jupiter. To petition some god outside the empire's religion for bread would undermine the entire system."[53] Christian symposium prayers surreptitiously challenged the imperial economic apparatus.[54] They rejected Caesar as chief benefactor of the empire and Jupiter as the Father of heaven. These kinds of prayers were subversive and treasonous because they called for the demise of an oppressive regime.

7.2.5 The Lord's Supper and Anti-Imperial Songs

All Roman banquets characteristically featured songs during the symposium portion of a formal supper.[55] Christian banquets were no exception.

53. Crosby, *Prayer*, 120.

54. Ibid.

55. Harland, *Associations*, 71–73, speaks to the importance of singing and music at association-sponsored meals. He writes, "Hymns were an elaborated, sung prayer that also honored the deities whose help was requested" (71). Plato, *Symposium*, is a

When believers gathered for the communal meal they also sang heartily during the symposium.[56]

Unlike modern denominations, the early church did not have a standardized hymnbook. Many of the songs that the Christians sang at their symposia were first embedded in the gospels and letters that comprise the NT. According to Taussig, the embedded NT songs followed the standard forms of other songs found in the Mediterranean region of the first century, only they contained Christian content.[57] When viewed in light of the political milieu, the patron-client system and the emperor cult that made up the social fabric of the Roman Empire, Christian symposium songs, which proclaimed Jesus to be the exalted Lord (the "little tradition"), stood in opposition to the ideological claims of the empire (the "great tradition"). As musical "hidden transcripts" they were subversive and counter-imperial in nature.[58] Often read aloud, prayed, or sung during the symposium, these embedded songs provided worshippers with a voice as they gathered for their weekly meals (Acts 4:23–26). Just as Roman symposium songs were sung throughout the empire to honor Caesar and implore the gods, so Christian songs served a similar purpose to honor God and Christ.

Rome used many means to control the masses, including military force, economic deprivation, stratification, and taxation. Outward domination, however, rarely succeeded in winning the hearts of the people. As long as the vanquished retained vivid "memories of life before exile," and as long as they dreamed of liberation and yearned for a return to their former existence, they were "a threat to the empire."[59] Until these memories can be replaced and the imagination "reshaped into the image of the empire, the people are still free."[60] Therefore, Rome sought to secure and

standard text that describes a typical Greek *deipnon*. He tells how after supper, Socrates and the other guests "had sung hymns to the god" (11). He also includes Pausanias's speech, which mentions "singing" during the symposium (18). As discussed in chapter 6, following tradition, Jesus not only teaches and engages his disciples in lively discussion at the symposium, but includes music. Matthew notes, "When they had sung the hymn, they went out to the Mount of Olives" (Matt 26:30; Mark 14:26).

56. Smith, *From Symposium*, 30, 179, 211–14.

57. Taussig, *In the Beginning*, 104.

58. As stated in chapter 2, "Christian" communal meals were not the only venues where anti-imperial sentiments were expressed musically. Other associations, composed of conquered peoples, often gathered to sing praises to their homeland or national deities. The main difference between Christian symposium songs and those of other associations was that the content of the Christian songs proclaimed Jesus to be the cosmic ruler of the universe.

59. Walsh and Keesmaat, *Colossians Remixed*, 82.

60. Ibid.

monopolize the imagination of its subjects.[61] Meals eaten in the name of Caesar, libations poured out to the Roman deities, and symposium activities, particularly songs exalting empire and emperor, were successful methods used to capture the hearts of the masses and win their loyalty. One might liken the positive results to the enthusiastic patriotism produced by American Independence Day celebrations with their cookouts, abundance of beer, fireworks displays, flag waving, and rousing songs that pull at the heart strings. Only the callous can resist the power of such emotion.

The Use of Psalms in the Christian Symposium

In describing a typical Christian symposium at Corinth, Paul writes, "When you come together, each has a hymn (ψαλμὸν), a lesson, a revelation, a tongue, or an interpretation" (1 Cor 14:26). Singing of hymns is but one of many symposium activities one might expect to experience at a communal meal. Hengel asserts that Hellenized Jewish believers would interpret ψαλμὸν in light of its use in the LXX to mean a song from the Psalter.[62] If such is the case, the Corinthians sang OT Psalms during the symposium portion of their community meal.

By their very nature Psalms are meant to be sung. Most are praise hymns that extol and glorify God. Anderson remarks, "Considering that the psalms were intended to be recited or sung to musical accompaniment, it is not surprising they are cast in poetic form . . ."[63] This structure made them easy to memorize and sing when put to music.

The admonition to a congregation in Asia Minor, "Do not get drunk with wine, for that is debauchery" (Eph 5:18a) also fits the context of a banquet symposium, especially when it is followed by the words, "but be filled with the Spirit, as you sing psalms (ψαλμοῖς) and hymns (καὶ ὕμνοις) and spiritual songs (καὶ ᾠδαῖς πνευματικαῖς) among yourselves, singing and making melody to the Lord in your hearts" (5:18b).[64]

In the context of a congregational gathering in which prayer, healing and confession take place, and hence a Lord's Supper, James adds these instructions: "Are any cheerful? They should sing songs of praise (ψαλλέτω)" (Jas 5:13).

61. Ibid.
62. Hengel, "Hymn and Christology," 174.
63. Anderson, *Out of the Depths*, 21.
64. Spiritual songs will be discussed later in this section.

New Testament writers quote or allude to dozens of Psalms in their Letters to the churches. While it is impossible to determine exactly which Psalms were sung during worship, we know that certain ones are quoted more often than others in the text of the NT: Psalm 2, for example, is referenced nine times; Psalm 8, four times; Psalm 22, eleven times; Psalm 69, twelve times, Psalm 91, five times; Psalm 110, thirty-three times; and Psalm 118, fourteen times. Since the Psalter was the hymnbook of the OT, it is probable that nascent Christian congregations used the Psalms in a similar manner.

Several popular Psalms, known as "Royal Psalms," announce God's reign over the nations.[65] The way they are referenced and quoted in the NT often suggests that the early church interpreted them from a messianic perspective, proclaiming that God raised Jesus to reign over his kingdom. Moyise, however, giving Psalm 8 as an example, argues that Christians did not unanimously view all such Psalms in the NT "as inherently messianic."[66] Whether the church looked at Royal Psalms through a christological lens or merely acknowledged that God ruled the cosmos, each ψαλμὸν may have been sung at one time or another during the Christian symposium. In either case, to sing of God and/or Christ ruling the world would be an affront to Roman ideology. To sing of one's allegiance to the kingdom of God rather than to the empire in a Roman banquet setting was seditious political activity.

Hymns and Spiritual Songs

While several songs are located in the Gospels and General Epistles, this section will limit its discussion to those embedded in what are commonly called the Pauline Epistles. When the congregation heard the instructions read, "Be filled with the Spirit, as you sing psalms and hymns and spiritual songs among yourselves, singing and making melody to the Lord in your hearts" (vv. 18b–19), they would discern that these instructions referred to the proper way to conduct oneself during a symposium.[67]

---

65. Chilton, *Pure Kingdom*, 31–55, examines thoroughly the scope of the kingdom in the Book of Psalms. He then proceeds to show how Jesus' understanding of the kingdom was based on the same characteristics found in the Psalms.

66. Moyise and Menken, *Psalms in the New Testament*, 186.

67. In non-Christian Greco-Roman banquets, songs also accompanied the libation. Paeans were offered as praises to the various gods as the libations were being poured out to them. Taussig, *In the Beginning*, 104–10, believes that christological hymns accompanied similar libations made to Christ at the pivot point of the meal.

Besides Psalms they sang "hymns and spiritual songs." To what do these terms refer? Smith and Klinghardt list two genres of songs associated with Greco-Roman meals: a *paean* and a *skolion*.[68] A *paean* was praise or prayer sung at a private meal such as a wedding and formal dinner or at a public feast and was addressed to a deity like Apollo or Artemis.[69] A *skolion* was a metric song accompanied by a lyre or pipe, sung during the symposium and spoke of valiant political acts.[70]

Christian *hymns* like *paeans* were addressed to God and/or Christ, and *songs* like *skolions* contained lyrics that extolled mighty acts of victory. The song of Moses (Exod 15:1–8 quoted in Rev 15:1–4) is an example of a *skolion*, and thus was a likely choice as a symposium song. The early church was not the first to use it this way. According to Philo the *Therapeutae* sang the victory song at their Passover feasts.[71]

While Christian hymns and songs may have technically differed from one another, they were both political in nature because they addressed God or spoke about his mighty acts in salvation history. With this understanding, hymns and songs can be deigned the Christian equivalent of their Roman counterparts and would have been sung at the Lord's Table. Scrutiny will be given to determine the anti-imperial content of the following three songs.

Philippians 2:6–11

After admonishing the church at Philippi to follow a path of humility, Paul quotes a well-known Christian hymn/song[72] which points to Jesus as Lord and victor over his enemies:

As discussed in a previous chapter, this researcher finds no support that believers ever poured wine onto the ground as a sacrifice to Christ. A much stronger case can be made for the Christian hymns being sung during the symposium portion of the meal.

68. Smith, *From Symposium*, 30; Klinghardt, *Gemeinschaftsmahl und Mahlgemeinschaft*, 118–20.

69 Gurgel, "Running Head," 4–5.

70. Smith, *From Symposium*, 30; Klinghardt, *Gemeinschaftsmahl*, 118–20.

71. Philo, *Contempl. Life*, XI, 84–88.

72. Because Phil 2:6–11 does not praise God in the form of a *paean*, a minority of commentators are reluctant to identify the text as a hymn, but as prose only. See Collins, "Psalms, Philippians," 361–72. Also see Fee, *Philippians*, 191–97, who characterizes the paragraph as "exalted prose." On the other hand, Martin, *Hymn of Christ: Philippians 2:5–11*, devotes an entire volume to exploring the nature and interpretation of this paragraph as a christological hymn. Martin and Hawthorne, *Philippians*, 99–100, note that there is an "almost universal agreement" that this passage

who, though he was in the form of God,
> did not regard equality with God
> as something to be exploited [grasped],
but emptied himself,
> taking the form of a slave,
> being born in human likeness.
> And being found in human form,
he humbled himself and became obedient
> to the point of death—even death on a cross.

Therefore God also highly exalted him
> and gave him the name
> that is above every name,
so that at the name of Jesus
> every knee should bend,
> in heaven and on earth and under the earth,
and every tongue should confess
> that Jesus Christ is Lord,
> to the glory of God the Father (Phil 2:6–11).

No scholarly consensus exists regarding the origin of this song. Was it written by Paul or did it exist already and he merely quoted it to support a point?[73] If quoted, Paul's readers were likely familiar with the content, and singing it already at communal meals.[74] This song not only evokes memory of Christ, but contains strong anti-imperial political language. Most commentators, however, miss this aspect of the song because they approach it from a theological perspective, giving little attention to its sociohistorical context. The mass of literature dealing with this passage far exceeds the scope of this book, but the main interpretations need to be noted in order to compare them to an anti-imperial rendering of the text. Gorman succinctly summarizes the eight major interpretations of the hymn.[75] They include that the hymn:

1. offers a christological interpretation of the fourth Servant hymn of Isaiah

---

"constitutes a signal example of a very early 'hymn' of the Christian church." O'Brien, *Philippians*, 186, describes these verses "as an early Christian hymn in honor of Christ" and says they constitute the "most important section in the letter to the Philippians."

73. Lohmeyer, *Der Brief an die Philipper, Kolosser und an Philemon*, 90–91, for instance, argues that Phil 2:6–11 contains non-Pauline words and style.

74. Martin, *Hymn of Christ*, 28, 94–95 supports Lohmeyer by placing the hymn in a "Eucharistic context."

75. Gorman, *Elements of Biblical Exposition*, 130–31.

2. speaks of Christ's pre-existence, incarnation, and glorification
3. compares and contrasts the Christ with Adam, who grasped for godhood[76]
4. presents a Christian reinterpretation of a Gnostic redeemer myth[77]
5. portrays Christ as emptying himself of deity and operating only as a human
6. represents Christ as the ultimate example of self sacrifice and humility
7. depicts Christ as sovereign Lord who is worthy of worship
8. promises resurrection and eternal life to all based on Christ's resurrection

Rather than accepting one of these standard theological perspectives, another option is open to the interpreter. He or she can view it through the lens of history and treat it as a song that mimics other songs being sung at symposia throughout the empire that exalt Caesar. Only this song contains a Christian and therefore countercultural response to Roman ideology. When one examines the text in its historical context, she or he discovers the phrase "equality with God" (ἴσος θεός) to be a designation used equally to describe the Roman emperor (considered to be the Son of Jupiter, Rome's highest god), and thus the song becomes a subversive political statement as much as a theological one.[78]

As leader of Rome, Caesar ruled on behalf of god. When Paul opened the song and ascribed the same descriptive phrase (ἴσος θεός) to Jesus, he insulted Roman sensitivities, since they believed no one deserved the same status as the emperor.[79] But unlike the emperor, Jesus did not exploit his position as Son of God (God's kingly representative), but chose rather to live a humble existence, taking the status of a slave. Even when facing crucifixion he did not use his authority or resort to force to defeat his adversaries and free himself from the executioner's stake, but trusted God

76. Dunn, *Christology*, 114–21, presents a convincing case for this view, which is very attractive from both biblical and theological perspectives.

77. Käsemann, "A Critical Analysis of Philippians 2:5–11," 25–48. Lack of evidence exists that Gnosticism existed at the time this epistle was written.

78. Heen, "Phil 2:6–11 and Resistance to Local Theocratic Rule," 125.

79. Jesus was charged before the Roman governor with claiming to be a king, a role reserved for Caesar (Luke 23:2); thus, he was a usurper and a threat to the nation. Likewise, at Thessalonica, the outraged mob charges Jason's house and accuses Paul of "acting contrary to the decrees of Caesar, saying there is another king—Jesus" (Acts 17:7).

for the outcome. In fact, the song reveals that his "death" was an act of obedience to God (v. 8). This means that the one whom Rome crucified was fulfilling God's will. While Pilate, on behalf of Caesar, exercised the full force of the empire, Jesus exercised the full faith of the kingdom of God.

The second stanza declares that God vindicated and exalted him above his adversaries to the status of "Lord" (vv. 9–11). This section opens with the word "therefore," showing that exaltation is the result of Jesus having chosen a path of obedient submission to God. In the end, he is given the status for which he does not seek. "Jesus, not Caesar, has been a servant and is now to be hailed as *kyrios*."[80] To assert that "Jesus is Lord" meant that Caesar was not! This pronouncement was an insult to both Rome and those Jewish elites who conspired with them to put Jesus to death. While they sought to destroy him, God's desire was to exalt him.

It was such assertions that "put Paul on a collision course" with governmental authorities.[81] According to Acts, during his evangelistic visit to Philippi, a mob hauls Paul and Silas before the magistrate and accuses him of "teach[ing] customs which are not lawful for us being Roman to receive or observe" (Acts 16:21).

Ironically, God gives "a name that is above every name" (v. 9) to the one that Rome charges as being a fraud and pretender. In reality Caesar is the "pretender to a throne that rightfully belongs to Jesus."[82]

As Lord of the cosmos "every knee" is morally obligated to bow at the name of Jesus and "every tongue" to confess that the one rejected and put to death by the Jewish and Roman elites is Messiah and Lord. That includes Caesar, the Senate, the high priests, the Sanhedrin, and the demon powers behind them. One can easily see how such a message would not be well received by the power brokers who use domination to control the masses.

Had the church not taken the song's words so seriously, the idea that Jesus was Lord would have seemed ludicrous. Yet this was what the churches regularly sang about in their symposia and the message they proclaimed to the masses—that Jesus is Lord of all! Is it any wonder the church was fervent in its mission, or that Rome and the Temple were just as fervent in their opposition?

When believers raised their voices in song at the communal meals they were committing subversive acts of resistance toward imperial Rome.

80. Wright, "Paul's Gospel and Caesar's Empire," 174.
81. Borg, *Jesus: Uncovering the Life*, 279.
82. Heen, "Phil 2:6–11 and Resistance," 150.

By declaring a common criminal to be Lord of the universe they challenged the emperor's divine right to represent heaven on earth. Given that believers sang these anti-imperial songs behind closed doors, they were able to spread their subversive doctrine clandestinely without immediate threat of retaliation from the government. However, they knew their actions were potentially volatile, should word hit the streets. Believing that they, like their master, might be called upon to suffer and face death for their obedience to God's mission, they did not retreat but placed their lives in the hands of God who could either intervene or vindicate them in the resurrection.

The purpose or thrust of this song is found in the verses immediately preceding it: "Do nothing from selfish ambition or conceit, but in humility regard others as better than yourselves. Let each of you look not to your own interests, but to the interests of others. Let the same mind be in you that was in Christ Jesus" (Phil 2:3–5). Jesus' followers are exhorted to follow his example. The pathway of self-sacrifice, not self-importance, is the door to exaltation. The way of peace and victory is counterintuitive to normal human thinking that stresses self-promotion and trusts devious means to get ahead. Christ's kingdom offers a counter-imperial ethic, an alternative to Caesar's, in which one trusts God for the outcome.[83]

Verse 15 further attests to the political nature of this song's message. Paul admonishes the believers to "shine like stars in the world" (φαίνεσθε ὡς φωστῆρες ἐν κόσμῳ) while they live "in the midst of a crooked and perverse generation" (μέσον γενεᾶς σκολιᾶς καὶ διεστραμμένης). Georgi notes that these two instructions are similar to the political instructions Cicero offered to the excellent political leaders of his day.[84] Paul presents the same advice as Cicero, but gives it to the church, and he equates the empire with the perverted world from which the church will one day be rescued.

The church saw itself as an alternative *polis* to the Roman ideal. Rome's time was limited. By raising Jesus from the dead, God exposed Rome's use of force and violence as an ineffective means of bringing peace. The church, which gave its loyalty to Christ alone, represented reality from God's perspective. It was a present manifestation of the future kingdom, which would be revealed in God's time. Empowered by the eschatological

---

83. Another even more subtle trap for Christ's followers is the danger of adopting a triumphal attitude, which motivates them to exploit their relationship to God and to embrace a militant form of Christianity that is out to conquer the world. This is the opposite of what Jesus did and is what Paul is opposing in Phil 2:6–11.

84. Georgi, *Theocracy*, 72–78.

Spirit, it knew it could not fail in its mission. With the resurrection of Christ, the new creation had already begun. The future belonged to him and to his followers.

As the small Jesus movement, scattered throughout the empire and comprised mainly of disenfranchised and marginal peasants, along with a smattering of elites, sang praises to their Lord above Caesar and to their kingdom over Rome, they formed their identity as the end-time people of God who were willing and ready to follow the example of their master. Mealtime was the experience that gave them a voice and bonded them together.

Believing that Jesus was Lord over the entire world, his followers gave him allegiance and united together under his rule to carry out his kingdom agenda. The churches of the Mediterranean were not merely a cabal of like-minded people who passively waited to be taken out of the world and transferred to paradise. They viewed themselves as Christ's active agents preparing the world for his return when he would set up his universal kingdom and every knee would bow.

Colossians 1:15–20

The letter to the Colossians contains another embedded song that Christians likely sang regularly at their banquets.[85] When read in light of Roman domination, rather than as an answer to some form of proto-Gnostic heresy, one can discern that each stanza is actually a challenge to Rome's imperial claim of supremacy over the world. In this context, Col 1:15–20 constitutes a hymn/song of subversion. It contains terms and titles usually associated with Caesar alone. That means everyone in the empire would be familiar with language of the Colossian hymn. The shock would not come until they realized the lyrics were exalting Christ instead of Caesar.

> He is the image of the invisible God, the firstborn of all creation;
> for in him all things in heaven and on earth were created, things
> visible and invisible, whether thrones or dominions or rulers
> or powers—all things have been created through him and for

---

85. Just as some scholars question the nature of Phil 2:6–11as being a hymn, Col 1:15–20 faces similar scrutiny. Dunn, *Epistles to the Colossians and to Philemon*, argues, "The marks of hymnic or poetic form are clear enough" (83). Klinghardt, "Chances and Limitations," 2, on the other hand, takes a different view and expresses his conviction that both texts along with John 1:1–14 were "written text for readers, but were never sung." He does affirm, however, that songs were part of ritual meals and that a need exists for scholarly exploration of this much neglected topic (3). Refer back to footnote 58 for further discussion.

him. He himself is before all things, and in him all things hold
together.

He is the head of the body, the church; he is the beginning,
the firstborn from the dead, so that he might come to have
first place in everything. For in him all the fullness of God was
pleased to dwell, and through him God was pleased to reconcile
to himself all things, whether on earth or in heaven, by making
peace through the blood of his cross (Col 1:15–20).

This christological hymn, divided into two strophes, speaks of Christ's
twofold relationship to: 1) creation (vv. 15–17) and 2) the church (vv.
18–20).[86] When viewed in context of empire, it becomes apparent that the
hymn's lyrics are subversive and anti-imperial in substance and design.
Just as Moses' song of victory on the heels of the Passover/Exodus helped
to evoke Israel's new social imagination as an alternative society living
under the reign of God, so does the Colossian hymn.

STROPHE ONE

First in relation to creation, the song identifies Christ, not Caesar, as God's
representative, i.e., "the image (εἰκὼν) of the invisible God" (v. 15). Images
of Caesar permeated the entire empire.[87] Everywhere one turned Caesar
was there. His "divine" image appeared on coins, statuary, frescoes, jew-
elry, and paintings located in the marketplace, city square, public baths,
gymnasia, palaces, and temples to name a few.[88] The all-pervading image
made it seem as if Caesar was omnipresent. As the "son of god" (Zeus/
Jupiter), he represented god on earth.

---

86. While acknowledging that this passage can be interpreted from a purely theological standpoint, dealing with such issues as hypostasis, proto-Gnosticism, angelic
intermediaries between heaven and earth, etc., one is left with the conundrum that
Dunn, *Colossians*, 86, voices: "It remains unclear what light the passage sheds on the
situation at Colossae. Why should this hymn be cited, and why here?" This is an unset-
tling dilemma because there must be a reason and a setting for the hymn. Reading
the hymn as a response to emperor worship and Roman domination provides both
the logic and the historical context. For more traditional interpretations the reader is
directed to Dunn, op cit; Harris, *Colossians and Philemon*; Schweizer, *Colossians*; Wall,
Colossians and Philemon; Wright, *Epistles of Paul to the Colossians and to Philemon*.

87. Walsh and Keesmaat, *Colossians Remixed*, 63, drawing upon Zanker, *Power
of Images*, 266–73, provide a long list of private and public places where the image of
Caesar could be found.

88. Walsh and Keesmaat, *Colossians Remixed*, 63.

Second, the song claims that Christ created "all things" in the universe. That means that everything ("visible and invisible") owes its existence to him—*"thrones or dominions or rulers or powers"*—including Caesar, the Senate, native retainers and the powers that stand behind the empire (v. 16a). Nothing is excluded, heavenly or earthly. This is expressly political language.

Third, "all things" exist to serve him, i.e., they owe Christ their allegiance (v. 16b). They were "created through him and *for* him." While Caesar and his cohorts are oblivious to this fact, the singing church is well aware it belongs to and lives for Christ. This inside information means that Christ's peasant-disciples understand the nature of reality better than the Roman and Jewish elites.

Finally, Christ not Caesar brings about order and keeps the world from falling into chaos (v. 17). The stanza rings out, "in him all things hold together." In other words, he is the bringer of peace.

STROPHE TWO

Strophe two makes four key points regarding Christ and his relationship to redemption. First, Christ is "head of the body, the church," i.e., the ruler of a new humanity or society. This authority comes through his resurrection (he is "the firstborn from the dead)." The stated purpose is "so that he might come to have first place in everything." In a world where "divine" Caesar is head of the body politic and has preeminence over all political structures and social institutions, those hearing this song would immediately recognize that Paul is "contrasting Jesus with Caesar."[89] This song could only be seen as "treasonous."[90]

Second, the subversive hymn links Christ's preeminence to God's good pleasure: "For in him all the fullness of *God was pleased* to dwell" (v. 19) and "and through him *God was pleased* to reconcile to himself all things, whether on earth or in heaven" (v. 20). This means that Christ is God's authorized and empowered earthly representative who brings about peace. Such a claim challenges both the claims of Caesar and his goal of universal *Pax Romana*.

89. Ibid., 89.

90. Ibid., 11. Walsh and Keesmaat make a compelling case throughout their book that Colossians is a subversive text that calls for its readers to embrace an alternative kingdom vision for living that liberates rather than to accept the empire's vision that enslaves. Like other commentators, however, they do not connect Col 1:15–20 to its possible use as a symposium song.

Third, God's peace plan "to reconcile to himself all things" is accomplished through Christ's humiliating death ("by making peace through the blood of his cross"), and not through Caesar's powerful and successful military campaigns or policies of domination (v. 20b). Since universal peace comes through God's Spirit-led man, particularly his act of suffering, then Caesar's aspiration for peace through force is doomed to fail. In fact, the resurrection of Christ revealed its utter failure to maintain peace through "law and order." Thinking it could quash the Jesus movement, Rome used its most fearful and powerful weapon—crucifixion of the leader—to drive fear into the hearts of Jesus' followers. His resurrection not only exposed the limitations of power to accomplish the desired goal, but galvanized the disciples into a faithful company who trusted God to defeat Roman tyranny. Although the hymn never mentions the emperor by name or title, hearers and singers would immediately understand it to be contrasting Christ with Caesar because the lyrics make references to the "image of God," "firstborn," and "first place," all monikers which Roman society attributed to Caesar alone.[91]

In relationship to Christ, Paul uses the comprehensive phrase "all things" four times in the song, along with such phrases as "all creation" and "all the fullness of God." The mention of "thrones or dominions or rulers or powers" (v. 16), which modify "things visible and invisible" (v. 15), likely refers to both human and demonic rulers.[92] When Christ's rule is placed in the context of "heaven and earth," nothing remains over which he does not have authority.[93] In comparison to God's ultimate plan in Christ, Caesar's efforts must have seemed miniscule and insignificant.

As believers sang Col 1:15–20 during their meals, they must have sensed that they were participants in events of historic proportions. Rome's days were numbered. The kingdom of God would prevail.

First Timothy 3:16

First Timothy 3:14–16 contains a portion of another familiar hymn, both subversive in purpose and anti-imperial in design, which Paul quotes

91. Ibid., 89–90.

92. For purposes of this essay, the exact identity of these powers is not essential to the argument that Christ and God rule the world, not Caesar and the Roman deities. Many scholars have sought to identify these categories, among them Caird, *Principalities and Powers*; Berkhof, *Christ and the Powers*; Wink, *Naming the Powers*; Yoder, *Politics of Jesus*; Boyd, *God at War*.

93. Walsh and Keesmaat, *Colossians Remixed*, 91.

in his correspondence to Timothy. Like many other songs and hymns found in the Epistles, it is impossible to determine its source.[94] After giving instructions regarding the qualifications for deacons and elders,[95] he reminds his young protégé, "I hope to come to you soon, but I am writing these instructions to you so that, if I am delayed, you may know how one ought to behave in the household of God, which is the church of the living God, the pillar and bulwark of the truth" (1 Tim 3:14–15). The purpose clause ἵνα εἰδῇς πῶς δεῖ ἐν οἴκῳ θεοῦ ἀναστρέφεσθαι ("that . . . you may know how one ought to behave in the household of God") not only places a moral obligation on the readers to obey, but identifies the location where the expected obedience is to take place: ἐν οἴκῳ, which he describes as the ἐκκλησία θεοῦ ζῶντος ("church of the living God"). By equating the "*household* of God" with the "*church* [or association] of the living God," Paul uses metaphors that are familiar to his readers. Homes served as places of pagan worship throughout the empire where loyalty to the imperial "house of the emperor" was reinforced.[96] The "implicit contrast" between the house of God and the house of Caesar would not go unnoticed. God, not Caesar, is the father to whom loyalty is to be given.[97] As the "pillar and bulwark of the Truth" the church is to guard the truth, which Marshall identifies as the gospel.[98]

These instructions are followed by the song of affirmation that likely contains the core content of the gospel:

> Without any doubt, the mystery of our religion is great:
> He was revealed in flesh,
> vindicated in spirit,
> seen by angels,

---

94. Towner, *Timothy and Titus*, 277.

95. Ehrensperger, "Striving for Office," 1–19 examines critically and answers convincingly the commonly held belief that 1 Tim 3:1–17 affirms a hierarchical order within the house church which tended toward superiority of leaders over members and eventually to possible domination, thus following the organizational pattern found in homes throughout the empire, which also served as cultic centers of worship with the father as head. Rather than accommodating the culture, Ehrensperger views the structure as "a mere survival strategy" (10). While a discernable hierarchy does appear in 3:1–17, Christian leaders were expected to serve rather than lord over their charges. In one sense, the house church mimics imperial practices, but in doing so, turns the system on its head with the leaders serving rather than dominating. In this manner, the church is practicing a hidden form of resistance.

96. Ibid., 8.

97. Ibid., 14.

98. Marshall, *Pastoral Epistles*, 521.

proclaimed among Gentiles,
believed in throughout the world,
taken up in glory (1 Tim 3:16).

When exegetes attempt to derive the meaning of this text without giving consideration to the politico-sociological atmosphere in which it was written, they correctly interpret it through a christological lens, but usually against the background of either pre-Gnosticism or some form of Hellenistic Judaism or Christianity.[99] But when read in light of Roman imperialism, the six-strophe hymn takes on an altogether different meaning. Here is how the hymn might be understood when interpreted in this way.

The hymn's prosaic opening, καὶ ὁμολογουμένως μέγα ἐστὶν τὸ τῆς εὐσεβείας μυστήριον ("Without any doubt, great is the mystery of religion"), takes on a more precise meaning when it is remembered that this letter is being sent to Ephesus, the capital of a great mystery religion and the site of the Temple of Diana. It was here that Paul started a riot, culminating with citizens crying out: "Great is Diana of the Ephesians" (Acts 19). In Roman mythology Diana was Jupiter's daughter and Apollo's twin sister. When seen in this historical light, the text counters the claim that Diana is great. Thus, this song contradicts the claims of the empire.

The poetic portion begins with the singular relative masculine pronoun "He" and contextually refers to Christ. Paul then unveils the "mystery" of the Christian faith by using six main verbs to depict what has happened to Jesus. First, Christ was shown to be a man ("revealed in flesh"). The messiah was not a mythical or apocalyptic figure but a real person who lived "among humankind."[100]

Second, he was ἐδικαιώθη ἐν πνεύματι ("vindicated in spirit"), i.e., God declared innocent the one whom Jewish and Roman elites put to death as a fraud and an insurrectionist. In doing so, they condemned God's chosen spokesperson. But God declared him not guilty by raising him from the dead.

Third, he was ὤφθη ἀγγέλοις ("seen by angels"), which means he was seen either by heavenly beings at his ascension, demonic beings over whom he triumphed or by earthly messengers at his resurrection. Either way, they attested to the fact that he rose from the dead.

99. For a summary and evaluation of the various interpretations, see Gundry, "The Form, Meaning and Background of the Hymn," 203–22. Gundry gives no consideration to Roman religious ideology when seeking to understand the text, and thus in this writer's opinion, misses the hymn's political significance and anti-imperial nature.

100. Towner, *Timothy and Titus*, 279.

Fourth, he was ἐκηρύχθη ἐν ἔθνεσιν ("proclaimed among the Gentiles"), i.e., the nations. The eyewitnesses successfully spread the news of Christ's resurrection beyond the boundaries of Palestine, across the entirety of the empire to the very nations that Rome has conquered and claimed as her own. The gospel has even reached Rome.

Fifth, he was ἐπιστεύθη ἐν κόσμῳ ("believed in throughout the world)." Many throughout the Roman Empire who once gave their allegiance to Caesar had now submitted to Christ as Lord. The kingdom agenda was succeeding. Rome's stranglehold on the world was tenuous and her plans unraveling.

Sixth, he was ἀνελήμφθη ἐν δόξῃ ("taken into glory)," i.e., God exalted him to the ultimate place of authority, placing Christ at his right hand from which he reigns over heaven and earth.

These lyrics make a radical claim—the Jewish messiah, by the power and approval of God, reigns as Lord over the cosmos. As his authority spread far and wide and his following increased, Caesar's declined. From Paul's perspective, Christ could not be defeated, since he was "taken into glory" and sat down in the presence of God. This revolutionary mealtime song would be a source of strength for the disciples and motivate them to be faithful to Christ, regardless of the cost.

The very essence of the song challenges Rome's ideology. One can only imagine the response when the letter with this embedded song reached Ephesus and was read aloud at mealtime. Possibly one saint raised her voice in song and others joined in as they rejoiced in their symposium celebration.

7.3 Conclusion

The thesis of this chapter was that at mealtime believers experienced and practiced kingdom ethics among themselves. The Lord's Supper provided a safe venue and opportunity for them to express their love for God and each other through tangible means and to exercise Spirit-empowered gifts as God manifested his presence in their midst. By their actions, Christians broke with acceptable Roman banquet protocols that were instituted to uphold the socioeconomic and political platforms of the empire. Rather than embracing a patron/client model of feasting, based on a rigid caste-like system, the followers of Jesus strove to practice classless fellowship that included slaves reclining side by side with elites, women taking leadership roles, and everyone ministering to the Lord and each other.

In addition, this chapter demonstrated that anti-imperial prayers were offered, texts were read aloud, and songs were sung that exalted Christ as Lord rather than Caesar. Chapter 8 will take an in-depth look at prophecy as an anti-imperial Christian symposium activity through which God guided the church as they waited for Rome's demise and the kingdom's arrival.

8

Prophecy as an Anti-Imperial Meal Activity

8.1 Introduction

THE FIRST CHRISTIANS GATHERED together at meals, where they garnered strength and support from each other to live in a world hostile to the kingdom of God. These meals followed the pattern of a typical Roman banquet, which included first and second tables, i.e., the supper proper followed by the symposium; but, instead of gathering to honor Caesar or a pagan deity, they met in the name of their exalted Lord Jesus. When they came together they expected Christ to manifest his power through the gifts of the Holy Spirit, which served as evidence that he was among them. During the symposium portion of the banquet, Christians prayed, worshipped, received instruction, and ministered to each other.

Hence, a first-century-CE Lord's Supper was an anti-imperial celebration. For twenty-first-century believers, the thought of a meal being a countercultural event seems foreign. This is mainly due to the modern practice of "eating on the run" and equating food with sustenance rather than with societal mores.

In the ancient world the meal was "about much more than eating."[1] It was a social institution, serving to reinforce the Roman way of life, i.e., social stratification, patronage, Rome's divine right to rule the world, and so forth. When viewed in this context one discerns why Christian meals

---

1. Taussig, *In the Beginning*, 22.

in general and symposium activities in particular were considered to be counter-imperial.

Chapter 2 mentioned the symposium activities found in non-Christian meals, showing them to consist of drinking mixed wine, oracles, lectures, dancing, theatrics, musical entertainment, corporate singing, readings, and occasional sexual escapades, to name a few, sponsored by the patron-host, who often served as the symposiarch.[2]

According to Philip Harland, a leading researcher on voluntary associations in the Mediterranean of the first- and second-centuries CE, prophetic utterances were also a part of the symposium. Association members used this portion of the banquet as a venue to make sacrifices to their patron gods and seek their advice. Harland cites one instance where members of a builders' guild appealed to Apollo about whether or not they should begin a construction project on a theatre in Miletus. Apollo responds through the voice of a prophet and calls for them to offer libations to Athena and Herakles.[3]

Much like its Roman counterpart, the Christian banquet featured prophetic speech. In his Lord's Supper discourse (1 Cor 11–14), Paul discusses the use of prophecy more than any other symposium pursuit. He indicates that prophecy is an acceptable and expected activity for a Christian symposium, and has uplifting value to all participants (1 Cor 14:3). At the same time, the inspired words served to subversively undermine the empire and its agenda. Rather than calling upon participants to seek advice or pay homage to the authorized Roman gods, Christian prophecy exalted Christ as Lord and served as a vehicle through which God revealed his divine will to the diners, which often stood opposed to the Roman imperialistic agenda.

---

2. Although everyone in the empire participated in banquets, most were either peasant farmers or urban artisans who eked out a living without the aid of a patron, living in small houses or tenement apartments. In such cases, banquets were likely cooperative events with each participant contributing to the meal. Apart from the absence of a patron, peasant banquets followed the pattern of every Roman banquet: a meal (with poorer quality of food) and a symposium. In other words, they copied the behavior of their overlords.

Oakes, *Reading Romans*, 44–45, however, points out that while all non-elites were poor there were different levels of poverty. For example, among artisans, a cabinet-maker was better off economically than a stone worker, and might own a house with a "rear-facing dining room," where he could host a meal. He might even serve as a patron of some sort to other craft workers.

3. Harland, *Associations*, 69–70.

To date, no scholarly study has examined first-century Christian prophecy within a mealtime context. For instance, while Aune, Gillespie, and Grudem adequately define prophecy and even place it within a general worship setting, they fail to examine it as a vital symposium activity.[4] This is likely due to the fact that research comparing Christian communal meals to Roman meals is a relatively recent undertaking. Because the discipline is so new, even the most respected contemporary scholars in this field, such as Hal Taussig and Dennis Smith, have yet to address this issue in a satisfactory manner.[5] To this author's knowledge this chapter will be the first attempt to examine Christian prophecy as a counter-imperial symposium activity.

The following statement serves as a thesis for this chapter: Prophecy, as an anti-imperial praxis, played a prominent role during Christian symposia. The discussion will be limited to selected texts which place prophecy within this setting. It will not examine instances of prophetic utterances which occur outside the locus of a meal.

Prophecy in the NT appears to be regarded as divinely inspired utterance which came by revelation, was addressed to God's people at mealtime, and given to provide knowledge of God's will. It is referred to as a gift of the Holy Spirit and is to be used for the benefit of the Christian community (1 Cor 12:10, 28; 13:1; 14:1–4). While the person who gives a prophecy might be called a prophet, he or she does not necessarily hold the office of a prophet. Boring describes a "Christian prophet" as an "inspired spokesperson for the risen Jesus, who received intelligible messages that he or she felt impelled to deliver to the Christian community, or as a representative of the community, to the general public."[6]

---

4. Gillespie, *First Theologians*, a revision of Gillespie's doctoral dissertation from Claremont Graduate School (CA), does not mention the Lord's Supper or symposium. For Gillespie prophecy in the first century took place during the worship service, which is left undefined and assumed to be like modern-day worship experience. Grudem's PhD dissertation, *Gift of Prophecy in 1 Corinthians*, assumes prophecy's place is within a local church worship, but like Gillespie, he fails to link it to the symposium. Aune's *Prophecy in Early Christianity*, considered one of the most comprehensive and detailed studies on prophecy in modern times, fails to mention its connection to the Lord's Supper. He does establish, however, that prophecy is mainly manifested during the gathering of the saints.

5. While doing exemplary research, Taussig, *In the Beginning*, 47, and Smith, *From Symposium*, only mention in passing that prophecy was a symposium activity.

6. Boring, *Continuing Voice of Jesus*, 38.

8.2 Prophecy in the Book of Acts

The Gospel of Luke and the Acts of the Apostles comprise a two-part narrative of Christianity's beginnings.[7] The latter volume opens with an explanation that whereas the Gospel of Luke chronicled selected events in Jesus' life until he ascended to God's right hand, Acts will chronicle his continued and active ministry on earth through the Spirit (Acts 1:1–2). Thus, Peter explains to the confused bystanders who have just witnessed an outbreak of tongues and prophecy that these manifestations came from the exalted Lord Jesus as he "poured out" the eschatological Spirit upon his followers (Acts 2:33).

This opening scene in Acts sets the stage for the remainder of the book and declares in graphic style that the one whom Rome executed as an insurrectionist is alive and continues to work wonders. Through the energizing presence of his Spirit, Christ now resides in the midst of his followers, and his ministry cannot be stopped.

Since the Gospel of Luke places prophetic words on Jesus' lips (Luke 9:21; 17:20–37; 18:31–33; 21:7–37), it is no surprise to find Jesus speaking through prophecy to his church in the Book of Acts (2:33; 3:22; 4:29–30; 9:11–16; 10:13–15; 23:11).

Acts identifies by name nine persons as prophets or individuals who prophesy.[8] There are an additional four references to anonymous or unnamed prophets (Acts 2:17–18; 11:27; 19:1–6; 20:23). Aune makes a distinction between those who hold the office of prophet and those who occasionally prophesy. The latter he places within "a congregational setting."[9] This might be shortsighted since in Acts prophets also ordinarily prophesy in a group or communal setting (Acts 11:27–28; 13:1–3; 15:32; 21:18).

Some prophecies were predictive in nature (Acts 11:17; 20:23; 21:10–11), while other prophetic utterances provided direction for ministry (Acts 13:1–3; 16:6–10). On one occasion a Spirit-inspired message helped resolve the issues facing the Jerusalem Council (Acts 15:28). Most commonly, prophecies offered comfort to believers or exhorted them to persevere in the faith (Acts 15:32).

---

7. For a discussion on the historicity of Acts, see chapter 4n118. For an excellent discussion of the genre of Acts see Witherington, *Acts*, 4–14.

8. Agabus (Acts 11:27–28; 21:10–11), Barnabas, Simeon, Niger, Lucius, Manaen, and Saul (13:1), Judas and Silas (15:32), Philip's four daughters (21:8–9).

9. Aune, *Prophecy*, 195.

Since prophecy emanates from the Lord and reveals God's will to his people, over against Rome's agenda, it can be identified by both its purpose and content as counter-imperial.

8.2.1 Pentecost: The Outpouring of the Spirit and Eschatological Manifestations

As one hundred and twenty followers of Jesus gathered in Jerusalem, most likely to celebrate the Jewish Feast of Pentecost, they were all caught off guard when "suddenly from heaven there came a sound like the rush of a violent wind, and it filled the entire house where they were sitting. Divided tongues, as of fire, appeared among them, and a tongue rested on each of them. All of them were filled with the Holy Spirit and began to speak in other languages, as the Spirit gave them ability" (Acts 2:1–4). Bewilderment followed as a crowd began to assemble, with some declaring the events to be miraculous and others labeling them as drunken antics (vv. 5–14). In an effort to clarify matters, Peter stands and assures them that the phenomenon is not the result of overindulgence, and then proceeds to explain:

> No, this is what was spoken through the prophet Joel:
> "In the last days it will be, God declares,
>   that I will pour out my Spirit upon all flesh,
>   and your sons and your daughters shall prophesy,
>   and your young men shall see visions,
>   and your old men shall dream dreams.
> "Even upon my slaves, both men and women,
>   In those days I will pour out my Spirit;
>   and they shall prophesy" (Acts 2:16–18).

In some sense, Peter views the outpouring of the Spirit and the accompanying manifestations as the fulfillment of God's purposes for earth. Whereas Joel speaks of these events as taking place "hereafter" (Joel 2:28), Peter identifies them with the "last days," and thus gives them "a sharper eschatological note than Joel."[10] These words instill a sense of urgency for the disciples' mission.[11] For the early church, the era leading up to the consummation of the kingdom would be characterized by dreams, visions, and prophecy, which in this instance, at least, involved Spirit-inspired

10. Spencer, *Journeying Through Acts*, 45.
11. Ibid.

utterances "about God's deeds of power" (2:11) that each person clearly understood in his or her own tongue. The prophecies would transcend gender ("your sons *and* daughters shall prophesy"), age ("your young men . . . and your old men . . ."), social classifications ("*Even* upon *slaves* . . . shall prophesy"), and all ethnic categories ("upon all flesh").

Peter links the unusual manifestations to Jesus' death at the hands of the Romans and their surrogates, and his vindication by God through the resurrection, which gave him victory over his enemies (Acts 2:22–31). As Spencer observes, "After suffering (unjustly) the utter shame of crucifixion, he was elevated to the place of highest honor in the universe."[12] Peter brings his sermon to a climax with these words, "Therefore *being exalted to the right hand of God*, and having received from the Father the promise of the Holy Spirit, *He poured out this which you see and hear*" (v. 33). Bruce remarks, "He who had earlier received the Spirit for the public discharge of his own earthly ministry had now received the Spirit to impart to his representatives, in order that they might continue, and indeed share in, the ministry which he had begun."[13] Peter then quotes Ps 110:1, "The Lord said to my Lord, 'Sit at My right hand till I make your enemies your footstool'" and concludes, "Therefore, let all the house of Israel know assuredly that God has made this Jesus whom you crucified, both Lord and Christ" (vv. 34–36).

The sermon on Pentecost is a strong exhortation that, contrary to Rome's claim, Jesus was not defeated, but now reigns and is in the process of bringing his enemies to their knees. He cannot be stopped. From his throne on high he is directing and supernaturally empowering his earthly disciples to do his bidding. Through his representatives, the reigning Lord now offers his enemies a choice: submit to his rule, receive forgiveness and the gift of the Spirit, or in time become his footstool. The course of history is set.

The eschatological nature of Peter's Spirit-initiated communication, which extols Christ and pronounces judgment on the empire, marks it as anti-imperial.

Throughout the Book of Acts, Luke records numerous instances where the Lord speaks to his people through prophetic means to guide and console them as they seek to advance the cause of his kingdom in direct opposition to the will of the empire and its cohorts (Acts 9:4–12;

12. Ibid., 48.
13. Bruce, *Acts*, 67.

10:9–17; 11:27–30; 13:1–2; 15:32; 16:6–10; 18:9–10; 20:22–23; 21:4–9; 22:7–17; 26:14–19; 27:23–25).

A brief examination of prophetic utterances given within a symposium setting will now be undertaken.

8.2.2 Acts 11—Agabus the Prophet

The first mention of Christian prophets occurs in Acts 11, after Barnabas's and Saul's year-long ministry at the local church in Antioch:[14] "At that time prophets came down from Jerusalem to Antioch. One of them named Agabus stood up and predicted by the Spirit that there would be a severe famine over all the world; and this took place during the reign of Claudius. The disciples determined that according to their ability, each would send relief to the believers living in Judea; this they did, sending it to the elders by Barnabas and Saul" (Acts 11:27–30). From the text one readily discovers that Barnabas and Saul are teaching within a congregation setting[15] which means that their ministry likely takes place during the symposium or "second tables," after the evening meal was eaten. In this setting Agabus, a traveling prophet from Jerusalem, stands and predicts a famine "over all the world" during the rule of the Roman emperor Tiberius Claudius, who reigned 41–54 CE (v. 29). "Wandering prophets were part and parcel of early Christianity in Syria (Acts 21:10; *Did.* 12:1–5), just as settled prophets (Acts 13:1–3; 21:8–9; *Did.* 11:1–2)."[16] Whether traveling or local, Christian prophets ministered within the congregation setting. Since Luke is a serious student of history, he knows that no worldwide famine occurred at this time. Therefore, he likely uses οἰκουμένην ("the world") in a hyperbolic sense, a practice not unusual for his day.[17] Torrey, however, believes that Luke incorrectly uses οἰκουμένην to refer to "the land," i.e., Judea.[18] Talbert asserts that grain shortages were common in the

---

14. Fitzmyer, *Acts*, 481.

15. Aune, *Prophecy*, 266. The Western text connects verses 27 and 28 through the use of the additional words: "and there was much rejoicing; and when we gathered together, one of them Agabus, by name spoke . . ." See Bruce, *Acts*, 229–30.

16. Talbert, *Reading Acts*, 116. Likewise, Witherington, *Acts*, 372.

17. Winter, "Acts and Food Shortages," 65–69.

18. Torrey, *Composition and Date of Acts*, 21, suggests that in translating from Aramaic, the language spoken by Agabus, into the Greek, Luke incorrectly chooses *oikoumene* to refer to Judea. Also see Bruce, *Acts*, 230, who mentions a Judean famine between 45 and 48 CE, when Helena, queen-mother of Adiabene and a Jewish proselyte, distributed food and money to authorities in Jerusalem for famine relief.

first-century Roman world and quotes Seneca, "We were threatened with
. . . lack of provisions . . . very nearly at the cost of the city's destruction
and famine and the general revolution that follows famine."[19] Witherington holds that "in all the world" can naturally be translated "in the whole
Empire" and places the famine between 45–46 CE or slightly thereafter.[20]
Whatever the case, the prophetic revelation from the exalted Lord motivates the believers to send relief to the church at Jerusalem.

By mentioning the reign of Claudius, Luke is doing more than placing the prophecy within an historical timeline. He is also identifying the
prophecy as anti-imperial. As emperor, Claudius was the ultimate patron
of his people. He was the first ruler since Augustus to be deified.[21] Yet,
Christ, not Claudius, has foreknowledge of the tragedy ahead and inter-
venes to meet the needs of his people. Where Claudius and the Roman
gods fail to anticipate the needs and make provisions, Christ is available
to help. The prophecy harkens back to the time Yahweh supernaturally
informed Joseph of a famine that was to spread over the earth. Apart from
divine intervention, Pharaoh and his gods would have been caught off
guard. In each instance, the God of Abraham, Isaac, and Jacob takes care
of his people and those who follow his prophetic advice.

It may be difficult for twenty-first century believers to visualize a
Christianized Greco-Roman banquet where prophecies, revelations, drama, and the like took place. Therefore, they have a tendency to project back
onto the text their own personal worship experiences and then interpret
the narrative through that grid. When doing so, the scene in Acts 11 looks
more like a modern church service with a few hundred people sitting in
rows of seats, singing a few songs, hearing a sermon, and, if the imagination has a charismatic bent, at the appropriate time someone rises and
gives a prophetic word while everyone else listens and then says, "Amen."

Such was not the case. The symposium section of a Christian banquet was a dynamic smorgasbord of "supernatural" activity. The list of
appropriate displays includes prophecies, revelations, words of knowledge, healings, and miracles, each producing a profound effect upon the
participants, assuring them that God was in control of the world and he

19. Seneca, *On the Shortness of Life*, 18.5. Referencing other ancient sources Talbert, *Reading Acts*, 117, suggests that serious widespread shortages occurred throughout the reign of Claudius.

20. Witherington, *Acts*, 368–72, explores the various causes for famine during the
first century.

21. Fitzmyer, *Acts*, 482.

was providing them with a foretaste of the kingdom to come (1 Cor 12:28; 14:26).

8.2.3 Acts 21—Prophecy in Caesarea

On his way to Jerusalem, Paul travels through Caesarea where he stops by the home of Philip, the former table server and evangelist from Jerusalem, who was driven from that city at the time of persecution (Acts 8:1–4). Luke mentions specifically that Phillip "had four unmarried daughters who had the gift of prophecy" (Acts 21:9).[22] They were living evidence that Joel's prophecy about the end-times was indeed being fulfilled. The only place in Roman society where they could have demonstrated their inspired speech would have been the gathering of the saints, which may have met in their home. Paul certainly allowed for it (1 Cor 11:10) under certain circumstances. Paul and his team stay with Philip and receive hospitality from his hand for several days. During a gathering of believers, which likely included eating the Lord's Supper, there arrived on the scene "a prophet named Agabus . . . from Judea" (Acts 21:10), who was mentioned previously in Acts 11:27–28. Luke recalls the incident vividly: "He came to us and took Paul's belt, bound his own feet and hands with it, and said, 'Thus says the Holy Spirit, This is the way the Jews in Jerusalem will bind the man who owns this belt and will hand him over to the Gentiles'" (Acts 21:11).

This dramatic and sobering prophetic enactment caused the church members to urge Paul not to go to Jerusalem, lest a horrible fate befall him (v. 12). But when Paul declared his willingness to suffer and die for Christ, the people acquiesced and said, "The Lord's will be done" (vv. 13–14).

Again the prophecy is spoken in the context of a Christian gathering, i.e., a meal. Because Luke does not specifically mention a *deipnon* or a symposium in describing these events most commentators miss the context. Luke's readers, however, understood that when believers gather they do so to share a Christianized Greco-Roman banquet. Therefore, it would be redundant and not necessary for Luke to mention the obvious. In applying the principles of hermeneutics to a text, the interpreter must be a student of history and culture. Otherwise, some basic assumptions will be missed and the text misinterpreted.

22. In the Hebrew Scriptures only four women are identified as prophetesses: Miriam (Exod 15:20), Deborah (Judg 4:4), Huldah (2 Kgs 22:14), and Noadiah (Neh 6:14).

While the prophecy is precise and correct—Paul will be arrested in Jerusalem and handed over to the Gentiles—the initial reaction of the Christian listener is unwarranted (v. 12). Paul alone seems to grasp that to suffer or even die for Christ is not a defeat. Although it may appear that Rome and her confederates will be victorious, in the end, Paul knows that he and all others who suffer for the gospel's sake will be vindicated. In following their Lord in death, they too will be exalted. The presence of the Spirit in this meeting is a sign that God's eschatological plan is in place and will come to pass in due time.[23]

This prophecy does not catch Paul off guard. Only a short time before his arrival in Caesarea, he had passed through Miletus where he met and dined with the Ephesian elders and reminded them. "The Holy Spirit testifies to me in every city that imprisonment and persecutions are waiting for me. But I do not count my life of any value to myself, if only I may finish my course and the ministry that I received from the Lord Jesus, to testify to the good news of God's grace" (Acts 20:23–24).

That the "Spirit testifies . . . in every city" (v. 23) indicates that whenever Paul stops to greet the brethren, have a meal with them and wish them farewell, the Spirit motivates the prophets to say the same thing—he will face a mortal enemy, the native elites who collaborate with imperial Rome. Some, claiming to be speaking by the Spirit, advise against his going to Jerusalem (Acts 21:4), but warnings do not stop Paul from keeping his appointment. He knows that in the end, the kingdom will prevail.

8.3 Prophecy in First Corinthians

Although First Corinthians follows the Book of Acts in the NT canon, it was actually written first. Therefore, what it says about prophecy is the first record on the subject. Supporting the thesis of this chapter, First Corinthians places prophecy in the meal context and describes it as an anti-imperial praxis.

8.3.1 First Corinthians 11—Egalitarian Prophecy

First Corinthians 11:2–16 is an important text when examining the issue of prophecy as a symposium activity. Careful consideration will be given to the entire passage.

23. Talbert, *Reading Acts*, 191.

I commend you because you remember me in everything and maintain the traditions just as I handed them on to you. But I want you to understand that Christ is the head of every man, and the husband is the head of his wife, and God is the head of Christ. Any man who prays or prophesies with something on his head disgraces his head, but any woman who prays or prophesies with her head unveiled disgraces her head—it is one and the same thing as having her head shaved. For if a woman will not veil herself, then she should cut off her hair; but if it is disgraceful for a woman to have her hair cut off or to be shaved, she should wear a veil. For a man ought not to have his head veiled, since he is the image and reflection of God; but woman is the reflection of man. Indeed, man was not made from woman, but woman from man. Neither was man created for the sake of woman, but woman for the sake of man. For this reason a woman ought to have a symbol of authority on her head, because of the angels. Nevertheless, in the Lord woman is not independent of man or man independent of woman. For just as woman came from man, so man comes through woman; but all things come from God. Judge for yourselves: is it proper for a woman to pray to God with her head unveiled? Does not nature itself teach you that if a man wears long hair, it is degrading to him, but if a woman has long hair, it is her glory? For her hair is given to her for a covering. But if anyone is disposed to be contentious—we have no such custom, nor do the churches of God.

This text which deals specifically with women exercising the gift of prophecy is not without controversy. Walker rejects the authenticity of the text and labels it a later non-Pauline interpolation that breaks with the flow of the letter.[24] He bases his argument on the observation that First Corinthians 8–10 deals with eating and drinking, and the same theme is picked up in 1 Cor 11:17–33; thus, the discussion in verses 3–16 seems to be out of place. Horsley agrees and feels that "without this paragraph the letter flows smoothly from 8:1—11:2 on to 11:17–34,"[25] although he does not state categorically that it is an interpolation.

24. Walker, "1 Corinthians 11:2–16," 95–111, also offers additional, but lesser, reasons why he feels verses 2–16 are not part of the original text, including a judgment that this paragraph contradicts Paul's other teaching on male and female relationships (106). This begs the question. In other passages is Paul dealing with men and women relationships in general or in the context of mealtime as he does in 1 Cor 11:2–16? Context is everything.

25. Horsley, *Corinthians*, 152.

Most commentators, however, hold to the originality of the text, and if one views chapters 10–14 inclusively as dealing with various problems associated with communal meals, then the paragraph fits in nicely, and Walker's arguments are weakened.[26] In the more immediate context, 1 Cor 11:2—14:40 comprises a section that opens and closes with a discussion of women,[27] and their exercise of liturgical gifts (particularly prayer and prophecy) during mealtime.[28] Hence, this writer feels the text is worth consideration.

Modern commentators have wrestled with the meaning of this seemingly complicated text that deals with male/female relationships, authority, head coverings, creation, and angels, among other interconnected but confusing topics. The interpretations are varied and disparate, often depending on the theological agenda of the commentator. For the purposes of this study, the writer will examine the paragraph in the context of the Lord's Supper and will not seek to address the various theological problems surrounding the text. Paul's discourse centers on one issue in particular—that of women wearing a head covering when they pray and prophesy. The two verbs "pray" and "prophesy" place the activities within a worship setting[29]—hence, a Lord's Supper. Not wearing one brings shame upon their "figurative" or metaphorical heads, i.e., husbands.[30] This becomes apparent when one sees the structure of Paul's argument:

11:4 Every man who prays or prophecies	v. 5 Every woman who prays or prophesies
11:7a On the one hand, the man . . .	v. 7b On the other hand, the woman . . .
11:7 A man ought not (οὐκ ὀφείλει) the head	v. 10 A woman ought (ὀφείλει) . . . the head
11:11a Neither a woman apart from the man	v. 11b Neither a man apart from the woman
11:12a For just as the woman . . .	v. 12b Thus also the man

26. An example is Hays, *Corinthians*, 181–82. Hays, like the writer of this paper, sees 11:2—14:40 as constituting "the next major block of the letter."

27. Fiorenza, "Rhetorical Situation," 155.

28. While the entire section is not limited to the subject of women's issues, it devotes a significant space to them.

29. Fee, *Corinthians*, 505, astutely observes, "One may pray privately; but not so with prophecy." While the former is directed toward God, the latter is directed toward the Christian community.

30. Keener, *Corinthians*, 92.

| 11:13 It is shameful for a woman to pray to God uncovered | (No Parallel) |
| 11:14b On the one hand (μὲν) the man | 11:15 On the other hand (δὲ) the woman |

Garland remarks about this structure, "Paul oscillates back and forth with statements about men and women, but the pattern is broken in 11:13 with a statement about the woman and none about the man. This interruption highlights the crux of the whole argument . . . women are praying to God uncovered."[31] Although men are mentioned along with women in this passage, they are not the issue. Paul is speaking specifically to the matter of how women should act when the church gathers for worship.[32] The force or thrust of the text is found in the only imperative in the entire paragraph: "She should wear a veil" (11:6).

Paul therefore is addressing the issue of decorum or proper etiquette to be followed by women [and men] when they prophesy. Decorum was important to all Greco-Roman banquets and no less so among Christian communal meals.[33] As previously discussed in chapter 2, decorum refers to the manner in which people conducted themselves during the *deipnon* and symposium according to prescribed rules in order to assure a good experience for all diners.[34] Guidelines applied to giving deference to those with higher rank, how and when one spoke, the consumption of wine, among other things, which if followed, would be conducive to fellowship (*koinonia*), friendship (*philia*), and pleasure (*hedone*).

Another concern may be that devotees of Dionysus and Cybele often prophesied with their hair hanging down. Paul does not want the eschatological women at Corinth to emulate such practices.[35]

Paul prescribes a set of rules for the Christian banquet which he feels will facilitate a positive outcome. With regard to the symposium practice of prophecy, he first allows for egalitarian participation: ("Any *man* who prays or prophesies," v. 4; "any *woman* who prays or prophesies," v. 5).[36] This was counter to Roman customs that restricted women from

31. Garland, *Corinthians*, 507.
32. Taussig, *In the Beginning*, 158.
33. Smith, *From Symposium*, 45–46, 51–62.
34. See chapter 2, section 2.6.
35. Lang, *Sacred Games*, 376.
36. That both men and women are praying and prophesying together and must abide by certain rules, places these activities within a congregational context, hence, a Lord's Supper.

participating fully and equally in the *deipnon* and symposium. As noted already, eschatological outpouring of the Spirit on all flesh—male and female, slave and free, citizen or alien—made the Christian meal different from those being eaten by society at large. First, it was an inclusive event. All who named Christ as Lord were invited to attend. Second, it was a supernatural event.[37] The presence of the Holy Spirit empowered receptive participants to speak on behalf of God, heal the sick, and compose and sing spirit-inspired songs, among other astounding acts.

Paul's main regulation regarding married women who wished to prophesy was that they covered their heads when doing so (v. 6, "she should" and v. 10, "she ought"). Evidently, the lack of decorum on the part of the eschatological women "tended to eliminate distinctions between the sexes . . . which had not yet been abrogated even though the new age had been inaugurated."[38] It is not within the purview of this exposition to discuss the theological reasons for such instructions or to discuss the nature of the veil, but simply to emphasize that women during the "already, but not yet" aspect of the kingdom were free to exercise their spiritual endowments at mealtime.[39] While Paul advocates a present Christian hierarchy

37. It should be noted, however, that Paul likely viewed pagan manifestations as supernatural in nature, but demonic in origin, and included uncontrolled frenzies. Christian manifestations should be orderly and characterized by self-control to distinguish them from their pagan counterparts.

38. Fee, *Corinthians*, 502, suggests that some women were arguing for the right to prophesy without their head being covered just like men (498). Jesus taught that when the kingdom arrived in its fullness the distinction between the sexes would no longer exist (Luke 20:35).

39. It may be that Paul's instruction for married women to cover their heads is aimed only at those within the *ekklesia* at Corinth, and is not applicable to all Christian women everywhere. Evidently some of the "eschatological women" at Corinth thought the kingdom had arrived in which there was "no male and female." As a result, they abandoned their wifely responsibilities for more spiritual endeavors. Seeing themselves as transcending sexual roles, they removed their veils. Paul may be attempting to rectify the situation by calling upon these women to demonstrate their married status by wearing a head covering, while still being free to exercise their gifts during the symposium. Since Philip had four unmarried daughters who prophesied, one doubts that these head covering rules would apply to them. Another reason for requiring head coverings may be to keep in check any sensual desires that an uncovered head may engender among the males in attendance, such as was prevalent in the pagan symposia in the temples of Dionysus and Isis where women with loose hair, possessed by the gods, spoke ecstatically tossing the head and hair. Loose hair was the mark of a loose woman. An additional reason for the admonition could be that many aristocratic women who sported expensive and elaborate hairdos left their heads uncovered. Against this background, Paul's instructions could be seen as countercultural. See MacDonald, *There is No Male or Female*, 81–91 and Keener, *Corinthians*, 90–94 for

(God, Christ, husband, wife, vv. 3, 8–9), he "does not require *subordination* of women . . . but a symbolic *distinction* between the sexes."[40] In doing so, he rejects Rome's hierarchical order (Jupiter, emperor, patrons, clients, et al.) that includes subjugation to one's superiors.[41] Coincidentally, he also concludes that despite gender distinctions, men and women both possess equal social status before God and have a reciprocal relationship with each other.[42] This is made clear when Paul writes, "Nevertheless, in the Lord woman is not independent of man or man independent of woman. For just as woman came from man, so man comes through woman; but all things come from God" (1 Cor 11:11–12). One gender does not have advantage over the other in the church, since both male and female have been water and Spirit baptized (1 Cor 10:3–4). According to Paul's understanding of the gospel, women as well as men have been liberated and empowered by the Spirit "to participate vocally in worship."[43]

While Paul advocates gender distinction, he also "supports a functional equality"[44] among the sexes. This differs from Roman imperial ideology, which relegated women to subservient roles. On those rare occasions when they attended a banquet, they were separated from the main activities and not allowed to recline during the *deipnon* or participate in symposium events unless as part of the "hired" entertainment.[45]

---

fuller discussions on the meaning of removing the veil.

40. Hays, *Corinthians*, 183 (emphasis in the original), concludes that Paul's "immediate concern is . . . to avoid bringing *shame* on the community" by either the men or women. Just as a woman who prophesies with an uncovered head breaks with etiquette, so does the man who covers his head (v. 4). A contemporary example, Hays offers, might be of a man who shows up to a formal dinner wearing a baseball cap. His actions would be viewed as rude and irreverent.

41. Although the man is called the "head" of the woman, according to Barrett, *Corinthians*, 248–49, this designation does not refer to a hierarchical structure that places man over the woman as her lord (*kurios*) in the sense that the Romans understood the term, but that man is the source of her being.

42. Marshall, *Corinthians*, 811. While Paul rejects the Roman concept of status and subjugation, he offers an alternative hierarchical structure based on reciprocal love and servanthood.

43. Horrell and Adams, "The Scholarly Quest for Paul's Church at Corinth," 34.

44. Hays, *Corinthians*, 189.

45. Wire, *Corinthian Women Prophets*, 96–97, deals with women at Christian communal meals. She makes the case that they were full participants and reclined at the table. That they were prophesying shows that they were in positions of leadership. This differed significantly from Roman meals, even those attended by the elites, where women were given more freedom.

The Christian meal was inclusive in scope and egalitarian in design. It provided an opportunity for all members of the *ekklesia* to join in the Lord's Supper as full participants and minister as they were energized by the Spirit of Christ. When male and female disciples of Christ gathered to eat, they functioned according to their new identities and not according to the ones dictated by the empire, which classified them in terms of superior or inferior. William S. Campbell argues convincingly that while distinctions (male/female, slave/free, rich/poor, young/old) among believers were not obliterated, they were viewed in a new perspective, their relationship to each other now based on their unity in Christ.[46] Operating with a fresh understanding and within new boundaries at the meal table, the church offered the watching world an alternative view of reality, a reality that would one day be universally actualized.[47]

8.3.2 First Corinthians 12—Nature of the Gift

Since First Corinthians 10–14 is set within a context of the Lord's Supper, Paul feels constrained to address the nature of the spiritual gifts that are operating during the symposium. At no time does he suggest that the gifts should cease being used, but he does speak to their proper use. On this matter he does "not want them to be uninformed" or ignorant (1 Cor 12:1). He reminds the Corinthians of their past identity as "pagans" (ἔθνη, i.e., Gentiles) who were "led astray" or swept away by idolatry when they participated in Roman banquets (v. 2).[48] Paul may be conjuring up an image of a people who as pagans were overtaken by a spirit and lost control of themselves during a festal occasion.

Concerned that these former ecstatics may come again under the sway of false gods or other spirits, he offers them an objective standard by which to judge all utterances: "No one speaking by the Spirit of God ever says, 'Let Jesus be accursed'" (v. 3a). Conversely, he adds, "No one can say 'Jesus is Lord' except by the Holy Spirit" (v. 3b). From these verses one concludes that all "inspired" utterances are not qualitatively equal or originate from the same source. Most likely, Paul does not suspect that Jesus

46. Campbell, *Paul and the Creation of Christian Identity*, 163–73.

47. Paul admonishes the Corinthian women to follow the mealtime decorum exemplified in all the churches in maintaining a distinctive female identity by wearing a head covering while participating equally with their male counterparts in the Lord's Supper celebration (v. 16).

48. First Corinthians 10 deals specifically with idols at mealtime. Those to whom Paul writes, prior to their conversion, participated in idolatrous activities at mealtime.

has been cursed at the Lord's Table, but is using "a rhetorical antithesis" to the inspired declaration that "Jesus is Lord."[49]

For Paul this confession involved more than mere words. It revealed one's allegiance to Jesus. Such an announcement meant these former pagans were now standing against empire and standing with the kingdom of God.

Therefore, the banquet, the very social institution that the state used to mold people into compliance with its will, was now being used by God to promote an alternative reality. Hays concludes, "Only where the Lordship of Jesus is authentically confessed can we know that the Holy Spirit is at work."[50]

As Paul proceeds in his discussion, he focuses on God as the source of all legitimate gifts [God=Spirit=Lord], but by his repeated use of the term "varieties" stresses their diversity. "Now there are varieties of gifts, but the *same Spirit*; and there are varieties of services, but the *same Lord*; and there are varieties of activities, but it is the *same God* who activates all of them in everyone" (vv. 4–6). Paul readily acknowledged that when the early believers gathered to eat the Lord's Supper, the Spirit of Christ was among them and ministered through them to others at the meal table. That they expected this as well is evident from Paul's exhortation, "To each is given the manifestation of the Spirit for common good" (1 Cor 12:7). The various gifts were given to various persons. No one is left out, and no one stands above another at mealtime. These God-given gifts should not be considered personal possessions for one's enjoyment, but as endowments of stewardship to be used in service to the community.[51] Paul then offers a sampling of spiritual manifestations: "To one is given through the Spirit the utterance of wisdom, and to another the utterance of knowledge according to the same Spirit, to another faith by the same Spirit, to another gifts of healing by the one Spirit, to another the working of miracles, to another prophecy, to another the discernment of spirits, to another various kinds of tongues, to another the interpretation of tongues. All these are activated by one and the same Spirit, who allots to each one

49. Horsley, *Corinthians*, 168–69. Fee, *Corinthians*, 579, however, leaves open the remote possibility that such cases were actually taking place in the Corinthian assembly. In such a case, to curse Jesus was tantamount to taking sides with the Roman dominators and their native Jewish collaborators.

50. Hays, *Corinthians*, 208, also points out that "the simple confession 'Jesus is Lord' remains the Spirit-inspired watchword that separates the work of the Holy Spirit from the work of deceiving spirits" (218).

51. Ibid., 219.

individually just as the Spirit chooses" (1 Cor 12:8–11). Paul makes two things clear. First, the gifts are selected and distributed by the sovereign God to individuals within the community. Therefore, there is not room for boasting. Second, these gifts are more than natural abilities. They are Spirit-energized χάρισμα (vv. 4–11), which are to be ministered during the Christian meal.

In offering a rationale for these various manifestations, Paul uses the metaphor of a single human body with its many parts, which work together in unison. He then applies the analogy to the relationship the church has to Christ, "For just as the body is one and has many members, and all the members of the body, though many, are one, so it is with Christ" (1 Cor 12:12). Horsley says "Christ" refers to "the community loyal to Christ."[52] If he is correct, then "Christ" in this instance is simply being used as a synonym for *ekklesia*. But if "Christ" refers to the exalted Lord, then Paul describes the relationship between Christ and his church as being analogous to a body. If the latter is correct, Paul shows that the church is not just another association but is united in some way with Christ as its head. He goes on to say, "For in the one Spirit we were all baptized into one body—Jews or Greek, slaves or free—and we were made to drink of the one Spirit" (v. 13). It is through the act of baptism that all believers entered into union with Christ through the Spirit and now the same Spirit indwells them all, producing an egalitarian church (see Gal 3:28). This vital union with each other and Christ makes them one. Christ is present and ministers to and through the *ekklesia* for the common good whenever it gathers.

The representative list of spiritual gifts[53] shows how the Corinthian followers of Christ participated in the symposium portion of the meal, both individually and collectively. This section will focus only on prophetic utterances.

The gift of prophecy was one way the exalted Lord manifested his presence. In this context prophecy refers to speaking an inspired word on behalf of God or Christ, his authorized envoy, to the gathered *ekklesia*. Therefore, when the congregation came together, it could expect to receive instruction, exhortation, and ministry from Christ through his Spirit. If Christ was ministering, he was alive and Rome had not stopped him. He, not Caesar, therefore was the Lord who provided supernatural wisdom, knowledge, discernment, health, and all that pertained to life.

---

52. Horsley, *Corinthians*, 171.

53. Within the Corinthian letter, Paul includes six other lists (12:28, 29–30; 13:1–3, 8; 14:6, 26. Other NT passages also contain lists, including Rom 12: 6–8).

Following the meal, the symposium allowed for continued drinking of wine, discussion and entertainment. Paul does not explain how some diners might have yielded themselves as vessels through whom the risen Lord could communicate, only that the Lord's Supper was the locus where the exalted Christ spoke to his gathered followers through the mouth of the prophets. This fits in with Luke's explanation that his former treatise (the Gospel of Luke) told of "all that Jesus *began* to do and to teach until he was taken to heaven," while Acts tells of his continued ministry. That Paul expected the saints to encounter Christ at the supper is beyond dispute.

They were, however, responsible for testing the validity of the "utterance." Paul identifies those with the gift of "discernment of spirits" (1 Cor 12:10) as especially qualified to judge a prophetic word.

Since the remaining verses in 1 Corinthians 12 offer little additional insight into the particular place of prophecy at mealtime, only a few concluding observations are needed. First, Paul notes that the various parts of the body,[54] even those which seem to be insignificant, are important: "The members of the body that seem to be weaker are indispensable, and those members of the body that we think less honourable we clothe with greater honour, and our less respectable members are treated with greater respect; whereas our more respectable members do not need this. But God has so arranged the body, giving the greater honour to the inferior member, that there may be no dissension within the body, but the members may have the same care for one another" (1 Cor 12:22–25). The implication by analogy is that those within the *ekklesia*, which is a localized manifestation of the kingdom of God, have value regardless of their status or gender. In fact God bestows extra honor to those who receive no such honor in the empire.

Second, Paul concludes this chapter with a litany of gifts, including tongues, miracles, healing, and prophecy, among others, and emphasizes that no one possesses them all (vv. 27–30). Some, like prophecy, are more desirable than others. Therefore, he advises, "strive for the greater gifts" (v. 31a). Then adds, "And I will show you a still more excellent way" (v. 31b).

8.3.3 First Corinthians 13—The More Excellent Way

Paul sandwiches his exposition of love in between his two discussions of spiritual gifts (1 Cor 12, 14), and offers "love as the sine qua non of the

---

54. Horsley, *Corinthians*, 167, believes that Paul uses the metaphor "body" in a political manner, i.e., "body politic."

Christian life" and as the guiding principle that "must govern the exercise of all the gifts of the Spirit."[55] Love is the corrective needed to end the Corinthian confusion at mealtime. Paul is not interested in stopping the use of spiritual gifts but wants to regulate them. Since the scope of this book is limited to discussing the anti-imperial nature of the Christian communal banquet and not the abuses of spiritual gifts in general, it will give attention only to the place of love as the controlling ethic of the meal as it relates to the prophetic gift.

A typical pagan banquet served to unite Roman citizens and subjects of the empire around the guiding principle of the *Pax Romana* and to mold them into compliant vassals of the state. In exchange for Caesar's protection and resources, people at mealtime poured their libations in honor to Caesar, accepted their prescribed status in the social order, and acted accordingly.

The Christian meal, operating on the principle of *agapé*, offered a counter-imperial worldview of reality and reflected what it was like to live under the *theou basileia* or government of God. Paul is not concerned with the proper use of gifts during *worship* in general but during the symposium in particular as the Christian alternative to the Roman banquet. This community meal was to operate on ethical principles quite different from other societal meals.

First Corinthians 10–14 deals with three identifiable problems: first, the infiltration of pagan practices into the meal; second, the stratification between the elites and the peasant-class; third, the spiritual pride and confusion resulting from those extolling tongues above all other gifts. The end result is that the church at Corinth is divided into factions. For Paul, love is the solution, both love for God and each other.

Agapé is portrayed as an ethical quality that should accompany one's actions, and serve as an antidote to the Corinthian way of doing things, which might be characterized as self-consuming and attention-seeking. Love describes unreserved self-sacrificial service toward God and others. Paul does not present love as an advanced or superior gift, but as a pathway (1 Cor 12:31B), "a manner of life within which all the gifts are to find their proper place."[56] Thus, Paul's instructions should be viewed as both a reprimand and as a corrective to the Corinthians' present course of action.

Paul opens with the words: "If I speak in the tongues of mortals and of angels, but do not have love, I am a noisy gong or a clanging cymbal.

---

55. Hays, *Corinthians*, 221; Fee, *Corinthians*, 636.
56. Hays, *Corinthians*, 222.

And if I have prophetic powers, and understand all mysteries and all knowledge, and if I have all faith, so as to remove mountains, but do not have love, I am nothing. If I give away all my possessions, and if I hand over my body so that I may boast, but do not have love, I gain nothing" (1 Cor 13:1–3). To make his case without sounding like a prosecuting attorney, Paul takes upon himself the hypothetical role of the one who abuses the gifts: "If I speak . . . if I have prophetic powers . . . if I have all faith . . . if I give away all my possessions . . . if I hand over my body . . . ." Regardless of the marvels performed or the sacrifice made, unless the actions are done in love, i.e., without seeking praise or attention to one's self, Paul twice decrees, "I am nothing."

When Paul likens loveless earthly and heavenly languages to noisy gongs and clanging cymbals, he has something in mind with which his Corinthian readers are familiar. He is not speaking in a vacuum. The *Testament of Job*, which predated Paul's letter by forty years or more, contained a well-known account of Hemera, one of Job's daughters, who is given the ability to praise God in the tongues of angels (*T. Job* 48:1–3).[57]

With regard to the "clanging cymbal," Paul likely has in mind a picture of the ecstatic Dionysian cultic banquets, where priestesses banged their bronze cymbals and worked themselves into a wild-eyed frenzy, losing all awareness of their surroundings.[58]

Corinth was known as a center for the manufacture of quality bronze products, especially its vases.[59] The term "gong" (χαλκὸς), which is not used elsewhere with reference to a musical instrument, likely refers to a vase-like megaphone used by actors to project or amplify their voices to the audience sitting in the theater.[60]

What Paul is likely saying is that if I could speak even in the most exalted ways possible (the tongues of angels), without love, it would be nothing more than "the empty echo of an actor's speech or the noise of

57. *Testament of Job*, 865–66.

58. According to Deiss, *Herculaneum*, 133, bas-relief from Herculaneum, dated from the late-first-century BCE, depicts cymbal players twirling ecstatically as they participate in Dionysian banquets. Strabo (ca. 64 BCE–24 CE), *Geogr.* X 3.7 identifies such activity as "Bacchic frenzy" which includes "uproar and noise" from "cymbals and drums."

59. Hays, *Corinthians*, 223. See also Keener, *Corinthians*, 108.

60. Hays, *Corinthians*, 223.

frenzied pagan worship."[61] "The most gifted individuals without love are worthless."[62]

Since Paul lists "prophetic powers" among the symposium gifts, which when operated apart from love produces no favorable outcome, the remaining verses of 1 Corinthians 13 will be analyzed to determine the proper use of prophecy. This will be done by matching characteristics of love with Paul's example of the proper use of prophecy in 1 Corinthians 14.

Between his treatment of the superiority of love (vv. 1–3) and the temporality of gifts (vv. 8–13), Paul lists the attributes of love, which serve as the antithesis of the way the Corinthians have behaved at mealtime. The manifestation of these virtues during the symposium will assure civility, and serve to regulate the gifts for the benefit of all. Love acts as a template against which the Corinthians can judge their behavior during the second course of the dinner.

Virtue 1–"Love is patient" (v. 4)

Virtue 2–"Love is kind"

Virtue 3–"Love is not envious"

Virtue 4–"Love is not boastful"

Virtue 5–"Love is not arrogant"

Virtue 6–"Love is not rude" (v. 5)

Virtue 7–"Love does not insist on its own way"

Virtue 8–"Love is not irritable or resentful"

Virtue 9–"Love does not rejoice in wrongdoing, but rejoices in the truth" (v. 6)

Virtue 10–"Love bears all things" (v. 7)

Virtue 11–"Love believes all things"

Virtue 12–"Love hopes all things"

Virtue 13–"Love endures all things"

Paul uses the final virtue of endurance to segue into his next discussion of mealtime gifts. He states, "Love never ends. But as for prophecies, they will come to an end; as for tongues, they will cease; as for knowledge, it will come to an end. For we know only in part, and we prophesy only in

61. Ibid. Also see Fee, *Corinthians*, 632.
62. Keener, *Corinthians*, 108.

part; but when the complete comes, the partial will come to an end" (1 Cor 13:8–10). Paul places his discussion of love and gifts in eschatological perspective. God's people live and minister "between the times," in the eschatological "already" but "not yet" advent of God's kingdom. God's kingdom has been inaugurated with the death and resurrection of Jesus and the subsequent outpouring of the Spirit, but the final consummation will not come until the *parousia*, when God will be "all in all" (see 15:20–28). Love spans both the already and not yet. Thus, the gifts of the spirit at suppertime will give way one day to the full manifestation of the kingdom where love continues to dominate.

Paul then uses an analogy to compare and contrast the "already" and the "not yet" aspects of the kingdom: "When I was a child, I spoke like a child, I thought like a child, I reasoned like a child; when I became an adult, I put an end to childish ways. For now we see in a mirror dimly, but then we will see face to face" (vv. 11–12a). Presently ("now") believers through the exercise of spiritual gifts only get a skewed or partial glimpse into God's mind and will, "but then" the fullest expression of God's character shall be known, as characterized by love. For God is love. The proleptic kingdom is like child's play compared to the future kingdom, when believers will stand in the presence of God. Paul concludes, "Now I know only in part; then I will know fully, even as I have been fully known. And now faith, hope, and love abide, these three; and the greatest of these is love" (vv. 12b–13). The contrast between the "now" and "then" in verse 12 speaks of the contrast between the present age and the age to come, the contrast between knowing only "in part" now and knowing "fully" then.[63] This supports and reemphasizes his statement in verses 9–10: "For we know only in part, and we prophesy only in part; but when the complete comes, the partial will come to an end." The gifts, which manifest the kingdom "in part" for now, will give way "when the complete" arrives. Hence the Corinthians are instructed to come behind in "no gift (χαρίσματι) eagerly awaiting (ἀπεκδεχομένους) the revelation (ἀποκάλυψιν) of Lord Jesus Christ" (1 Cor 1:7). The gifts are presently needed to build up the people of God until the kingdom comes in its fullness. There is continuity between the incomplete kingdom and its fullness in the future. The former gives way to the latter. While gifts as a manifestation of God's power are important for the present, love as a manifestation of God's character is essential. To paraphrase Barth: "When the sun comes up, other lights are no longer needed."[64]

63. Hays, *Corinthians*, 229.
64. Barth, *Resurrection of the Dead*, 86.

Thus Paul admonishes the church, "Pursue love and strive for the spiritual gifts, and especially that you may prophesy" (14:1). In this way, they can avoid patterning their communal meals after the unruly pagan banquets of their past, and model them after Jesus' example at the Last Supper whose actions at the meal table were motivated by selfless love (1 Cor 11:23–25).

The love ethic is what sets the Lord's Supper apart from all other Roman banquets, where one's status was recognized, Caesar was honored, and self-consumption the rule.

Paul's bottom line is that spiritual gifts not tempered by love are meaningless. The meal must be characterized by love. Hence, it is a love feast. Paul will later close this letter with a triad of related admonitions: 1) "Let all that you do be done in love" (16:14); 2) "Let anyone be accursed who has no love for the Lord. Maranatha!" (16:23); and 3) "My love be with all of you in Christ Jesus" (16:24). This threefold conclusion shows that love dominates Paul's thinking regarding the communal meal.

8.3.4 First Corinthians 14—Regulating the Mealtime Gifts

That prophecy occurred within the symposium in 1 Corinthians 14 is supported by the way Paul places it with other symposium activities such as teaching (vv. 6, 19, 26), singing (vv. 15, 26), and tongues (vv. 4–6, 13, 18–23, 26, 39). Ecstatic utterances, as already noted, were commonplace at Roman banquets, especially at Dionysian meals.

Within the Corinthian fellowship, confusion ruled the day during the second tables. Many Corinthians equated speaking in tongues with spirituality, and used the Lord's Supper as an occasion to display their prowess, possibly in a competition with each other according to Hellenistic inculcation. Rather than commending them for vibrant worship, Paul admonishes them for being self-centered, immature, and causing disorder during the symposium festivities:

> For those who speak in a tongue do not speak to other people but to God; for nobody understands them, since they are speaking mysteries in the Spirit. On the other hand, those who prophesy speak to other people for their building up and encouragement and consolation. Those who speak in a tongue build up themselves, but those who prophesy build up the church. Now I would like all of you to speak in tongues, but even more to prophesy. One who prophesies is greater than one who speaks

> in tongues, unless someone interprets, so that the church may
> be built up (1 Cor 14:2–5).

Paul's concern with those speaking in tongues is that "nobody understands them" (v. 2a), "they are speaking mysteries" (v. 2b), and they "build themselves up" (v. 4a). The manifestation is useless to other diners "unless someone interprets" v. (5a), which evidently is not happening.[65] "On the other hand" Paul commends "those who prophesy" for their utterance can be understood, builds up, encourages, and consoles the church (vv. 3–5). Paul concludes that those who prophesy in the gathering have "greater" value to the church than those who speak in tongues (v. 5). This is because they are following his earlier call, "But strive for the greater gifts" (12:31).

Paul compares speaking with tongues to a "flute" or "harp" that gives off an uncertain sound, whose tune cannot be discerned by the listeners (v. 7). The mention of the flute and harp is significant because they were the standard instruments used to entertain during a typical Greco-Roman symposium,[66] thus linking tongues (without interpretation) to a defective symposium activity. But he extols the use of prophecy during the symposium for "building up the church" (vv. 6, 12).

In verses 13–21 Paul characterizes those who exercise tongues, apart from interpretation as "children in . . . thinking" (v. 20), who produce confusion among the dinner guests. He writes, "If, therefore, the whole church comes together and all speak in tongues, and outsiders or unbelievers enter, will they not say that you are out of your mind?" (v. 23).[67] But then he adds: "But if all prophesy, an unbeliever or outsider who enters is reproved by all and called to account by all. After the secrets of the unbeliever's heart are disclosed, that person will bow down before God and worship him, declaring, 'God is really among you'" (vv. 24–25).

Here Paul presents a hypothetical situation (whether likely or unlikely cannot be determined) where a person on the margins attends the

---

65. Paul is not opposed to *glossolalia*, which he believes to be a valid spirit-motivated gift (v. 2). He even believes it has a place in the symposium when it is accompanied by interpretation. Since tongues is characterized as speaking to God (v. 2), it is a form of prayer. When uttered publicly in order for others to say, "Amen" it must be understood (v. 16). This is why interpretation is necessary. Otherwise, tongues should be used privately to praise and offer thanksgiving to God (v. 19).

66. Plato, *Symp.* 176E; Xenophon, *Symp.* 2.1, 2.21, 3.1.

67. Hays, *Corinthians*, 229–30, identifies the outsiders' reaction as thinking they had entered a "mystery cult that whips its partisans into a frenzy of frothy enthusiasm." The phrase "out of your mind" means temporary, not permanent insanity.

Christian banquet.[68] He has an adverse response to tongues (v. 23), but a life-changing experience results from the prophecy (vv. 24–25). In language reminiscent of Isa 45:14, Paul envisions Gentiles coming to recognize Yahweh through prophetic utterances.[69] Hays observes: "Thus, when the church prophesies authentically, it becomes the instrument through which God accomplishes the eschatological conversion of the nations—or at least a foretaste of that final event. In short, Paul sees prophecy as a powerful tool of evangelism, but he sees tongues (in public worship) as a hindrance to making the gospel understood."[70] As a symposium activity, the evangelistic use of prophecy fits easily into the category of anti-imperial praxis. The declaration that "God is *really* among you" shows that God's presence at the meal was a shocking reality to the outsider. The one who had previously bowed to Caesar as Lord, switches allegiances. Now Jesus is his new Lord. What can be more counter-imperial than this?

In his final instructions to the congregation at Corinth, Paul describes his conception of an ideal symposium:

> What should be done then, my friends? When you come together, each one has a hymn, a lesson, a revelation, a tongue, or an interpretation. Let all things be done for building up. If anyone speaks in a tongue, let there be only two or at most three, and each in turn; and let one interpret. But if there is no one to interpret, let them be silent in church and speak to themselves and to God. Let two or three prophets speak, and let the others weigh what is said. If a revelation is made to someone else sitting nearby, let the first person be silent. For you can all prophesy one by one, so that all may learn and all be encouraged. And the spirits of prophets are subject to the prophets, for God is a God not of disorder but of peace (1 Cor 14:26–33).

Paul's concern is that order prevails during the symposium, rather than confusion. All members are free to exercise their gifts, as long as they are Spirit-prompted and seek to build up the church. The meeting can include singing (a hymn), exposition (a lesson), a mystery (a revelation), prayer and praise (a tongue, an interpretation), and exhortation (a prophecy). As shown in chapter 2, the phrase, "When you come together" locates

---

68. Since this person is called an "outsider," Paul may be identifying him as an uninvited guest or party crasher; a literary character who commonly appears in Greco-Roman descriptions of symposia.

69. According to Keener, *Corinthians*, 115, the cry, "God is with you" likely "recalls the confession of Gentiles bowing to God's servants in Is 45:14 (cf. Zech 8:23)."

70. Hays, *Corinthians*, 239.

these activities within the context of the Lord's banquet, since these exact words are used to describe the setting of the communal meal (1 Cor 11:17, 18, 20, 33).[71]

Since Paul said that "we prophesy only in part" (1 Cor 13:9), prophecy was not a full disclosure of God's will and therefore had to be submitted for evaluation (1 Cor 14:29). Those with the gift of discernment were expected to serve in this role. The evaluation was based on the content of the prophecy, namely the declaration that "Jesus is Lord." Such a notion stood opposed to the accepted acclamation that "Caesar is Lord."

The political and eschatological implications of prophecy placed it in the category of an anti-imperial activity, which was uttered during the Lord's Supper and celebrated Christ's superiority over Caesar. The empire's days were numbered and a new age had been inaugurated.

Whenever another prophet received a word from God, the current speaker was to yield the floor (v. 30). In this manner, the body is edified (v. 31). Those ministering gifts were not caught up in a frenzy, but could control their actions (v. 32), since God's ways are orderly and peaceful (v. 33). The description provided in verses 28–33 gives insight into the interaction that took place during the symposium.[72]

If things got out of hand, as they often did at Corinth, it was evidence that God was not at work. As Paul reminded the church, "Anyone who claims to be a prophet, or to have spiritual powers, must acknowledge that what I am writing to you is a command of the Lord. Anyone who does not recognize this is not to be recognized" (vv. 37–38).

Chapter 14 concludes as it began, i.e., on a positive note, encouraging the believers to prophesy: "So, my friends, be eager to prophesy, and do not forbid speaking in tongues; but all things should be done decently and in order" (vv. 39–40). Since Paul promotes prophecy as a gift to be desired

71. See chapter 2, "The Roman Banquet as a Model for the Lord's Supper."

72. Verses 33b–36 include the following admonitions: "As in all the churches of the saints, women should be silent in the churches. For they are not permitted to speak, but should be subordinate, as the law also says. If there is anything they desire to know, let them ask their husbands at home. For it is shameful for a woman to speak in church. Or did the word of God originate with you? Or are you the only ones it has reached?" This controversial passage comes in direct conflict with 11:2–16, which permits women to pray and prophesy during the symposium if they cover their heads. Both Fee, *Corinthians*, 699–708, and Hays, *Corinthians*, 245–48, believe the paragraph to be a gloss which was "introduced into text by the second- or third-generation of Pauline interpreters who compiled the pastoral epistles" (Hays, *Corinthians*, 247), although they offer other views as well, none of which solve the conflict.

by all members, it should be considered an acceptable symposium activity, one that ministers to both believer and unbeliever alike.

8.4 First Thessalonians 5:19–22

While Paul's letter to the Corinthians addresses issues related uniquely to their situation, the principles upon which his instructions are founded have universal application. With regard to prophecy, he tells the eschatological women that his directives and correctives are based on practices common to all "the churches of God" (1 Cor 11:16). Therefore, one would expect to find Paul offering similar advice to other churches where spiritual gifts are causing concern within a congregation. Such is the case at Thessalonica. In fact, First Thessalonians (ca. 49 CE) is "the earliest surviving piece of Christian literature" written by Paul[73] and thus predates his First Letter to the Corinthians by three to five years.

8.4.1 Instructions Regarding Prophecy

The key passage for consideration is 1 Thess 5:19–22, which includes five imperatives, all of which relate to prophetic manifestations within the Christian community,[74] and which "are intended to be read together."[75] The commands are divided into two sets. The first set is composed of two negative commands, with the latter expanding upon the first. The second set, comprised of three positive commands, tells the Thessalonians what they should do:

> Do not quench the Spirit.
> Do not despise the words of prophets,
>   but test everything;
>   hold fast to what is good;
>   abstain from every form of evil (1 Thess 5:19–22).

From the text itself, it is difficult to determine what kind of problem the Thessalonians were having with prophecy. Is Paul offering corrective or preventive advice? Is prophecy being abused within the congregation, as in Corinth, causing some within the congregation to be leery of it? Are these Gentile converts on the verge of falling into frenzies reminiscent of

73. Aune, *Prophecy*, 190.
74. Ibid., 219.
75. Fee, *Thessalonians*, 217.

their old pagan idolatry (1:9) and thus need to be prevented from doing so?[76] Or is the opposite the case? Are they now fearful of participating in Spirit-motivated ecstatic speech, which remind them of their pagan rituals of ecstasy? Or perhaps misguided advice and direction in the past has been conveyed to the church through false prophecies, leading to confusion among the disciples.[77] Whatever the specific problem, the solution is not disuse of spiritual gifts but their proper use.[78] For Paul, "pneumatic activity" is an eschatological sign of the last days, and thus should be an expected and welcomed occurrence whenever the Thessalonian Christians gather to worship.[79]

Since Paul designates "the Spirit" (τὸ πνεῦμα) as the source of the prophecy (v. 19), the Thessalonians' opposition or abuse of it means that they are stifling God's attempt to communicate with the congregation during the symposium. Paul is attempting to offer either preventive or corrective advice.

The first command is "Quench not the Spirit" (v. 19). The verb μὴ σβέννυτε, a negative present active imperative secondd person plural, can have a meaning of either, "Do not habitually quench or extinguish the Spirit" or "Stop quenching the Spirit," the latter indicating that they were currently doing so.

When "quench" is used in a literal sense, it "applies to the extinguishing of a flame of some sort, such as that of a fire (Mark 9:48)."[80] Paul uses it here in a metaphorical sense, implying that the divine flame or activity of God's Spirit can be doused or dampened.

76. Paul reminds the Thessalonians of how upon hearing the gospel, they "turned to God from idols, to serve a living and true God" (1 Thess 1:9). Possibly they are uncomfortable with ecstatic prophecies, which seem all too similar to their old idol practices. According to Fee, *Thessalonians*, 218, Paul may be trying to counter these reservations by offering guidelines for valid and acceptable forms of prophecy which emanate from the Spirit of God.

77. A few months later Paul will have to write another letter to the Thessalonians because erroneous prophecies about the arrival of the Day of the Lord have caused confusion within the congregation (2 Thess 2:1–2). The writer is aware of the controversy surrounding the authorship of 2 Thessalonians. For an excellent survey of the issues, see Jewett, *Thessalonian Correspondence*, 3–18, who concludes, "The evidence concerning the authenticity of 2 Thessalonians is equivocal, with the likelihood remaining fairly strongly on the side of Pauline authorship" (16–17). No more can be said of the epistle than it falls into the category of "probably Pauline" (16).

78. Fee, *Thessalonians*, 220.

79. Wanamaker, *Thessalonians*, 201.

80. Morris, *Thessalonians*, 175.

That the Spirit's ministry can be opposed and hampered by the community shows that it is not "an irresistible force, but rather susceptible to human resistance."[81] As Paul says to the Corinthians, "the spirits of the prophets are subject to the prophets" (1 Cor 14:32).

With the second exhortation in verse 20, "Despise not the words of the prophet" (προφητείας μὴ ἐξουθενεῖτε), Paul provides a clue as to how they are quenching the Spirit. The plural noun "words" (προφητείας), being in the accusative case and lacking a definite article, suggests that certain of the Thessalonians are treating the very utterances "as of no account,"[82] which may reflect more accurately the meaning of ἐξουθενεῖτε than the NRSV rendering of "despise." By treating lightly the inspired instructions they quench the Spirit, and miss out on the exalted Christ's will for the church. Since προφητείας μὴ ἐξουθενεῖτε, like Paul's first admonition (v. 19), is also negative present active imperative second person plural, it might be translated, "Stop your continuous disregard for prophetic utterances."

Although the identity of the despising culprits cannot be found in verses 19–23, Jewett hypothesizes that opposition likely comes from the leadership within the congregation, whom Paul appointed to organize and lead the church in his absence, and whose authority was being challenged by a charismatic element within the church.[83] In 1 Thess 5:12–13, Paul instructs those with charismatic gifts to give deference to his appointed leaders: "But we appeal to you, brothers and sisters, to respect those who labour among you, and have charge of you in the Lord and admonish you; esteem them very highly in love because of their work. Be at peace among yourselves" (vv. 12–14a).

Based on the immediate context and the relationship between verses 12–14 and 19–23, Jewett makes a strong case, which leads one to draw a comparison between Corinth and Thessalonica.[84] Like the ecstatics in Corinth, those in Thessalonica receiving eschatological revelations and guidance directly from the Spirit feel little or no need to submit to their human leaders. Conversely, the leadership views the prophetic utterances as a hindrance to church order and a brazen challenge to their authority;

81. Gillespie, *First Theologians*, 49.

82. Wanamaker, *Thessalonians*, 202.

83. Jewett, *Thessalonian Correspondence*, 175.

84. Some like Wanamaker, *Thessalonians*, 203, believe Jewett is "reading the Corinthian situation into the Thessalonian correspondence," but there is no evidence for this accusation. The context (1 Thess 5:12–23) makes the comparison plausible, if not certain.

hence, they despise or treat prophetic utterances with little regard. Paul therefore, must address both camps.

Paul offers a corrective in verse 21 by issuing a third command, "but test everything" (πάντα δὲ δοκιμάζετε). The adversative "but" (δὲ) is the only conjunction in the text, and it links the problem (vv. 19–20) with the solution (v. 21). "Even though they must not quench the Spirit by showing contempt for prophetic utterances, neither must they simply accept every kind of utterance of this kind as from the Spirit."[85] On the contrary the prophecy must be put to the test. This is the same solution Paul gives to the Corinthians (1 Cor 14:29). In the immediate context, "everything" (πάντα) refers to the prophetic utterances; since the antecedent is "prophetic utterances" (πάντα is προφητείας). While no specific reason is given why the prophecies should be tested, F. F. Bruce notes, "The gift of prophecy lent itself to imitation, and it was important that counterfeit prophets should be detected."[86] What at first glance may appear to be good, in fact may be detrimental to the Jesus community. Not all manifestations which claim to come from the risen Christ actually have their source in him.

The verb "test" (δοκιμάζετε), as a present active imperative second person plural, places the burden of responsibility upon the members of the *ekklesia* and not on prophets only.[87] Regardless of initial apprehensions, the Thessalonians are to receive the spoken prophecies and then scrutinize them. This tradition of testing prophecy is carried over from the OT (Deut 18:21–22).

How does the congregation go about to test (δοκιμάζετε) or examine prophecy? If Paul's subsequent instructions to the Corinthians and Thessalonians are any indication, those with the gift of discernment are to weigh the prophecy to determine if it proclaims Jesus as Lord (1 Cor 12:4), comforts and edifies the saints (1 Cor 14:3), and conforms to the traditions which have been passed down by word or epistle (2 Thess 2:15). Those that do not pass muster are to be rejected as originating from a source other than the Spirit, either human or demonic. The NT is filled with warnings about false prophets and teachers who bring messages contrary to Christ. Such counterfeiters are to be ferreted out and exposed (2 Pet 2:1; 1 John 4:1; Jude 4; Rev 2:2, 20).

---

85. Fee, *Thessalonians*, 221.

86. Bruce, *Thessalonians*, 125–26.

87. Paul gave similar instructions about judging or testing prophecy to the Corinthians (1 Cor 14:29).

Rather than attempting to discover the genus of the prophecy, Paul seems to recommend examining the content of the prophecy. It may be that prophetic messages have caused confusion in the church. In a second letter to the Thessalonians, for instance, the writer corrects a false teaching that the "Day of the Lord" has already dawned, when he writes "we beg you, brothers and sisters, not to be quickly shaken in mind or alarmed, either *by spirit* or by word or by letter, as though from us, to the effect that the day of the Lord is already here" (2 Thess 2:2). The phrase "by spirit" likely refers to an "oracular utterance of a prophet."[88]

Once the prophetic content is judged, Paul gives two further instructions in verses 21b–22, one a positive and the other a negative: 1) "hold fast to what is good" (τὸ καλὸν κατέχετε) and 2) "abstain from every form of evil" (ἀπὸ παντὸς εἴδους πονηροῦ ἀπέχεσθε). These imperatives deal with the results of the testing. The goal is to discern God's will for the community. The Jesus community should embrace (κατέχετε) the prophecies which prove to be beneficial and avoid (ἀπέχεσθε) those which are detrimental. Paul used the same strong verb (ἀπέχεσθε) in 1 Thess 4:3 when he exhorted, "This is the will of God . . . that you abstain (ἀπέχεσθε) from fornication." The verb carries the idea of "separation" or avoidance.[89]

Although some commentators place the terms "good" and "evil" in ethical categories and interpret these two admonitions to be general ethical instructions on how to conduct one's life, such explanations strip the exhortations from their context. As Marshall rightly observes, "a sudden transition" from a specific discussion about prophecy "to an ethical principle is improbable."[90]

Aune in his analysis of these instructions draws three conclusions: 1) The Spirit was the source and cause of the prophecy; 2) Prophecy was a customary activity during worship; and 3) Prophecy caused consternation within the church at Thessalonica.[91] He also mentions that these three characteristics were notable of "prophetic activity" in other "Christian communities" as well.[92]

---

88. Aune, *Prophecy*, 220.

89. Morris, *Thessalonians*, 179.

90. Marshall, *Thessalonians*, 159. Marshall has a fuller discussion of this matter on pp. 157–59.

91. Aune, *Prophecy*, 191.

92. Ibid.

8.4.2 The Lord's Supper as the Locus of the Prophecy

The main point made thus far is that Paul gave similar instructions to the Thessalonians as he did to the Corinthians. The locus for the prophecies issuing forth at Thessalonica is obviously a congregational setting.[93] In the next few paragraphs the author will seek to narrow the venue to the Lord's Supper. Such a task is a difficult one because many scholars, like their ministerial and lay contemporaries, have a tendency to impose an anachronistic understanding of worship upon the first-century church. While most correctly conceive that the church met together in homes, they imagine a circle of chairs, a preacher, some singing, and ministering of gifts, something similar to what one might expect to find happening in a contemporary cell group or home church. Only in the last two decades has a more realistic model surfaced thanks to the scholars Dennis Smith, Matthias Klinghardt, Hal Taussig, and others associated with the Meals in the Greco-Roman World study group of the SBL, who have made a convincing case that believers assembled to eat a communal meal in the form of a Roman banquet. Thus, a more likely picture of early worship has emerged that not only places first-century worship in homes but at the Lord's Table. The Christian banquet was the locus of worship.

In the verses immediately preceding the admonitions about prophecy, but in the same paragraph, are found three positive commands dealing with God's will, which comfortably fit into a communal meal setting:

> Rejoice always,
> pray without ceasing,
> give thanks in all circumstances; for this is the will of God in
> Christ Jesus for you (1 Thess 5:16–18).

Gillespie, citing James M. Robinson on 1 Thess 5:16–22, states that this section "represents an embryonic *church order*."[94] Meeks also finds in these verses a charismatically free order of worship that was observed by the earliest churches.[95] This is likely the case, and fits nicely with the understanding that worship centered upon the Christian banquet. A comparison can be made between Paul's instructions here (vv. 16–22) and his instructions to the Corinthians about prayer, thanksgiving, and the gifts of

93. Ibid., 219.

94. Gillespie, *First Theologians*, 42. Italics in the original. While neither Robinson nor Gillespie would have conceived of the worship as being centered on the Lord's Supper, at least they place the paragraph in the context of a worship setting.

95. Meeks, *First Urban Christians*, 150.

the Spirit, all of which were made within the context of the Lord's Supper (1 Cor 11:23–25; 14:13–17). In both cases, he speaks about order in worship. Since he relates his Corinthian comments to a *deipnon*/symposium setting, it is likely that this serves as the context here as well.

His charge to the Thessalonians to "give thanks" (εὐχαριστεῖτε) also fits with his description of Jesus' activities of the Last Supper "having *given thanks* he broke bread," (καὶ εὐχαριστήσας ἔκλασεν), upon which the Eucharist was modeled (1 Cor 11:24).

It would be natural for Paul, having founded the church at Thessalonica on his second missionary journey, to recline at the table with them in Roman fashion. On such occasion he would have taught the new believers how to eat the Lord's Supper as a counterculture celebration. Hence, these former idolaters would now be eating in the name of the exalted Lord rather than Caesar and paying homage to the God of Israel instead of Jupiter. Their symposium activities would be Christ-oriented and Spirit-empowered. Luke records in Acts 17 that Paul and Silas ministered successfully for three weeks in the synagogue at Thessalonica before opposition from jealous Jews forced them out. Along with the new believers they moved to the home of Jason, which likely became their new base of operation (Acts 17:2–7a). It takes little to imagine Jason serving as the host at mealtime.

The charge to "rejoice" (χαίρετε) or be cheerful may also be related to "hymnic praise,"[96] which was a standard symposium activity at all Roman banquets, Christian or otherwise.[97]

If the series of admonitions (vv. 16–22) are about how to conduct themselves when they come together, then the meal becomes the likely setting for prophecy.

8.4.3 The Prophetic Word is Anti-Imperial

Paul opened his Letter to the Thessalonians by commending them for living an exemplary life despite the cost involved: "And you became imitators of us and of the Lord, for in spite of persecution you received the word with joy inspired by the Holy Spirit" (1:6). Since Paul characterized

---

96. Gillespie, *First Theologians*, 41, again refers to Robinson on this point.

97. Plutarch, *Quaest. conv.* 708D, discusses the importance of friends rejoicing together at mealtime. The relationship of hymns to cheerfulness is found in Jas 5:13: "Are any cheerful? They should sing songs of praise." See chapter 7, which discusses this relationship.

"the word" as "inspired by the Holy Spirit," it was likely a prophetic word. That it resulted in "persecution" points to its anti-imperial content. This is borne out by the charges leveled against the evangelists when they first ministered in Thessalonica. An angry mob "set the city in an uproar," stormed the house of Jason, dragged him into the street, and shouted, "These people who have been turning the world upside down have come here also, and Jason has entertained them as guests. They are *all acting contrary to the decrees of the emperor, saying that there is another king named Jesus*" (Acts 17:5–7). Luke tells how the "people and the city officials were disturbed when they heard this" (v. 8). Jason was then arrested, and Paul and Silas were secretly led out of the city at night (vv. 9–10). The nature of the charges against the missionaries strengthens the argument that their prophetic word had an anti-imperial flavor.

8.5 Symposia Prophecy in the Apocalypse

The Apocalypse opens with the author identifying his message as a prophecy from the exalted Lord: "The revelation of Jesus Christ, which God gave him to show his servants what soon must take place. He made it known by sending his angel to his servant John, who testified to the word of God and the testimony of Jesus Christ, even to all he saw. Blessed is the one who reads the words of this prophecy and blessed are they who hear and keep what is written in it for the time is near" (Rev 1:1–3). As in 1 Cor 14:30, this text characterizes "prophecy" as a "revelation" (ἀποκάλυψις) from the risen Lord, which is delivered to the church by a Spirit-inspired person. The revelatory message involves a disclosure of God's will for the future, which previously has been concealed from view or understanding. New Testament writers use the term mystery (μυστήριον) when referring to the heretofore hidden message (1 Cor 15:51; Rom 11:25; Rev 1:20), whose content is often eschatological in nature. To the Romans Paul writes, "The proclamation of Jesus Christ, according to the revelation of the mystery that was kept secret for long ages but is now disclosed" (Rom 16:25–26). He delivers a similar message to the churches at Ephesus and Colossae, respectively: "The plan of the mystery hidden for ages in God who created all things" (Eph 3:9). "The mystery that has been hidden throughout the ages and generations but has now been revealed to his saints" (Col 1:27).

In the opening paragraph of the Apocalypse, Christ unfolds the future to "his servant John," who in turn "testified" (ἐμαρτύρησεν) to the message, which he described as "the word of God" (τὸν λόγον τοῦ θεοῦ) "and" (καὶ) "the testimony of Jesus Christ" (μαρτυρίαν Ἰησοῦ Χριστοῦ). Most likely John uses καὶ to mean "even," thus equating "the word of God" and "the testimony of Jesus" (1:2, 9; 6:9; 20:4), with the latter phrase understood as a subjunctive genitive, i.e., "the testimony borne by Jesus."[98] That Christ is the one giving the prophecy (Rev 6:9; 11:7; 12:11; 20:4) and does so by speaking in the first person (Rev 1:8, 17–20; 2; 3; 16:15; 22:7–20) seems to confirm this view. By identifying the revelation that he receives and delivers as "the word of God," John acknowledges himself to be a "prophet in the tradition of OT prophets who received the word of God (Hos 1:1; Joel 1:1; Jer 1:2, 4, 11)."[99] Like prophets of old, John "saw" the message unfold before his eyes (Amos 1:1; Hab 1:1). The revelator then preserves the prophecies by putting them in "written" form, assuring that they safely reach their destination and intended audience without alteration (Rev 22:18–19). These written prophecies are to be read aloud and heard. "Such an arrangement was necessary since only a small number of Christians in the churches of Asia could read, probably about one out of ten."[100] Hence John's first of seven beatitudes: "Blessed is the one who reads the words of this prophecy and blessed are they who hear and keep what is written in it" (v. 3). Both the one who reads[101] and those who heed the prophecy are promised a blessing. The audience to whom the prophecy is addressed must be obedient immediately because "the time is near" when the events described will come to pass. Likewise, the phrases "the words of this prophecy" (v. 3) and "the word of God" (v. 2) are synonymous, giving the prophecy its divine authority.

The recipients are the "seven churches which are in Asia" (v. 4), i.e., the Jesus communities in the Lycus Valley (Revelation 2–3), which are identified by name (2:1, 8, 12, 18; 3:1, 7, 14) and by the formula, "Let anyone who has an ear listen to what the Spirit is saying to the churches" (Rev 2:7, 11, 17, 29; 3:6, 13, 22). As noted by Aune, John expects his prophecy

98. Aune, *Revelation 1–5*, 19.

99. Ibid. When John falls to worship an angel who has just shown him the new heaven and new earth, the angel reprimands him and identifies John as one of "the prophets" (Rev 22:9).

100. Thompson, *Revelation*, 48.

101. To read audibly was likely the norm in the ancient world; even individuals read aloud to themselves. Aune, *Revelation 1–5*, 20–21, explores the ancient practice of audibly reading texts to audiences, which included seeking to interpret the text and choosing words whose sounds convey its meaning. Interestingly, the verb ἀναγινώσκων carries the meaning "to distinguish between, to recognize, to know accurately, to acknowledge" as well as "to read," showing that the lector did much more than recite words.

"to be read aloud in a service of worship (1:2; 22:18)."[102] This likely places the reading in a symposium setting. To the church at Laodicea, Christ exhorts, "Listen! I am standing at the door, and knocking; if you hear my voice and open the door, I will come into you and eat with you, and you with me" (3:20), and thus places the reading in the context of a communal meal (see 8.6 Excursus that follows).

Since the anti-imperial tenor of the prophecy is self evident throughout the entirety of Revelation and has been adequately discussed in many critical commentaries, the reader can refer to those sources. For the purposes of this thesis, only a brief overview will be given.

John opens his greetings on an anti-imperial note by identifying the exalted Jesus as the earth's ultimate king: "Grace to you and peace from him who is and who was and who is to come, and from the seven spirits who are before his throne, and from Jesus Christ, the faithful witness, the firstborn of the dead, and the ruler of the kings of the earth" (vv. 4–5). While most commentaries characterize John's greeting as typical of other salutations of the era, secular or Christian, they fail to place it in its sociopolitical context. Rather than identify the words "grace" and "peace" as a dual Greek/Hebrew greeting addressed to readers from both backgrounds, they should be understood in light of the sociopolitical context. It was Jupiter and Caesar, his earthly representative, who guaranteed peace (protection=*Pax Romana*) and bestowed grace (favor) upon the people of the Roman Empire. Caesar as Lord was the ultimate patron of the empire and distributed divine blessings.

John says that "grace" and "peace" originates from "him who is and who was and who is to come, and from the seven spirits who are before his throne, and from Jesus Christ, the faithful witness, the firstborn of the dead, and the ruler of the kings of the earth" (vv. 4–5). Whether this is a reference to the triune God (Father, Son, and Holy Spirit) or the eternal God and those who represent him, John makes the case that God, not Jupiter, is the fountainhead of all blessings. By describing Jesus as Christ (messiah), followed by the threefold designation of "faithful witness, firstborn of the dead, and the ruler of the kings of the earth," John implies that Jesus alone possesses the divine right to rule the world. Although Rome and her collaborators executed him as a false messiah and political insurrectionist, God has vindicated Jesus by raising him from the dead and giving him a position over all earthly rulers.

102. Aune, *Prophecy*, 275; Howard-Brook and Gwyther, *Unveiling Empire*, xxi.

272

This anti-imperial message must have been music to the ears of the persecuted believers. Rome's most brutal weapon—execution—was exposed as ineffective against the power of God. Since Jesus was "the first-born of the dead," his followers can face persecution and death head-on, yet remain faithful, knowing that they too will be raised to eternal life. Neither Rome's heavy hand nor the devil's murderous plots can hinder God's kingdom plans.

John's greeting that elevates God's reign above Rome's concludes with a cacophony of praise to the one who "made us to be a kingdom of priests, serving his God and Father" (v. 6), indicating that faithful believers have obtained "already" a position of authority in the present kingdom as they await for arrival of the "not yet" kingdom, which will come at the *parousia*. At such time, the interim reign will give way to the fullness of God's reign over the earth. This is confirmed when John turns to see an amazing sight:

> Look! He is coming with the clouds;
>> every eye will see him,
>> even those who pierced him;
>> and on his account all the tribes of the earth will wail.
> So it is to be. Amen (v. 7).

A voice then is heard declaring, "'I am the Alpha and the Omega,' says the Lord God, who is and who was and who is to come, the Almighty" (1:9). This divine irruption will mark an end to humankind's rebellious rule. Could any message be more anti-imperial than these prophetic symposium words? To prepare his readers for the prophecy which follows, John explains: "I, John, your brother who share with you in Jesus the persecution and the kingdom and the patient endurance, was on the island called Patmos because of the word of God and the testimony of Jesus. I was in the spirit on the Lord's day, and I heard behind me a loud voice like a trumpet saying, 'Write in a book what you see and send it to the seven churches, to Ephesus, to Smyrna, to Pergamum, to Thyatira, to Sardis, to Philadelphia, and to Laodicea'" (vv. 9–11). Three of the seven churches, Ephesus, Smyrna, and Pergamum, were located in "the three greatest cities in the Roman province of Asia."[103] Laodicea, the richest city in Phrygia, was known as a center for banking, textile, and medicine.[104] By mentioning that he, like his readers, suffers persecution for the cause of Christ and the kingdom ("I . . . share with you in Jesus the persecution"), John portrays the Roman Empire as opposing the Jesus communities in

103. Aune, *Revelation 1–5*, 137.

104. Richard, *Apocalypse*, 62.

Asia. Since the region of Asia for the most part welcomed Roman rule, embraced the culture, and enthusiastically supported the imperial cult, Rome's hostility was most likely directed only at those churches that refused to adopt Roman ideology and proclaimed Jesus to be Lord and the kingdom of God supreme.[105] Because of her cooperation with Rome, Asia as a whole prospered, which may explain the wealth found in the assembly at Laodicea, and John's rebuke (Rev 3:17).

Whether John is an itinerant prophet and evangelist, or an exile for his faith, he does not retaliate, but faces opposition with "patient endurance" as he waits for the promised deliverance at the eschaton. The prophecy which follows is addressed to the seven churches that also face persecution at the hands of the empire.

The exalted Lord prophetically addresses in geographical order the seven churches of the Lycus Valley, starting with Ephesus and ending with Laodicea. Christ commends and encourages all the churches (except for Sardis and Laodicea who live off their past reputations, but have since conformed to the world) to endure in the midst of suffering (2:1, 9, 13, 19, 25; 3:10). He also makes eschatological promises to all who overcome their present circumstances (2:7, 11, 17, 26–27; 3:5, 12, 21). These promises include "permission to eat from the tree of life that is in the paradise of God" (2:7), "authority over the nations—even as I also received authority from my Father" (2:26–27), and "a place with me on my throne, just as I myself conquered and sat down with my Father on his throne" (3:21), among others. Each anti-imperial promise is related in some way to emerging victorious over the Roman Empire. At the consummation of the age, God's rule will be universally recognized, his people vindicated, and Jesus will be recognized as Lord of all.

Since Jesus makes these eschatological promises to those who conquer "just as I myself conquered," their success is cross-centered and belongs only to those who trust God for the outcome when faced with persecution, suffering and even death.

Thus the apocalyptic prophecies, which will be read at the Second Tables, challenges the emperor's claim to rule the world, asserting that Christ alone is God's anointed choice as king. He, not Caesar, is Savior and Lord. Therefore, Caesar is a usurper who does Satan's bidding. And his days are numbered.

---

105. For an excellent discussion of the socio-political environment in Asia at the time of the Apocalypse, see Howard-Brook and Gwyther, *Unveiling Empire*, 87–119.

8.6 Excursus: Revelation 3:20

In his admonition to the church at Laodicea, Christ brings together prophecy and the Lord's Supper:

> To the angel of the church in Laodicea write:
>
> "These are the words of the Amen, the faithful and true witness, the ruler of God's creation. 'I know your deeds, that you are neither cold nor hot. I wish you were either one or the other! So, because you are lukewarm—neither hot nor cold—I am about to spit you out of my mouth. You say, I am rich; I have acquired wealth and do not need a thing. But you do not realize that you are wretched, pitiful, poor, blind and naked. I counsel you to buy from me gold refined in the fire, so you can become rich; and white clothes to wear, so you can cover your shameful nakedness; and salve to put on your eyes, so you can see. Those whom I love I rebuke and discipline. So be earnest, and repent. Here I am! I stand at the door and knock. If anyone hears my voice and opens the door, I will come in and eat with him, and he with me. To him who overcomes, I will give the right to sit with me on my throne, just as I overcame and sat down with my Father on his throne. He who has an ear, let him hear what the Spirit says to the churches" (Rev 3:14–22, NIV).

8.6.1 Overview of Revelation 3:14–22

In order to interpret Rev 3:14–22 correctly, one must not lose sight that this passage is first and foremost a prophecy from the exalted Lord to the church at Laodicea, which is to be read when the church gathers for a communal meal. Without such an understanding, many erroneous interpretations are possible.

After identifying himself as a "ruler of God's creation" and the one who gives a "faithful and true witness" (v. 14), Jesus excoriates the church members for their haughty, self-sufficient, and opulent lifestyles, declaring that their attitudes and actions sicken him (vv. 15–16). Their indulgence and life of ease has led to self-deception: "But you do not realize that you are wretched, pitiful, poor, blind and naked" (v. 17). Their Lord then invites them "to buy from me gold refined in the fire, so you can become rich; and white clothes to wear, so you can cover your shameful nakedness; and salve to put on your eyes, so you can see" (v. 18), a scene reminiscent of Yahweh inviting his wayward people to enter the covenant of David and live (Isa 55:1–3). Motivated by compassion, Jesus calls upon the complacent Laodiceans to take immediate remedial action: "Be earnest and repent" (v. 19).

Verse 20 opens with Christ, declaring, "ἰδού," variously translated "Here I am" (NIV), "behold" (NASV, NKJV), and "listen" (NRSV). The one whom Christ addresses in this verse is likely John the Revelator who is commanded to pay special attention as the scene unfolds before his eyes. He looks to see a most unusual sight—that of the Savior standing outside the assembly and knocking on the door to gain entry.[106]

Beginning with verse 20b the verbs change from second person plural, "you all" (vv. 14–20a) to third person singular, "s/he" (vv. 20b–22), which indicates that Jesus is speaking to individuals: "If anyone hears (ἐάν τις ἀκούσῃ) my voice and opens the door, I will come in and eat with him, and he with me" (v. 20). According to Osborne while the pronoun τις can technically apply to the church as a unit, in the Book of Revelation, "it is always singular and in every case is individualistic."[107]

The same "love" that leads Christ to "discipline" the backsliders (v. 19) now motivates him to reach out in reconciliation in (v. 20).

Next, Christ promises the "one who overcomes . . . the right to sit with me on my throne" (v. 21). This victorious individual should be understood as the one who conquers by remaining faithful to God in the midst of suffering and potential martyrdom, just as Jesus had demonstrated. He concludes his remarks with, "He (τις) who has an ear, let him hear what the Spirit says to the churches" (v. 22).

8.6.2 Exegesis of the Text

As a text, Rev 3:14–22 would not be difficult to understand were it not for verses 19–21. As the exegete attempts to interpret these verses she or he confronts several difficulties. The first difficulty is contextual. How does Rev 3:20 relate to verses 19 and 21? Is it related to verse 19 only, verse 20 only, or to both? How one resolves this difficulty will determine his or her interpretation of the text.

---

106. By translating ἰδού as "Listen" the NRSV implies that Christ is addressing the church at Laodicea. Whether the addressee is John, the church or both, Christ calls attention to the fact that he stands and knocks at "the door."

107. Osborne, *Revelation*, 217.

The second difficulty is linguistic in nature. What is the nature of "the door"? Does it refer metaphorically to the door of the human heart or the door of the church, or is it simply another way of saying that Christ is trying to get the church's attention? This question is not easy to answer.

Finally, what does Jesus mean when he announces his desire to "eat" with the respondent(s)? Does he want to fellowship with them now as they eat the Lord's Supper, or join them in the messianic banquet during the kingdom age, or both?

8.6.3 Three Views

Although there are many ways to look at Rev 3:19–20, there are three predominate views. Each view is determined by: 1) the relationship between the verses, 2) the identity of "the door," and 3) the meaning of "eat."

1. The *Present Fellowship View* contextually links verse 20 ("If anyone hears my voice and opens the door, I will come in and eat with him, and he with me") to verse 19 ("Be earnest and repent"), placing the events contemporaneous with each other.

Thus the one who repents of his or her participation in the Laodicean sins is the one with whom Christ eats, which metaphorically represents fellowship.[108] According to Charles, Osborne, Harrington, and others, "the door" upon which Christ knocks and seeks entry is the human heart.[109] This concept has been popularized by Holman Hunt's classic painting *The Light of the World*[110] as well as by Bill Bright's gospel booklet, "The Four Spiritual Laws," which directs the penitent reader to open his heart's door to Christ.[111] Louis A. Brighton sees the loving appeal (v. 19) as a "gospel

---

108. Osborne, *Revelation*, 213; Hemer, *Letters to the Seven Churches*, 206–7.

109. Charles, *Revelation*, 100, writes, "He [Christ] comes to each individual and seeks an entrance into his heart." Osborne, *Revelation*, 212, agrees, "Christ is presently at the 'door' of each one's heart announcing himself and knocking." Harrington, *Revelation*, 75, expresses the same sentiment, "The lover turns (v. 20) from the Church to the individual Christian and seeks an entry into the human heart."

110. Hunt's *The Light of the World*, based on John 12:46, depicts Christ, lantern in hand, standing at a door with no outside handle or knob. He can only enter if someone on the inside opens the door. "Holman Hunt experienced a conversion during the painting of this picture. He wrote of this experience in a letter to a friend, Thomas Combe, in August 1853" (Reddish, *Revelation*, 83). The original oil painting is located in the Keble Collection, University of Oxford.

111. Bright, "Four Spiritual Laws," 9–10.

invitation" to the lost,[112] but Mounce,[113] Beasley-Murray,[114] Beale,[115] and Charles[116] do not limit Christ's entrance to initial salvation, believing it also includes a desire to reestablish an intimate fellowship with one who has strayed from the fold. Mounce, representative of this view, writes, "In their blind self-sufficiency they had, as it were, excommunicated the risen Lord from their congregation. In an act of unbelievable condescension he requests permission to enter and reestablish fellowship."[117] Those holding to this view often point to the Song of Solomon 5:2,[118] which portrays a husband knocking at the door of the bedchamber, encouraging his wife to express her continued love for him, which she seems hesitant to do.

Beale finds support for the fellowship in Luke 12:36–37, which speaks of household servants opening the door to their master who knocks upon his return from a wedding feast, despite the fact that Luke clearly relates the parable to the *parousia*.[119]

The weakness of this view is that elsewhere in the NT the phrase "come in to him" never means to enter "into" a person's heart, but refers to entering a house or a room, where a person is located (see Mark 15:43; Acts 10:3; 16:40; 17:2, etc.). Christ is never portrayed as seeking entrance into a person's heart, although Jesus promises his abiding presence to those who love him and keep his word (John 14:24).

2. The *Eschatological View* contextually links verse 20 ("I will come in and eat with him and he with me") to verse 21 ("He who overcomes, I will grant to him to sit down with Me on My throne"), placing both verses in the future. Beckwith describes the dining experience as "altogether eschatological" without any present application, eucharistic

112. Brighton, *Revelation*, 101.

113. Mounce, *Revelation*, 113–14, states that it is "best to interpret the saying as personal and present rather than ecclesiastical and eschatological" (114). Mounce seems to interpret the text anachronistically with a twenty-first century individualistic mindset.

114. Beasley-Murray, *Revelation*, 106–7.

115. Beale, *Revelation*, 307–8, remarks, "This is not an invitation for the readers to be converted but to renew themselves in a relationship with Christ that has already begun, as is apparent from v 19" (308). Yet, he leaves open the possibility that some of the church members never had a relationship to Christ.

116. Charles, *Revelation*, 100–101.

117. Mounce, *Revelation*, 113, also sees the possibility that this verse has both Eucharistic and eschatological overtones. His main point, however, is that whether present or future, the reference to eating has to do with fellowship.

118. Beale, *Revelation*, 308; Mounce, *Revelation*, 114 (fn. 46).

119. Beale, *Revelation*, 308.

or otherwise.[120] Like Osborne, Roloff turns to the parable in Luke 12:35–38 for support, but uses it to endorse an eschatological interpretation of Rev 3:20. He observes that three common features are found in both Rev 3:20 and the Lukan passage: "the knocking by the master, the opening of the door by the servants who have remained awake, and the reward of these servants with a meal prepared by the returning master."[121] Since the parable concludes with the exhortation, "Therefore, you also be ready for the Son of Man is coming at an hour you do not expect" (v. 40), the same should be seen as the thrust of Christ's invitation in Rev 3:20. Those Laodiceans responding positively will join in the messianic meal. Those ignoring the warning will be spat out or judged (v. 16).

Another support for this position is found in the various other eschatological passages that feature a meal motif (Isa 25; Matt 8:11; 26:29; Mark 13; Luke 14:15; 22:18, 30; Jas 5:9; Rev 19:9). Revelation 19:9 is especially significant since it speaks of a future wedding feast attended by Christ's disciples, followed by these same believers sitting on thrones as judges and rulers (Rev 20:4 and 22:5). Hence, in light of the wider context, Rev 3:20–21 must be interpreted as referring to events occurring after the *parousia*.

A further support for the eschatological view is found in the future tenses of the main verbs, "I will come in," "[I will] eat," "I will grant," etc. Osborne questions this assumption, noting that future tense verbs alone do not prove the validity of the eschatological view, since future verbs are often used in the NT simply to call upon readers to make immediate decisions.[122] He adds, "This fellowship may well anticipate the future messianic banquet, but it cannot be restricted to that event. It is more likely that this carries on the impact of verse 19. If anyone 'repents' and 'opens the door' to Christ, present fellowship will result."[123]

According to the eschatological view, metaphorically the door must be the door of the heart or the church.

3. The *Lord's Supper View, Present and Proleptic* contextually links verse 20 ("Look, I stand at the door . . .") to verse 19 ("Repent . . .") as well as to 20 ("To him that overcomes . . ."), giving it both a present relevance

---

120. Beckwith, *Apocalypse*, 491.

121. Roloff, *Revelation*, 65, readily admits that the present Eucharist "is an allusion to the imminent coming of the Lord and anticipation of the future meal with him in its perfection."

122. Osborne, *Revelation*, 213.

123. Ibid., 217.

and future application.[124] Swete, recognizing both present and future aspects of Rev 3:20, maintains, "If any individual gives heed to the call of Christ and opens the door, Christ will enter the dwelling and exchange with such a one the fellowship of intimate communion in that endless feast of Love of which the Eucharist is the earnest."[125] But the Lord who desires to be present at the communal meal with the repentant one, also promises that the restored believer will sit with him at the messianic banquet.

This combined understanding finds support in Christ's instruction to his disciples during the Last Supper, when he says: 1) the present Passover will find its fulfillment in the kingdom at which time he will again eat it with his followers (Luke 22:16), and 2) "You are those who have stood by me in my trials; and I confer on you, just as my Father has conferred on me, a kingdom, so that you may eat and drink at my table in my kingdom, and you will sit on thrones judging the twelve tribes of Israel" (Luke 22:28–30). Paul likewise connects the present eating of the Lord's Supper to the future when he reminds his readers, "For as often as you eat this bread and drink the cup, you proclaim the Lord's death until he comes" (1 Cor 11:26).

The Lord's Supper, therefore, is presently eaten and looks forward to the Lord's return when he subdues all his enemies, sets up the kingdom of God, and invites the overcomers to sit at his banquet table where they will experience perfect intimacy with their God (Isa 25:6; 55:1–3; Luke 22:30; Matt 26:29; Rev 19:9). Like the Passover, which the Jews ate as a memorial of past deliverance (Exodus) and as a foretaste of future deliverance (messianic banquet), so Christians celebrate the Lord's Supper.

Here the word "eat" (δειπνήσω), variously translated "dine" and "sup," carries the idea of eating a full evening meal, which in the context of the church community is the Lord's Supper. The verb form δειπνήσω appears only three times in the NT, and each time in the context of the Lord's Supper. Its cognate nouns, likewise, appear in the NT in the context of the Lord's Supper (Luke 22:20; John 13:2; 1 Cor 11:20, 21, 25). Caird concludes that the passage "has a Eucharistic flavor about it. The mention of supper with Christ could hardly fail to conjure up pictures of the last supper in the upper room and subsequent occasions when the meal had been re-enacted as the symbol of Christ's continuing presence."[126]

124. Caird, *Revelation*, 58.

125. Swete, *Apocalypse*, 64.

126. Caird, *Revelation*, 58.

Therefore, churches receiving this correspondence would have naturally understood the mention of dining to be a reference to the Lord's Supper or Love Feast, a real meal, undertaken in the name of the Lord, in which church members gathered at the end of the day or first of the week to break bread, fellowship, and worship God through Christ Jesus.

According to Osborne, the use of "I stand" (ἕστηκα) in the perfect tense "as always has a present force"[127] and implies that Christ has been standing at "the door," waiting patiently for admittance. This kindly request for entrance can be viewed as counter-imperial action. As Hemer explains, Laodicea had a long and difficult relationship with Rome dating back to the first-century BCE that resulted in Rome assessing high tribute and excessive taxation upon the city. In addition, whenever Roman soldiers and aristocrats visited the region, they forcibly entered people's homes and used them as a residence and bases of operation as long as they were in the city. The owners had little recourse but to comply with the strong-arm tactics. In contrast to a forced entry, Jesus knocks patiently waiting to be invited inside.[128]

Since the verb "knock" (κρούω) is a present, active, indicative, it implies continuous action and portrays the excluded Lord standing outside for a period of time trying to gain entrance to the church that has excommunicated him. His efforts go unnoticed as the self-centered, self-satisfied congregation gathers for the communal meal, gorging itself with the delicacies of life like the church at Corinth. While claiming to lack nothing, the Laodicean church, in reality, is "wretched, miserable, poor, blind and naked" (v. 17), and lacks the most important thing—the Lord's presence. Undeterred, Christ stands patiently waiting for a response, ever ready to join in a communal meal with any individual who opens the door.

When Christ declares he knocks at a door he may be referring to an image recognizable to the Laodiceans. Situated at the crossroads of one of the most important intersections in Asia Minor, Laodicea had four city gates that opened up to a busy trade route. Hemer observes that "The inhabitants must have been very familiar with the belated traveler who 'stood at the door and knocked' for admission" into the city.[129] If this event serves as a background, Jesus might be identifying with the weary sojourner seeking refreshment and a meal from God's people. This has support from Jesus own parabolic teaching in Matt 25:34–35: "Then the

---

127. Osborne, *Revelation*, 212.

128. Hemer, *Letters to the Seven Churches*, 202–6.

129. Ibid., 204.

king will say to those on his right hand, 'Come you blessed of my Father; inherit the kingdom prepared for you from the foundation of the world: for I was hungry and you gave me food. I was thirsty and you gave me drink. I was a stranger and you took me in . . .'"

The door could be the door of the home where the church gathers to eat and worship.[130] Or it may not be a door at all but a metaphorical way of saying, "Look, I am here. Recognize my presence. Allow me to speak through the gift of prophecy and minister in your assembly through the other gifts of the spirit."[131]

As Keener observes, the Laodiceans devour their "fabulous dinners without the presence of Christ (3:20), who dwells only with the contrite and broken (Isa 57:16; 66:2; James 4:6)."[132] The Laodicean church, in essence, finds itself in a situation similar to the Corinthians who assemble for the Lord's Supper, but end up eating their own supper not the Lord's because wealthy members choose to satisfy their own appetites, while ignoring the needs of the less fortunate members. While going through the motions of eating the Lord's Supper, the church has turned inward. It has lost its purpose for existence. No longer do the believers gather to commune with each other and their Lord. Hence, they will miss out on the eschatological meal as well. The invitation to rule with Christ in his future (not yet) kingdom is offered only to those who repent and eat with him in the present (already) kingdom.

Since a conditional clause ("If any one hears . . . and opens the door") follows the pleading ("I knock . . ."), there is no guarantee that the invitation will be heeded. The one who opens the door to Christ will have table fellowship with him. However, only those with "ears to hear" will obey and answer the door (v. 22). Smalley points out that this interpretation is more in line with the OT picture of Yahweh who seeks a relationship with a wayward people and constantly holds out his inviting hand (Isa 65:1–2; Hos 2:16–23).[133]

---

130. Caird, *Revelation*, 57–58.

131. This may be the better explanation, since Christ introduces his remarks to the seven churches in this way: "These are the words of him who holds the seven stars in his right hand, *who walks among* the seven golden lampstands" (Rev 2:1). If Christ is already in the midst of the church gatherings, then his presence has virtually gone unnoticed and his knocking is an attempt to get their attention. This could mean that Spirit-empowered ministry at the communal banquet is lacking (Rev 2:4–5). The churches are not hearing what "the Spirit says" to them.

132. Keener, *Revelation*, 167.

133. Smalley, *Revelation*, 101.

Dumb

The force of the conditional clause, "If anyone hears . . . and opens the door" (ἐάν τις ἀκούσῃ . . . καὶ ἀνοίξῃ τὴν θύραν), indicates that the promise "I will come in and eat (δειπνήσω) with him" will be executed immediately. Thus it has a present fulfillment. The repentant church member, who only a few verses before was about to be spit out and judged, finds himself forgiven, having fellowship with Christ at the Lord's Table, while the remainder of the recalcitrant church misses out, despite sitting at the same table.

One must not forget that this verse is part of the prophecy given to John by the exalted Lord, which is written down and delivered with the expectation that it will be read to all "the churches" on behalf of Christ ("hear what the Spirit says *to the churches*").

Could it be that the courier entrusted to carry the letters to the seven churches departs Patmos and takes a circuitous route, stopping first at Ephesus and concluding at Laodicea? If so, is it not likely that the messages delivered to the seven churches are related?

In his prophetic exhortation to the Ephesians the exalted Lord commends them for testing and rejecting false apostles in their midst (Rev 2:2) and for enduring persecution in his name (3:3), but he scolds them because they have abandoned (ἀφῆκες) or forsaken their "first love" (Rev 2:4). If "first love" or "*the* love (τὴν ἀγάπην) you had at the first" (NRSV) is not a reference to some kind of vague emotional feeling, but to the love feast (i.e., the Lord's Supper where kingdom benevolence is demonstrated) then the messages to Laodicea and Ephesus are indeed related. In the following verse, Christ calls them to repent and "do *the works* you did at first" (v. 5), thus equating "first love" and "first works." What they had abandoned were acts of charity, most likely toward the needy, and at the very least, during mealtime.[134] When the church abandons its love for the brethren, it stops functioning rightly as a church. Christ then calls them to "remember from what they have fallen" and threatens to remove its "menorah" unless they "repent" (v. 5).[135] Interestingly, Christ concludes

134. Other commentators have made the connection between first love and first works, but have not related them to the Lord's Supper or love feast. For instance, Mounce, *Revelation*, 88, says that "first love . . . includes both love of God and love of mankind at large, but seems to refer mainly to their love for one another (as in II Jn 5)." Boring, *Revelation*, 96, describes love as "the active care of others" and equates it "with 'works' in 2:4–5." Osborne, *Revelation*, 115, says the first love is the love they had for each other soon after their conversions. Beale, *Revelation*, 230, emphatically states, "The idea is that they no longer expressed their former zealous love for Jesus *by witnessing for him in the world*" (emphasis in original).

135. Aune, *Revelation 1–5*, 147.

with a promise to the Ephesians: "To everyone who conquers, I will give permission to eat from the tree of life that is in the paradise of God" (2:7). In doing so, he places his eschatological promise in the context of eating. To eat of the tree or at the messianic table speaks metaphorically of receiving eschatological salvation or eternal life.[136]

In the context of his message to the church at Thyatira, Christ possibly links prophecy and the love feast. He first praises: "I know your works—your love, faith, service, and patient endurance. I know that your last works are greater than the first" (2:19). Here was a church living out its commitment at the communal meal in the midst of difficult times. Then he voices his concern: "But I have this against you: you tolerate that woman Jezebel, who calls herself a prophet and is teaching and beguiling my servants to practice fornication and to eat food sacrificed to idols" (v. 20). The communal meal would have served as the venue for these false prophecies to come forth. The church had not been diligent to judge her prophecies aright.

A similar message is delivered to the church at Pergamum: "But I have a few things against you: you have some there who hold to the teaching of Balaam, who taught Balak to put a stumbling-block before the people of Israel, so that they would eat food sacrificed to idols and practice fornication" (Rev 2:14). Here is another reference to wrong eating, based on the erroneous advice of a local prophet. If such is the case, the prophecy would have been given during the symposium portion of the banquet. A possible motivation for accepting these aberrant prophetic messages was so Christians in the church "could participate in the economic, political, and social life of the empire. Such participation took place in associations and guilds where emperor worship was the common ideology and eating meat sacrificed to idols was a common practice."[137] In other words, these believers wanted to fit comfortably into the empire. Believers had to choose which Lord they would serve—Caesar or Jesus.

The writer of Hebrews warns against forsaking the assembly of ourselves (Heb 10:25). Could he likewise be speaking of forsaking the God-intended purpose of the assembly, i.e., participation at the Lord's Table where compassion and self-sacrifice are manifested? Jude exhorts, "Woe to them. For they have gone in the way of Cain, have run greedily in the error of Balaam for profit . . . These are spots in your *love feasts*, while

136. This is confirmed in several extrabiblical apocalyptic writings, including *1 Enoch* 24:3—25:6; *T. Levi* 18:9–12; *T. Dan* 5:12.

137. Richard, *Apocalypse*, 53.

they feast with you without fear, *serving only themselves.*" He characterizes these persons as "clouds without water" and places the entire discussion in eschatological perspective: "The Lord comes with ten thousand of his holy ones to execute judgment on all, to convict all who are ungodly among them of all their ungodly deeds (or works)." He closes, "*But you beloved . . . keep yourselves in the love* of God, looking for the mercy of our Lord Jesus Christ unto eternal life" (Jude 11–12). The message seems to be the same throughout.

8.7 Conclusion

The thesis of this chapter was that anti-imperial prophetic utterances served a prominent role during the Christian symposium. Energized by the Spirit of God, church members proclaimed an anti-imperial vision, namely that God raised Jesus from the dead, exposing Rome's impotence against the power of God. They announced the lordship of Christ, foretold of Rome's demise, and exhorted the suffering believers to persevere as they awaited eschatological vindication.

To support the thesis, this chapter examined the content of the prophetic speeches in Acts, First Corinthians, First Thessalonians, and the Book of Revelation, showing: 1) that they were given in a meal setting, whether delivered spontaneously in the moment or written out and read aloud at a later date and 2) that they were counter-imperial in purpose.

9

Conclusion

THIS BOOK HAS INVESTIGATED previously unexplored territory by situating the first-century Christian meal as an off-stage political act of non-violent resistance, i.e., a hidden transcript that challenged Rome's "great tradition" and offered a Christian social vision in its place.

By applying James C. Scott's categories of hidden and public transcripts to the Lord's Supper, this writer has been able to formulate a thesis that the Lord's Supper was an anti-imperial practice. The irony is that Christians used the same banquet—employed by Rome as a vehicle of enforcing and advancing its social vision—to oppose Caesar and his agenda of world domination.

The Lord's Supper celebrated the inauguration of God's kingdom in Christ and served as a venue where Christians could invite their curious friends to dine and experience for themselves the firstfruits of the kingdom (1 Cor 14:26). Because the structure was like other Roman meals, the visitor would not enter totally unfamiliar territory. The inclusive, egalitarian atmosphere was likely very attractive to a guest living on the margins. The symposium activities had a subversive political quality, since the community raised its voice in praise to Jesus as Lord and proclaimed an eschatological vision that differed entirely from Rome's.

Hopefully, this thesis produces a paradigm shift in the way academics think about the Lord's Supper. The author encourages other scholars to pick up where he left off. Additional research needs to be done on ways that ministry gifts, beyond prophecy, functioned in the symposium as anti-imperial activities. Moreover, research is needed on the anti-imperial nature of the Lord's Supper based on expanded texts. For example, when viewed from a dining room rather than a courtroom perspective, James 2:1–9 lends itself to such analysis. No less important is the practical application of this research. How should an understanding of the Lord's Supper in the first century impact communion services in the twenty-first century?

Bibliography

Adams, Edward, and David G. Horrell, eds. *Christianity at Corinth: The Quest for the Pauline Church*. Louisville: Westminster John Knox, 2004.

Albright, W. F., and C. S. Mann. *Matthew*. The Anchor Bible 26. Garden City, NY: Doubleday, 1971.

Allen, C. Leonard. *The Cruciform Church: Becoming a Cross-Shaped People in a Secular World*. 2nd ed. Abilene, TX: Abilene Christian University Press, 1990.

Anderson, Bernhard W. *Out of the Depths: The Psalms Speak for Us Today*. Louisville: Westminster John Knox, 2000.

Arias, Mortimer. *Announcing the Reign of God*. Philadelphia: Fortress, 1984.

Aristeas. "The Letter of Aristeas." In *The Lost Books of the Bible and the Forgotten Books of Eden*, 140–176. Cleveland, OH: Collins/World, 1977.

Arnold, Clinton E. *The Colossian Syncretism: The Interface Between Christianity and Folk Belief at Colossae*. Grand Rapids: Baker, 1996.

Ascough, Richard. *Paul's Macedonian Associations: The Social Context of Philippians and 1 Thessalonians*. Tübingen: Mohr Siebeck, 2003.

Assmann, Hugo. *Theology for a Nomad Church*. Translated by Paul Burns. Maryknoll, NY: Orbis, 1976.

Athenaeus. *The Deipnosophists*. 7 vols. Translated by Charles Burton Gulick. LCL. Cambridge: Harvard University Press, 1969.

Augustus. "Res Gestae." In *Rome: Sources in Western Civilization*, edited by William G. Sinnigen, 104–13. New York: Free Press, 1965.

Aulen, Gustaf. *Christus Victor: A Historical Study of the Three Main Types of the Idea of the Atonement*. Translated by A. G. Hebert. New York: Macmillan, 1969.

Aune, David E. *The Cultic Setting of Realized Eschatology in Early Christianity*. Supplements to *NovT* 28. Leiden: Brill, 1972.

———. *The New Testament in Its Literary Environment*. Philadelphia: Westminster, 1987.

———. *Prophecy in Early Christianity and the Ancient Mediterranean World*. Grand Rapids: Eerdmans, 1991.

———. *Revelation 1–5*. Word Biblical Commentary 52. Dallas: Word, 1997.

———, ed. *The Gospel of Matthew in Current Study*. Grand Rapids: Eerdmans, 2001.

Baker, David W., ed. *Looking into the Future: Evangelical Studies in Eschatology*. Grand Rapids: Baker, 2001.

Balch, David L. *Roman Domestic Art and Early House Churches*. WUNT 228. Tübingen: Mohr Siebeck, 2008.

———. "Zeus, Vengeful Protector of the Political and Domestic Order: Frescoes in Dining Rooms N and P of the House of the Vettii in Pompeii, Mark 13:12–13, and 1 Clement 6:2." In *Picturing the New Testament*, edited by Annette Weissenrieder et al., 67–95. WUNT 2/193. Tübingen: Mohr Siebeck, 2005.

Balch, David L., and Carolyn Osiek, eds. *Early Christian Families in Context: An Interdisciplinary Dialogue*. Grand Rapids: Eerdmans, 2003.

Banks, Robert. *Paul's Idea of Community: The Early House Churches in their Historical Setting*. Homebush West, Aus.: Lancer, 1979.

Barber, Michael. *Singing in the Reign: The Psalms and the Liturgy of God's Kingdom*. Steubenville, OH: Emmaus Road, 2001.

Barclay, William. *And Jesus Said: A Handbook on the Parables of Jesus*. Philadelphia: Westminster, 1970.

Barrett, C. K. *A Commentary on the First Epistle to the Corinthians*. Peabody, MA: Hendrickson, 1987.

———. *The Gospel According to St. John*. 2nd ed. Philadelphia: Westminster, 1978.

———. *Jesus and the Gospel Tradition*. Philadelphia: Fortress, 1968.

Barrow, R. H. *The Romans*. Baltimore: Penguin, 1949.

Barth, Karl. *The Resurrection of the Dead*. Translated by H. J. Stenning. London: Hodder & Stoughton, 1933.

———. *The Teaching of the Church Regarding Baptism*. Translated by Ernest A. Payne. London: SCM, 1954.

Barth, Markus. *Rediscovering the Lord's Supper*. Atlanta: John Knox, 1988.

Bartholomew, Craig G., and Michael W. Goheen. *The Drama of Scripture: Finding Our Place in the Biblical Story*. Grand Rapids: Baker, 2004.

Bartholomew, Craig G., Joel B. Green, and Anthony C. Thiselton, eds. *Reading Luke: Interpretation, Reflection, Formation*. Scripture and Hermeneutic 6. Grand Rapids: Zondervan, 2005.

Bauckham, Richard. *The Bible in Politics: How to Read the Bible Politically*. Louisville: Westminster John Knox, 1989.

———. *Moltmann: Messianic Theology in the Making*. Basingstoke, UK: Marshall Pickering, 1987.

———. *The Theology of the Book of Revelation*. Cambridge: Cambridge University Press, 1993.

Beale, G. K. *The Book of Revelation: A Commentary on the Greek Text*. Grand Rapids: Eerdmans, 1999.

Beasley-Murray, George R. *The Book of Revelation*. The New Century Bible Commentary 43. Grand Rapids: Eerdmans, 1978.

———. *Jesus and the Kingdom of God*. Grand Rapids: Eerdmans, 1986.

———. "Jesus and the Kingdom of God." *Baptist Quarterly* 32 (July 1987) 141–46.

———. *John*. Rev. ed. Word Biblical Commentary 36. Nashville: Thomas Nelson, 1999.

———. "The Kingdom of God in the Teaching of Jesus." *Journal of the Evangelical Theological Society* 35 (March 1992) 19–30.

———. *Preaching the Gospel from the Gospels*. Peabody, MA: Hendrickson, 1996.

Beavis, Mary Ann. *Jesus and Utopia: Looking for the Kingdom of God in the Roman World*. Minneapolis: Fortress, 2006.

Beckwith, Isbon T. *Apocalypse of John: Studies in Introduction with Critical and Exegetical Commentary*. New York: Macmillan, 1919.

Beker, J. Christiaan. *The Triumph of God: The Essence of Paul's Thought.* Translated by Loren T. Stuckenbruck. Minneapolis: Fortress, 1990.

Benko, Stephen. *Pagan Rome and Early Christians.* Bloomington: Indiana University Press, 1986.

Berkhof, Hendrikus. *Christ the Meaning of History.* Translated by Lambertus Buurman. Grand Rapids: Baker, 1979.

————. *Christ and the Powers.* Translated by John Howard Yoder. Scottdale, PA: Herald, 1977.

Berkhof, Louis. *The Kingdom of God: The Development of the Idea of the Kingdom, Especially Since the Eighteenth Century.* Grand Rapids: Eerdmans, 1951.

Berryman, Phillip. *Liberation Theology: The Essential Facts About the Revolutionary Movement in Latin America and Beyond.* Philadelphia: Temple University Press, 1987.

Beyerhaus, Peter P. J. *God's Kingdom and the Utopian Error.* Wheaton, IL: Crossway, 1992.

Bieler, Andrea, and Luise Schottroff. *The Eucharist: Bodies, Bread, and Resurrection.* Minneapolis: Fortress, 2007.

Black, Matthew. "The Kingdom of God Has Come." *Expository Times* 63 (1951–52) 289–90.

Bloesch, Donald G. *The Last Things: Resurrection, Judgment, Glory.* Downers Grove, IL: InterVarsity, 2004.

Blomberg, Craig L. *Contagious Holiness: Jesus' Meals with Sinners.* Downers Grove, IL: InterVarsity, 2005.

————. *Interpreting the Parables.* Downers Grove, IL: InterVarsity, 1990.

————. *Matthew.* The New American Commentary 22. Nashville: Broadman, 1992.

————. "A Response to G. R. Beasley-Murray on the Kingdom." *Journal of the Evangelical Theological Society* 35/1 (1992) 31–36.

Bock, Darrell L. "Current Messianic Activity and the OT Davidic Promise: Dispensationalism, Hermeneutics and NT Fulfillment." *Trinity Journal* NS 15/1 (1994) 55–87.

————. *Jesus According to the Scriptures: Restoring the Portrait from the Gospels.* Grand Rapids: Baker, 2002.

————. *Luke 9:51—24:53.* Baker Exegetical Commentary of the New Testament 2. Grand Rapids: Baker, 1996.

Bokser, Baruch M. *The Origins of the Seder: The Passover Rite and Early Rabbinic Judaism.* Berkeley: University of California Press, 1984.

Bond, Helen K. *Caiaphas: Friend of Rome and Judge of Jesus?* Minneapolis: Westminster John Knox, 2004.

Bonhoeffer, Dietrich. *The Communion of the Saints.* Translated by R. Gregor Smith. New York: Harper & Row, 1963.

————. *Life Together.* Translated by John W. Doberstein. New York: Harper & Row, 1954.

Borg, Marcus J. "Jesus and Eschatology: A Reassessment." In *Images of Jesus Today*, edited by James H. Charlesworth and Walter P. Weaver, 42–67. Faith and Scholarship Colloquies 3, Florida Southern College. Valley Forge, PA: Trinity, 1994.

————. *Jesus: Uncovering the Life, Teaching, and Relevance of a Religious Revolutionary.* San Francisco: HarperCollins, 2006.

————. "A Temperate Case for a Non-Eschatological Jesus." *Forum* 2/3 (1986) 81–102.

Borg, Marcus J., and John Dominic Crossan. *The Last Week: What the Gospels Really Teach About Jesus's Final Days in Jerusalem*. San Francisco: HarperCollins, 2006.

Boring, M. Eugene. *The Continuing Voice of Jesus: Christian Prophecy and the Gospel Tradition*. Louisville: Westminster John Knox, 1991.

———. *Revelation*. Interpretation. Louisville: John Knox, 1989.

Bornkamm, Günther. *Jesus of Nazareth*. Translated by Irene and Fraser McLuskey with James M. Robinson. New York: Harper & Row, 1960.

Boyd, Gregory A. *God at War: The Bible and Spiritual Conflict*. Downers Grove, IL: InterVarsity, 1997.

———. *Satan and the Problem of Evil*. Downers Grove, IL: InterVarsity, 2001.

Braaten, Carl E. *The Flaming Center: A Theology of Christian Mission*. Philadelphia: Fortress, 1977.

Bradshaw, Paul F. *Eucharistic Origins*. New York: Oxford University Press, 2004.

Braun, Willi. "The Greco-Roman Meal: Typology of Form or Form of Typology." Paper presented at the annual meeting of the SBL Meals in the Greco-Roman World Seminar. Atlanta, GA, November 2003.

Breech, James. *The Silence of Jesus: The Authentic Voice of the Historical Man*. Philadelphia: Fortress, 1983.

Bright, Bill. "Four Spiritual Laws." Orlando: Campus Crusade for Christ, 1994.

Bright, John. *The Kingdom of God*. Nashville: Abingdon, 1981.

Brighton, Louis A. *Revelation*. Concordia Popular Commentary. Saint Louis, MO: Concordia, 1999.

Brooks, James A. "The Kingdom of God in the New Testament." *Southwestern Journal of Theology* 40/2 (1998) 21–37.

Brower, Kent E., and Mark W. Elliott, eds. *Eschatology in Bible and Theology: Evangelical Essays at the Dawn of a New Millennium*. Downers Grove, IL: InterVarsity, 1997.

Brown, Raymond E. *The Birth of the Messiah*. New York: Doubleday, 1977.

———. *The Gospel According to John (i–xii)*. 2nd ed. The Anchor Bible 29. Garden City, NY: Doubleday, 1978.

Bruce, F. F. *The Book of Acts*. Rev. ed. New International Commentary on the New Testament. Grand Rapids: Eerdmans, 1988.

———. *1 & 2 Thessalonians*. Word Biblical Commentary 45. Waco, TX: Word, 1982.

———. *The Gospel of John*. Grand Rapids: Eerdmans, 1983.

Brueggemann, Walter. *Biblical Perspectives on Evangelism: Living in a Three-Storied Universe*. Nashville: Abingdon, 1993.

———. *Genesis*. Interpretation. Atlanta: John Knox, 1982.

———. *Hope within History*. Atlanta: Westminster John Knox, 1987.

———. *Israel's Praise: Doxology Against Idolatry and Ideology*. Minneapolis: Augsburg/Fortress, 1988.

Brumberg-Krause, Jonathan. *Memorable Meals: Symposia in Luke's Gospel, the Rabbinic Seder, and the Greco-Roman Literary Tradition*. Unpublished manuscript, 2003. Online: http://www.wheatoncollege.edu/academic/academicdept/religion/MemorableMeals/mm_tc.htm.

Bryan, Christopher. *Render to Caesar: Jesus, the Early Church, and the Roman Superpower*. London: Oxford University Press, 2005.

Buchanan, George Wesley. *Jesus: The King and His Kingdom*. Macon, GA: Mercer University Press, 1984.

Bultmann, Rudolf. *History and Eschatology*. Edinburgh: Edinburgh University Press, 1957.

———. *Jesus and the Word*. Translated by Louise Pettingbone and Erminie Huntress. New York: Scribner's, 1934.

———. "The Primitive Christian Kerygma and the Historical Jesus." In *The Historical Jesus and the Kerygmatic Christ*, edited and translated by C. E. Braaten and R. A. Harrisville, 15–42. Nashville: Abingdon, 1964.

Burge, Gary M. *The Anointed Community: The Holy Spirit in Johannine Tradition*. Grand Rapids: Eerdmans, 1987.

———. *John: The NIV Application Commentary*. Grand Rapids: Zondervan, 2000.

Burkert, Walter. "Oriental Symposia: Contrasts and Parallels." In *Dining in a Classical Context*, edited by William J. Slater, 7–24. Ann Arbor: University of Michigan Press, 1991.

Burrus, Virginia, ed. *Late Ancient Christianity*. Vol. 2 of *A People's History of Christianity*. Minneapolis: Fortress, 2005.

Butts, J. R. "Probing the Polling: Jesus Seminar Results on the Kingdom Sayings." *Forum* 3/1 (1987) 98–128.

Cadbury, H. J. *The Making of Luke-Acts*. London: SPCK, 1961.

Caird, G. B. *Principalities and Powers: A Study in Pauline Theology*. London: Oxford University Press, 1956.

———. *Revelation of Saint John*. Peabody, MA: Hendrickson, 1999.

Campbell, Charles L. *The Word Before the Powers*. Louisville: Westminster John Knox, 2002.

Campbell, J. Y. "The Kingdom of God Has Come." *Expository Times* 48 (1936–37) 91–94.

Campbell, William S. *Paul and the Creation of Christian Identity*. London: T. & T. Clark, 2006.

Caragounis, Chrys C. "Kingdom of God/Heaven." In *Dictionary of Jesus and the Gospels*, edited by J. B. Green, S. McKnight, and I. H. Marshall, 417–30. Downers Grove, IL: InterVarsity, 1992.

———. "The Kingdom of God, Son of Man and Jesus' Self-Understanding." *Tyndale Bulletin* 40 (1989) 3–23, 223–38.

Carey, Greg. *Sinners: Jesus and His Earliest Followers*. Waco, TX: Baylor University Press, 2009.

Carson, D. A. *Matthew*. The Expositor's Bible Commentary 8. Grand Rapids: Zondervan, 1984.

Carter, Warren. *Matthew and Empire: Initial Explorations*. Harrisburg, PA: Trinity, 2001.

———. Review of *Christ and Caesar: The Gospel and the Roman Empire in the Writings of Paul and Luke* by Seyoon Kim. *Review of Biblical Literature* (July 2009). Online: http://www.bookreviews.org/pdf/6957_7550.pdf.

———. *The Roman Empire and the New Testament: An Essential Guide*. Nashville: Abingdon, 2006.

Castro, Emilio. *Freedom in Mission: The Perspective of the Kingdom of God: An Ecumenical Inquiry*. Geneva: World Council of Churches, 1985.

———. *Sent Free: Mission and Unity in the Perspective of the Kingdom*. Risk 23. Geneva: World Council of Churches, 1985.

Charles, R. H. *The Revelation of St. John*. Edinburgh: T. & T. Clark, 1920.

Chester, Tim. *From Creation to New Creation*. Waynesboro, GA: Paternoster, 2003.

Chilton, Bruce. *God in Strength: Jesus' Announcement of the Kingdom*. Studien zum Neuen Testament und seiner Umwelt. Series B, vol. 1. Freistadt, Aut.: F. Plöchl, 1979.

———. *Pure Kingdom: Jesus' Vision of God*. Grand Rapids: Eerdmans, 1996.

———. "Regnum Dei Deus Est." *Scottish Journal of Theology* 31 (1978) 261–70.

———, ed. *The Kingdom of God in the Teaching of Jesus*. Issues in Religion and Theology 5. Philadelphia: Fortress, 1984.

Chilton, Bruce, and J. I. H. McDonald. *Jesus and the Ethics of the Kingdom*. Grand Rapids: Eerdmans, 1987.

Cho, Youngmo. *Spirit and Kingdom in the Writings of Luke and Paul: An Attempt to Reconcile these Concepts*. Milton Keynes, UK: Paternoster, 2005.

Cicero. *De Divinatione*. Translated by W. A. Falconer. LCL 154. Cambridge, MA: Harvard University Press, 1923.

———. *Pro Flacco*. In *Orations*. Rev. ed. Translated by C. Macdonald. LCL 324. Cambridge, MA: Harvard University Press, 1976.

Clark, K. W. "Realized Eschatology." *Journal of Biblical Literature* 59 (1940) 367–83.

Clowney, Edmund P. "The Politics of the Kingdom." *Westminster Theological Journal* 61/2 (1979) 291–310.

Cochrane, Arthur C. *Eating and Drinking with Jesus: An Ethical and Biblical Inquiry*. Philadelphia: Westminster, 1974.

Colautti, Federico M. *Passover in the Works of Josephus*. Leiden: Brill, 2002.

Collins, Adela Yarbro. "Psalms, Philippians, and the Origins of Christology." *Biblical Interpretation* 11 (2003) 361–72.

Collins, John J. *The Scepter and the Star: The Messiahs of the Dead Sea Scrolls and Other Literature*. New York: Doubleday, 1995.

Conyers, A. J. *The End: What Jesus Really Said About the Last Things*. Downers Grove, IL: InterVarsity, 1995.

Conzelmann, Hans. *First Corinthians: A Commentary on the First Epistle to the Corinthians*. Hermeneia. Minneapolis: Fortress, 1975.

Corley, Kathleen E. *Maranatha: Women's Funerary Rituals and Christian Origins*. Minneapolis: Fortress, 2010.

———. *Private Women, Public Meals: Social Conflict in Synoptic Tradition*. Peabody, MA: Hendrickson, 1993.

Cotter, Wendy. "The Collegia and Roman Law: State Restrictions on Voluntary Associations, 64 BCE—200 CE." In *Voluntary Associations in the Graeco-Roman World*, edited by John S. Kloppenborg and Stephen G. Wilson, 74–89. New York: Routledge, 1996.

Coutsoumpos, Panayotis. *Paul and the Lord's Supper: A Socio-Historical Investigation*. Studies in Biblical Literature 84. New York: Peter Lang, 2005.

Cranfield, C. E. B. "Thoughts on New Testament Eschatology." *Scottish Journal of Theology* 35/6 (1982) 497–512.

Crosby, Michael H. *The Prayer that Jesus Taught Us*. Maryknoll, NY: Orbis, 2003.

Crossan, John Dominic. *The Birth of Christianity: Discovering What Happened in the Years Immediately after the Execution of Jesus*. San Francisco: Harper Collins, 1998.

———. *God and Empire: Jesus Against Rome, Then and Now*. San Francisco: Harper Collins, 2007.

———. *The Historical Jesus: The Life of a Mediterranean Jewish Peasant.* San Francisco: Harper Collins, 1992.

———. *In Parables: The Challenge of the Historical Jesus.* New York: Harper & Row, 1973.

———. "Roman Imperial Theology." In *In the Shadow of Empire: Reclaiming the Bible as a History of Faithful Resistance,* edited by Richard A. Horsley, 59–73. Louisville: Westminster John Knox, 2008.

Crossan, John Dominic, and Jonathan Reed. *In Search of Paul: How Jesus's Apostle Opposed Rome's Empire with God's Kingdom.* San Francisco: Harper Collins, 2004.

Crump, David. *Knocking on Heaven's Door: A New Testament Theology of Petitionary Prayer.* Grand Rapids: Baker, 2006.

Cullmann, Oscar. *Christ and Time.* Translated by Floyd V. Filson. London: SCM, 1951.

———. *Jesus and the Revolutionaries.* New York: Harper & Row, 1970.

———. *Peter: Disciple, Apostle, Martyr.* Translated by Floyd V. Filson. New York: Meridian, 1958.

———. *Salvation in History.* London: SCM, 1967.

———. *The State in the New Testament.* New York: Scribner's, 1956.

Danker, F. W. *Jesus and the New Age: A Commentary on Luke's Gospel.* Rev. ed. Philadelphia: Fortress, 1988.

D'Arms, John H. "Slaves at Roman Convivia." In *Dining in a Classical Context,* edited by William J. Slater, 171–83. Ann Arbor: University of Michigan Press, 1991.

Davids, Peter H. "The Kingdom of God Come with Power." *Criswell Theological Review* 2/1 (2004) 15–33.

Davies, W. D., and Dale C. Allison Jr. *An Exegetical and Critical Commentary on the Gospel According to Saint Matthew.* International Critical Commentary 3. Edinburgh: T. & T. Clark, 1997.

Davis, William Stearns. *A Day in Old Athens.* Boston: Allyn & Bacon, 1914.

Deiss, Joseph J. *Herculaneum: Italy's Buried Treasure.* New York: Crowell, 1966.

Demaris, Richard E. *The New Testament in Its Ritual World.* London: Routledge, 2008.

DeSilva, David A. *Honor, Patronage, Kinship, and Purity: Unlocking New Testament Culture.* Downers Grove, IL: InterVarsity, 2000.

Dessau, H., trans. *Corpus Inscriptionum Latinarum.* Berlin: Berlin-Brandenburg Academy of Sciences and Humanities, 1966.

Dibelius, Martin. *Jesus.* Translated by Charles B. Hedrick and Frederick C. Grant. Philadelphia: Westminster, 1949.

Dio Cassius. *Roman History.* Vol. 7. Translated by Ernest Cary. LCL 257. Cambridge: Harvard University Press, 1924.

Dio Chrysostom. *Orations.* Vol. 7. Translated by Donald Andrew Russell. Cambridge: Cambridge University Press, 1992.

Dionysius of Halicarnassus. *Roman Antiquities.* Rev. ed. LCL 634. Cambridge: Harvard University Press, 1943.

Dittenberger, Wilhelmus, ed. *Orientis Graeci Inscriptiones Selectae.* Reprint. Chicago: Ares, 2001.

Dix, Dom Gregory. *The Shape of the Liturgy.* London: Continuum, 2000.

Dodd, C. H. *Apostolic Preaching and its Developments.* London: Hodder & Stoughton, 1944.

———. *The Parables of the Kingdom.* New York: Scribner's, 1961.

Donovan, Vincent J. *Christianity Rediscovered.* Maryknoll, NY: Orbis, 2000.

Driver, John. *Images of the Church in Mission*. Scottdale, PA: Herald, 1997.

Dulling, Dennis C., "Kingdom of God, Kingdom of Heaven." In vol. 4 of the *Anchor Bible Dictionary*, edited by D. N. Freedman, 49–96. 6 vols. New York: Bantam Doubleday Dell, 1992.

Dunn, James D. G. *Baptism in the Holy Spirit*. Philadelphia: Westminster, 1970.

———. *The Christ and the Spirit*. Grand Rapids: Eerdmans, 1998.

———. *Christology in the Making*. London: SCM, 1980.

———. *The Epistles to the Colossians and to Philemon*. New International Greek Testament Commentary. Grand Rapids: Eerdmans, 1996.

———. *The Evidence for Jesus*. Philadelphia: Westminster, 1985.

———. "Spirit and Kingdom." *Expository Times* 82 (1970–71) 36–40.

Edwards, David L. *The Last Things Now*. Valley Forge, PA: Judson, 1970.

Edwards, George R. *Jesus and the Politics of Violence*. New York: Harper & Row, 1972.

Ehrensperger, Kathy. *Paul and the Dynamics of Power: Communication and Interaction in the Early Christ-Movement*. Library of New Testament Studies. London: T. & T. Clark, 2007.

———. "Striving for Office and Exercise of Power in the 'House of God': Reading in 1 Tim 3:1–16 in Light of 1 Cor 4:1." Paper presented at the annual meeting of the SBL. New Orleans, LA, November 2009.

Eller, Vernard. *In Place of Sacraments: A Study of Baptism and the Lord's Supper*. Grand Rapids: Eerdmans, 1972.

———. *Proclaim Good Tidings: Evangelism for the Faith Community*. Elgin, IL: Brethren, 1987.

———. *The Promise: Ethics in the Kingdom of God*. Garden City, NY: Doubleday, 1970.

Elliott, Neil. "The Apostle Paul and Empire." In *In the Shadow of Empire*, edited by Richard A. Horsley, 97–116. Louisville: Westminster John Knox, 2008.

Ellis, E. Earle. *The Gospel of Luke*. New Century Bible Commentary. Grand Rapids: Eerdmans, 1981.

Esler, Philip F. *Community and Gospel in Luke-Acts: The Social and Political Motivations of Lucan Theology*. Cambridge: Cambridge University Press, 1989.

Eusebius. *Ecclesiastical History*. Translated by Kirsopp Lake. LCL 153. Cambridge MA: Harvard University Press, 1926.

Evans, Craig A. *Luke*. New International Biblical Commentary. Peabody, MA: Hendrickson, 1990.

Farrow, Douglas. *Ascension and Ecclesia: On the Significance of the Doctrine of the Ascension for Ecclesiology and Christian Cosmology*. Grand Rapids: Eerdmans, 2000.

Fee, Gordon D. *The First and Second Letters to the Thessalonians*. New International Commentary on the New Testament. Grand Rapids: Eerdmans, 2009.

———. *The First Epistle to the Corinthians*. New International Commentary on the New Testament. Grand Rapids: Eerdmans, 1987.

———. *God's Empowering Presence*. Peabody, MA: Hendrickson, 1994.

———. *Paul, the Spirit, and the People of God*. Peabody, MA: Hendrickson, 1996.

———. *Paul's Letter to the Philippians*. New International Commentary on the New Testament. Grand Rapids: Eerdmans, 1995.

Feeley-Harnik, Gillian. *The Lord's Table: The Meaning of Food in Early Judaism and Christianity*. Washington DC: Smithsonian, 1994.

Filson, Floyd V. *Jesus Christ the Risen Lord: A Biblical Theology Based on the Resurrection.* Nashville: Abingdon, 1941.

Finger, Reta Halteman. *Of Widows and Meals: Communal Meals in the Book of Acts.* Grand Rapids: Eerdmans, 2007.

Fitzmyer, Joseph A. *The Acts of the Apostles: A New Translation with Introduction and Commentary.* The Anchor Bible 31. New York: Doubleday, 1998.

———. *The Gospel According to Luke I–IX: Introduction, Translation, and Notes.* The Anchor Bible 28. New York: Doubleday, 1982.

———. *The Gospel According to Luke, X–XXIV.* The Anchor Bible 28A. Garden City, NY: Doubleday, 1985.

Flandrin, Jean-Louis, and Massimo Montanari. *Food: A Culinary History from Antiquity to the Present.* New York: Columbia University Press, 1999.

Foner, Eric. *Forever Free: The Story of Emancipation and Reconstruction.* New York: Vintage, 2005.

France, R. T. *The Gospel of Matthew: An Introduction and Commentary.* Grand Rapids: Eerdmans, 1985.

Fredriksen, Paula. *Jesus of Nazareth: King of the Jews.* New York: Vintage, 1999.

Fuellenbach, John. *The Kingdom of God: The Message of Jesus Today.* Maryknoll, NY: Orbis, 1995.

Garland, David E. *1 Corinthians.* Baker Exegetical Commentary on the New Testament. Grand Rapids: Baker, 2003.

———. *Reading Matthew: A Literary and Theological Reading of the First Gospel.* New York: Crossroad, 1993.

Gärtner, B. E. "The Person of Jesus and the Kingdom of God." *Theology Today* 27 (1970) 32–43.

Geertz, Clifford, ed. *Myth, Symbol, and Culture.* New York: Norton, 1971.

Georgi, Dieter. *Theocracy in Paul's Praxis and Theology.* Minneapolis: Fortress, 1991.

Gillespie, Thomas W. *The First Theologians: A Study in Early Christian Prophecy.* Grand Rapids: Eerdmans, 1994.

Glancy, Jennifer. *Slavery in Early Christianity.* Minneapolis: Fortress, 2006.

Glasson, T. F. "The Temporary Messianic Kingdom and the Kingdom of God." *Journal of Theological Studies* NS 41 (1990) 515–25.

Gloer, W. Hulitt. *Eschatology and the New Testament.* Peabody, MA: Hendrickson, 1988.

Goldsworthy, Graeme. *According to Plan: The Unfolding Revelation of God in the Bible.* Downers Grove, IL: InterVarsity, 2002.

———. *The Goldsworthy Trilogy.* Waynesboro, GA: Paternoster, 2000.

Gorman, Michael J. *Elements of Biblical Exposition.* Rev. ed. Peabody, MA: Hendrickson, 2009.

Gottwald, Norman K. "Early Israel as an Anti-Imperial Community." In *In the Shadow of Empire*, edited by Richard A. Horsley, 9–24. Louisville: Westminster John Knox, 2008.

———. *The Tribes of Yahweh: A Sociology of Religion of Liberated Israel 1250–1050 BCE.* Sheffield, UK: Sheffield Academic Press, 1999.

Gowan, Donald E. *Eschatology in the Old Testament.* Philadelphia: Fortress, 1986.

Grassi, Joseph. *Broken Bread and Broken Bodies: The Lord's Supper and World Hunger.* Rev. ed. Maryknoll, NY: Orbis, 2004.

Gray, John, ed. *The Biblical Doctrine of the Reign of God.* Edinburgh: T. & T. Clark, 1979.

————. "Hebrew Conception of the Kingship of God." *Vetus Testamentum* 6 (1956) 268–85.

Green, Joel B. *The Gospel of Luke*. New International Commentary on the New Testament. Grand Rapids: Eerdmans, 1997.

Grenz, Stanley. *Prayer: The Cry for the Kingdom*. Rev. ed. Peabody, MA: Hendrickson, 1988.

Grudem, Wayne. *The Gift of Prophecy in 1 Corinthians*. Washington DC: University Press of America, 1982.

Guder, Darrell L., ed. *Missional Church: A Vision for the Sending Church*. Grand Rapids: Eerdmans, 1998.

Gundry, Robert H. "The Form, Meaning and Background of the Hymn Quoted in 1 Timothy 3:16." In *Apostolic History of the Gospels, Biblical and Historical Essays Presented to F. F. Bruce*, edited by W. Ward Gasque and Ralph P. Martin, 203–22. Exeter, UK: Paternoster, 1970.

————. *Matthew: A Commentary on His Handbook for a Mixed Church Under Persecution*. 2nd ed. Grand Rapids: Eerdmans, 1994.

Gurgel, Autumn. "Running Head: Roots and Theories of the Doctrine of Ethos." Online: http://www.charis.wlc.edu/publications/symposium_spring03/gurgel.pdf.

Gutierrez, Gustavo. *A Theology of Liberation*. Translated by Caridad Inda and John Eagleson. Maryknoll, NY: Orbis, 1973.

Guy, Laurie. "The Interplay of the Present and Future in the Kingdom of God (Luke 19:11–44)." *Tyndale Bulletin* 48/1 (1997) 119–37.

Haenchen, Ernst. *John 1*. Translated by Robert W. Funk. Hermeneia. Minneapolis: Fortress, 1984.

————. *John 2*. Translated by Robert W. Funk. Hermeneia. Minneapolis: Fortress, 1984.

Hahn, Scott. *Understanding "Our Father": Biblical Reflections on The Lord's Prayer*. Steubenville, OH: Emmaus Road, 2002.

Hagner, Donald A. *The Jewish Reclamation of Jesus: An Analysis and Critique of Modern Jewish Study of Jesus*. Grand Rapids: Zondervan, 1984.

————. *Matthew 14–28*. Word Biblical Library 33B. Dallas: Word, 1995.

Hanson, K. C., and Douglas E. Oakman. *Palestine in the Time of Jesus: Social Structures and Social Conflicts*. 2nd ed. Minneapolis: Fortress, 2009.

Harink, Douglas. *Paul Among the Postliberals: Pauline Theology Beyond Christendom and Modernity*. Grand Rapids: Brazos, 2003.

Harkness, Georgia. *Understanding the Kingdom of God*. Nashville: Abingdon, 1974.

Harland, Philip A. *Associations, Synagogues, and Congregations: Claiming a Place in Ancient Mediterranean Society*. Minneapolis: Fortress, 2003.

————. *Dynamics of Identity in the World of the Early Christians*. London: T. & T. Clark, 2009.

Harrington, Daniel J. *The Gospel of Matthew*. Sacra Pagina 1. Collegeville, MN: Liturgical, 1991.

Harrington, Wilfrid J. *Revelation*. Sacra Pagina 16. Collegeville, MN: Liturgical, 1993.

Harris, Murray J. *Colossians and Philemon*. Exegetical Guide to the Greek New Testament. Grand Rapids: Eerdmans, 1991.

Harvey, Anthony E. *Jesus and the Constraints of History*. Philadelphia: Westminster, 1982.

Hauerwas, Stanley. *The Peaceable Kingdom*. Notre Dame, IN: University of Notre Dame Press, 1983.

———. *Performing the Faith: Bonhoeffer and the Practice of Nonviolence*. Grand Rapids: Brazos, 2004.

Hauerwas, Stanley, and William H. Willimon. *Resident Aliens: Life in the Christian Colony*. Nashville: Abingdon, 1989.

Hay, David M. *Glory at the Right Hand: Psalm 110 in Early Christianity*. Nashville: Abingdon, 1973.

Hays, Richard B. *First Corinthians*. Interpretation. Louisville: John Knox, 1997.

———. *The Moral Vision of the New Testament*. New York: HarperCollins, 1996.

Heen, Erik M. "Phil 2:6–11 and Resistance to Local Theocratic Rule." In *Paul and the Roman Imperial Order*, edited by Richard A. Horsley, 125–49. Harrisburg, PA: Trinity, 2004.

Hemer, Colin J. *Letters to the Seven Churches of Asia in the Local Setting*. Grand Rapids: Eerdmans, 1989.

Hendrickx, Herman. *The Parables of Jesus*. New York: Harper & Row, 1986.

Hengel, Martin. "Hymn and Christology." In *Papers on Paul and Other New Testament Authors*, edited by E. A. Livingstone, 174. *SNT* Supp. 3. Sheffield, UK: JSOT, 1980.

Herzog, William R., II. *Jesus, Justice and the Reign of God: A Ministry of Liberation*. Louisville: Westminster John Knox, 2000.

———. "On Stage and Off Stage with Jesus of Nazareth: Public Transcripts, Hidden Transcripts, and Gospel Texts." In *Hidden Transcripts and the Arts of Resistance*, edited by Richard A. Horsley, 41–60. Atlanta: SBL, 2004.

———. *Parables as Subversive Speech*. Louisville: Westminster John Knox, 1994.

Hicks, John Mark. *Come to the Table: Revisioning the Lord's Supper*. Orange, CA: Leafwood, 2002.

Hiers, Richard H. *The Historical Jesus and the Kingdom of God: Present and Future in the Message and Ministry of Jesus*. Gainesville: University of Florida Press, 1973.

———. *The Kingdom of God in the Synoptic Tradition*. Gainesville: University of Florida Press, 1970.

Higgins, A. J. B. *The Lord's Supper in the New Testament*. Studies in Biblical Theology 6. London: SCM, 1952.

Hippolytus. *The Apostolic Tradition of Hippolytus*. Translated by Burton Scott. New Haven: Archon, 1962.

Homer. *Odyssey*. Translated by Robert Fagles. New York: Penguin, 2006.

Horace. *The Complete Odes and Epodes*. Translated by David West. Oxford: Oxford University Press, 2008.

———. *Satires, Epistles, and Ars Poetica*. Translated by Rushton Fairclough. LCL. Cambridge: Harvard University Press, 1970.

Horbury, William. *Jewish Messianism and the Cult of Christ*. London: SCM, 1998.

Horrell, David G., and Edward Adams. "The Scholarly Quest for Paul's Church at Corinth: A Critical Study." In *Christianity in Corinth: The Quest for the Pauline Church*, edited by Edward Adams and David G. Horrell, 1–43. Louisville: Westminster John Knox, 2004.

Horsley, Richard A. *1 Corinthians*. Abingdon New Testament Commentaries. Nashville: Abingdon, 1998.

———. *Hidden Transcripts and Arts of Resistance: Applying the Work of James C. Scott to Jesus and Paul*. Atlanta: SBL, 2004.

————. "Jesus and Empire." In *In the Shadow of the Empire*, edited by Richard A. Horsley, 75–96. Louisville: Westminster John Knox, 2008.

————. *Jesus and Empire: The Kingdom of God and the New World Disorder.* Minneapolis: Fortress, 2003.

————. *Jesus and the Spiral of Violence: Popular Jewish Resistance in Roman Palestine.* San Francisco: Harper & Row, 1987.

————. *Jesus in Context: People, Power, and Performance.* Minneapolis: Fortress, 2008.

————. *The Message and the Kingdom.* Minneapolis: Fortress, 2002.

————. *Paul and Empire: Religion and Power in Roman Imperial Society.* Harrisburg, PA: Trinity, 1997.

————. *Paul and Politics: Ekklesia, Israel, Imperium, Interpretation.* Harrisburg, PA: Trinity, 2000.

————. *Paul and the Roman Imperial Order.* Harrisburg, PA: Trinity, 2004.

————, ed. *In the Shadow of Empire: Reclaiming the Bible as a History of Faithful Resistance.* Louisville: Westminster John Knox, 2008.

Horsley, Richard A., and John S. Hanson. *Bandits, Prophets, and Messiahs: Popular Movements at the Time of Jesus.* San Francisco: Harper & Row, 1988.

Horsley, Richard A., and Neil Asher Silberman. *The Message and the Kingdom: How Jesus and Paul Ignited a Revolution and Transformed the Ancient World.* Minneapolis: Fortress, 1997.

Howard-Brook, Wes, and Anthony Gwyther. *Unveiling Empire: Reading Revelation Then and Now.* Maryknoll, NY: Orbis, 1999.

Hunter, Archibald M. *The Parables Then and Now.* Philadelphia: Westminster, 1971.

Jeffers, James S. *The Greco-Roman World of the New Testament: Exploring the Background of Early Christianity.* Downers Grove, IL: InterVarsity, 1999.

Jeremias, Joachim. *The Eucharistic Words of Jesus.* London: SCM, 1966.

————. *New Testament Theology.* New York: Scribner's, 1971.

————. *Rediscovering the Parables.* New York: Scribner's, 1966.

Jewett, Robert. *Romans.* Hermeneia. Minneapolis: Fortress, 2006.

————."Tenement Churches and Communal Meals in the Early Church: The Implications of a Form-Critical Analysis of 2 Thessalonians 3:10." *Biblical Research* 38 (1993) 23–43.

————."Tenement Churches and Pauline Love Feasts." *Quarterly Review* 14/1 (1994) 43–58.

————. *The Thessalonian Correspondence.* Philadelphia: Fortress, 1986.

Johnson, Dennis E. *The Message of Acts in the History of Redemption.* Phillipsburg, NJ: P & R, 1997.

Johnson, Luke Timothy. "Book of Luke-Acts." In *Anchor Bible Dictionary*, edited by D. N. Freedman, 4:406. New York: Bantam Doubleday Dell, 1992.

————. *The Gospel of Luke.* Sacra Pagina 3. Collegeville, MN: Liturgical, 1991.

Jonge, Henk Jan de, "The Early History of the Lord's Supper." In *Religious Identity and the Invention of Tradition.*, edited by Jan Willem van Henten and Anton Houtepen, 209–37. Leiden: Brill, 2001.

Jonge, Marinus de. *God's Final Envoy: Early Christology and Jesus' Own View of His Mission.* Grand Rapids: Eerdmans, 1998.

Josephus. *The Complete Works of Josephus.* Translated by William Whiston. Peabody, MA: Henrickson, 1988.

Just, Arthur A. *The Ongoing Feast: Table Fellowship and Eschatology at Emmaus.* Collegeville, MN: Liturgical, 1993.

Justin, Martyr, Saint. *Apology* 1. Translated by Marcus Dods and George Reith. In *Ante-Nicene Fathers* 1, edited by A. Roberts, J. Donaldson, and A. Coxe. Buffalo: Christian Literature, 1885.

Kahl, Brigitte. "Acts of the Apostle." In *In the Shadow of Empire: Reclaiming the Bible as a History of Faithful Resistance*, edited by Richard A. Horsley, 137–56. Louisville: Westminster John Knox, 2008.

Kallas, James. *Jesus and the Power of Satan.* Philadelphia: Westminster, 1958.

Karkkainen, Veli-Matti. *An Introduction to Ecclesiology: Ecumenical, Historical and Global Perspectives.* Downers Grove, IL: InterVarsity, 2002.

Karlson, William, Jr. "Syncretism: The Presence of Roman Augury in the Consecration of English Monarchs." PhD diss., Baylor University, 2007.

Karris, Robert J. *Luke: Artist and Theologian.* New York: Paulist, 1985.

Käsemann, Ernst. "A Critical Analysis of Philippians 2:5–11," *Journal for Theology and the Church* (1968) 25–48.

———. "The Eschatological Royal Reign of God." In *Your Kingdom Come: Mission Perspectives Report on the World Conference on Mission and Evangelism: Melbourne Australia, 12–15 May, 1980*, 61–71. Geneva: World Council of Churches, 1980.

Kaufman, Peter Ivan. *Redeeming Politics.* Princeton, NJ: Princeton University Press, 1990.

Kaylor, R. David. *Jesus the Prophet: His Vision of the Kingdom on Earth.* Louisville: Westminster John Knox, 1994.

Keck, Leander E. "The Spirit and the Dove." *New Testament Studies* 17 (1970–71) 41–67.

Keener, Craig S. *A Commentary on the Gospel of Matthew.* Grand Rapids: Eerdmans, 1999.

———. *1–2 Corinthians.* New Cambridge Bible Commentary. Cambridge: Cambridge University Press, 2005.

———. *The Gospel of John: A Commentary.* 2 vols. Peabody, MA: Hendrickson, 2003.

———. *Revelation: The NIV Application Commentary.* Grand Rapids: Zondervan, 2000.

Kibble, David G. "The Kingdom of God and Christian Politics." *Themelios* 7/1 (1981) 24–32.

Kim, Seyoon. *Christ and Caesar: The Gospel and the Roman Empire in the Writings of Paul and Luke.* Grand Rapids: Eerdmans, 2008.

King, Philip J., and Lawrence E. Stager. *Life in Biblical Israel.* Louisville: Westminster John Knox, 2001.

Kinsler, Ross, and Gloria Kinsler. *The Biblical Jubilee and the Struggle for Life.* Maryknoll, NY: Orbis, 1999.

Kittel, Gerhard, and Gerhard Friedrich, eds. *Theological Dictionary of the New Testament.* Translated by Geoffrey W. Bromiley. 10 vols. Grand Rapids: Eerdmans, 1964–1976.

Klaiber, Walter. *Call and Response: Biblical Foundations of a Theology of Evangelism.* Nashville: Abingdon, 1997.

Klein, Günther. "The Biblical Understanding of the 'Kingdom of God.'" Translated by Richard N. Soulen. *Interpretation* 26 (1972) 387–418.

Kline, Meredith G. *Kingdom Prologue: Genesis Foundations for a Covenantal Worldview.* Overland Park, KS: Two Age, 2000.

Klinghardt, Mathias. "Chances and Limitations of Ritual Analysis of Early Christian Meals." Paper presented at the annual meeting of the SBL Meals of the Greco-Roman World Study Group. New Orleans, LA, November 2009.

———. *Gemeinschaftsmahl und Mahlgemeinschaft: Soziologie und Liturgie Fruehchristlicher Mahlfeiern.* Tübingen: Francke, 1996.

Kloppenborg, John S., and Stephen S. Wilson, *Voluntary Associations in the Graeco-Roman World.* New York: Routledge, 1996.

Koenig, John. *The Feast of the World's Redemption: Eucharistic Origins and Christian Mission.* Harrisburg, PA: Trinity, 2000.

———. *New Testament Hospitality: Partnership with Strangers as Promise and Mission.* Philadelphia: Fortress, 1985.

Kollmann, Bernd. *Ursprung und Gestalten der frühchristlichen Mahlfeier.* Göttingen: Vandenhoeck & Ruprecht, 1990.

Köstenberger, Andreas J. *John.* Baker Exegetical Commentary on the New Testament. Grand Rapids: Baker, 2004.

Kraus, C. Norman. *An Intrusive Gospel? Christian Mission in the Postmodern World.* Downers Grove, IL: InterVarsity, 1998.

Kraybill, Donald B. *The Upside-Down Kingdom.* Scottdale, PA: Herald, 1978.

Kraybill, J. Nelson. *Apocalypse and Allegiance: Worship, Politics, and Devotion in the Book of Revelation.* Grand Rapids: Brazos, 2010.

Krieder, Alan, Eleanor Kreider, and Paulus Widjaja. *A Culture of Peace: God's Vision for the Church.* Intercourse, PA: Good Books, 2005.

Kulp, Joshua. *The Schechter Haggadah: Art, History and Commentary.* Brooklyn: Lambda, 2009.

Kümmel, W. G. *Promise and Fulfilment: The Eschatological Message of Jesus.* London: SCM, 1957.

Ladd, George Eldon. "The Kingdom of God: Reign or Realm?" *Journal of Biblical Literature* 81 (1962) 230–38.

———. "The Life Setting of the Parables of the Kingdom." *Journal of Bible and Religion* 31 (1962) 193–99.

———. *The Presence of the Future: The Eschatology of Biblical Realism.* Grand Rapids: Eerdmans, 1974.

Lang, Bernhard. *Sacred Games: A History of Christian Worship.* New Haven, CT: Yale University Press, 1997.

Larsen, Lillian. "Early Christian Meals and Slavery." Paper presented at the annual meeting of the SBL Meals of the Greco-Roman World Study Group. Boston, MA, November 2008.

LaVerdiere, Eugene. *Dining in the Kingdom of God: The Origins of the Eucharist According to Luke.* Chicago: Liturgy Training, 1994.

Leithart, Peter J. *Blessed Are the Hungry: Meditations on the Lord's Supper.* Moscow, ID: Canon, 2000.

———. *The Kingdom and the Power: Rediscovering the Centrality of the Church.* Phillipsburg, NJ: Presbyterian and Reformed, 1993.

Lenski, Gerhard. *Power and Privilege: A Theory of Stratification.* 2nd ed. Chapel Hill: University of North Carolina Press, 1984.

Leonhard, Clemens. *The Jewish Pesach and the Origins of the Christian Easter.* Studia Sacra 35. Berlin: de Gruyter, 2006.

Liebenberg, Jacobus. *The Language of the Kingdom and Jesus.* New York: de Gruyter, 2001.

Lietzmann, Hans. *Mass and the Lord's Supper.* Translated by Dorothea H. G. Reese. Leiden: Brill, 1953.

Lindar, Barnabas. *Jesus, Son of Man: A Fresh Examination of the Son of Man Sayings in the Gospels in the Light of Recent Research.* Grand Rapids: Eerdmans, 1984.

Livy. *History of Rome.* Vols. 1–2. Translated by B. O. Foster. LCL 114. Cambridge, MA: Harvard University Press, 1919.

Lohfink, Gerhard. *Jesus and Community: The Social Dimension of Christian Faith.* Translated by John P. Galvin. Philadelphia: Fortress, 1984.

Lohmeyer, Ernest. *Der Brief an die Philipper, Kolosser und an Philemon.* Göttingen: KEK, 1962.

Lucian. *The Works of Lucian of Samosata.* Vol. 4. Translated by H. W. Fowler and F. G. Fowler. Oxford: Clarendon, 1905.

Lundström, Gösta. *The Kingdom of God in the Teaching of Jesus: A History of Interpretation from the Last Decades of the Nineteenth Century to the Present Day.* Translated by Joan Bulman. London: Oliver & Boyd, 1963.

Luz, Ulrich. *Matthew 21–28: A Commentary.* Translated by James E. Crouch. Hermeneia. Minneapolis: Fortress, 2005.

Lyall, Francis. *Slaves, Citizens, Sons: Legal Metaphors in the Epistles.* Grand Rapids: Zondervan, 1984.

MacDonald, D. R. *There is No Male or Female: The Fate of the Dominical Saying in Paul and Gnosticism.* Philadelphia: Fortress, 1987.

MacDonald, Nathan. *Not by Bread Alone: The Use of Food in the Old Testament.* New York: Oxford University Press, 2008.

Mack, Burton L. "The Kingdom Sayings in Mark." *Forum* 3/1 (1987) 3–47.

———. "The Kingdom That Didn't Come." In *SBL Seminar Papers*, edited by David J. Lull, 608–35. Atlanta: Scholars, 1988.

———. *A Myth of Innocence: Mark and Christian Origins.* Minneapolis: Fortress, 1988.

Malherbe, Abraham J. *Social Aspects of Early Christianity.* 2nd ed. Philadelphia: Fortress, 1983.

Malina, Bruce J. *The Social Gospel of Jesus: The Kingdom of God in Mediterranean Perspective.* Minneapolis: Fortress, 2001.

Malina, Bruce J., and John J. Pilch. *Social-Science Commentary on the Book of Acts.* Minneapolis: Fortress, 2008.

Maloney, Elliott C. *Jesus' Urgent Message for Today: The Kingdom of God in Mark's Gospel.* New York: Continuum, 2004.

Manson, T. W. *The Sayings of Jesus.* London: SCM, 1957.

———. *The Teaching of Jesus.* Cambridge: Cambridge University Press, 1931.

Marcus, Joel. "Entering into the Kingly Power of God." *Journal of Biblical Literature* 107 (1988) 663–75.

———. *The Mystery of the Kingdom.* SBL Dissertation Series 90. Atlanta: Scholars, 1986.

———. *The Way of the Lord: Christological Exegesis of the Old Testament in the Gospel of Mark.* Louisville: Westminster John Knox, 1992.

Marshall, Christopher D. "Kingdom Come: The Kingdom of God in the Teaching of Jesus." *Journal of the Christian Brethren Research Fellowship* 120 (1990) 7–25.

Marshall, I. Howard. *Eschatology and the Parables.* London: Tyndale, 1963.

Bibliography

———. *1 and 2 Thessalonians*. New Century Bible Commentary. Grand Rapids: Eerdmans, 1983.

———. *The First Epistle to the Corinthians*. New International Greek Testament Commentary. Grand Rapids: Eerdmans, 2000.

———. *The Gospel of Luke: A Commentary on the Greek Text*. New International Greek Testament Commentary. Grand Rapids: Eerdmans, 1978.

———. "The Hope of a New Age: The Kingdom of God in the New Testament." *Themelios* 11/1 (1985) 5–15.

———. *Last Supper and Lord's Supper*. Vancouver, BC: Regent College, 1980.

———. *New Testament Theology: Many Witnesses, One Gospel*. Downers Grove, IL: InterVarsity, 2004.

———. *The Pastoral Epistles*. International Critical Commentary. Edinburgh: T. & T. Clark, 1999.

Martin, Ralph P. *A Hymn of Christ: Philippians 2:5–11 in Recent Interpretation and in the Setting of Early Christianity*. Grand Rapids: InterVarsity, 1997.

———. *Worship in the Early Church*. Grand Rapids: Eerdmans, 1974.

Martin, Ralph P., and Gerald F. Hawthorne. *Philippians*. Revised and expanded. Word Biblical Commentary 43. Nashville: Nelson, 2004.

Matthews, Shelly, and E. Leigh Gibson, eds. *Violence in the New Testament*. London: T. & T. Clark, 2005.

McGowan, Andrew. *Ascetic Eucharists: Food and Drink in the Early Christian Ritual Meals*. Oxford: Clarendon, 1999.

———. "Is There a Liturgical Text in this Gospel? The Institution Narratives and their Early Interpretive Communities." *Journal of Biblical Literature* 118 (1999) 73–87.

McGready, Wayne O. "Ekklesia and Voluntary Associations." In *Voluntary Associations in the Graeco-Roman World*, edited by John S. Kloppenborg and Stephen S. Wilson, 69–70. New York: Routledge, 1996.

McIver, Robert K. "The Parable of the Weeds among the Wheat (Matt. 13:24–30, 36–43) and the Relationship between the Kingdom and the Church as Portrayed in the Gospel of Matthew." *Journal of Biblical Literature* 114 (1995) 643–59.

McKinion, Steven A., ed. *Life and Practice in the Early Church: A Documentary Reader*. New York: New York University Press, 2001.

McKnight, Scot. *A New Vision for Israel: The Teachings of Jesus in National Context*. Grand Rapids: Eerdmans, 1999.

Meeks, Wayne A. *The First Urban Christians: The Social World of the Apostle Paul* New Haven, CT: Yale University Press, 2003.

Meier, John P. *A Marginal Jew: Rethinking the Historical Jesus, Volume Two: Mentor, Message and Miracles*. New York: Doubleday, 1994.

Mendenhall, George E. *Law and Covenant in Israel and the Ancient Near East*. Pittsburgh: Biblical Colloquium, 1955.

Merrill, Eugene H. "Covenant and the Kingdom: Genesis 1–3 as Foundation for Biblical Theology." *Criswell Theological Review* 1/2 (1987) 295–308.

Metzger, Bruce, ed. *The Oxford Annotated Apocrypha*. New York: Oxford University Press, 1965.

———. *A Textual Commentary on the Greek New Testament*. New York: United Bible Society, 1971.

Meyer, Ben F. *One Loaf, One Cup: Ecumenical Studies of 1 Cor 11 and Other Eucharistic Texts*. New Gospel Studies 6. Macon, GA: Mercer University Press, 1993.

Millar, Fergus. *The Roman Near East, 31 B.C.–A.D. 337.* Cambridge, MA: Harvard University Press, 1993.

Minear, Paul S. *The Kingdom and the Power: An Exposition of the New Testament Gospel.* Philadelphia: Westminster, 1950.

Moloney, Francis J. *The Gospel of John.* Sacra Pagina 4. Collegeville, MN: Liturgical, 1998.

Moltmann, Jürgen. *Theology of Hope.* Translated by James W. Leith. New York: Harper & Row, 1967.

Moltmann, Jürgen, Nicholas Wolterstorff, and Ellen T. Charry. *A Passion for God's Reign.* Edited by Miroslav Volf. Grand Rapids: Eerdmans, 1998.

Morris, Leon. *The First and Second Epistles to the Thessalonians.* Rev. ed. Grand Rapids: Eerdmans, 1991.

———. *The Gospel According to John.* Grand Rapids: Eerdmans, 1971.

Mounce, Robert H. *The Book of Revelation.* Rev. ed. Grand Rapids: Eerdmans, 1977.

———. *Matthew: A Good News Commentary.* New International Biblical Commentary. San Francisco: Harper & Row, 1985.

Mowinckel, Sigmund. *He That Cometh: The Messiah Concept in the Old Testament and Later Judaism.* New York: Abingdon, 1954.

Moyise, Steve, and Maarten J. J. Menken, eds. *The Psalms in the New Testament.* London: T. & T. Clark, 2004.

Mulholland, James. *Praying Like Jesus: The Lord's Supper in a Culture of Prosperity.* New York: HarperCollins, 2001.

Müller-Fahrenholz, Geiko. *The Kingdom and the Power: The Theology of Jürgen Moltmann.* Minneapolis: Fortress, 2001.

Munck, Johannes. *Paul and the Salvation of Mankind.* Atlanta: John Knox, 1977.

Nerney, Catherine T., and Hal Taussig. *Re-Imaging Life Together in America: A New Gospel of Community.* Lanham, MD: Sheed & Ward, 2002.

Nolan, Albert. *Jesus Before Christianity.* Maryknoll, NY: Orbis, 1976.

Nolland, John. *The Gospel of Matthew: A Commentary on the Greek Text.* Grand Rapids: Eerdmans, 2005.

———. *Luke 1:1—9:20.* Word Biblical Commentary 35A. Dallas: Word, 1989.

———. *Luke 9:21—18:34.* Word Biblical Commentary 35B. Dallas: Word, 1993.

———. *Luke 18:35—24:53.* Word Biblical Commentary 35C. Dallas: Word, 1993.

———. "The Role of Money and Possession in the Parable of the Prodigal Son (Luke 15:11–32)." In *Reading Luke: Interpretation, Reflection, Formation,* edited by Craig G. Bartholomew, Joel B. Green, Anthony C. Thiselton, 178–209. London: Paternoster, 2005.

Oakes, Peter. *Reading Romans in Pompeii: Paul's Letter at Ground Level.* Minneapolis: Fortress, 2009.

O'Brien, Peter T. *The Epistle to the Philippians.* New International Greek Testament Commentary. Grand Rapids: Eerdmans, 1991.

O'Neill, J. C. "The Kingdom of God." *Novum Testamentum* 35 (1993) 130–41.

Osborne, Grant R. *Revelation.* Baker Exegetical Commentary on the New Testament. Grand Rapids: Baker Academic, 2002.

Otto, Rudolf. *The Kingdom of God and the Son of Man: A Study in the History of Religion.* Translated by Floyd V. Filson and Bertram L. Woolf. London: Lutterworth, 1951.

Pamment, Margaret. "The Kingdom of Heaven According to the First Gospel." *New Testament Studies* 27 (1981) 211–32.

Pannenberg, Wolfhart. *Jesus—God and Man.* London: SCM, 1968.

———. *Theology and the Kingdom of God.* Philadelphia: Westminster, 1969.

———, ed. *Revelation as History.* Translated by David Granskou. New York: Macmillan, 1968.

Pate, C. Marvin. *The End of the Age Has Come: The Theology of Paul.* Grand Rapids: Zondervan, 1995.

Patrick, Dale. "The Kingdom of God in the Old Testament." In *The Kingdom of God in 20th-Century Interpretation,* edited by Wendell Willis, 67–79. Peabody, MA: Hendrickson, 1987.

Peels, H. G. L. "The Kingdom of God in the Old Testament." *In die Skriflig* 35/2 (2001) 173–89.

Perrin, Norman. *Jesus and the Language of the Kingdom: Symbol and Metaphor in New Testament Interpretation.* Philadelphia: Fortress, 1976.

———. *The Kingdom of God in the Teaching of Jesus.* Philadelphia: Westminster, 1963.

———. *Rediscovering the Teachings of Jesus.* New York: Harper & Row, 1967.

Perry, John Michael. *Exploring the Evolution of the Lord's Supper in the New Testament.* Kansas City, MO: Sheed & Ward, 1994.

Philo. *On the Contemplative Life.* Vol. 9. Translated by F. H. Colson. LCL 363. Cambridge, MA: Harvard University Press, 1941.

———. *On the Embassy to Gaius.* Vol 10. Translated by F. H. Colson. LCL 379. Cambridge, MA: Harvard University Press, 1962.

Pigott, Susan M. "The Kingdom of the Warrior God: The Old Testament and the Kingdom of Yahweh." *Southwestern Journal of Theology* 40/2 (1998) 5–20.

Pixley, George V. *God's Kingdom.* Maryknoll, NY: Orbis, 1981.

Plato. *The Symposium on Love or the Banquet.* Translated by Percy B. Shelley. Mount Vernon, NY: Peter Pauper, 1944.

Pleins, J. David. *The Social Visions of the Hebrew Bible: A Theological Introduction.* Louisville: Westminster John Knox, 2001.

Pliny. *The Letters to the Younger Pliny.* Translated by Betty Radice. New York: Penguin, 1963.

Pliny the Elder. *Natural History.* Translated by H. Rackham. LCL 394, Cambridge, MA: Harvard University Press, 1952.

Plutarch. *Isis and Osirus.* In *Moralia,* vol. 5. Translated by Frank Cole Babbitt. LCL 306. Cambridge, MA: Harvard University Press, 1936.

———. *Table-Talk.* In *Moralia,* vol. 8. Translated by P. A. Clement and H. B. Hoffleit. LCL 424. Cambridge, MA: Harvard University Press, 1969.

Potgieter, P. C. "The Consummation of the Kingdom of God: Reflections on the Final Victory of Christ as Portrayed in Paul's First Epistle to the Corinthians." *In die Skriflig* 35/2 (2001) 215–24.

Prevost, Jean-Pierre. *How to Read the Prophets.* London: SCM, 1995.

Price, S. R. F. *Rituals and Powers: The Roman Imperial Cult in Asia Minor.* New York: Cambridge University Press, 1987.

Pritchard, James B. *The Ancient Near East in Pictures.* 2nd ed. Princeton, NJ: Princeton University Press, 1969.

———, ed. *Ancient Near Eastern Texts Relating to the Old Testament with Supplement.* 3rd ed. Princeton, NJ: Princeton University Press, 1969.

Ramsay, W. M. *The Letters to the Seven Churches of Asia.* New York: A. C. Armstrong, 1904.

Rasmusson, Arne. *The Church as Polis*. Rev. ed. Notre Dame, IN: University of Notre Dame Press, 1995.

Reddish, Mitchell G. *Revelation*. Smyth and Helwys Bible Commentary. Macon, GA: Smyth & Helwys, 2001.

Revell, Louise. *Roman Imperialism and Local Identities*. Cambridge: Cambridge University Press, 2008.

Richard, Pablo. *Apocalypse: A People's Commentary on the Book of Revelation*. Maryknoll, NY: Orbis, 1995.

Richter, Sandra L. *The Epic of Eden: A Christian Entry into the Old Testament*. Downers Grove, IL: InterVarsity, 2008.

Ridderbos, Herman N. *The Gospel According to John: A Theological Commentary*. Translated by John Vriend. Grand Rapids: Eerdmans, 1977.

Rieger, Joerg. *Christ and Empire: From Paul to Postcolonial Times*. Minneapolis: Fortress, 2007.

Ringe, Sharon H. *Jesus, Liberation, and the Biblical Jubilee*. Eugene, OR: Wipf & Stock, 2004.

Roberts, Chris. *Heavy Words Lightly Thrown: The Reason Behind the Rhyme*. New York: Gotham, 2004.

Roberts, Harold. *Jesus and the Kingdom of God*. London: Epworth, 1955.

Roberts, Vaughan. *God's Big Picture: Tracing the Storyline of the Bible*. Downers Grove, IL: InterVarsity, 2002.

Robinson, Anthony B., and Robert W. Wall. *Called to Be Church: The Book of Acts for a New Day*. Grand Rapids: Eerdmans, 2006.

Roller, Matthew B. *Dining Posture in Ancient Rome: Bodies, Values, and Status*. Princeton, NJ: Princeton University Press, 2006.

Roloff, Jürgen. *The Revelation of John*. Translated by John E. Alsup. Continental Commentary Series. Minneapolis: Fortress, 1993.

Roussel, Pierre, and Marcel Launey, eds. *Inscriptions de Delos, nos 1497–2879*. Paris: H. Champion, 1937.

Rowe, C. Kavin. *World Upside Down: Reading Acts in the Graeco-Roman Age*. New York: Oxford University Press, 2009.

Saldarini, Anthony J. *Pharisees, Scribes and Sadducees in Palestinian Society*. Wilmington, DE: Michael Glazier, 1988.

Sanders, E. P. *The Historical Figure of Jesus*. New York: Penguin, 1993.

———. "Jesus and the Kingdom: The Restoration of Israel and the New People of God." In *Jesus, the Gospels, and the Church: Essays in Honor of William R. Farmer*, edited by E. P. Sanders, 225–39. Macon, GA: Mercer University Press, 1987.

———. *Paul and Palestinian Judaism*. Philadelphia: Fortress, 1977.

Sartre, Maurice. *The Middle East Under Rome*. Translated by Catherine Porter and Elizabeth Rawlings. Cambridge, MA: Harvard University Press, 2005.

Saucy, Mark. "The Kingdom-of-God Sayings in Matthew." *Bibliotheca Sacra* 151 (1994) 175–97.

Schiffman, Lawrence H. *Texts and Tradition: A Source Reader for the Study of the Second Temple and Rabbinic Literature*. New York: KTAV, 1997.

Schmemann, Alexander. *The Eucharist: Sacrament of the Kingdom*. Translated by Paul Kachur. Crestwood, NY: St. Vladimir's Seminary Press, 2000.

Schmidt, Dan. *Taken by Communion: How the Lord's Supper Nourishes the Soul*. Grand Rapids: Baker, 2003.

Bibliography

Schnackenburg, Rudolf. *God's Rule and Kingdom*. Translated by John Murray. New York: Herder & Herder, 1963.

Scholer, David M., ed. *Social Distinctives of the Christians in the First Century: Pivotal Essays by E. A. Judge*. Peabody, MA: Hendrickson, 2008.

Schultz, Hans Jürgen, ed. *Jesus in His Time*. Translated by Brian Watchorn. Philadelphia: Fortress, 1971.

Schussler Fiorenza, Elisabeth. "Rhetorical Situation and Historical Reconstruction in 1 Corinthians." In *Christianity at Corinth: The Quest for the Pauline Church*, edited by Edward Adams and David G. Horrell, 145–160. Louisville: Westminster John Knox, 2004.

Schweitzer, Albert. *The Mystery of the Kingdom of God: The Secret of Jesus' Messiahship and Passion*. Translated with introduction by Walter Lowrie. New York: Schocken, 1964.

———. *The Quest of the Historical Jesus: A Critical Study of Its Progress from Reimarus to Wrede*. Translated by William Montgomery. New York: Macmillan, 1961.

Schweizer, Eduard. *The Letter to the Colossians*. Translated by Andrew Chester. London: SPCK, 1982.

Scott, Bernard Brandon. *Hear Then the Parables: A Commentary on the Parables of Jesus*. Minneapolis: Fortress, 1989.

Scott, Ernest F. *The Kingdom of God in the New Testament*. New York: Macmillan, 1931.

Scott, James C. *Domination and the Arts of Resistance: Hidden Transcripts*. New Haven, CT: Yale University Press, 1990.

Scott, Margaret. *The Eucharist and Social Justice*. Mahwah, NJ: Paulist, 2009.

Seccombe, David Peter. *The King of God's Kingdom: A Solution to the Puzzle of Jesus*. Carlisle, UK: Paternoster, 2002.

Segal, Judah Ben-Zion. *The Hebrew Passover: From Earliest Times to A.D. 70*. London Oriental Series 12. London: Oxford University Press, 1963.

Seneca, Lucius Annaeus. *On the Shortness of Life*. Translated by John H. Basore. LCL. London: William Heinemann, 1932.

Sharman, Henry Burton. *Son of Man and Kingdom of God: A Critical Study*. New York: Harper, 1943.

Sheehan, Thomas. *The First Coming: How the Kingdom of God Became Christianity*. New York: Random House, 1986.

Shepherd, Massey H., Jr. *The Paschal Liturgy and the Apocalypse*. Richmond, VA: John Knox, 1960.

Shires, Henry M. *The Eschatology of Paul in Light of Modern Scholarship*. Philadelphia: Westminster, 1966.

Simonetti, Manlio, ed. *Matthew 14–28*. Ancient Christian Commentary on Scripture 1B. Downers Grove, IL: InterVarsity, 2002.

Smalley, Stephen S. *The Revelation to John: A Commentary on the Greek Text of the Apocalypse*. Downers Grove, IL: InterVarsity, 2005.

Smith, Dennis E. *From Symposium to Eucharist: The Banquet in the Early Christian World*. Minneapolis: Fortress, 2003.

———. "The Greco-Roman Banquet as a Social Institution." Paper presented at the annual meeting of the SBL. Atlanta, GA, November 2003.

———. "Meals and Christian Origins." Paper presented at the annual meeting of the SBL. Toronto, ON, November 2002.

————. "Response to Andrew McGowan's Article on Rethinking Eucharistic Origins." Paper presented at the annual meeting of the SBL. San Diego, CA, November 2007.

————. "A Review of Hal Taussig's *In the Beginning was the Meal*." Paper presented at the annual meeting of the SBL Meals in the Greco-Roman World seminar. New Orleans, LA, November 22, 2009.

Smith, Dennis E., and Hal E. Taussig. *Many Tables: The Eucharist in the New Testament and Liturgy Today*. London: SCM, 1990.

Snyder, Howard A. *The Community of the King*. Rev. ed. Downers Grove, IL: InterVarsity, 2004.

Soards, Marion L. *The Speeches in Acts: Their Content, Context, and Concerns*. Louisville: Westminster John Knox, 1994.

Spencer, F. Scott. *Journeying Through Acts: A Literary-Cultural Reading*. Peabody, MA: Hendrickson, 2004.

Stackhouse, John G., Jr. *Finally Feminist: A Pragmatic Understanding of Gender*. Grand Rapids: Baker, 2005.

Standhartinger, Angela. "Response to Hal Taussig's *In the Beginning was the Meal*." Paper presented at the annual meeting of the Meals in the Greco-Roman World Study Group. New Orleans, LA, November 11, 2009.

————. "Rethinking the Eucharistic Origins: Response to the Work of Andrew McGowan." Paper presented at the annual meeting of the SBL Meals in the Greco-Roman World Study Group. Atlanta, GA, November 2002.

Starr, Chester G. *The Emergence of Rome as Ruler of the Western World*. 2nd ed. Ithaca, NY: Cornell University Press, 1953.

Stegemann, Ekkehard W., and Wolfgang Stegemann. *The Jesus Movement: A Social History of Its First Century*. Minneapolis: Fortress, 1999.

Stein, Siefried. "The Influence of Symposia Literaure on the Literary Form of the Pesach Haggadah." *Journal of Jewish Studies* 7 (1957) 13–44.

Stendahl, Krister. "New Testament for the Doctrine of the Sacraments." In *Gospel and Sacrament*, edited by Günther Gassmann and Vilmos Vajta, 56. Minneapolis: Augsburg, 1970.

Stevens, Marty E. *Temples, Tithes, and Taxes: The Temple and Economic Life in Ancient Israel*. Peabody, MA: Hendrickson, 2006.

Storkey, Alan. *Jesus and Politics: Confronting the Powers*. Grand Rapids: Baker, 2005.

Strabo. *Geography*. Vol. 8. Translated by Horace Leonard Jones. LCL 267. Cambridge, MA: Harvard University Press, 1917.

Strack, Hermann L., and Paul Billerbeck. *Kommentar zum Neuen Testament aus Talmud and Midrash*. Munich: Beck, 1922.

Strecker, George. *The Sermon on the Mount*. Translated by O. C. Dean Jr. Nashville: Abingdon, 1988.

Streett, Daniel R. "Food, Fellowship and Favoritism: Early Christian Meals as the Setting for James 2:1–9." Paper presented at the regional meeting of the Southwest Commission on Religious Studies. Irving, TX, March 2010.

Suetonius. *The Twelve Caesars*. Rev. ed. New York: Penguin, 1979.

Sullivan, Clayton. *Rethinking Realized Eschatology*. Macon, GA: Mercer University Press, 1988.

Swete, Henry B. *Apocalypse of Saint John*. Reprint. Eugene, OR: Wipf & Stock, 1999.

Syme, Ronald. *The Roman Revolution*. Rev. ed. New York: Oxford University Press, 2002.

Bibliography

Talbert, Charles H. *A Literary and Theological Commentary on the Fourth Gospel and Johannine Epistles*. Rev. ed. Macon, GA: Smyth & Helwys, 2005.

———. *Reading Acts: A Literary and Theological Commentary on the Acts of the Apostles*. New York: Crossroad, 1977.

———. *Reading Luke: A Literary and Theological Commentary on the Third Gospel*. New York: Crossroad, 1982.

Tannehill, Robert C. *The Narrative Unity of Luke–Acts: A Literary Interpretation*. Philadelphia: Fortress, 1986.

Tatum, W. Barnes. *In Quest of Jesus: A Guidebook*. Atlanta: John Knox, 1982.

Taussig, Hal. *In the Beginning Was the Meal: Social Experimentation and Early Christian Identity*. Minneapolis: Fortress, 2009.

Tenney, Merrill C. *The Gospel of John*. The Expositor's Bible Commentary 9. Grand Rapids: Zondervan, 1981.

Testament of Job. In *The Old Testament Pseudepigrapha: Apocalyptic Literature and Testaments*, edited by James H. Charlesworth. Translated by R. P. Spittler, 865–66. New York: Doubleday, 1983.

Thatcher, Tom. *Greater Than Caesar: Christology and Empire in the Fourth Gospel*. Minneapolis: Fortress, 2009.

Theissen, Gerd, and Annette Merz. *The Historical Jesus: A Comprehensive Guide*. Minneapolis: Fortress, 1996.

Thielicke, Helmut. *The Waiting Father*. New York: Harper & Row, 1959.

Thiselton, Anthony C. *The First Epistle to the Corinthians*. New International Greek Testament Commentary. Grand Rapids: Eerdmans, 2000.

Thompson, Leonard L. *Revelation*. Abingdon New Testament Commentaries. Nashville: Abingdon, 1998.

Torrey, Charles Cutler. *The Composition and Date of Acts*. Cambridge, MA: Harvard University Press, 1916.

Towner, Philip H. *The Letters to Timothy and Titus*. New International Commentary on the New Testament. Grand Rapids: Eerdmans, 2006.

Travis, Stephen H. *Christian Hope and the Future*. Downers Grove, IL: InterVarsity, 1980.

———. *End of Story? What Jesus Said About the Future of the World*. Leicester, UK: InterVarsity, 1997.

Treier, Daniel J. "The Fulfillment of Joel 2:28–32: A Multiple-Lens Approach." *Journal of the Evangelical Theological Society* 40/1 (March 1997) 13–26.

Turner, Seth. "The Interim, Earthly Messianic Kingdom in Paul." *Journal for the Study of the New Testament* 25/3 (2003) 323–42.

Twelftree, Graham H. *People of the Spirit: Exploring Luke's View of the Church*. Grand Rapids: Baker, 2009.

Udoh, Fabian E. *To Caesar What Is Caesar's: Tribute, Taxes, and Imperial Administration in Early Roman Palestine, 63 B.C.E.–70 C.E.* Brown Judaic Studies 343. Providence, RI: Brown University, 2005.

VanderKam, James C. *The Book of Jubilees: Guides to Apocrypha and Pseudepigrapha*. Sheffield, UK: Sheffield Academic Press, 2001.

Vermes, Geza. *The Changing Faces of Jesus*. London: Penguin, 2000.

———. *The Complete Dead Sea Scrolls in English*. New York: Penguin, 1997.

———. *Who's Who in the Age of Jesus*. London: Penguin, 2005.

Vetta, Massimo. "The Culture of the Symposium." In *Food: A Culinary History from Antiquity to the Present*, edited by Jean-Louis Flandrin and Massimo Montinari, 96–105. New York: Columbia University Press, 1999.

Virgil. *The Aeneid*. Translated by Robert Fagles. New York: Penguin, 2008.

Volf, Miroslav. *The End of Memory: Remembering Rightly in a Violent World*. Grand Rapids: Eerdmans, 2006.

Vos, Geerhardus. *The Kingdom of God and the Church*. Nutley, NJ: Presbyterian & Reformed, 1972.

———. *The Pauline Eschatology*. Grand Rapids: Eerdmans, 1953.

Wagner, J. Ross. *Heralds of the Good News: Isaiah and Paul in Concert in the Letters to the Romans*. Boston: Brill, 2002.

Wainwright, Geoffrey. *Eucharist and Eschatology*. New York: Oxford University Press, 1981.

Waldner, Mike M. "Christian Mission in Eschatological Perspective: Promoting the Dynamic of Eschatology for Missionary Motivation." DMiss diss., Fuller Theological Seminary, 1987.

Walker, W. O. "1 Corinthians 11:2–16 and Paul's View Regarding Women." *Journal of Biblical Literature* 94 (1975) 95–111.

Wall, R. W. *Colossians and Philemon*. The IVP New Testament Commentary Series 12. Downers Grove, IL: InterVarsity, 1993.

Walsh, Brian J., and Sylvia C. Keesmaat. *Colossians Remixed: Subverting the Empire*. Downers Grove, IL: InterVarsity, 2004.

Waltke, Bruce K. "The Irruption of the Kingdom of God." *Criswell Theological Review* N.S. 2/1 (2004) 3–13.

Waltke, Bruce K., and Charles Yu. *An Old Testament Theology*. Grand Rapids: Zondervan, 2007.

Wanamaker, Charles. *The Epistles to the Thessalonians: A Commentary on the Greek Text*. Grand Rapids: Eerdmans, 1990.

Warren, Rick. *The Purpose-Driven Church*. Grand Rapids: Zondervan, 1995.

Webb, William J. *Slaves, Women, and Homosexuals*. Downers Grove, IL: InterVarsity, 2001.

Weiss, Johannes. *Jesus' Proclamation of the Kingdom of God*. Translated and edited by Richard H. Hiers and David L. Holland. Philadelphia: Fortress, 1971.

Wengst, Klaus. *Pax Romana and the Peace of Jesus Christ*. Translated by John Bowden. Philadelphia: Fortress, 1987.

Wenham, David. "How Jesus Understood the Last Supper: A Parable in Action." *Themelios* 20/2 (1995) 11–15.

———. *The Parables of Jesus*. Downers Grove, IL: InterVarsity, 1989.

———. "The Purpose of Luke-Acts: Israel's Story in the Context of the Roman Empire." In *Reading Luke: Interpretation, Reflection Formation*, edited by Craig Bartholomew et al., 79–103. Grand Rapids: Zondervan, 2005.

White, L. Michael. "Taste and Space: Archeology and Adaptation in Roman Dining Practice." Paper presented at the annual meeting of the SBL Meals in the Greco-Roman World seminar. Toronto, ON, November 2002.

White, R. E. O. *The Night He Was Betrayed*. Grand Rapids: Eerdmans, 1982.

Wilder, Amos. *Eschatology and Ethics in the Teaching of Jesus*. New York: Harper, 1939.

Williams, Ritva H. *Stewards, Prophets, Keepers of the Word: Leadership in the Early Church*. Peabody, MA: Hendrickson, 2006.

Bibliography

Willis, Wendell Lee. *Idol Meat in Corinth: The Pauline Argument in 1 Corinthians 8 and 10.* Eugene, OR: Wipf & Stock, 2004.

———, ed. *The Kingdom of God in 20th-Century Interpretation.* Peabody, MA: Hendrickson, 1987.

Wilson, Marvin R. *Our Father Abraham: Jewish Roots of the Christian Faith.* Grand Rapids: Eerdmans, 1996.

Wink, Walter. *Naming the Powers: The Language of Power in the New Testament.* Philadelphia: Fortress, 1984.

———. *The Powers That Be: A Theology for a New Millennium.* New York: Doubleday, 1998.

———. *Unmasking the Powers: The Invisible Forces that Determine Human Existence.* Philadelphia: Fortress, 1986.

Winter, Bruce W. "Acts and Food Shortages." In *The Book of Acts in Its Graeco-Roman Setting,* edited by David W. J. Gill and Conrad Gempf, 2:59–78. Grand Rapids: Eerdmans, 1994.

———. *Seek the Welfare of the City: Christians as Benefactors and Citizens.* Grand Rapids: Eerdmans, 1994.

Wire, Antoinette Clark. *The Corinthian Women Prophets: A Reconstruction through Paul's Rhetoric.* Minneapolis: Fortress, 1995.

Witherington, Ben, III. *The Acts of the Apostles: A Socio-Religious Commentary.* Grand Rapids: Eerdmans, 1998.

———. *The Gospel of Mark: A Socio-Rhetorical Commentary.* Grand Rapids: Eerdmans, 2001.

———. *Jesus, Paul and the End of the World: A Comparative Study of New Testament Eschatology.* Downers Grove, IL: InterVarsity, 1992.

———. *Making a Meal of It: Rethinking the Theology of the Lord's Supper.* Waco, TX: Baylor University Press, 2007.

———. *Matthew.* Smyth and Helwys Bible Commentary. Macon, GA: Smyth & Helwys, 2006.

———. *Revelation.* The New Cambridge Bible Commentary. Cambridge: Cambridge University Press, 2003.

Woolf, Greg, ed. *Ancient Civilizations: The Illustrated Guide to Belief, Mythology, and Art.* San Diego: Tender Bay, 2005.

Wright, N. T. *The Epistles of Paul to the Colossians and to Philemon.* Tyndale New Testament Commentaries. Grand Rapids: Eerdmans, 1986.

———. *Jesus and the Victory of God.* Minneapolis: Fortress, 1996.

———. *The Meal Jesus Gave Us: Understanding Holy Communion.* Philadelphia: Westminster John Knox, 2003.

———. *The New Testament and the People of God.* Minneapolis: Fortress, 1996.

———. "Paul's Gospel and Caesar's Empire." In *Paul and Politics: Ekklesia, Israel, Imperium, Interpretation,* edited by Richard A. Horsley, 160–83. Harrisburg, PA: Trinity, 2000.

———. *The Resurrection of the Son of God.* Minneapolis: Fortress, 2003.

———. *What Saint Paul Really Said: Was Paul of Tarsus the Real Founder of Christianity?* Grand Rapids: Eerdmans, 1997.

Xenophon. *Anabasis.* Books 1–4. Edited by Maurice W. Mather and Joseph William Hewitt. Norman: Oklahoma University Press, 1979.

————. *Xenophon in Seven Volumes.* Vol 4. Tranlsated by E. C. Marchant and O. J. Todd. Cambridge, MA: Harvard University Press, 1979.

Yoder, John Howard. *Body Politics: Five Practices of the Christian Community before the Watching World.* Scottdale, PA: Herald, 2001.

————. *The Politics of Jesus.* Grand Rapids: Eerdmans: 1972.

Zanker, Paul. *The Power of Images in the Age of Augustus.* Translated by Alan Shapiro. Ann Arbor: University of Michigan Press, 1990.

Scripture Index